Critical Acclaim for *Best Dives of the Caribbean*

". . . the bible of Caribbean dive-travel . . . I highly recommend it"
Christopher Lofting, The Travel Show, WOR Network Radio

"It's super!... a great reference and we love it."
Dive Travel Magazine

"A terrific guide. . . "
John Clayton, The Travel Show, KABC Radio, Los Angeles

". . . a must have. . . for divers, snorkelers or those who just love to float in liquid turquoise"
Brenda Fine, Travel Editor, *The New York Law Journal*

". . . great dive spots. . . ."
Suzanne Durant, *Caribbean Travel and Life*

". . . a good travel planner from a diver's point of view. . . ."
Jill Schensul, Travel Editor, *The Record*

". . . opens a new world of adventure to anyone with a mask and snorkel."
Pat Reilly, travel writer, *Commerce Magazine*

". . . the best coverage of the subject matter I've seen, and incredibly easy to read. . . essential for the serious or beginning diver."
Dr. Susan Cropper, DVM, Society of Aquatic Veterinarians

". . . details more than 200 of the finest dive sites in the Caribbean. . . ."
Bill Smith, *Dive Travel News*, ICS Scuba

"Don't plan a dive without it!. . . Concise and informative. . . one of the few bargains of the decade."
Wendy Canning Church, Divers Exchange International

"It's a trustworthy publication. . . ."
Indepth/Undercurrent

Acknowledgements

The authors thank all of *Best Dives'* contributors, correspondents, photographers and researchers (identified throughout the book) for their enormous effort in preparing material for this edition.

A special thanks to Janice Brink, Dennis Eidson, Anita, Amanda, Neal and KenLiggett, Underwater Sports of New Jersey; Rick and Lisa Ocklemann, Puerto Rico and Guadeloupe; JoAnn and Jonathan Pannaman, BVI snorkeling; Alvin Jackson, Honduras; Bret Gilliam, Joe Giacinto, Dive BVI; Barbara Swab, Frank Holler, Holler Swab & Partners; Auston MacLeod, Julian Rigby, Kenneth Samuel, H.V. Pat Reilly, Marilyn and Tim Benford, Ellis Chaderton, St. Kitts and Nevis; Mark Padover, St. Eustatius; Bob Di Chiara; Susan and Rick Sammon, CEDAM; Dr. Susan Cropper; Dee Scarr, Touch the Sea, Bonaire; Brenda Fine; Karen and Dennis Sabo, Landfall Productions; Aruba Tourism; Christopher Lofting, Maria Shaw, Cayman Brac; Mike Emmanuel, Little Cayman; Lucy Portlock, Pelagic Pleasure, USVI; Dave Farmer, Michael Young, Barbados; Erwin F. Eustacia, Ivan Englentina, and Eva Van Dalen, Michel Angelo Harms, Curaçao Tourism; Dominique & Leroy French, St. Martin; Tom McKelvey; Finn Rinds, Tobago; Gareth Edmonson-Jones, José E. Rafols, Efra Figueroa, Puerto Rico; Iain I. Grummitt, Thomas L.C. Peabody, Anguilla; Jim Spencer; Joan Borque, Saba; Karolin Kolcuoglu, St. Lucia; Luana Wheatley, Michelle Pugh, Mike Meyers, Monica Leedy, Myron Clement, Guadeloupe; Tom Burnett, Walter Frischbutter, Dominican Republic; Christopher Wright, Jamaica.

NOTE: This publication is intended only as a guide. Additional information should be obtained prior to visiting each area. Every effort has been made to obtain accurate and up-to-date information for this publication. However, considering the sheer magnitude of the research included, all information could not be confirmed immediately prior to press time.

The authors, contributors, and publishers of this guide assume no liability for its use.

In memory of Jon.

BEST DIVES

of the

CARIBBEAN

Third Edition

Joyce & Jon Huber

HUNTER PUBLISHING, INC,
30 Mayfield Ave, Edison, NJ 08818
☎ 800-255-0343; fax 732-417-1744
www.hunterpublishing.com

Ulysses Travel Publications
4176 Saint-Denis, Montréal, Québec
Canada H2W 2M5
☎ 514-843-9882, ext. 2232; fax 514-843-9448

Windsor Books
The Boundary, Wheatley Road, Garsington
Oxford, OX44 9EJ England
☎ 01865-361122; fax 01865-361133

ISBN 1-58843-575-7
© Joyce Huber

For complete information about the hundreds of travel guides offered by Hunter Publishing, visit our website at www.hunterpublishing.com.

All rights reserved. No part of this publication may be reproduced, stored in a retrieval system, or transmitted in any form, or by any means, electronic, mechanical, photocopying, recording, or otherwise, without the written permission of the publisher.

This guide focuses on recreational activities. As all such activities contain elements of risk, the publisher, author, affiliated individuals and companies disclaim responsibility for any injury, harm, or illness that may occur to anyone through, or by use of, the information in this book. Every effort was made to insure the accuracy of information in this book, but the publisher and author do not assume, and hereby disclaim, liability for any loss or damage caused by errors, omissions, misleading information or potential travel problems caused by this guide, even if such errors or omissions result from negligence, accident or any other cause.

Cover photo: *Hawksbill turtle at Columbia Profundo wall,*
© Randy Hodge

All interior color photos courtesy of the authors
unless otherwise indicated.

Maps by Joyce Huber

1   2   3   4

Contents

Introduction

Before the creation of underwater viewing equipment, early Caribbean travelers caught merely a glimpse of the world beneath the sea. But, once they did, the idea of subsea exploration really caught on. By the 1930s, rubber goggles with glass lenses and face masks became a standard part of many a tropical traveler's wardrobe and a new wave of adventure travel took root. And, though much has changed since those early days, the fascination of the sea and its splendid inhabitants are still romancing and captivating visitors the way they always have.

Dive vacations have since evolved into a major part of Caribbean travel. There are now resorts, travel agents, tour operators and yacht charters that cater exclusively to divers and snorkelers. Many all-inclusive resorts have added scuba lessons and tours. There is even a cruise ship with an all-dive itinerary. Sailing afficionados find hull-to-hull pick-up service offered by the dive shops. Novice sailor-divers can rent a yacht with a captain who doubles as a dive instructor and a reef-and-wreck tour guide. The biggest consideration left for the traveler is deciding where to go.

Best Dives of the Caribbean is designed to help you wade through this endless wonder of vacation choices. Whether you are a snorkeler, a novice diver or an experienced ocean explorer, you'll find a unique choice of destinations, diver-friendly accommodations and dive services to pick from. We've added several adventure destinations to this edition and expanded others to include more dive and snorkeling sites, a wider choice of accommodations, eateries and après-dive activities.

You'll find suggestions for the best time of year to visit each island and where to write, call or e-mail for additional information.

Dive and snorkeling sites have been carefully described and rated for various skill levels by the top dive operators of each area and double-checked by a member of our own US-based panel of dive-travel experts. Rules and etiquette for diving individual marine parks and reserves are listed throughout the guide.

If we've overlooked one of your favorite spots, write and tell us about it and we'll take another look for the next edition. In the meantime we hope you find *Best Dives of the Caribbean* a useful addition to your diver's bookshelf.

E-mail for the author may be addressed to bestdives@aol.com.

Planning Your Trip

To plan your best dive vacation, consider first the type of trip that interests you most. It may be a stay at a luxury resort, a week's tour on a live-aboard yacht or an excursion into the wilderness. Then check the best time of year to go. A week of bad weather or rough seas can turn any vacation sour. Most areas experience a predictable rainy season. And, though no one can guarantee the weather, each chapter discusses local weather patterns and suggests a best time of year to go.

Finally, consider your budget. You'll note a wide range of live-aboards and land accommodations throughout this guide, plus the appropriate contact for additional information at the end of each chapter.

All rates are quoted in US dollars unless otherwise stated, and are subject to change without notice.

SCUBA CERTIFYING ORGANIZATIONS

Locations for scuba instruction near your home may be obtained from one of the following organizations:

IDEA (International Diving Educators Association), PO Box 8427, Jacksonville, FL 32239-8427. ☎ 904-744-5554.

NAUI (National Association of Underwater Instructors), PO Box 14650, Montclair, CA 91763. ☎ 800-553-6284, www.naui.org.

PADI INTERNATIONAL (Professional Association of Diving Instructors), 1251 E. Dyer Rd., Suite 100, Santa Ana, CA 92705-5605. ☎ 800-729-7234; 714-540-7234, www.padi.com.

PDIC INTERNATIONAL (Professional Diving Instructors Corporation), PO Box 3633, Scranton, PA 18505. ☎ 570-342-1480; fax 570-342-6030; info@PDIC-INTL.com, www.pdic-intl.com.

SSI (Scuba Schools International), 2619 Canton Court, Fort Collins, CO 80525. ☎ 970-482-0883, www.divessi.com.

YMCA (National YMCA Scuba Program), 101 N. Wacker Drive, Chicago, IL 60606, ☎ 800-872-9622; scuba@ymca.net, www.ymcascuba.org.

CRUISES AND PACKAGE TOURS

Hundreds of dollars can be saved by choosing a package tour offered by dive-tour operators, airlines, resorts and dive shops. For example, one package to Guadeloupe includes airfare and hotel for $100 less than the airfare alone. Package tours with diving are listed throughout this guide.

Be sure to read the fine print carefully when you are comparing tours, and to allow for the potential added costs of transfers, sightseeing tours, meals, auto rentals, acceptable accommodations, and taxes. Tanks and weights may or may not be included. Also ask whether extra airline weight allowances are included for dive gear.

HANDICAPPED DIVERS

Handicapped divers will find help and information by contacting the **Handicapped Scuba Association** (HSA). The association has provided scuba instruction to people with physical disabilities since 1975. Over 600 instructors in 24 countries are HSA-trained. HSA has developed the "Resort Evaluation Program" to help handicapped divers select a vacation destination. They check out facilities and work with the staff and management to ensure accessibility. Once a resort is totally accessible it is certified by HSA.

For a list of HSA-certified resorts, group-travel opportunities and more information on HSA's programs, instruction and activities, visit their Website at www.hsascuba.com. Contact HSA International, 1104 El Prado, San Clemente, CA 92672; ☎ 949-498-4540; hsa@hsascuba.com.

MONEY

Most large resorts, restaurants and dive operators will accept major credit cards, although you risk being charged at a higher rate if the local currency fluctuates. Travelers' checks are accepted almost everywhere and often you'll get a better exchange rate for them than cash. It's always a good idea to have some local currency on hand for cabs, tips and small purchases.

INSURANCE

Many types of travel insurance are available covering everything from lost luggage and trip cancellations to medical expenses. Because emergency medical assistance and air ambulance fees can run to several thousand dollars, it is wise to be prepared. Trips purchased with some major credit cards include life insurance.

Divers Alert Network (DAN) offers divers' health insurance for $35 a year plus an annual membership fee of $25, $35 for a family. Any treatment required for an accident or emergency which is a direct result of diving, such as decompression sickness (the bends), arterial gas embolism or pulmonary baro-trauma is covered up to $125,000. Air ambulance to the closest medical care facility, recompression chamber care and in-patient hospital care are covered. Lacking proof of insurance or the ability to pay, a diver may be refused transport and may be refused treatment. For more information write to DAN, PO Box 3823, Durham, NC 27710, www.diversalertnetwork.org.

In a diving emergency contact local EMS, then call ☎ 919-684-8111, 919-684-4DAN (collect), 800-446-2671 (toll-free), 919-684-9111 (Latin America Hotline).

Non-diving travel-related accidents are NOT covered by this insurance. For assistance with non-diving emergencies call the **International Emergency Hotlines Travel Assistance for Non-Diving Emergencies**,

☎ 1-800-DAN-EVAC (1-800-326-3822). If outside the US, Canada, Puerto Rico, Bahamas, British or US Virgin Islands, ☎ 919-684-3483 (collect).

For non-emergency medical questions, call ☎ 800-446-2671 or 919-684-2948, Monday to Friday, 9 am-5 pm (ET). All other inquiries, ☎ 800-446-2671 or 919-684-2948, fax 919-490-6630 or (medical) 919-49303040.

International SOS Assistance is a medical assistance service to travelers who are more than 100 miles from home. For just $55 per person for seven to 14 days, or $96 per couple, SOS covers air evacuation and travel-related assistance. Evacuation is to the closest medical care facility, which is determined by SOS staff doctors. Representative Michael Klein states that SOS has and will send out a private LearJet if necessary to accommodate a patient. Hospitalization is NOT covered. Standard **Blue Cross and Blue Shield** policies do cover medical costs while traveling. For information, write to International SOS Assistance, Box 11568, Philadelphia, PA 19116; ☎ 800-523-8930 or 215-942-8226, www.intsos.com, jfahy@intsos.com.

Lost luggage insurance is available at the ticket counter of many airlines. If you have a homeowner's policy, you may already be covered. Be sure to check first with your insurance agent.

Keep a list of all your dive equipment and other valuables, including the name of the manufacturer, model, date of purchase, price and serial number, if any, on your person when traveling. Immediately report any theft or loss of baggage to the local police, hotel security people or airline and get a copy of that report. Both the list and the report of loss or theft will be needed to collect from your insurance company. Do not expect airlines to cheerfully compensate you for any loss without a lot of red tape and hassle. Regardless of the value of your gear the airline pays by the weight ($9 per pound) of what is lost. Be sure to tag your luggage with your name and address. Use a business address if possible.

DOCUMENTS

Carry your personal documents on you at all times. Be sure to keep a separate record of passport numbers, visas, or tourist cards in your luggage.

SECURITY

Tourists flashing wads of cash and expensive jewelry are prime targets for robbers. Avoid off-the-beaten-track areas of cities, especially at night. Do not carry a lot of cash or wear expensive cameras or jewelry. Keep alert to what's going on around you. Stay with your luggage until it is checked in with the airlines. Jewelry should be kept in the hotel safe.

Rental cars have become a target for robbers, more so in the US than the Caribbean, but a few incidents of "bump-n-rob" crimes have been reported in the islands. To avoid problems, try to rent a car without rental agent markings.

If someone bumps into your car, do not stop. Drive to a police station and report the incident. Do not stop for hitchhikers or to assist strangers.

DRUGS

Penalties for possession of illegal drugs are very harsh (selling drugs is still cause for public hanging in some areas) and the risk you take for holding even a half-ounce of marijuana cannot be stressed enough. Punishment often entails long jail terms. In certain areas, such as Mexico, your embassy and the best lawyer won't be much help. You are guilty until proven innocent.

CAMERAS

Divers traveling with expensive camera gear or electronic equipment should register each item with customs *before* leaving the country.

SUNDRIES

Suntan lotion, aspirin, antihistamines, decongestants, anti-fog, or mosquito repellent should be purchased before your trip. These products are not always available and may cost quite a bit more than you pay for them at home.

FIRST AID

Every diver should carry a small first aid kit for minor cuts, bruises or ailments. Be sure to include a topical antihistamine ointment, antihistamine tablets, seasickness preventive, decongestant, throat lozenges, Bandaids, aspirin and diarrhea treatment.

SUNBURN PROTECTION

Avoid prolonged exposure to the sun, especially during peak hours, 10 am to 3 pm. Because most dive trips occur during peak hours, whenever possible, opt for trips on dive boats with sun canopies, use sunblock lotions or a sunscreen with a protection factor of at least 15, select a hat with a wide brim, and wear protective clothing of fabrics made to block the sun's ultraviolet rays. The following manufacturers offer catalogs featuring comfortable, protective clothing: **Sun Precautions Inc.**, Everett WA, ☎ 800-882-7860; **Solar Protective Factory**, Sacramento CA, ☎ 800-786-2562; **Koala Konnection**, Mountain View CA, ☎ 888-465-6252.

DIVER IDENTIFICATION

Most dive operations require that you hold a certification card and a logbook. A check-out dive may be required if you cannot produce a log of recent dives.

GEAR

Uncomfortable or ill-fitting masks, snorkels, and other personal diving gear can make your dive a miserable experience. You can greatly reduce the possibility of these problems by buying or renting what you need from a reliable dive shop or specialty store before departure. Snorkeling gear, especially, is often expensive to rent away from home.

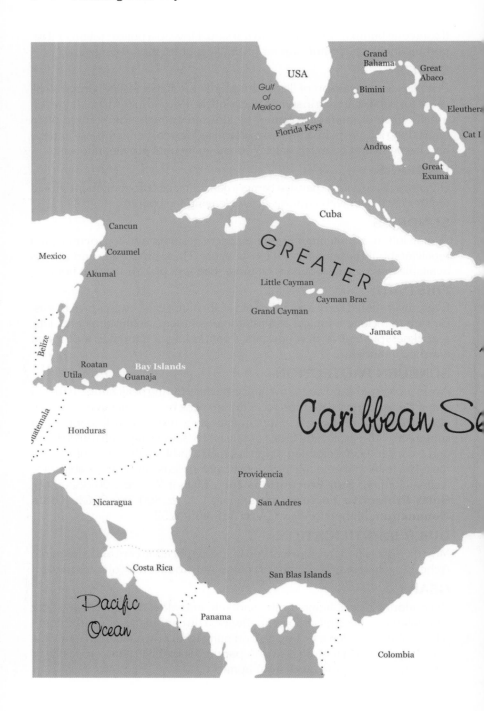

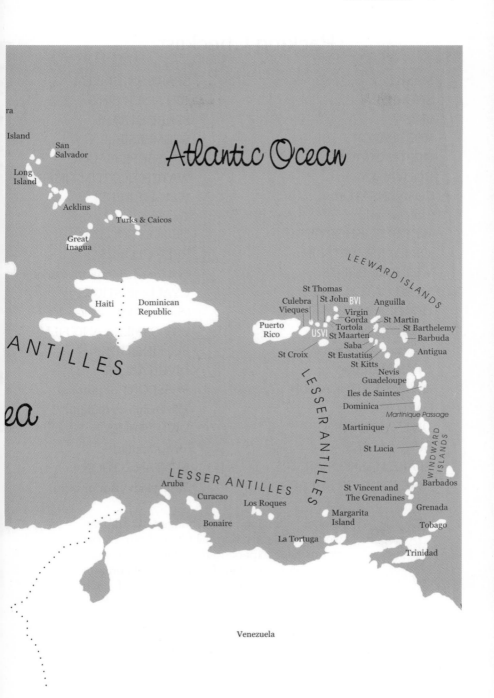

Packing Checklist

___ MASK

___ SNORKEL

___ FINS

___ REGULATOR

___ DEPTH GUAGE

___ BOUYANCY
COMPENSATOR
(stab jacket)

___ WET SUIT, SHORTIE
OR LYCRA WETSKIN

___ WET SUIT BOOTS

___ MESH CATCH BAG

___ U/W DIVE LIGHTS

___ DRAMAMINE or other
seasickness preventative

___ GEAR MARKER

___ DIVER CERTIFICATION
CARD (C-card)

___ DIVER LOG BOOK

___ SUNGLASSES

___ SPARE MASK STRAP

___ DIVE KNIFE OR SHEARS

___ SPARE SNORKEL
RETAINER RING

___ SPARE STRAPS

___ SUBMERSIBLE
PRESSURE GAUGE

___ WATCH/BOTTOM TIMER

___ WEIGHT BELT
(no lead)

___ DE-FOG SOLUTION

___ REEF GLOVES
(not for use in marine parks)

___ CYALUME STICKS
(chemical light sticks)

___ U/W CAMERA AND FILM

___ FISH ID BOOK

___ DIVE TABLES

___ PASSPORT or proof of
citizenship as required

___ DIVE TABLES
(or computer)

___ SUNTAN LOTION

___ HAT (with visor or brim)

 Global warming has changed Caribbean weather. Islands normally free from winter storms have experienced colder air and water temperatures during January and February. Desert islands, normally dry year-round, have been hit with storms and shifting winds in February for the first time.

If you plan a vacation during January or February, check weather in your planned destination before packing. You may want to consider a full wetsuit.

Anguilla

The island of Anguilla (pronounced Ann-GWIL-A) is one of the Caribbean's best-kept secrets. Though sailing buffs have enjoyed its secluded bays and coves for decades, divers are just discovering its rich coral walls, great wrecks and miles of shallow snorkeling gardens.

Sitting just five miles from St. Martin and 190 miles east of Puerto Rico, Anguilla is the northernmost of the Leeward Islands in the Eastern Caribbean. It is small, just 16 miles long and three miles wide, with one main road that threads through picturesque villages, rows of Indian cottages, and colorful fruit and vegetable stands. Scattered along its craggy coast are 30 white sand beaches.

Delightfully tranquil, this crown colony is devoid of mammoth shopping centers, casinos, and crowds. Just 7,000 residents and a few thousand free-roaming goats comprise the local population.

Physically, Anguilla is predominantly low-lying, formed of limestone and coral with patches of mangrove and freshwater ponds. Small cliffs on its north side are habitat to a variety of tropical birds, as are nearby out islands where you can spot the red-billed tropic bird, royal terns, kingfishers, laughing gulls, frigates and blue-faced boobies.

Anguilla's capital, **The Valley**, is a tiny strand of pastel shops, government buildings and colorful houses.

Sandy Ground – just west of The Valley – on the northwest end, is the main yacht and cruise-ship harbor. It is the jumping-off point for sail-snorkeling cruises and west-end dive trips. Adjacent to Sandy Ground is **Road Bay**, a small strip of land with an ocean beach on one side and a maze of salt ponds that attract a multitude of tropical birds on the other.

When to Go

 The best time to visit Anguilla is from mid December to May. Tropical storms bringing an annual rainfall of 35 inches are a threat from late July to October, though most storms occur during September.

Air and water temperatures are agreeable for diving year-round. Average air temperature is 80°F. Water temperatures range from 79° to 85°F.

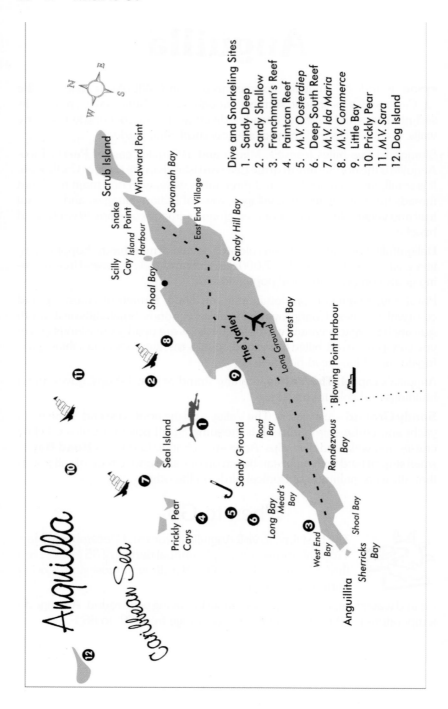

Anguilla

Caribbean Sea

Dive and Snorkeling Sites
1. Sandy Deep
2. Sandy Shallow
3. Frenchman's Reef
4. Paintcan Reef
5. M.V. Oosterdiep
6. Deep South Reef
7. M.V. Ida Maria
8. M.V. Commerce
9. Little Bay
10. Prickly Pear
11. M.V. Sara
12. Dog Island

Best Dive & Snorkeling Sites

Wreck diving and out-island snorkeling prevail over Anguilla's subsea activities, though new sites are being opened on the east end of the island where coral caves and chutes shelter a robust fish population.

Eight of the 25 sites regularly visited by The Dive Shop, the island's west-end operator, are wrecks that were intentionally sunk to create artificial reefs. Anguillan dive masters boast the largest number of diveable wrecks in the eastern Caribbean – all in warm, clear water.

☆☆ **Stoney Ground Marine Park**, Anguilla's first underwater heritage site, surrounds an 18th-century Spanish warship, *El Buen Consejo*. Dive tours of the site are offered by **Shoal Bay Scuba and Watersports**. Tours are fully guided and begin with a video and presentation on the site's history. The wreckage includes several 10-foot canons, anchors, bronze religious medals and other interesting artifacts.

☆☆☆ The wreck of the **MV *Oosterdiep*** is one of the newest sites. It is a 130-foot freighter resting at 80 feet, about 2½ miles out from Road Bay. Intact and upright, it attracts schooling yellowtail, schoolmaster snapper, Atlantic spadefish, flying gurnard, stingrays and small fish. Penetration is not allowed without specialty certification and under the supervision of local dive masters.

☆☆☆ **Sandy Deep**, a mini wall and the favorite reef dive, is lush with hard and soft corals, gorgonians, and abundant fish life and lobsters (no collecting). Not recommended for snorkeling, but good for the novice, with depths from 15 to 60 feet. Sea conditions vary depending on the time of year.

☆☆☆ **Frenchman's Reef**, a collapsed limestone cliff off the southern point of West End Bay, is Anguilla's best snorkeling and novice-diver spot. Depths are from the surface to 40 feet. The submerged terrain is mixed coral, boulders and sand. There are spectacular swim-throughs, ledges and caverns – a "Whitman's Sampler" of West Indies marine life. Seas are calm, visibility good.

☆☆☆☆ The wall at **Dog Island**, 10 miles northwest of Road Bay, is an outstanding dive with depths from 15 to 80 feet. The wall's rock and coral face is riddled with nooks and crannies where you'll find octopi, turtles, arrow crabs, basket sponges, slender tube sponges, shrimp and lobsters. Sea fans and gorgonians abound. Fish include horse-eye jacks, chub, parrotfish, huge grey and French angels, blacktip and nurse sharks. Stingrays bury themselves in the sandy bottom. The surface over the wall is usually too choppy for snorkeling, but other areas around Dog Island – Bay Rock, for example – are popular snorkeling spots when seas are calm. The boat ride is about 30 minutes.

⭐⭐ **Little Bay Reef** is a sheltered 15- to 25-foot reef, ideal for novice divers, students and snorkelers. The bottom is a mix of coral, sand and turtle grass. There is excellent micro-life, including nudibranchs and lettuce slugs, seahorses, turtles, octopi, barber shrimp and lobsters. The reef is a stone's throw from shore but access other than by boat entails a rugged climb down a rocky footpath to the beach. **The Dive Shop, Ltd.** offers snorkelers drop-off and pick-up service to the beach at Little Bay.

Noted underwater photographer Paul Humann shot extensively here for his famous book, *Reef Creatures*.

⭐⭐⭐ **Shoal Bay East** is the best water-entry snorkeling and scuba site. There are two reefs, one directly off the beach that parallels the beach for some distance and another one a little farther out. Depths range from the surface to 80 feet.

⭐⭐ The wreck of the **MV *Commerce*** is another freighter scuttled by dive masters Peabody and Grummitt. This 130-foot ship was sunk in 1986 off Limestone Bay on the Northwest coast. Depth is 45 to 80 feet. Great for photography, dramatic remains of the ship sparkle with schools of barracuda, golden sergeant majors, queen angels, green and spotted morays, stingrays and spiny lobsters. Macro subjects proliferate. Seas are variable; usually a light chop with an occasional current. Bottom terrain is boulder coral and sand.

⭐⭐⭐⭐ Marine life is superb at **Deep South Reef**, a patch reef displaying beautiful brain-coral formations. A profusion of soft, pastel corals and gorgonians blend with the vibrant reds and oranges of the reef. Purple tube sponges, barrel sponges and sea fans are abundant. Triggerfish, trumpetfish, parrotfish, angels, jacks, southern stingrays, spotted drums, wrasses, blue tangs, crabs and lobsters are in residence. Depths are 55 to 80 feet. Good visibility. Seas vary with winds. Deep South is a short boat trip, about a mile, from the south end of Road Bay.

⭐⭐⭐⭐ **Paintcan Reef** is named for colorful splashes of strawberry and vase sponges that adorn the magnificent hard-coral structures of this patch reef. Fish life, too, is excellent, with glimpses of black durgon, blacktip and nurse shark, walls of grunts, morays, jacks, copper sweepers, barracuda, and schools of silversides and sergeant majors. Pink-tipped anemones, and iridescent tube sponges cluster along the walls of the reef. Hawksbill turtles are recurrent visitors. *Paintcan* is about three miles north of Road Bay, a 15-minute boat trip. Depths are from 55 to 80 feet. Sea conditions vary. Recommended for experienced divers.

⭐⭐⭐⭐ The **MV *Sara***, a freighter scuttled by the government to create an artificial reef, is impressive by size alone – over 230 feet long. The *Sara* provides a fantastic backdrop for underwater photographs. Grunts, goatfish, barjacks, stingrays and small schooling fish frequent the area. Depth is 80 feet. It is about 2½ miles north of Road Bay. Seas are usually choppy.

☆☆☆ Another favorite of macro photographers is the wreck of the **MV Ida Maria**. Scuttled in 1986 by dive masters Peabody and Gummitt, this 110-foot freighter sits on the sand at 60 feet. The deteriorating hull is over-grown with plate, pencil and clinging corals, anemones and sponges – home to seahorses, octopi, urchins, arrow crabs, banded cleaner shrimp, lavender shrimp and sea cucumbers. Huge green moray eels and lobsters peek out from the cracks along the bottom. Fish life and visibility are outstanding. Seas vary with weather. The *Ida Maria* is about six miles north of Limestone Bay.

☆☆☆ **Prickly Pear Reef** is an underwater canyon characterized by ledges and caverns. One formation resembling a chimney is a beautiful backdrop for underwater portraits. There are schooling goatfish, crabs, lobster, barracuda, friendly angels and grouper, squirrelfish, long nose butterflyfish, tarpon, man-grove snapper and grunts. Nurse sharks rest on the sandy bottom under the ledges. Depths range from 40 to 70 feet. Prickly Pear is west of the MV *Sara* – about six miles out from Long Bay.

☆ **Sandy Shallow** is recommended for novice divers. A garden of soft cor-als and gorgonians slopes from 30 to 70 feet. Seas are usually calm. Small schooling tropicals and invertebrates populate this spot.

Snorkeling

Catamaran and mono-hull sailboats leave Road Bay daily for snorkeling/picnic jaunts to **Little Bay**, on Anguilla's north-west coast; **Prickly Pear Cays,** six miles out of Road Bay; **Shoal Bay**, on the south end of Anguilla; **Scilly Cay**; **Dog Is-land**, 10 miles north of Road Bay and **Sandy Island**, the most popular out-island snorkeling destination. Tiny Sandy Island is surrounded by living reef from waist deep to 10 feet.

Beach snorkeling is good at **Barnes Bay**, West End, if you don't mind climb-ing down the crag from the Coccoloba Hotel. When winds and seas are calm, good snorkeling exists off the beach behind **Shoal Bay Villas**.

Spearfing and **collecting** is prohibited in Anguilla.

Dive Operators

Anguillan Divers, **Ltd.**, in Meads Bay, dives the reefs and dropoffs on the east end of Anguilla. PADI certifications. Rates are $50 for a one-tank dive, $70 for two one-tank dives, $135 for three one-tank dives. Snorkelers may join the trips for $15. Special snorkeling excursions that include a beach barbecue are offered. Prices vary with meal choice. ☎ 264-497-4750, www.anguillandivers.com.

Shoal Bay Scuba, the Valley, offers reef and wreck diving, PADI certification and open-water referrals. Their custom dive boat has a head, shower and dry area. Divers are given a clean beach towel, fruit and beverages. A one-tank boat dive costs $50, two-tank $80; ☎ 264-497-4371, http://shoalbayscuba.ai/, sbscuba@anguillanet.com.

Additional snorkeling cruises can be arranged through **Enchanted Island Cruises, Ltd.**, Road Bay. Enchanted Island operates a 50-foot catamaran, *Wildcat*, and a 31-foot monohull, *Counterpoint;* ☎ 264-497-3111. Also try **Sandy Island Enterprises**, Road Bay, with three Shauna power boats and a 26-foot sailboat, *Ragtime*; ☎ 264-497-6395; or **Suntastic Yacht Services**, Road Bay, with a 37-foot yacht, *Skybird*, and 30-foot powerboat, *Sunrise*; ☎ 264-497-6847.

Where to Stay

 Accommodations range from low- to mid-priced inns and cottages to luxurious resorts. A 10% service charge is added to resort bills in lieu of gratuities, and 8% government tax is added onto rooms only. Diving and snorkeling packages are offered through the dive operator. Website for more hotels: www.rendezvousbay.com or anguilla-vacation.com.

Syndans Apartments are clean, attractive studios overlooking Sandy Ground Beach and Road Salt Pond. Winter rates are $90 to $150 per day. ☎ 264-497-3180, fax 264-497-5381.

Shoal Bay Villas offers 26 one-bedroom, beachfront suites with full kitchen, private patio with hammock, ceiling fans (some with A/C). Freshwater pool. Terrific snorkeling reef off the beach. Dive packages with a room for two start at $1,550 for five nights. Winter room rates are from $270 per night; summer from $175 per night. ☎ 264-497-2671, fax 264-497-2901, www.sbvillas@anguillanet.com.

The Mariners is a West Indian-style beachfront cottage complex at Sandy Ground. Choose from rooms or cottages, each with a veranda, refrigerator, ceiling fan, telephone and private bath. Winter rates for a double are $190-$320; summer, $125-$165. Dive packages, tennis, pool, restaurant. Romantic. PO Box 139, Sandy Ground, Anguilla, BWI; ☎ 264-497-2671, fax 264-497-2901.

Anguilla Great House Beach Resort, built in the style of a West Indian plantation house, sits on Rendezvous Bay, where you can see St. Martin on the nearby horizon. Features include an open-air restaurant, pool, beach bar and snorkeling off the mile-long beach. Suites have well-equipped kitchenettes. Winter rates for a double run from $250 per day for a room, $440 with meals for two; summer, $165 for a double, $360 with meals. Money-saving dive packages from $830 per person for six nights and five dives. ☎ 800-583-9247 or 264-497-6061, www.anguillagreathouse.com, flemingw@anguillanet.com.

La Sirena is an intimate hideaway overlooking Mead's Bay on the southwest portion of the island. Choose between guest rooms and villas, all with ocean views, balcony, ceiling fans, phone and minibars. Restaurant, bar, two freshwater pools and **Anguilla Divers Ltd.** on site. Rates for a double are from $140 in summer; $230 in winter. Five-night dive packages start at $760 to $1,245. ☎ 800-331-3358; direct, 264-497-6827. Write to PO Box 200, Mead's Bay, Anguilla BWI; www.la-sirena.com; lasirena@anguillanet.com.

The Ferryboat Inn is a small family-operated inn on the south side of the island. Snorkeling and swimming off the beach. Well-equipped apartments are adjacent to the beach. Restaurant. Rates are from $140 per day in winter, $78 in summer, for a one-bedroom apartment, double occupancy. Skiing, cruises, windsurfing, Sunfish and catamarans are included in the rates. Rooms are clean, modern and attractive. ☎ 264-264-497-6613; http://online.offshore.com.ai/ferryboatinn; ferryb@anguillanet.com.

Carimar Beach Club, Meads Bay, features suites with fully equipped kitchens, island décor, ceiling fans, hair dryers and A/C. The resort sits on a lovely stretch of beach. April 1 through November 15, dive packages for seven nights in a one-bedroom, beachview apartment start at $910 per person; higher in season. ☎ 800-235-8667, or 264-497-6881; www.carimar.com; carimar@anguillanet.com.

The Inns of Anguilla is a group of 23 hotels, guest houses, apartments and villas offering attractively priced accommodations from $85 per night. For a list, description, brochures and rates of the inns, ☎ 800-553-4939, fax 264-497-2710 or write to The Anguilla Tourist Office, PO Box 1388, One Coronation Avenue, The Valley, Anguilla. BWI. In the UK: Anguilla Tourist Office, WINDOTEL, 3 Epirus Road, London SW6 7UJ, ☎ 01-937-7725, fax 938-4793; atbtour@candw.com.ai.

Sightseeing & Other Activities

Sailing, **deep-sea fishing**, **sunset cruises**, **birdwatching** at Little Bay and Crocus Bay, **shelling** and **relaxing** are the main activities on Anguilla. Plans for a movie theater and museum are in the works.

Anguilla's sightseeing spots are the **Wallblake Historic House** near the Roman Catholic Church; the **prison at Crocus Hill**, the old **Warden's Place** in the Valley; the **Fountain Cave** area, the **Devonish Cotton Gin Gallery**, **Road Bay** and **Sandy Ground**, where you'll find the dive shop and fishing boats.

Anguilla does not have a tourist-oriented nightlife, but a 15-minute ferry ride to **St. Martin** brings you to a wealth of duty-free shops, casinos and evening entertainment. Ferries leave Blowing Point for Marigot, St. Martin, every 40 minutes from 7:30 am till 11 pm. ☎ 497-6853 for information.

For guided archaeological tours write to PO Box 252, Anguilla, in advance of your trip. Deep-sea fishing can be arranged at Road Bay and Island Harbor, glass bottom boat cruises are from Shoal Bay and Island Harbour (☎ 4155); sunset cruises to out islands are offered by **Enchanted Island Cruises**, ☎ 497-3111.

Dining

Anguilla's leading French eatery, **Hibernia** at Island Harbour, offers dining on a huge veranda overlooking the sea. Choice menu picks include smoked Caribbean fish, grilled crayfish in lemongrass sauce, grilled snapper in honey and garlic, and chestnut ice cream. Open for lunch and dinner. ☎ 497-4290. Major credit cards.

Uncle Ernie's in Shoal Bay is a laid-back beach bar and restaurant where you can get a beer for one dollar. Selections include barbecued chicken, fish or ribs with chips. ☎ 497-3907.

Reefside, a friendly beachfront complex adjacent to Shoalbay Villas, opens every day for breakfast, lunch and dinner. Offers grilled lobster, steaks, steamed shrimp and tropical drinks. Catch the beach barbecue on Wednesday, Friday and Sunday from noon to 3 pm. ☎ 497-2051. Major credit cards.

Fat Cat in George Hill packages hors d'oeuvres, entrées, salads, and desserts ready to heat in the oven or microwave. Call ahead for picnics, special entrées or special-occasion cakes. ☎ 497-2307. American Express accepted.

Ships Galley on the beach at Sandy Ground features sumptuous West Indian dishes – stewed whelks (shellfish) with sweet potatoes, scampi, grilled snapper and lobster. Open for breakfast, lunch and dinner. ☎ 497-2040. Major credit cards.

Vegetarian dishes with a Mexican flair are offered at **Que Pasa** in Sandy Ground, where the chef whips up stuffed mushrooms, chili-potato soup, enchiladas in red chili sauce, quesadillas and burritos for lunch and dinner. Lobster, chicken, pork and beef are available for all dishes. Take-out and delivery service. ☎ 497-3171. Major credit cards.

For American food stop at the **Paradise Café** in Katouche, ☎ 497-3200, or enjoy luxurious Anguillian surroundings at **The Old House** at George Hill, ☎ 497-2228. **KoalKeel**, in The Valley, specializes in Caribbean seafood, ☎ 497-2930.

Facts

Helpful Phone Numbers: Police, ☎ 497-2333. Princess Alexandria Hospital, ☎ 497-2551/1552.
Nearest Recompression Chamber: Saba (38 miles).

Airlines: *Wallblake Airport*, ☎ 264-497-2719. International airports serving Anguilla are at St. Maarten, San Juan and Antigua. St. Kitts and St. Thomas also have scheduled feederline services. **WINAIR** has flights from St. Maarten, St. Thomas. **American Eagle** links with flights from San Juan. **LIAT** connects to St. Kitts and Antigua. Flying time to Anguilla from St. Maarten is seven minutes; from San Juan and Antigua, one hour; from St. Thomas, 45 minutes; from St. Kitts, 35 minutes.

Ferry Service: From Marigot Bay, St. Martin, to Blowing Point takes 15-20 minutes. Ferries depart at approximately 40-minute intervals during the day. There is one evening ferry that departs Blowing Point at 6 pm and Marigot, St. Martin, at 7:30. Fare: US$15 day; US$17 night.The ferries vary, but are small, none take vehicles, and all protect you from the weather. The crossing is about 20 to 30 minutes each way and ferries run every half hour during daylight. The ferry deposits you on the waterfront in Marigot, the French side. You show your passport (usually no forms to complete) and you are in France! To return, you pay the French a $4 tax. There is a landing card to fill out for Anguilla. *Don't miss the last ferry at 7 pm.*

Driving: On the left. Driver's license required. US$10 for visitor's permit. May be obtained at the police station or any car-rental agency.

Documents: Passports and onward ticket are required of all visitors.

Customs: Visitors may bring in duty-free one carton of cigarettes or cigars, one half-pound of tobacco, one bottle of liquor, and four ounces of perfume.

If you are sailing your own boat, you must clear customs and immigration at Blowing Point, across from Marigot, St. Martin or at Sandy Ground.

Currency: The EC (Eastern Caribbean) dollar. US$1=EC$2.68 (variable).

Language: English.

Climate: Average temperature is 80°F. Rainfall averages 35 inches per year.

Clothing: Lightweight casual dress. Nudity, including topless swimming and sunbathing, is forbidden. Wearing swimwear off the beach without a coverup is frowned upon.

Electricity: 110 volts AC, 60 cycles.

Time: Atlantic Standard (Eastern Standard + 1 hr).

Departure Tax: US$10 Airport; US$2, Ferry Port.

Religious Services: Methodist, Anglican, Baptist, Seventh Day Adventist, Roman Catholic, Church of God and the Apostolic Faith Churches.

Additional Information: *Anguilla Tourist & Information Office*, PO Box 1388, One Coronation Avenue, The Valley, Anguilla BWI; ☎ 800-553-4939, fax 264-497-2710, www.anguilla-vacation.com.

Antigua & Barbuda

Set smack in the center of the Caribbean, Antigua & Barbuda, a two-island nation, offer visitors the best of England's charm, great diving and a wealth of enticing resorts.

Antigua, a 108-square-mile island, populated by 76,000 people, is the largest of the two and of the Leeward Islands. Its capital, St. John's, is the hub of tourist activity with a bustling cruise-ship terminal, duty-free shops, full-service dive shops, fast-food and gourmet restaurants. Formerly a thriving sugar cane producer, the island has given way to a booming tourist industry since its independence from the British Crown in 1981. Physically, the island is circular and ringed by 365 secluded beaches, coves, bays and small harbors. Gentle hills to the south slope down to a beautiful turquoise sea pierced by miles of coral shoals. Beneath the surface lies a rocky terrain of coral cliffs, caves and buttresses, an oasis to thousands of fish, rays and shellfish. Shallow reefs and countless wrecks surround the island.

Barbuda, 26 miles north of Antigua, is considered one of the last frontiers of the Caribbean. It is a beautifully undeveloped and pristine low-coral island where there are no paved roads, few hotel rooms and only a handful of restaurants. Miles of secluded, untouched pink sand beaches meld into a sea of well-developed reefs teeming with lobster, hawksbill turtles, conch, and fish. Conservation efforts protect large tracts of coral banks with marine-park status. Barbuda is also habitat to the **Frigate Bird Sanctuary**, one of the largest in the world.

History

 The islands' history dates back to 1775 BC, when the *Ciboney* tribe inhabited the land. In 1493, on his second voyage to the New World, Christopher Columbus sighted and named Antigua in homage to the miracle-working Santa Maria de la Antigua of Seville. More than a century later, in 1632, an English party from St. Kitts landed on the island and claimed it for the British Crown – a relationship that would remain in force until 1981, when Antigua gained full independence.

Dive and Snorkeling Sites

1. Shirley Heights
2. Cades Reef
3. Monkshead
4. Wreck of the *Andes*

5. Sunken Rock
6. Diamond Marine Park
7. Wreck of the *Jettias*

Best Dive & Snorkeling Sites

Diving Antigua

Antigua's dive and snorkeling sites are one to two miles offshore, no more than a five-minute boat ride in most cases, along a barrier reef that surrounds nearly all of the island. Dive shops frequent the south- and west-coast reefs where visibility is good, seas are dependably calm and currents mild, but new areas are continually opening up. Depths range from shallow to dropoffs of more than 2,000 feet. Dive shops offer both scuba and snorkeling tours. Scuba divers must show a certification card.

☆☆☆ **Shirley Heights**, off the south coast, is one of the island's most spectacular areas. Jagged cliffs, coral buttresses, huge boulders and sheer dropoffs form the subsea terrain. Residents include eagle rays, schools of spadefish and turtles, with frequent sightings of mantas and dolphins. Huge mackerel and kingfish pass through. Depths are from 10 to 100 feet. Visibility is usually excellent.

☆☆☆ **Cades Reef**, a five-mile shelf off Antigua's southwest corner, is Antigua's largest reef structure. It has 25 or more different dive and snorkeling sites that vary in depth from 20 to 90 feet. Examples are **Lemon Ridge**, with depths from 20 to 45 feet; **The Chimney**, home to huge pillar coral formations inhabited by margate, squirrelfish, nurse sharks, morays; and the **The Pillars**, at 50 to 80 feet, where you'll see queen angelfish, triggerfish, black durgons, spotted and green moray eels.

The ridges and valleys of this reef are shot through with small caves hiding lobsters, crabs and small fish. Forests of elkhorn and staghorn coral provide shelter to an abundant fish population, including huge grouper, eagle rays, throngs of grunts and sergeant majors, parrotfish, stingrays, snapper and barracuda. Visibility often exceeds 100 feet when seas are calm.

☆☆☆☆ **Monkshead** is a sandy coral passage in the center of Cades which is populated by garden eels, large stingrays and jacks. Spearfishing, or collecting shells, shellfish and coral are prohibited.

The Wreck of the *Andes*, an old freighter, lies in 20 feet of water at the bottom of Deep Bay, 100 yards off the west coast. She went down in 1905 when a cargo of cotton and pitch caught fire. Abundant with fish, the hull and scattered remains are overgrown with plate corals, orange and red sponges. Good for snorkeling and diving in summer. Visibility during a swell can go down to zero.

☆☆☆ **Sunken Rock**, just five minutes off the south coast, is one of the island's most popular dive sites when sea conditions permit. The dive starts at 30 feet and drops off to 150 feet. Hundreds of coral crevices and ledges attract huge rays, amberjack, and barracuda. Recommended for experienced ocean divers.

☆☆☆ **Diamond Bank**, located 2½ miles off the north coast of Antigua, is a large shallow barrier reef complex riddled with small caves, boulders, overhangs and canyons. Marine life is prolific, with huge rays, nurse sharks, morays, lobster, queen helmuts, conch, and tropicals. Depths range from shallow to about 100 feet. Trips are weather-dependent. Usually choppy.

The Wreck of the *Jettias*, a 310-foot steamship that hit the reefs in 1917, rests in 25 feet of water and offers dramatic photo opportunities when

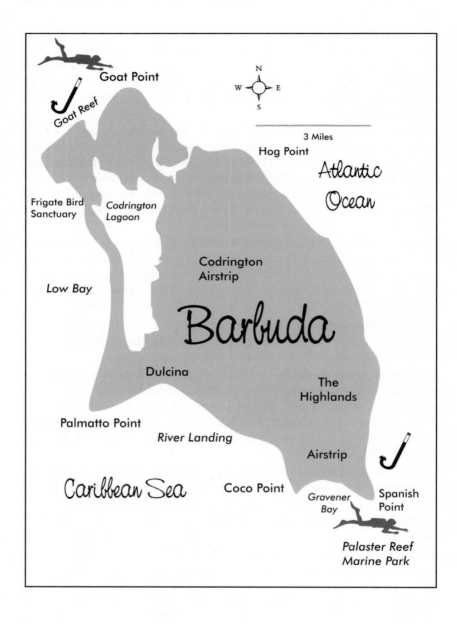

weather and visibility permit. This area is subject to swells and silting during high winds. Summer is the best time to dive the *Jettias*.

Snorkeling Antigua

When seas are calm, good shore snorkeling may be found in **Half Moon Bay** in Saint Philip Parish, off the beaches of the **Galley Bay Hotel** at Deep Bay, **Pineapple Beach Hotel** at Long Bay on the Southeast coast, the **Hawksbill Beach Resort** at Five Islands Village, just south of Deep Bay, and the **Sandpiper Reef Hotel**. (The Galley Bay and Sandpiper hotels were not open at press time, but you can still use the beaches). Check with local dive shops for wind and current conditions before entering the water.

Boone's Reef, located one mile offshore from Dickenson Bay, is a protected reef area, good for beginning and experienced snorkelers. The reef starts at two feet and drops off to 25 feet. Juvenile and schooling fish abound. Visibility varies with sea conditions. Snorkeling boats depart from Dickenson Bay.

Diving Barbuda

The dense reefs fringing Barbuda are largely unexplored. There are no dive shops on the island, but experienced snorkelers can swim to **Palaster Reef**, off Palmetto Point on the southwest tip of the island. More than 100 shipwrecks have been documented off Barbuda's coast. Charter day-trips from Antigua can be easily arranged.

Antigua Dive Operators

Aquanaut Diving Centres are at the St. James' Club and the Galleon Beach Club, ☎ 268-460-5000, aquanaut@candw.ag. Or try **Dive Antigua Scuba Center** at the Pineapple Beach Resort, English Harbour, offering tours and rentals, ☎ 268-729-4698, www.antiguascuba.com; or **Dive Antigua**, ☎ 268-462-3483, www.diveantigua.com.

Dockyard Divers at English Harbour visits the south-coast dive and snorkeling sites, ☎ 268-460-1178, fax 268-460-1179, VHF channel 68. Others are **Jolly Dive** at Club Antigua, ☎ 268-462-0061, and **Pirate Divers** at the Lord Nelson Beach Hotel, ☎ 268-462-3094.

Ultramarine Antigua, Hodges Bay, has dive trips to the south and west sides of the island. Kids' programs and a full range of certification courses are offered. ☎ 268-463-3483, www.h2oantigua.com.

Catamarans such as the **Wadadli Cats** (☎ 462-2980) offer excellent sail-snorkeling trips. Lunch, drinks and equipment are included in the price.

Where to Stay

Antigua

Antigua is not a "diver's island" and has no dedicated dive resorts, but those listed either have dive operators on the premises, are associated with diving, or are located near popular dive or snorkeling areas.

 8.5% room tax and 10% service charge are added to accommodation rates. Some resorts include them in their package rates. Some do not. Check with individual operations; www.antigua-barbuda.org.

The Grand Royal Antiguan Beach & Tennis Resort, located on Deep Bay at the entrance of St. John's Harbor, features three restaurants, four bars, eight tennis courts, a watersports center, freeform pool with swim-up bar, white sand beach, children's activities and nightly entertainment. It has 262 spacious rooms (12 poolside cottages), each with air conditioning, phones, color TV, key card locks. Marker buoys for the wreck of the *Andes*, 100 yards offshore, can be seen from the alfresco restaurant on Andes Bay. Diving is arranged by the desk with a nearby dive shop. Room-only rates for a double are $150 in summer, $190 in winter. Hotel ☎ (800) 858-4618, direct 268-462-3733. Write PO Box 1322, Deep Bay, Antigua, WI, www.grandroyalantiquan.com, reservations@grandroyalantigual.com.

Curtain Bluff Resort sits on a dramatic, 13-acre seaside bluff on Antigua's southern shore. This all-inclusive resort is the closest jump-off point to Cades Reef diving. The property slopes down to two coves, one calm and good for snorkeling, the other with rolling surf. Amenities include 61 beachfront rooms and suites. Dive shop on premises offers boat tours only. Certification courses, if desired, can be arranged with nearby shops. Rates cover the room, all meals for two, bar service, afternoon tea and hors d'oeuvres, mail service, water-skiing, scuba diving (two dives per day – gear included), a snorkeling trip to Cades Reef each morning, deep-sea fishing, sailing, tennis, golf, squash and croquet. Summer and fall rates (October 18 to December 18; April 15 to October 17th) are $595 per day for two; winter rates (January 2 to April 14), $850 per day for two. 10% gratuities and 8.5% tax not included. ☎ 888-268-4227, direct 268-462-8400, fax 268-462-8409, www.curtainbluff.com.

Set on Antigua's southernmost tip, the **Galleon Beach Club and Hotel** offers one- and two-bedroom cottages and suites with fully equipped kitchens. Rooms overlook Freeman's Bay and English Harbour. Dive shop, restaurant and bar on premises. Winter rates for a one-bedroom suite start at $305 per night. Two-bedroom cottage for up to four people, $385 per night. Diving and meals are extra. ☎ 268-460-1024, www.galleonbeach.com; galleonbeach @candw.ag.

The **Copper and Lumber Store Hotel** is a rustic 17th-century brick building restored as an intimate 14-suite hostelry, located in Nelson's Dockyard. Each individually decorated room features beamed ceilings and dormer windows overlooking the harbour with luxurious Persian rugs, period antiques, four-poster beds and mahogany baths with brass fixtures. Ferry service to Galleon Beach for scuba. No beach. ☎ 268-460-1058, www.copperandlumberhotel.com, or book through your travel agent.

The lagoon off **The Galley Bay Resort** is a favorite snorkeling spot. This plush resort offers scuba, but can arrange for reef trips through nearby shops. Galley Bay is a 70-room, all-inclusive resort set on 40 acres of landscaped ground between a half-mile sandy beach and a lagoon. Guests choose from a variety of splendid air-conditioned accommodations, including cottages with grass roofs. The resort has a freeform pool and a gourmet restaurant. Rates per couple start at $480 per day in summer, $600 per day in winter, and include all meals, drinks, and taxes. One-tank dives are $70. ☎ 800-858-4612, direct 268-462-0302, www.eliteislandresorts.com or www.antigua-resorts.com.

Another snorkelers' favorite, though expensive, is **Jumby Bay**, an exclusive, yet accessible, luxury resort on its own island, two miles north of Antigua. Off the beach lie beautiful coral patches and throngs of tropical fish. Jumby Bay offers 38 recently renovated suites with ocean views and secluded beaches. Rates include three meals, afternoon tea, unlimited cocktails, laundry and picnic service. Three snorkeling trips are made to Bird Island each week. Facilities include tennis, water-skiing and instruction, snorkeling, Sunfish sailboats, bicycles, croquet, putting green, bar and laundry service. Rates include three meals, afternoon tea, unlimited cocktails and laundry service. Winter rates are $1,050 per night, per couple for a stay of seven nights; summer rates are $900 per night per couple. 8.5% tax not included. Scuba diving extra. ☎ 800-421-9016; 268-462-6000, www.jumbybayresort.com.

Long Bay Hotel, on Long Bay, offers 18 rooms and six cottages. The resort offers dive trips with the Long Bay Dive Shop to nearby reefs and wrecks, snorkeling trips, tennis, two restaurants, a pretty beach. Winter rates average $255 per day. ☎ 800-291-2005, www.longbayhotel.com or www.longbay-antigua.com. **Long Bay Dive Shop**, ☎ 268-463-2005.

Allegro Pineapple Beach Club is an all-inclusive 125-room hotel on Long Bay Beach. Good snorkeling available over a shallow coral reef just off the beach. Winter rates, per night, start at about $350 for two; summer at $300, including meals for two, drinks, board surfing, sailboats, snorkeling gear, fishing, fitness center, tennis, beach, pool, and entertainment, and room tax. Scuba is not included in the resort's all-inclusive rates; dive packages with **Antigua Scuba Center** start at $230 for six dives. Book through travel agents or ☎ 800-345-0356 or 268-463-2006, www.allegroresorts.com.

Rex Halcyon Cove Resort on Dickenson Bay offers a choice of first-class rooms. Standard rooms at $230 per day for a double in summer, $280 per day in winter; rooms have double beds, shower, ceiling fan, phone and terrace. Superior rooms include a mini-fridge, cable TV, air conditioning. Diving is arranged at the desk. Recreational facilities include tennis, beach volleyball, shuffleboard and table tennis. All-inclusive rates are also available, though water-skiing, scuba and fishing are charged separately. Restaurants offer casual or fine dining. ☎ 800-255-5859, direct 268-462-0256, fax 268-462-0271.

Sandals Antigua, a luxurious resort village on Dickenson Bay, features lavish round suites known as *rondovals*, a dive shop, fitness center, five restaurants, five pools, five whirlpools, gorgeous white sand beach, swim-up bar, outdoor dancing and dining. Diving and snorkeling are part of its all-inclusive package, which also includes meals, land and watersports. Per-day, per-person rates start at $350 per person in winter, $325 in summer. ☎ 800-SANDALS (726-3257), UK 0171-581-9895; www.sandals.com.

St. James Club, on 100 acres of private peninsula, features 73 two-bedroom villas, 20 suites, 85 rooms, all with ocean or bay view. Amenities include three pools, two beaches, seven tennis courts, water-skiing, sailing, board surfing, horseback riding, and fitness center. There are also children's facilities, three restaurants, night club, casino, salon and shops. Scuba school, fishing and private marina. All-inclusive rates, including meals and accommodations (not diving) for two, range from $250 per night in summer, to $330 per night in winter. **Aquanaut Divers** on property. ☎ 800-858-4618, direct 268-460-5000, www.antigua-resorts.com.

Budget-minded divers will find lower rates and terrific inns and small resort online at www.antigua-vip.com. One favorite is the **Sandpiper Reef Resort**, with rates from $110 per room, per day. ☎ 268-462-0939, www.sandpiper-reef.com.

Barbuda

Palmetto Hotel, Barbuda. Located on Palmetto's Peninsula, to the southwestern side of Barbuda, this resort consists of a 63-room luxury hotel and 67 villas facing the ocean. The surroundings insure complete comfort and privacy. ☎ 268-460-0440, www.palmettohotel.com.

For additional Antigua accommodations visit www.antigua-barbuda.org.

Other Activities

A number of leisure cruises, most of which last the better part of a day and include lunch, sightseeing, snorkeling and other entertainment, sail Antigua's jagged coast. The *Servabo Fun Cruise*, a 70-foot Brixham gaff-rigged ketch based off the shore of Dickenson Bay, departs from Antigua Village. The *Jolly Roger Pirate Cruise*, Antigua's largest two-masted schooner, offers daily and Saturday evening cruises, ☎ 462-2064. The *Falcon*, an elegant catamaran, does sunset and day snorkeling cruises to Barbuda and Bird Island, a tiny, uninhabited nesting ground for red-billed tropic birds, sooty terns, brown noddies, and brown pelicans. Outstanding shallow snorkeling reefs skirt Bird Island's beach. Most hotels can arrange for any of these cruises.

Antigua's northeast trade winds are ideal for windsurfers of all abilities. The island's sheltered west coast is perfect for beginners, while on the east coast, the giant "Atlantic rollers" are challenging even for advanced surfers.

Windsurfing lessons for novices, intermediate, and advanced board surfers are offered at several hotels, including Jolly Beach Hotel's **Windsurfing Sailing School** and **Patrick Scales Water Sports** at Lord Nelson Beach Hotel.

Water-skiing, JetSkiing, and parasailing are offered at the **Wadadli Watersports Centre** at Buccaneer Cove and **Unlimited Hydro Sports** at Dickenson Bay and Jolly Beach.

Deep-sea fishing charters can be arranged through most hotels. Tennis courts are everywhere. **Viking Tennis Club**, ☎ 462-2260, is a private club that offers temporary membership for visitors. **Temo Sports**, ☎ 460-1781, a tennis and squash complex, has synthetic grass courts and two glass-backed squash courts. Squash is also offered at the **Bucket Club**, ☎ 462-3060.

Golf enthusiasts will enjoy Antigua's fine 18-hole, par-72 course at **Jolly Harbour Golf Club**, ☎ 462-7771 or 480-6950. Daily greens fees are $40 for 18 holes, $25 for nine holes; carts are $25 for 18 holes and $13 for nine.

Escorted horseback beach and cross-country tours are arranged at the **Wadadli Stables**, ☎ 462-2721, in St. John's.

Antigua's exquisite scenery, varied terrain and well-preserved monuments make excellent walking and hiking territory. The capital of St. John's is filled with interesting attractions and shops, and the national park at **Nelson's Dockyard** provides historic sightseeing opportunities. Mond's Hill, Boggy Peak, Fig Tree Drive, and Megaliths at Greencastel Hill are just a few of the hiking areas for adventurous souls.

Bicycles are another way to view Antigua's scenery. Mountain bikes can be rented for $10 per day from **Sun Cycles**, ☎ 461-0324.

Sightseeing

Antigua

Two major sightseeing areas are the capital city of St. John's on the northwestern side of the island and English Harbour on the south side. St. John's, with a population of 35,000, is the center of business and visitor activity. More than half of the country's hotels surround the capital city.

Situated on a hilltop overlooking the center of town, **St. John's Cathedral** was originally constructed in 1683 and replaced in 1745. It was rebuilt and re-consecrated in the 19th century after a shattering earthquake. Its unusual architecture features two Baroque-style towers. The **Museum of Antigua & Barbuda**, located in the Old Courthouse, exhibits artifacts tracing the rich history of the sister islands from pre-historic times through independence. **Government House** is the official residence of the Governor General for Antigua in St. John's. As such, it is not regularly open to the public, but is a fine example of 17th-century colonial architecture. **Fort James**, which once defended the entrance of St. John's Harbor, features weapons and other military details dating back to the American Revolution.

Other interesting things to see in and around St. John's include the **Public Market**, a semi-open-air mart that provides much local color and the opportunity to sample native produce. The **Antigua Rum Distillery,** which may be toured by prior arrangement, is at Deep Water Harbour. Cavalier and Old Mill Rums are made here. **Heritage Quay**, a shopping complex and cruise ship pier, offers a wide variety of duty-free shops, a casino, and a hotel. **Redcliffe Quay**, a restored arsenal, now houses shops and restaurants.

Many more historical buildings can be found on the other side of the island within the confines of **Nelson's Dockyard**. Built in 1784 at **English Harbour**, it served as the headquarters for Admiral Horatio Nelson, the commander of the Leeward Islands Squadron, during the days when a man's worth was measured by how quickly he could reload his musket.

Landmarks of the seamen's commitment to Antigua have been painstakingly restored and the area is now a national park. One landmark in particular is the **Copper and Lumber Store Hotel**, the former center of activity for purchasing construction materials. While the bottom served as a supply store, the upper floors were used as quarters for sailors whose ships were being hauled in for repairs. Today, those early quarters are elegant rooms of a Georgian hotel filled with period furnishings. Two other buildings, the old **Capstan House** and the **Cordage and Canvas Store,** have been restored for additional hotel space by the Copper and Lumber owners. **Admiral's Inn and**

Restaurant also provides accommodations and the opportunity for leisurely investigation.

The complex has two museums. **Admiral's House,** with its bust of Nelson framing the doorway, is an original structure full of Nelsonian mementos reminiscent of his era. **Clarence House**, the former home of Prince William Henry, Duke of Clarence, who later became King William IV, is a graceful Georgian stone residence overlooking the Dockyard. It is now home to Antigua's Governor General. When he is not in residence it is open to the public, and the caretaker provides visitors with a lively lecture on the house's origins and history. In modern times, it has served as the vacation residence of the late Princess Margaret.

To the north are the stately ruins of **Shirley Heights**, named for General Thomas Shirley, the former governor of the Leeward Islands. The fortress includes extensive fortifications, barracks, and powder magazines, which serve as great "lookout" points. On Sunday afternoons, Shirley Heights is a gathering spot where visitors can enjoy local reggae and steel bands and a tasty barbecue meal as they watch the sun set over the dockyard area. On the southern side of the Harbour, about a 10-minute walk from the dockyard, are the remains of **Fort Berkeley**, a small outpost with eight cannons.

In the center of the island lies Antigua's pioneer sugar plantation, **Betty's Hope Estate**, which introduced large-scale sugar cultivation and innovative methods of processing sugar. It was founded in the 1650s by Governor Keynell and granted to Christopher Codrington in 1688. The Codrington family were involved with Betty's Hope for more than 250 years until 1920. Both Christopher Codrington and his son served as Governor General of the Leeward Islands, developing the plantation as the seat of government during the late 17th and early 18th centuries. Two old windmill towers still stand, together with the walls and arches of the plantation's boiling house. A conservation project was recently completed that has handsomely refurbished this historic site.

Barbuda

 After the magnificent reefs that surround the island, Barbuda's **Frigate Bird Sanctuary** tops the list of sightseeing favorites. It is at the north end of Codrington Lagoon, and is only accessible by small boat. Here, the *Fregata magnificens* (Magnificent frigate birds) brood in mangrove bushes that stretch for miles. In olden days, sailors called the frigate bird the "man-o-war bird" and the "hurricane bird" because their eight-foot wingspan gives them enough power to soar as high as 2,000 feet above ground. Although visitors can see the birds throughout the year, the mating season, from September to February, is a brilliant spectacle, when the male frigate inflates a crimson pouch at his throat and breast in an attempt to attract the female. Chicks hatch from December to March and remain in the nest for up to eight months until they are strong enough to fly.

A visit to the sanctuary is a 45-minute trip in a wooden rowboat powered by a small outboard motor. The boats are piloted by Barbudians who cautiously navigate through the mangroves.

Barbuda's dry climate and abundant marine life attracts pelicans, warblers, snipes, ibis, herons, kingfishers, tropical mockingbirds, oyster catchers, and cormorants. Other wildlife found roaming the island are white-tailed deer, boars, donkeys, and red-footed tortoises. Unique to its marine life is the Barbudian lobster.

Besides snorkeling and bird watching, Barbuda offers some interesting attractions and activities. **Highland House** is the former estate of Sir William Codrington, the first lessee of Barbuda, when the annual rent to the crown was "one fatted sheep, on demand." **Dark Cave** has deep pools of clear water that extend approximately one mile underground, and at the **Caves at Two Foot Bay** visitors can climb down into a circular chamber through a hole in the roof to view faded Arawak drawings on the walls.

Several Antigua-based companies offer day-tours of Barbuda. Tour prices are approximately $120 per person. They include round-trip airfare, a tour with a visit to the Frigate Bird Sanctuary and lunch.

Dining

 The cuisine of Antigua & Barbuda has evolved from the tastes and foods of the many groups that make up the islands' West Indian heritage: Carib Indians, French, English, Africans, Spanish, Portuguese, Indian, Lebanese, and Syrian. The influence of these cultures, and the diversity of locally grown fruits and vegetables, combine to create a cuisine that will satisfy the most discerning palate.

A trip to the **public market** in St. John's is a delectable opportunity to sample the real riches of Antigua & Barbuda. Visitors will find a variety of fruits and vegetables, some that are familiar to many in North America, but known by a different name. For instance, a *green fig* is a small green banana that must be cooked before eating. *Christophine*, a large squash with pale green flesh, is boiled and served hot. The *breadfruit* is rounded with a hard green skin and soft inside, and is cooked and served as a vegetable or made into bread, pie, or pudding. The islands' most famous fruit is the *Antigua black pineapple*, a smaller, sweeter version of the Hawaiian variety.

Lobster, conch, cockles (mollusks), grouper, and red snapper are other local seafood delights.

Coconut Grove Beach Restaurant (☎ 462-0806) sits beneath swaying palm trees at the water's edge on Dickenson Bay, and offers fresh lobster, seafood and Caribbean dishes. Open for breakfast, lunch and dinner.

Amigos at Barrymore Beach Club, Runaway Bay (☎ 461-3304) is an inexpensive spot for Mexican-American dishes.

Alberto's at Willoughby Bay (☎ 460-3007) offers dining in a giant gazebo cooled by the Caribbean breeze. Local seafood, prepared with an Italian accent, includes conch salad, lobster, and pasta dishes, and the wine list features many Italian favorites.

Facts

Nearest Recompression Chamber: None on island.

Getting Here: *V.C. Bird International Airport* accommodates large aircraft, and passengers are served by a new and modern terminal. **Air Jamaica, American Airlines, BWIA, West Indies Airways, Continental Airlines** and **US Air** from the United States; **Air Canada** and **BWIA** direct from Canada; **British Airways** and **Virgin Atlantic** direct from London; **Lufthansa** direct from Frankfurt; **LIAT** and **Caribbean Star** fly inter-island.

Carib Aviation operates flights into Barbuda; ☎ 268-462-3147 or caribav@candw.ag for schedules.

Driving: On the left. A valid driver's license will secure a temporary license in Antigua at a nominal cost (US$20).

Documents: Passport and onward ticket.

Customs: Arriving passengers are allowed 200 cigarettes, one quart of liquor, and six ounces of perfume.

Currency: Antigua & Barbuda use the Eastern Caribbean dollar, also known as the "Bee Wee." The currency is tied to the US dollar at an average exchange rate of EC$2.65 to US$1, subject to fluctuation. Most major credit cards are accepted.

Taxes: Airport Departure Tax for stay-over visitors is US$20. An 8.5% government tax is added to all hotel bills. There is a 10% service charge added to bills in lieu of tipping. Elsewhere tipping is discretionary.

Climate: Antigua's temperatures range between an average of 76°F in January and February to 83°F in August and September. Rainfall averages 45 inches per year with relatively low humidity. The rainy season is September, October and November, but there are usually only short showers.

Clothing: Casual, light, loose-fitting cotton clothes are suggested. Generally, it's informal, but some hotels and casinos require jackets at night. Ladies are requested to wear skirts or slacks rather than abbreviated shorts or swimwear while in the city. Use a light wetsuit or wetskin for diving during winter.

Electricity: Dual voltage available in major hotels, 220 and 110 AC, 60 cycles.

Language: English with an island lilt – "No big ting."

Religious Services: Protestant, Roman Catholic, Seventh-Day Adventist.

Additional Information: *Antigua & Barbuda Department of Tourism* has offices in New York at 610 Fifth Avenue, Suite 311, NY, NY 10020, ☎ 212-541-4117; info@antigua-barbuda.org; and in Florida at 25 SE Second Avenue, Suite 300, Miami, FL 33131, ☎ 305-381-6762 or 800-268-4227, www.antigua-barbuda.org.

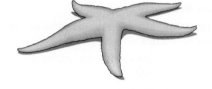

Aruba

Vacationers discovered Aruba in 1957, when the first cruise ship, *Tradewinds*, arrived. The island has since developed into a top tourist destination. Easy to reach, it is just 18 miles from Venezuela's coast – yet far enough away to escape the hustle and bustle of civilization.

And, it's easy to explore, both above and below the sea. Just 20 miles long and six miles wide, its luxury hotels and dive boats line up neatly along the western (leeward) shore – minutes from popular reef and wreck dives. The shops and sights of the capital, **Oranjestad**, are nearby too.

Aruba's sub-seascapes encompass dramatic wrecks, rocky shoals, and reefs. Coastal scenery is impressive, with miles of white, soft sand beaches along the western and southern shores. Huge rocks dot the eastern windward coast where a natural coral bridge rises from the sea to 25 feet and stretches more than 100 feet long. On shore, windswept divi divi trees (*watapana*) beautymark the rocky cliffs and wind-sculpted sand dunes.

Inland, Aruba presents a unique Caribbean landscape of cactus and aloe with gigantic boulders strewn about. Very low humidity and an average annual rainfall of only 20 inches explain the desert-like countryside. On the southeastern tip is Aruba's other city, **San Nicolas**.

Arubans themselves may be their country's best advertisements. Long secure in a solid economy with good education, housing and health care, the island's population of about 88,000 regard tourists as welcome guests. Even the national anthem celebrates a high regard for hospitality. The phrase *"Grandeza di bo pueblo ta su gran cordialidad"* translates as "The greatness of our people is their great cordiality." Thousands of past visitors would agree.

History

 Aruba's history is a tale of varied influences. The Spaniards had relatively low regard for the land they discovered and claimed in 1499. Like its neighbors, **Bonaire** and **Curaçao**, Aruba was officially declared an *isla inutil* (useless island). The Spanish found Arawak Indians of the Caiquetio tribe living there, just as they had in the Stone Age, and promptly shipped them off to Santo Domingo to work in the gold mines. About 11 years later, its discoverers turned Aruba into something of a large cattle ranch and some of the original inhabitants were brought back to work it.

Dive and Snorkeling Sites
1 Arashi Marine Park
2 Wreck of the *Antilla*
3 Malmok
4 Wreck of the
   Pedernales
5 South Airplanes
6 Harbour Reef
7 Tugboat Wreck
8 Barcadera Reef
9 Mike Reef
10 Mangel Halto Reef
11 Isla de Oro Reef
12 Natural Bridge

For awhile the Indians regained control of their land, but in 1636 it was taken over by the Dutch, who have remained in power ever since. Through 300 years of changing economic fortunes and various immigrations, the ABC islands (Aruba, Bonaire and Curacao) were part of the Netherlands Antilles, whose governor reported directly to the queen.

Europeans began to immigrate to Aruba in the late 1700s. At this time, Oranjestad was founded and named after the reigning Royal House of Orange. During the 19th century, many Venezuelans arrived, adding a decidedly Spanish influence to the small country.

In 1824, gold was discovered in Aruba. Visitors can still see remains of the smelting works at Bushiribana and Balashi. When gold mining no longer proved profitable, Aruban aloe plantations flourished. Then, in the 1920s, the oil industry arrived. The Lago refinery, a subsidiary of Standard Oil, was established just outside San Nicolas and remained the island's most important employer until its closing in the spring of 1985. Its influence is likely to be permanent, however. The resulting influx of Americans and others has made English a prominent second language, and Aruba's main thoroughfare, L.G. Smith Boulevard, is named for Lago's one-time general manager.

Politically, Aruba has made quiet and peaceful change. On January 1, 1986, the nation left the Netherlands Antilles to become a separate entity within the Kingdom of the Netherlands. Now Aruba has its own governor, appointed by the Queen. Local government is democratic, with an elected 21-member parliament and Council of Ministers.

Tourism in Aruba began in 1959 when the first hotel/casino, the **Aruba Caribbean** (restored to its former prominence by the Radisson company), opened its doors. However, the world truly began to discover the island in the mid 1960s. Hotels, casinos, restaurants, dive boats, shops and amusements have been popping up ever since.

Diving & Snorkeling Sites

Except for Renaissance Island, access to most of Aruba's dive and snorkeling sights is easiest by boat. All are a few minutes ride from shore on the leeward side, along the west and south coasts. Dive shops divide the area into north end (wrecks and rocks), and south end (reefs and artificial reefs). Three spots on the south shore are close enough to swim to, but attempting to find the channels and cuts through the shallow reefs is futile without a local guide.

☆☆ **Arashi**, a rocky reef offshore from the lighthouse at the northwest corner of the island, delights novice divers and snorkelers with throngs of juvenile fish, elkhorn and brain corals. Visibility is always 60 feet or better. Depths range from the shallows to 40 feet. Nice! Seas are calm with an occasional light surge. Boat access. Good for novice divers and snorkelers.

☆ **Arashi Airplanes** include a twin-engine Beechcraft at 35 feet and a Lockheed Lodestar at 60 feet – both purposely scuttled to create an artificial reef. Visibility is good enough to see the Beechcraft from the surface. Both wrecks are broken up. Small fish inhabit the engines and fuselages. Boat access. Good for new divers.

☆ A short distance from Arashi lies **Blue Reef** and *Debbie II*, a small tugboat at 70 feet. The reef starts at 50 feet and drops to a sandy shelf at 90 feet, where huge lobsters and a couple of stingrays hide out. In 1992, a 120-foot fuel barge was sunk as an additional feature. The wreck attracts schooling fish.

Purple, orange and green sponges decorate the reef. Depths are from 40 to 90 feet.

☆☆☆☆ Just south of Blue Reef sits one of Aruba's most unusual sights and most popular dives, the wreck of the 400-foot German freighter, **Antilla**. The ship was new when it was scuttled in 1940, when Germany invaded Holland.

Locally referred to as the "ghost ship," it is covered by giant tube sponges and brilliant orange cup corals. Her twisted, rusting steelwork extends upward from the main section to above the surface, making for intriguing photo opportunities. The remains of the hull are surrounded by big lobsters and angelfish, moray eels and throngs of silversides. Octopi and puffers are common. Outside, schools of yellowtail and sergeant majors sway with the gentle current.

The wreck lies about a mile offshore, just north of Palm Beach, in 60 feet of water. Visibility is between 50 and 70 feet. Snorkelers can circle the *Antilla's* superstructure.

☆☆ Just west of Palm Beach lies the wreck of the **Pedernales**, an oil tanker torpedoed by a German sub during WWII, then later cut into three pieces by the US military. The bow and stern were salvaged, towed to the US and welded together to create a new vessel, which joined the Normandy invasion fleet. The center section was left behind and now rests at 25 to 40 feet. A favorite of novice divers, the wreck is populated by parrotfish, yellowtails, grunts, squirrelfish, trumpetfish and a profusion of silversides. Boat access.

☆☆ **Barcadera Reef**, four miles south of Oranjestad, ranges from 20 to 90 feet. Excellent for snorkelers and divers, the reef supports dense stands of elkhorn and staghorn corals, finger corals, with wrasses, scorpionfish, blue and stoplight parrotfish, French angels, damselfish and pink-tipped anemones. The reef lies 600 yards from the shore at Barcadera Harbor. Boat dive.

☆☆☆☆ **Mangel Halto** ("tall mangrove"), three quarters of a mile south of Barcadera Harbor, can be reached by swimming out from the Mangel Halto Beach for 120 yards, but it's easier from a boat. The reef slopes from 15 ft to ledges and ridges at 110 ft that support an array of hard corals and encrusting sponges. Fish life includes copper sweepers, grunts, sergeant majors, lobsters, blue tangs, butterflyfish, stingrays and jacks. At depth, green morays, nurse sharks, tarpons and large barracudas inhabit small caves and overhangs. Nice for snorkeling and diving.

Just south of Mangel Halto lies the **Jane Sea**, an impressive 250-foot cement freighter intentionally sunk by local dive masters to attract fish. *Jane Sea's* bottom rests upright in 45 to 90 ft of water. Good for photography.

☆☆ **Isla de Oro Reef** lies off Savaneta, an old Aruban fishing village, near the south end of the island. This site is close to the mangrove-lined shore and is challenging for novice and experienced divers. There is always some current running; visibility is usually excellent. Resident yellowstingrays, lobsters, Spanish hogfish and French angelfish race the walls of star, brain and plate corals. At depth, sheet and leaf corals form ledges and caves – home to large morays and parrotfish. The reef begins at 20 feet and drops down to 125 feet. Boat access.

DePalm Island

 First-time snorkelers (of all heights) will find waist-high snorkeling outside of DePalm Island, a quarter-mile offshore from the Water & Electricity Plant – four miles south of Oranjestad along L.G. Smith Boulevard. A ferry to DePalm leaves the mainland every half hour. Half-day trips to DePalm with food, beverages and snorkeling equipment cost $45.

Snorkelers are immediately greeted by a dozen or more two-foot blue parrotfish looking for a handout. These fish meet you at the dock stairs and will leap up out of the water to eat offerings of bread or whatever munchies you tote. Feed with caution – they have sharp teeth! One surprised small snorkeler was chased back up the dock staircase by a few voracious fish.

More adventurous snorkelers swim out about 30 yards to find a dense coral reef, which gets more interesting the farther out you swim. The reef supports an abundance of fish – blue tangs, blue and stoplight parrotfish, triggerfish, sergeant majors, yellowtail and grunts. Depths range from four feet to a dropoff of 120 feet about 400 yards out.

Facilities on DePalm include a good bar and grill, showers, changing facilities and a snorkeling equipment rental shack. The restaurant sells fish food for $1. DePalm reef is great for scuba too, but more easily reached from a dive boat.

Renaissance Island

Renaissance Island, a watersports outpost owned by the Renaissance Resorts at Seaport Village, is reached by a short shuttle-boat ride. Guests of the resort may use the island for free. Others pay $50 for the day, which includes the shuttle to and from the resort, lunch and one cocktail. Coupons for the island are sold in the resort lobby. Snorkeling gear, rented on the island by **Redsail Sports**, ☎ 568-61603, costs $10 for a day's use (with a credit card guarantee for deposit). Moorings for dive kayaks were in the plans at press time. The island has a dive shop, beach restaurant, air-conditioned fitness center. Three separate beaches cater to families or adults (topless), with a special cove for honeymooners, divers and snorkelers.

☆☆☆ **Renaissance Airplanes**, 50 yards from the Renaissance Island main beach, is the site of two vintage twin-engine aircraft wrecks – both unclaimed drug runners – sunk to form an artificial reef and a fun dive. The wrecks, a Beechcraft 18 and a Convair 400, are intact and can be penetrated by divers. Inside are octopi, moray eels, lobsters and crabs. The Beech sits in 15 feet of water on a sloping reef, while the Convair lies in 40-60 feet. The oxidizing fuselages, good for video and still photography, are covered with a thin layer of clinging corals and hydroids. **Red Sail Sports** on the island rents equipment and offers guided tours and lessons. Normally calm with one- to two-foot swells and a mild current. Snorkelers can see the Beechcraft from the surface.

☆ **The Barge**, in 12 feet of water lying about 100 yards off Renaissance Island's main beach, makes for a fun snorkeling spot. Crowds of fish swarm the wreckage. Usually calm, with a one- to two-foot swell and light current. Check with the dive shop for current conditions. Swimming and snorkeling outside the protected lagoon is not recommended for small children, though swimming inside the lagoon is fine.

Windward-side Dives

☆☆☆ The *California*, a wreck off the northwest tip of the island, is for experienced divers and then recommended only during periods of extreme calm. Resting at 40 feet, the scattered remains of the wooden ship are draped in orange and yellow sponges, plate corals and anemones. Huge groupers, jewfish, lobsters, sharks and barracudas frequent the area. A dense reef of staghorn and pillar corals forms a breakwater beyond the wreck.

☆☆☆ The **Natural Bridge**, another north-shore adventure dive, rises from monster-size boulders adorned with black and soft corals. Gigantic basket sponges loom up from the bottom. Depths from 20 to 110 feet. Rough water and currents make this a choice for advanced divers only.

Where to Snorkel & Shore-dive

The best beach snorkeling from the mainland is off **Malmok**. Get there by driving north from Palm Beach along L.G. Smith Boulevard, the main coast road. There is usually a snorkeling boat moored offshore, which makes it easy to spot, or if you look straight out to sea you'll see the top of the *Antilla*. Park anywhere and walk down to the beach. Swim out from the shore about 10 feet to the rocks, where you'll find hordes of small reef fish. Always calm. Good for children, *but beware the spiny urchins hiding in the rocks*.

All of Aruba's beaches are open to the public, but a narrow strip directly behind the houses is private. Most homeowners have a sign marking where their back yard ends and the public beach begins.

Beach dives are best off Renaissance Island, but possible off the local beaches on the south end of the island. **Mangel Halto** – swim straight out to the breakwater, then about 45 yards to the reef; **Pos Chiquito** – swim to the left once out of the lagoon; **Santo Largo** – walk out about 200 yards till the water is deeper. All require a fairly long swim or walk through shallow water and you must be accompanied by an Aruban dive operator.

Caution: **Baby Beach**, outside the breakwater, is listed everywhere, including Aruba's Website, as a great beach dive. This is a beautiful, natural lagoon with shallow, calm water but, in fact, there's not much to see. There is absolutely nothing on the bottom but white sand, three juvenile yellowtails and an old sneaker, which may be gone by press time. Outside the breakwater there is a nice coral reef, but seas are often very rough and currents are frequently too strong to allow you to swim back to shore.

Inside the breakwater there is nothing but sand on the bottom – no fish, no coral. If you ignore our suggestion to pass it up and want to try it as a shore-dive, wait for a day when seas are calm and expect the current to carry you up the coast all the way to the Marina Pirata Country Club. Start from the southernmost corner of the parking lot.

 To call from outside Aruba you must use the country code 001-297 plus the seven-digit local number. On-island use just the last seven digits, beginning with the 5.

Dive Operators

Most Aruban dive shops offer scuba and/or snorkeling trips, certification and resort courses. One-tank dive trips start at $50; snorkeling tours from $25. Mask, fins and snorkel rent for about $12 per day, but may be included at no extra charge on a sail tour.

Set sail for a half- or full-day snorkel cruise aboard a racy catamaran with **Red Sail Sports**, ☎ 586-1603, www.redsailaruba.com; **DePalm Tours**, ☎ 582-4545, www.depalm.com; or **Pelican Watersports**, ☎ 583-1228, www.pelican-aruba.com.

Scuba courses, reef and wreck dive trips can be arranged through any hotel or direct through **Red Sail Sports**, ☎ 582-4500 or 800-255-6425; **Pelican Watersports**, ☎ 583-1228; **Aruba Pro Dive**, ☎ 582-5520, fax 583-7723; **DePalm Watersports**, ☎ 582-4545, fax 582-3012; **Native Divers**, ☎ 583-4763; and **Unique Watersports**, ☎ 586-0096.

Red Sail, Unique and Pelican are full-service shops. Pelican is on Palm Beach behind the Holiday Inn and offers gear rental, sail-snorkeling tours, courses and dive tours. Red Sail Sports offers a "Dive, Dive & More Dives" package that allows you to select and trade the number of dives and tanks that fit your schedule. Five tanks costs $150, with Nitrox $185. Three days of boat-dives with two-tank dives, tanks, weights and belt cost $217.

Red Sail Sports also tempts guests with water-skiing, JetSkis and WaveRunners, tubing, banana boat rides, Hobie Cat rentals, instruction and sailing with a captain, Sunfish and paddle boat rental and Sea Searcher floats. Their 35-foot catamaran, *Balia*, sets sail for morning snorkeling tours, as well as sunset and dinner cruises. Red Sail is at the Hyatt & Allegro Resorts, Palm Beach Marriott Resort, Palm Beach Renaissance Resort & Island, downtown in Seaport Village. Dive tours are top-notch, with a full pre-dive briefing, underwater guides and a rescue diver who remains on the boat. ☎ 582-4500 or 800-255-6425.

Unique Watersports at the Aruba Grand Resort (see above) features PADI courses, scuba and snorkeling tours.

Where to Stay

 A 19-22% government tax is added to all hotel bills.

Aruba's resorts come in two varieties – low rise and high rise. The low-rise dive-friendly resorts, Talk of the Town, Bucuti Beach and Manchebo Beach, are near town and the Seaport Village. The village is home to hundreds of beautiful shops and trendy waterfront bars and restaurants – all set in charming, pastel, gingerbread architecture. The high-rise resorts – Hyatt, Holiday Inn, Las Cabanas Beach Resort, farther north – are nearer to Malmok and the Lighthouse.

Bucuti Beach Resort touts beautiful Spanish architecture, a gorgeous, powder white beach and **The Pirate's Nest**, a unique restaurant built to resemble an 18th-century ship. Other amenities include an outdoor fitness center, pool, activities desk that will book dive and snorkeling excursions and on-site car rental. The resort's 71 guest rooms and suites range from $150 to $325 per night in summer, $255 to $440 in winter. All are clean, very comfortable and modern, with cable TV, phone, air conditioning, safe, king- or queen-size beds, ceiling fan, small refrigerators and a mini-bar. Friendly staff members attend to guests' every want. Meal plans for $44 per day include a full American breakfast daily and three-course meal at the Pirate's Nest or a choice of nine popular outside restaurants. Dive tours are arranged at the desk with **Red Sail Watersports**. ☎ 800-344-1212, or locally 583-1100, www.bucuti.com, bucuti@setarnet.aw, www.redsailaruba.com.

Manchebo Beach Resort, next to the Bucuti Beach Resort, has clean, modern rooms with cable TV, air conditioning, direct-dial phones, safes and in-room refrigerators. On-site are **Bistro Aruba**, a patio restaurant; **French**

Steak House; and **Pega Pega**, a beachside bar and grill open all day. Great beach! Summer room rates are $129 for a standard up to $159 for a superior; winter rates are $199 and $249 per room, per day. Optional all-inclusive package. Children under 16 stay free in room with parents. Gift shop, car rental, laundry, pool and snack bar. Dive and snorkeling trips are arranged with **Red Sail Watersports**. ☎ 800-223-1108, fax 310-440-4220 or direct 011-297-582-3444, www.manchebo.com.

The Hyatt Regency Aruba Resort, beachfront, sprawls across 12 acres of swaying palms with two outdoor whirlpools, a three-level swimming pool with cascading waterfalls and water slide.

On-site dining options include **Café Japengo** with pan-Asian cuisine, specializing in sushi and fresh seafood. **The Palms** offers a choice of seafood and grilled specialties, innovative salads, and spectacular sandwiches (with outdoor seating available). Or try the unique health drinks at **Kadushi Juice Bar** in front of the Palms Beach Bar. Other on-site dining and drinking includes **Alfresco Bar**, **Balashi Bar**, **TCBY**, **Café Piccolo**, **Ole**, **Ruinas Del Mar**, and 24-hour room service.

Each room has bathroom amenities, voice mail, clock radio, iron, mini bar, hair dryer, coffee maker, and cable television. Room rates per day in summer are from $240 to $300; in winter, $440 to $590. Slightly lower rates may be available through the resort Website. **Red Sail Watersports**, on site, offers a "Dive, Dive & More Dives" package that allows you to select and trade the number of dives and tanks that fit your schedule. Five tanks costs $150, with Nitrox $185; three days of boat-dives with two-tank dives, tanks, weights and belt, is $217.

The 600-room **Holiday Inn Sunspree Resort and Casino**, convenient to the dive boat docks, has recently undergone major renovation with a new lobby, additional restaurants, shopping arcade, laundry facilities and modernized rooms. Coffee makers, hair dryers, in-room safes, irons and ironing boards have been added to the guest rooms. Summer room rates range from $79.99 to $200 per night. Winter rates are from $196 to $349. Diving is arranged with **Pelican** or **DePalm Watersports** at the hotel's tour desk. ☎ 800-HOLIDAY or 297-586-3600, www.holidayinn-aruba.com or www.ichotelsgroup.com.

The Aruba Grand Resort, located on Palm Beach, features lovely, oversize rooms, most with ocean views, all with balconies or patios. Recently, a state-of-the-art fitness center was added, along with Internet kiosks in the lobby.

Guests choose from standard rooms with a king- or two queen-size beds, deluxe rooms with more sweeping ocean views, and one- or two-bedroom suites. All have a phone, safe, hair dryer, am/fm alarm clock and cable TV. This resort features a 24-hour front desk, free parking, fitness center, spa, shops, safe deposit box, fabulous alfresco and indoor restaurants, tennis, handicapped access, concierge, wide, white sand beach, meeting rooms, barber/beauty shop, Olympic-size freshwater pool, laundry and valet services. Baby sitting and child services as well.

Diving is arranged with on-site **Unique Water Sports** (☎ 297-825216), a PADI shop. Rates vary with type of room. Discounts with AARP, AAA and government cards can save quite a bit. Summer rates for a room for two range from $170 per night to $440 for a two-bedroom suite. Discounts can bring the rate as low as $99. Winter room rates climb to between $255 and $325. Scuba diving and snorkeling are additional. ☎ 011-297-58-63900, www.aruba-grand.com.

Wyndham Aruba Resort, **Spa & Casino** offers the charm of the Dutch Caribbean, a magnificent beach, casino, seaside pool, four restaurants, health club, spa, tennis and a host of outdoor pleasures. Guest rooms tout satellite TV, fully stocked mini bar, floor-to-ceiling windows and a private balcony with a spectacular view. Seaside pool. **Cuban Revue** restaurant serves island cuisine. This is a high-rise resort. If you are carrying much personal dive gear, request a ground-level guest room. ☎ 800-WYNDHAM, direct 011-297-864466, www.arubawyndham.com.

For a complete list of resorts, contact your travel agent or **The Aruba Tourism Authority**, L.G. Smith Boulevard 172, Eagle, Aruba or ☎ 800-TO-ARUBA. In the US, 1000 Harbor Boulevard, Weehawken, NJ 07086, ☎ 201-330-0800, fax 201-330-8757, www.aruba.com.

Other Activities

Outdoor-lovers will enjoy visiting Aruba's national park – where flamboyant scenery, tropical foliage and even wild goats and donkeys await. The **Arikok National Park** has two hiking trails. Free admission. One of the island's newest sport attractions is kite surfing. Do it or view it at **Aruba Boardsurfing** at Fishermen Huts, just north of Palm Beach. Aruba's constant trade winds create ideal conditions for board surfing off the eastern shoreline. Rentals and lessons available.

Sunset cruises, deep-sea fishing, island tours, para-sailing, and sightseeing can all be easily arranged at your hotel. Tennis is widely available.

There are two golf courses, one 18-hole professional caliber **Tierra del Sol** course and a nine-hole with oiled sand greens; the trade winds and an occasional goat as a live hazard make playing tricky. Equestrians can ride along the beach at **Rancho El Paso**, ☎ 873310.

While nightlife to many divers means suiting up after sunset for yet another dive, others will find endless entertainment on shore in the form of casino gambling, limbo shows and discos.

Those traveling with young children will enjoy a picnic at **Baby Beach** on the southwestern tip of the island. This is a beautiful, natural lagoon with shallow, calm water.

Sightseeing

A walking tour of Oranjestad would include the **harbor-side fruit market**; **Fort Zoutman** and **King Willem III Tower**, home to an Aruban heritage museum; the **Numismatic Museum** and the **Archaeology Museum**. Shopping abounds.

If you are opposed to organized tours, grab a road map and rent a car to tour the island. Directly east of the high-rise hotel strip, on the north shore, you'll find the **Chapel of Alto Vista** high above the sea on a most peaceful spot. It was built by Spanish missionary, Domingo Antonio Silvester, and serves as a ceremonial center. Stations of the cross border the steep, cactus-lined road to the chapel.

Driving east to Andicuri from Oranjestad will lead to the **Natural Bridge** (the largest of eight on the island), complete with gift and snack shops. The road is unpaved and bumpy in spots, but very scenic and photogenic at sunrise. Also worth a visit are the **Casibari and Ayo rock formations** – monstrous boulders that mystify geologists. Casibari is about halfway (three miles) between the Natural Bridge and Oranjestad. Ayo is about two miles from the Natural Bridge toward Casibari. At Casibari stone steps give access to a viewing platform on top. At the entrance, a formation named "**Dragon Mouth**," and resembling just that, can be seen. You can climb to the top and, on a clear day, see all of Aruba and the coast of Venezuela.

The **California Dunes** and **California Lighthouse** are at the northernmost tip of the island. The dunes are sand, but most of this area is barren and rocky. High winds have carved some interesting shapes in the rocks. Views from the lighthouse ridge are magnificent.

Dining

Fine Aruban restaurants are expensive, but meal plans offered by several resorts frequently allow money-saving dinner trade-ins at local restaurants.

Even so, expect to spend between $60 and $100 (US) on dinner for two at the hotel and seaside restaurants. Most eateries add a 15% service charge, which does not cover the tip. Tips are usually just a couple of dollars for good service.

For divers on a budget, fast-food chains are widely available. Hotel meal plans average $40 to $50 per person, per day, and may include vouchers, which are accepted by many outside restaurants. Check with your hotel.

All hotels have coffee shops and snack bars. Most also feature specialty restaurants that serve American, Continental and regional food. For outstanding native seafood dishes, don't miss **Brisas Del Mar Restaurant**, six miles south of Oranjestad at Savaneta 222 (turn right after the Esso station), ☎ 5847718; or **The Waterfront Crabhouse** at Seaport Marketplace, ☎ 5835858. For additional country flavor try **The New Old Cunucu House Restaurant**, which is set in a 70-year-old Aruban home, Palm Beach #150, ☎ 61666; or **Boonoonoos** on Wilhelmastraat #18, ☎ 831888. You can enjoy seafood or steaks inside a Dutch windmill, first built in 1804 in Holland then reconstructed on Aruba in 1960. This is the **Mill Restaurant** at J.E. Irausquin Boulevard #330 (open from 6 to 11 pm), ☎ 862060 – within walking distance from the high-rise hotels.

The Pirate's Nest at the Bucuti Beach Resort features a nice beach bar and a breakfast buffet for $13. The best steaks are found at **El Gaucho**, Wilhelmastraat #80, ☎ 823677, the **Holiday Inn Restaurant** and the French restaurant at the **Manchebo Beach Hotel**. Other notable dining spots such as **Scandals** and **Salt & Pepper**, are spread throughout the **Seaport Village**.

Facts

Helpful Phone Numbers: Police/ambulance, ☎ 824000. **Airport**, ☎ 824800. **Hospital**, ☎ 826034.

Nearest Recompression Chamber: Curaçao, 40 minutes by air. None on Aruba.

Getting Here: American Airlines offers direct daily flights from New York, twice daily from Miami and San Juan, Puerto Rico with connections from Boston, Philadelphia, New Jersey, Baltimore, Miami, Raleigh, Washington, Hartford, Providence, Chicago, Dallas, Detroit, Pittsburgh and other major US cities. **Continental** has direct flights from Newark, Boston and Miami. From the United Kingdom, **British Airways**, **Delta** and **Continental** fly here. From Venezuela, **Avensa**; from Europe, **KLM**; from Toronto, **Air Canada**.

Car Rentals: Hertz, ☎ 824545, 824400, airport 824886; **Dollar**, ☎ 822783, 831237, airport 825651; **Budget**, ☎ 828600, airport 825423; **AC&E Jeep**, ☎ 876373. Also **Thrifty**, ☎ 5855300; **Toyota**, ☎ 5834902; **Amigo**, ☎ 5883299.

Driving: On the right.

Language: The official language is Dutch, but residents speak Papiamento – a blend of Dutch, Spanish, Portuguese and English. English and Spanish are widely spoken.

Documents: A passport and onward ticket are required of US, Canadian and UK visitors.

Customs: Citizens of the United States who have been out of the US for a minimum of 48 hours and who have not used their respective duty-free allowance within 30 days are entitled to a $600 duty-free tax exemption. Families traveling together can pool their exemptions, meaning a couple with two children can bring back $2,400 worth of articles. Canadian citizens who have been outside Canada for a minimum of seven days are permitted a duty-free exemption of C$500. Canadian citizens are also permitted a duty-free exemption of $100 each time they are out of the country for more than 48 hours. Exemptions cannot be pooled with spouse and/or children.

Currency: The Aruban florin or guilder. AWG1=US$1.78 (variable); US dollars widely accepted.

Credit Cards: Widely accepted.

Service Charges: There is a 19-22% tax on room rates. The service charge on food and beverage is 12-15%, which should not be considered a tip. Tips are extra, but generally much lower than in the US.

Climate: Dry and sunny, with a year-round average temperature of 82°F. Showers of short duration are frequent during November and December. Aruba is outside the hurricane belt.

Clothing: Lightweight casual cottons. Informal for the most part, but dress-up clothes are advisable for a night out in one of the elegant restaurants, night clubs or casinos. Jackets are required for men at night in some casinos, night clubs and restaurants.

 Persons under 18 are not permitted in the casinos.

Airport Departure Tax: US$23.

Electricity: 110-120 volts AC, 60 cycles (same as in US).

Time: Atlantic Standard Time. Same as Eastern Daylight Saving Time, all year round.

Religious Services: Roman Catholic. Protestant (Dutch Reformed, Anglican, Evangelican, Methodist, Seventh Day Adventist, Church of Christ, Baptist), Jewish, Baha'i Faith.

Additional Information: *Aruba Tourism Authority*, L.G. Smith Boulevard 172, Eagle, Aruba, ☎ 2978, 23777, fax 2978 34702; 1000 Harbor Boulevard, Weehawken, NJ 07047, ☎ 800-TO-ARUBA or 201-330-0800, fax 201-330-8757, www.aruba.com.

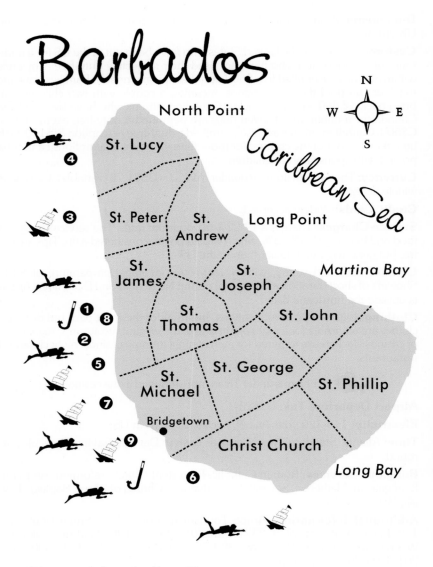

Barbados

North Point

St. Lucy

Caribbean Sea

St. Peter St. Andrew Long Point

Martina Bay

St. James St. Joseph St. John

St. Thomas

St. George St. Phillip

St. Michael

Bridgetown

Christ Church

Long Bay

Dive and Snorkeling Sites
1. Dottins Reef
2. Sandy Lane
3. The *Pamir*
4. Bright Ledge
5. The *Stavronikita*
6. Friar's Craig
7. Bell Buoy
8. Folkestone Park
9. The *Berwyn*

Barbados

Barbados, a tiny island just 21 miles long and 14 miles wide, offers remarkable contrasts, from its boulder-strewn northern coast to its serene Caribbean leeward coastline. Inland, hilly forests slope down to golden fields of sugarcane, corn, sweet potatoes, and yams. Stunning white sand beaches rim the island.

The easternmost island of the Lesser Antilles, Barbados boasts a unique range of natural and historic attractions, from its exquisite plantation "Great Houses" to vast caves filled with prehistoric formations. Its quaint colonial capital, Bridgetown, surprises visitors with upscale shopping and gourmet dining.

Despite 30 years of independence from Great Britain, Barbados still exudes a British atmosphere. A statue of Admiral Nelson graces Bridgetown's Trafalgar Square, and afternoon tea remains a custom for many hotels. Good diving and snorkeling exists off the southwestern shores. Gorgeous reefs flank the rocky east coast, but pounding seas and strong currents usually limit access to this area.

When to Go

Divers, both novice and experienced, are advised to visit Barbados between April and November, when they can expect calm seas and fabulous visibility on the barrier reef. This changes from December through March, when a "north swell" decreases visibility near shore and on the outer reefs.

During spring, summer and fall the island's shallow shipwrecks offer a variety of dive experiences. The best wrecks are found on the offshore barrier reef that extends along Barbado's western coast. Soft corals, sea fans, and sponges camouflage the sunken ship remains. Snorkelers enjoy soft sand beaches and shore access sites with friendly fish hovering about varied corals and sponges.

Best Dive & Snorkeling Sites

☆☆☆☆☆ **Dottins Reef**, a half mile off the coast of St. James Parish on the west coast, drifts along the shore from St. James to Bridgetown. It is the prettiest reef in Barbados with visibility at 100 feet or better. Basket sponges, sea fans, gorgonians, and thickets of staghorn and brain coral adorn the reef's canyons and walls. Depths start at 65 feet with some dropoffs to 130 feet. Reef residents include rays, turtles, barracuda, parrotfish, snapper and large grouper. Seas are generally calm.

☆☆☆ **Sandy Lane,** a deeper area off Dottin's Reef, is usually a drift dive. The walls, dotted with sponges and vibrant, clump corals, drop to 90 feet. Superb marine life abounds. A good spot for video photography. For experienced divers only.

☆☆☆ **Wreck of the *Pamir*,** located just 200 yards offshore, is easily accessible from the beach and is very open and uncluttered. This 150-foot ship was sunk in 30 feet of water by the Barbados dive shop operators to form an artificial reef. The ship's superstructure breaks the usually calm surface, making it perfect for snorkelers and snorkel-swimmers. Swarms of sergeant majors and butterflyfish inhabit the wreck. Nearby, about 60 yards out, is a small reef. Although visibility varies, seas are always calm. Dive operators request no spear fishing or collecting. An excellent dive for novices.

☆☆☆ **Bright Ledge Reef** is a narrow reef that wraps around the island's northern tip. Depths average 60 feet, with deep dropoffs on either side. Unsuitable for novices but generally a safe dive and particularly good for photography. Encounters with gigantic pelagics, turtles and rays are frequent, with dependable sightings of parrotfish, snapper, grouper, porgy, grunts, and glass eye snapper. The sea is generally calm unless there is a stiff wind or storm.

☆☆☆ The ***Stavronikita*,** a 360-foot freighter, was gutted by a fire at sea 14 years ago. After towing the sinking ship closer to shore, the government of Barbados sunk the smoldering mass where it would benefit divers and fishermen as an artificial reef. The wreck sits in 130 feet of water, the deck at 80 feet. Although the depth discourages most novice explorers, the ship is one of the island's most interesting dives. Its hull, covered with a colorful patchwork of small sponges and clinging corals, attracts schools of silversides and large pelagics. Very appealing to photographers.

☆☆ Nearby in shallow water lie the ***Conimara*,** an old PT boat, and the ***Lord Combermere*,** an old tug boat – both in 30 to 40 feet of water. Visibility varies. Good photo opportunities abound here as well. The wrecks can be reached from the shore after a 600-yard swim.

☆☆ **Friar's Craig** is a good dive for the novice although strong current may be occasionally encountered. This is another purposely sunken wreck. It lies in just 60 feet of water with the bridge at 30 feet, making it more accessible than the *Stavronikita*. Nearby **Asta Reef**, a shelter for throngs of fish, is often combined with a Friar's Craig dive. A short 600-yard swim from the southwest corner of Christ Church Parish will put you over the wreck and an adjacent reef, **Castle Bank.** Exercise extreme caution and check the current before diving. Numerous fish and usually great visibility.

☆☆☆ **Bell Buoy Reef**, located off St. Michael's Parish on the island's southwest, is a wall dive with a shelf at 40 feet, dropping off to a sandy bottom at 70 feet. The reef is alive with small critters amidst the shadows of large brain coral heads, sea fans, and vase sponges. Schools of small reef fish, turtles, and an occasional ray are in residence. During windy periods this spot can be wiped out by strong currents.

☆☆☆ **Caribbee Reef**, off the Caribbee Hotel, is a section of the fringing reefs that parallel the southwest shore. Lots of fish, giant barrel sponges, tube sponges and sea fans. Usually good visibility. Light surge. Good for experienced divers. Depths are 60 to 120 feet. This is a boat dive.

☆☆☆ **Folkestone Park** is the favorite beach/snorkeling site in Barbados. An underwater trail has been marked around the inshore reef. It is also the favorite area for boaters and JetSkiers, so the swimming and snorkeling area has been roped off to insure safety. Snorkel with or near a group. A 200-yard swim from the sandy beach will take you to a raft anchored over the wreckage of a small barge sitting in 20 feet of water. During winter when the North Swell rises, visibility can drop drastically for as long as two days. During the rest of the year, Folkestone is the number one snorkeling choice.

☆☆ The **Wreck of the *Berwyn*** is a 45-foot-long French tugboat that sunk in the early 1900s. It sits at the bottom of Carlisle Bay, 200 yards off the island's southwest shore at a depth of 25 feet. Encrusted with plate corals, the wreck is host to seahorses, frogfish, wrasses, arrow crabs and other small creatures. It is a favored snorkeling photo site with good visibility and calm sea conditions.

☆☆ The **Wreck of the *Eillion***, a former drug boat, was sunk June 8, 1996 to form part of the Carlisle Bay Marine park. The wreck, located near the *Berwyn*, sits at 110 feet, with the top at 55 feet. Lots of fish.

The ***Ce-Trek***, an old cement-constructed boat at a depth of 40 feet, sits near the *Berwyn*. A favorite of re-entry divers, the *Ce-Trek* has attracted hordes of fish and invertebrates since its sinking in 1986. She sits 300 yards offshore.

The *Berwyn*, *Eillion*, *Ce-Trek* and the *Fox* (a small wreck) are possible to see on one dive.

Two nice spots for beginning snorkelers are **Mullins Beach** and **Paynes Bay**. Both offer calm waters and ample parking.

Dive Operators

Dive shops are located along the southwest shore.

Bubbles Galore Barbados Dive Shop at the Sandy Beach Island Resort, Worthing, Christ Church, provides all levels of PADI training. Two-tank dives are offered every morning and afternoon. Complimentary drinks served on board their custom 31-foot Bertam dive boat. Night dives upon request. Specialty courses in Dan O2 Provider, Basic Nitrox, underwater photography, and navigation. All are offered in English, German, Italian, Spanish, French, Swedish, Norwegian and Russian. ☎ 246-430-0354, fax 246-430-8806, bubbles@caribsurf.com, www.funbarbados.com.

The Dive Shop Ltd., celebrating its 30th year on the island, offers daily trips at 10 am and noon with night dives twice a week. All staff members are certified by PADI, NAUI and/or ACUC. They are also DAN O2 certified. All levels of certification courses are taught. Shipwrecks *Berwyn* and *Ce-Trek* sit 300 yds from the shop. Rates are $55 for a one-tank dive, $90 for a two-tank dive. A 10-dive package costs $300 with equipment, $260 with your own equipment. Hotel/dive packages are available at the Island Inn Hotel and Cacrabank Beach Apartments. For additional information write or call Haroon Degia, The Dive Shop Ltd. Aquatic Gap, Bay Street, St. Michael, Barbados WI. ☎ 246-426-9947 or 800-348-3756, fax 246-426-2031, www.caribnet.net/diveshop, hardive@carib net.

Underwater Barbados, on Bay Street in St. Michael's Parish, visits all the best sites. Staff are medic first-aid trained and experienced dive instructors. PADI instruction. ☎ 246-426-0655, myoung@underwaterbarbados.com, www.underwaterbarbados.com.

Coral Isle Divers, on the Careenage in Bridgetown, operates a custom 40-foot power catamaran dive boat with a changing room, on-board washroom and shower, dry storage areas and plenty of deck space. They offer PADI and NAUI instruction. Complimentary soft drinks. ☎ 246-431-9068. coralis@caribnet.net.

Blue Reef Water Sports, St. James, offers reef and wreck trips, resort and certification courses. Their 28-foot boat carries 12 divers. ☎ 246-422-3133, fax 246-422-3133.

High Tide Watersports, at the Coral Reef Club Resort, tours aboard a custom-built, 30-foot dive boat, *Flyin' High*. This PADI shop offers one- and two-tank dives, night dives, snorkeling trips, and PADI instruction. Equipment sales and rentals, video camera. Gear storage. ☎ 246-432-0931.

WestSide Scuba Centre, Holetown, St. James, offers PADI courses, dive and snorkeling tours. Free transportation to and from your hotel. ☎ 246-432-2558.

Beginning and advanced dive tours and certification courses are also offered at **Willies Watersports**, St. Michael, ☎ 246-425-1060 or 246-422-4900; at

Dive Boat Safari at the Barbados Hilton, St. Michael, ☎ 246-427-4350; and at **Scotch & Soda**, ☎ 246-435-7375, peter@sunbeach.net.

Hazell's Water World Inc., in the Sandy Bank complex, Hastings, Christ Church, sells a wide range of scuba and snorkeling equipment. Repair service on dive equipment. ☎ 246-426-4043.

Atlantis Submarine, Shallow Draught, Bridgetown, dives to 150 feet, exploring the reefs and wrecks for 90 minutes. Divers on scooters outside the sub interact with the surroundings and can communicate with submarine guests. ☎ 246-436-8929.

Atlantis' 65-foot glass-hulled **Seatrec** (Sea Tracking and Reef Exploration Craft) features advanced glass-bottom viewing with in-cabin video monitors.

Reserve sail-snorkeling, sunset, lunch and dinner tours through **Jolly Roger Cruises**, Bridgetown, ☎ 436-6424, fax 429-8500; **Tiami Catamaran Sailing Cruises**, Bridgetown, ☎ 246-430-0900; mask and snorkel included.

Where to Stay

Most hotels and nightlife venues are on the south- and central-western coast of the island. There are no dedicated dive resorts, but all will arrange for diving. Several guest houses, cottages and apartments may be rented for $30 per night and up. A list with current rates is available from the **Barbados Board of Tourism**. In the US, ☎ 800-221-9831; in Canada, ☎ 800-268-9122 or 416-512-6569, fax 416-512-6581. In Barbados, ☎ 246-427-2623/4, fax 246-426-4080, www.barbados.org.

To book on the Internet, go to the Website, select "hotels," then click on e-mail to book reservations with the hotel of your choice.

Before booking on your own, check the travel section of your Sunday newspaper. Money-saving packages including airfare and choice hotels in Barbados are frequently featured by the large travel companies.

Divi Southwinds Beach Hotel sits on a half mile of white sand beach near the St. Lawrence Gap. It is surrounded by 20 acres of tropical gardens and features 166 guest rooms and air-conditioned suites, all having a patio and pool or ocean views. Beachside restaurants offer local and international dishes. Poolside bar and snackery. You are within walking distance of restaurants and nightlife. ☎ 800-367-3484, 607-277-3484 or write Divi Resorts, 6340 Quadrangle Drive, Suite 300, Chapel Hill, NC 27514-8900.

Almond Beach Club, an all-inclusive resort, features 131 air-conditioned guest rooms and suites with ocean or pool views. Gourmet meals are served at the elegant beachside restaurant; refreshments at a swim-up bar adjacent to the twin pools. All-inclusive rates per couple, per day, include meals, drinks, snorkeling, fishing, board surfing, kayaking. Winter (December 18 to March 31) rates per day, per couple, start at $660 for a standard room; summer rates start at $525. ☎ 800-4ALMOND. Dive trips are arranged at additional charge with the **Blue Reef Dive** shop.

Grand Barbados Beach Resort is a luxury, beachfront resort with scuba facilities on the premises. Located in Carlisle Bay, one mile from Bridgetown, the resort is just minutes from reef and wreck dives. Features are a fitness center, shopping arcade, coffee shop, two restaurants and bars, satellite TV, hair dryers, mini-safes, radio, phone, balconies, and meeting facilities. Mistral Windsurfing School. Dive packages for seven nights/six dives with breakfast and airport transfers are from $850 per person, based on a double. Summer room-only rates start at $225 for a double; winter at $240. ☎ 246-426-4000, fax 246-429-2400, www.grandbarbados.com.

Coral Reef Club, a small, luxury, beachfront resort with its own dive shop (High Tides Watersports) sits in 12 acres of gardens adjacent to a superb, white sand beach. All 70 lovely air-conditioned cottages and rooms feature secluded patios or balconies. Activities available to guests include cruises on the club's own 30-foot catamaran. Amenities include tennis court, pool, and shops. Alfresco restaurant overlooks the sea. Special nights include Bajan buffets and barbecue dinner with steel band, flaming limbo and exotic calypso dancers. Room rates start at $290 in summer per day for a double; from $420 in winter. ☎ 246-422-2372, fax 246-422-1776, coral@caribsurf.com, http://coralreefbarbados.com.

Coconut Court, a family-owned hotel two miles from Bridgetown, features ocean views, gift shop, restaurant. TV in rooms. Rates start at $100 per day in summer, $150 in winter. Dive trips arranged with Underwater Barbados. ☎ 246-427-1655.

Crane Beach Hotel, built in 1887 and restored to 20th-century plush, sits on four acres overlooking a half mile of beautiful coral sand beach. A gourmet restaurant, refreshment bar and four tennis courts are on the estate. Rates start at $105 per room in summer; from $160 in winter. Elegant rooms and apartments. ☎ 800-223-9815 or 246-423-6220, fax 246-423-5343, www.thecrane.com.

Long Beach Club on Chancery Lane in Christ Church features 24 simple rooms. Rates are from $65 in summer; from $100 in winter. ☎ 246-428-6890, fax 246-428-4957.

Sandy Beach Island Resort, Worthing, Christ Church, offers 128 air-conditioned, beachfront rooms. Diving with **Bubbles Galore Dive Shop**. Rates per person are $85 to $125 in summer, $120 to $200 in winter. ☎ 246-435-8000, fax 246-435-8053.

Sam Lord's Castle, a luxurious, waterfront Marriott resort in Long Bay, St. Phillip, on the Atlantic east coast, features 234 air-conditioned rooms with all amenities. Tennis courts. All-inclusive rates in summer range from $275 for a double to $330; winter from $350 to $475. ☎ 800-228-9290 or 246-423-7350, fax 246-423-5918. Diving with **Underwater Barbados**.

 For a list of 30 low-budget accommodations in Barbados, visit www.intimate hotelsbarbados.com or ☎ 246-436-2053.

Other Activities

The **Sandy Lane Golf Course** at the Sandy Lane Hotel in St. James (☎ 246-432-1145) offers a 45-hole championshiop golf cours and great views from the "signature" seventh hole. **The Royal Westmoreland Golf & Country Club** (☎ 246-419-7263) offers 18 holes of championshipship golf, contrasting challenges, stunning scenery and a succession of "feature holes." **Barbados Golf Club**, Durants, Christ Church resorts (☎ 246-428-8463) offers an 18-hole layout with two lakes and coral waste bunkers, par 72, restaurant, bar, warm-up nets. Green fee for 18 holes is $119, cart $13 Club rental $20; www.barbadosgolfclub.com. **Almond Beach Village** and **Club Rockley**, two of the island's all-inclusive resorts, offer nine-hole golf courses for visitors (*see* page 51 for contact info).

Horseback riding is offered by **Brighton Riding Stables**, ☎ 425-9381; **Caribbean International Riding Centre**, ☎ 422-7433; **Riding Beau Geste Farm**, ☎ 429-0139; or **Ye Olde Congo Road Stables**, ☎ 423-6180. Stables are near Bridgetown.

Deep-sea Fishing for dorado, wahoo, sailfish, tuna and marlin is easily arranged by the hotel desks. Call **Action/Cannon II,** ☎ 246-424-6107; **Blue Jay Charters**, ☎ 246-429-2326; *Blue Marlin*, ☎ 246-429-2326 or *Honey Bea III*, ☎ 246-428-5344.

Skyrider Parasail features a 32-foot boat with an integrated, self-contained launching and landing platform; ☎ 435-0570.

Windsurfing off the south coast can be arranged at the **Club Mistral**, Oistens **Barbados Windsurfing Club** at Maxwell and **Silver Rock Windsurfing Club** at Silver Sands. ☎ 428-2866.

Submarine tours of the reefs are offered aboard the 28-passenger *Atlantis*. ☎ 436-8929 or 800-535-6564.

Sightseeing

Ride on an electric tram into **Harrison's Cave** (☎ 438-6640) to explore beautiful underground waterfalls, mirror lake, and the rotunda room, where the walls of the 250-foot chamber glitter like diamonds. Or view exotic tropical birds and native monkeys at the **Oughterson House Barbados Zoo Park**. History buffs will delight in finding 17th-century military relics like antique cannons and signal towers around the island.

Through the Barbados National Trust's open house program, **Historical Great Houses** are open for public viewing from 2:30 to 5:30 pm. Entrance is $7.50. A bus tour that includes entrance and transportation from hotels is $18.75. ☎ 809-426-2421.

Shopping

 Barbados abounds with boutiques, galleries and shops, with department stores such as **Harrison's** and **Cave Shepherd & Co**. offering goods from around the world, particularly diamonds and Italian gold. Island specialties include handmade puppets and clay and wood figures along with colorful silk-screened prints and fabrics. Pepper sauce and Barbados rum are also high on the list of popular take-homes. Most shops are in or near Broad Street, Bridgetown.

Duty-free shops require visitors to produce their passport and airline ticket. Goods that cannot be bought over the counter dury-free are spirits, wines, tobacco, cigarettes, cigars, video sets, games, TV's and home computers.

Dining

 West Indian specialties and native seafood dishes such as grilled flying fish and lobster are featured throughout the island. Bajan delicacies include *cou-cou* (a cornmeal and okra dish), pepperpot (a spicy stew), and *jug-jug* (a mixture of Guinea corn and green peas). Whether you're looking for a romantic five-star restaurant, beachfront café or Bajan buffet, Barbados has an endless number of dining options for every palate and budget. Restaurants range from small, front-porch cafés to large, luxury hotel dining rooms. Many hotels – Sandy Lane for example – offer a barbecue served to the music of steel bands or open-air discos. Fast-food afficionados will enjoy **Chefette Drive-Thru**, Barbados' answer to the golden arches, open weekends from 10 am on Friday to midday Sunday. Chefette restaurants are located in Bridgetown on Fairchild Street,

Fontabelle, Broad Street, Heroes Square and Marhill Street. Also in the towns of Rockley, Wildey, Oistins and Holetown.

Josef's, located in St. Lawrence Gap, Christ Church, serves fabulous gourmet fish and continental cuisine in a grand native home with a garden overlooking the sea. Meals are under $25. ☎ 435-6541.

Pisces Restaurant, located in the St. Lawrence Gap on the waterfront, is noted for West Indian specialties and fabulous rum pie. ☎ 435-6564.

Waterfront Café, The Careenage, Bridgetown, serves Bajan specialties and Creole cuisine, including pepperpot and melts, plus tapas. Meals run between $25 and $40. Nice view of the docks. ☎ 427-0093.

"Nu-Bajan" cuisine is served at **Koko's** on Prospect, St. James. Meals are under $25. Seating overlooks the ocean. ☎ 424-4557.

Creole cuisine lovers should be sure to try the **Brown Sugar Restaurant** at the Aquatic Gap in St. Michael. Popular buffet lunch served in an old Barbadian home. Under $25. ☎ 427-2329.

Atlantis Resort, Bathsheba, St. Joseph, features a Bajan buffet on Sundays. Breathtaking views of the Atlantic surf. Under $25.

Additional favorites are **39 Steps** wine bar in Hastings, **Raffles** gourmet restaurant in Holetown, ☎ 432-6557, and the **Round House Inn** in Bathsheba for great margaritas, and gorgeous views of the Atlantic coast, ☎ 433-9678.

Facts

Helpful Phone Numbers: Police, ☎ 112; ambulance, ☎ 115.

Recompression Chamber: Located in St. Annes, Fort Garrison, St. Michael. Contact Dr. Brown or Major Gittens at ☎ 436-6185.

Getting Here: *From the US*: **American Airlines**, ☎ 800-433-7300, www.aa.com; **BWIA**, ☎ 800-523-0204; **Air Jamaica**, ☎ 800-523-5585; **US Airways**, www.usairways.com; and **Continental**, ☎ 800-523-3273; *from Canada*: **Air Canada** and **BWIA**; *from the UK*, **British Airways**, **BWIA** and **Virgin Atlantic**. *Inter-Island*: **BWIA** and **LIAT**. Barbados' ***Grantley Adams International Airport*** is modern and well kept.

Island Transportation: Taxi service is available throughout the island. (Note: cab fares should be negotiated before accepting service.) Local auto-rental companies are at the airport: **National**, ☎ 246-426-0603; **P&S**, ☎ 424-2907; **Corbins**, ☎ 427-9531; **Drive-A-Matic**, ☎ 422-3000; **Courtesy Rent A Car**, ☎ 431-4160.

Driving: Traffic keeps to the left in Barbados. Visting drivers must be over 25 years old and have a valid driver's license to obtain a permit to drive in Barbados.

Local Buses: There is a very good, inexpensive public transport system covering virtually the entire island.

Documents: Canadian and US citizens require a valid passport and return ticket in order to enter Barbados. Entry documentation is good for three months.

Customs: Personal effects of visitors, including cameras and sports equipment, enter duty free. Returning US citizens may take back free of duty articles costing a total of US$600 providing the stay has exceeded 48 hours and that the exemption has not been used within the preceding 30 days. One quart of liquor per person (over 21 years) may be carried out duty free. Not more than 100 cigars and 200 cigarettes may be included.

 Cameras and dive equipment should be registered with Customs **before** you leave the US.

Currency: Barbados dollar (BBD or Bds); US$1=Bds$1.98 (variable).

Climate: Temperatures vary between 75 and 85°F. Average rainfall is 59 inches.

Clothing: Lightweight casual clothing is recommended. A jacket for men may be desirable for visiting nightclubs or dressy resort restaurants. Swim suits, bikinis and short shorts are not welcome in Bridgetown shops or banks.

Departure Tax: BD $25 US$12.50.

Electricity: 110 volts AC, 50 cycles.

Time: Atlantic Standard (EST + 1 hr).

Language: English with a local dialect.

Taxes: A 10% service charge is added to the bill at most hotels. A sales tax of 5% is also added to hotel and restaurant bills.

Religious Services: Anglican, Baptist, Catholic, Methodist, Moravian, Seventh Day Adventist, Jehovah's Witnesses.

For Additional Information: *Barbados Board Of Tourism*: in New York, 800 Second Avenue, NY, NY 10017, ☎ 800-221-9831, 212-986-6510. In Florida, 150 Alhambra Circle, Suite 1270, Coral Gables, FL 33134. ☎ 305-442-7471, fax 305-567-2844. In Barbados, Harbour Road, Bridgetown, WI. ☎ 246-427-2623, 2624 or 800-744-6244, fax 246-426-4080, http://barbados.org.

Belize

Fascinating and exotic, Belize offers a world of tropical adventure to divers and snorkelers. The **Hol Chan Marine Preserve** is a small portion of the largest barrier reef in the western hemisphere, the **Mesoamerican Reef**, which extends along the Yucatán Peninsula of Mexico, the entire coast of Belize and parts of Guatemala and Honduras, second in size only to the Great Barrier Reef in Australia. Also in the reef area are the magnificent **Blue Hole**, a 1,000-foot-wide ocean sinkhole, and three beautiful atolls – **Lighthouse Reef**, the **Turneffe Islands** and **Glovers Reef**. Within the reef system are hundreds of uncharted islands.

Just 750 miles from Miami, Belize lies on the Caribbean coast of Central America between Guatemala and Mexico. Populated by a mere 200,000 people, it is a country of approximately 9,000 square miles. It has inland mountain ranges with peaks over 3,500 feet, dense tropical jungles, a coastline of mangrove swamps, and 266 square miles of offshore coral islands. The 185-mile-long Mesoamerican barrier reef parallels the shore from 10 to 30 miles out, with prime diving locations around the out islands.

Tours to Belize's out islands are still labeled "expedition" or "safari" rather than "vacation." Its offshore accommodations and facilities, except for Ambergris Caye, are considered primitive by Caribbean standards – few TVs, phones or automobiles on most of the islands – yet Belize's jungles and unspoiled reefs lure intrepid divers back again and again.

Visitors arriving in Belize City will find a safer environment than in the past, thanks to a special Tourist Police Force that has reduced crimes against tourists by 72%. Despite the improvement, it's still wise to avoid flashing expensive cameras, jewelry, or money around.

On the mainland outside Belize City one finds fairly rugged and varied terrain, alive with yellowhead parrots, giant iguanas, monkeys and a curious creature called the gibnut – described by Belizean author, Robert Nicolait, as a cross between a fat rabbit and a small pig.

The heart of dive tourism is **Ambergris Caye**, a bustling resort and fishing community, the largest of the out islands or "*cayes.*" Its main town, **San Pedro**, is a few hundred yards from the **Hol Chan Marine Preserve**, the northernmost point of the Mesoamerican Reef, and is the jumping-off point to Belize's smaller cayes and atolls. Ambergris is just 20 minutes by air from Belize City or an hour and 15 minutes by ferry (see end of chapter for transportation details). The northern portion of Ambergris is accessible by boat only, but plans for a road are under consideration. Transportation on Ambergris and the other islands is by golf cart or on foot.

A new area for divers is **Placencia**, a quaint fishing village located on a 16-mile coastal peninsula, 100 miles south of Belize City. There are some coral heads off the beaches, but a half-hour boat ride will bring you to **Laughing Bird Caye**, a small island surrounded by pristine reefs, and the remains of old wrecks. Several Spanish galleons went down in this area over the years and occasionally a gold piece washes up on the beach. Placencia is an intriguing new place to explore.

When to Go

Visit Belize during the dry season, from February to May. Annual rainfall ranges from 170 inches in the south to 50 inches in the north. Heaviest rainfall is from September to January. August is frequently dry.

The climate is subtropical, with constant brisk winds from the Caribbean Sea. Summer highs are rarely above 95°F, winter lows seldom below 60°. Bug repellent is always needed as mosquitoes and sand flies are a constant annoyance.

Belize has a long history of stable government. It is a member of the British Commonwealth, with a democratically elected government. The people are Creoles (African-European), Garifuna (African-Indian), Mestizo (Spanish-Indian), Maya and European. English is the official language and is widely spoken, as is Spanish.

History

Early inhabitants of Belize were the Maya, whose territory also included Mexico, Guatemala, Honduras and El Salvador. They left behind great ceremonial centers, pyramids and evidence of a dynamic people with advancements in the arts, math and science. The Maya inhabited Belize as early as 9000 BC and flourished as a master civilization until most of them mysteriously disappeared about 1000 AD. Theories about their fate range from massive death by natural disaster to speculation about spaceship travel to other planets. Remnants of this ancient culture show that Belize was a major trading center for the entire Mayan area. Today, a small population of Maya descendants inhabit the countryside.

At **Altun Ha** (30 miles north of Belize City), an excavated Maya center, spectacular jade and stone carvings have been unearthed, including an ornately carved head of *Kinisch Ahau*, the Mayan Sun God. This head, weighing 9.75 pounds and measuring nearly six inches from base to crown, is believed to be the largest Maya jade carving in existence. Also uncovered was the Temple of the Green Tomb, a burial chamber that contained human remains and a wealth of jade pieces, including pendants, beads, figures and jewelry. Side trips to this and other jungle archaeological sites are offered by most dive-tour operators.

During the 17th century, Belize was colonized by the British and the Spanish. In 1862, the settlement became an English colony known as British Honduras. It gained independence in 1981. Today, it is the only Central American nation where English is widely spoken.

Best Dive & Snorkeling Sites

The Mesoamerican Barrier Reef

☆☆☆ **Hol Chan Marine Preserve**, a five-square-mile reef area off the southern tip of Ambergris Caye, is characterized by a natural channel or cut that attracts and shelters huge communities of marine animals. Maximum depth inside the reef is 30 feet, allowing unlimited bottom time. The outside wall starts at 50 feet, then drops to depths greater than 150 feet. Schools of tropicals line the walls, with occasional glimpses of big turtles, green and spotted morays, six-foot stingrays, eagle rays, spotted dolphins and nurse sharks.

A constant flow of seawater through the cut promotes the growth of large barrel and basket sponges, sea fans, and beautiful outcroppings of staghorn and brain corals. Check tide charts before diving on your own; currents can be very strong in the channel at outgoing tides.

Diving all along the barrier reef is extraordinary. There are caves, dramatic overhangs, and pinnacles, all with superb marine life, though commercial fishing has taken its toll on the really big grouper, shark and huge turtles that were commonplace 10 years ago. The subsea terrain is similar throughout the area, with long channels of sand running perpendicular to the overall reef system. These cuts run to seaward allowing a constant change of nutrient-rich sea water to cleanse and feed the coral.

The inner reef, that area facing land, is shallow, with coral slopes that bottom out between 20 and 40 feet. Amidst its forests of stag horn and elkhorn are throngs of juvenile fish, barracuda, invertebrates, spawning grouper, stingrays, conch, nurse shark and small critters.

Diving the outer reef brings a better chance to see mantas, permits, jacks, black durgons, tuna, dolphin, turtles and sharks. Visibility is exceptional too. The reef profile outside is typically a sloping shelf to between 25 or 40 feet, which then plunges to 2,000 feet or more.

Live-aboard yachts that explore the entire coast are extremely popular in Belize, though local guides and tourist officials are working to attract more divers to their shore facilities and après-dive attractions.

The Atolls

 Atolls are ring-shaped coral islands or island groups surrounding a lagoon. Most are in the South Pacific and are often the visible portions of ancient, submerged volcanoes. But those in Belize are composed of coral and may have been formed by faults during the shifting of land masses.

All three – Lighthouse Reef, Glovers Reef and the Turneffe Islands – are surrounded by miles of shallow reefs and magnificent, deep dropoffs. The sheltered lagoons are dotted with pretty coral heads and are great for snorkeling and novice divers. Outside, visibility exceeds 150 feet and marine life is unrivaled. Generally, the islands are primitive, remote and largely uninhabited, with the bulk of the population made up of free-roaming chickens, though each location has at least one dive resort and a resident dive master.

☆☆☆☆ **The Turneffe Islands**, 35 miles from Belize City and beyond the barrier reef, are a group of 32 low islands bordered with thick growths of mangroves. The lower portion of the chain forms a deep V shape with **Cay Bokel** at the southernmost point. Reef areas just above both sides of the point are the favorite southern dive spots. Cay Bokel is where you'll find the **Turneffe Island Lodge**, a quaint resort offering dive services. West of the southern point are sheltered, shallow reefs at 20- to 60-foot depths. Along the reef are some old anchors overgrown with coral, a small, wooden wreck called the *Sayonara*, and a healthy fish population. Seas are rougher, currents stronger and the dives deeper to the east, but more impressive coral formations and large pelagics are found. The ridges and canyons of the reefs are carpeted by a dense cover of sea feathers, lacy soft corals, branching gold and purple sponges, anemones, sea fans and luxurious growths of gorgonians. Passing dolphins and rays are the big attraction as they upstage the reef's "blue-collar workers" – cleaner shrimp, sea cucumbers, patrolling barracuda, defensive damselfish, schooling yellowtail, grunts and coral crabs. Snorkeling and diving are excellent, with outstanding water clarity, protected areas, and diverse marine life.

Rendezvous Point at the northernmost point is equal in subterrain and diver interest, but is more often visited by fishermen. Much of the northern area is shallow mangrove swamp where tarpon, bonefish, shrimp and lobster proliferate.

☆☆☆☆☆ The most popular atoll, and that most visited by dive boats, is **Lighthouse Reef.** It lies 40 miles from Belize City and is the outermost of the

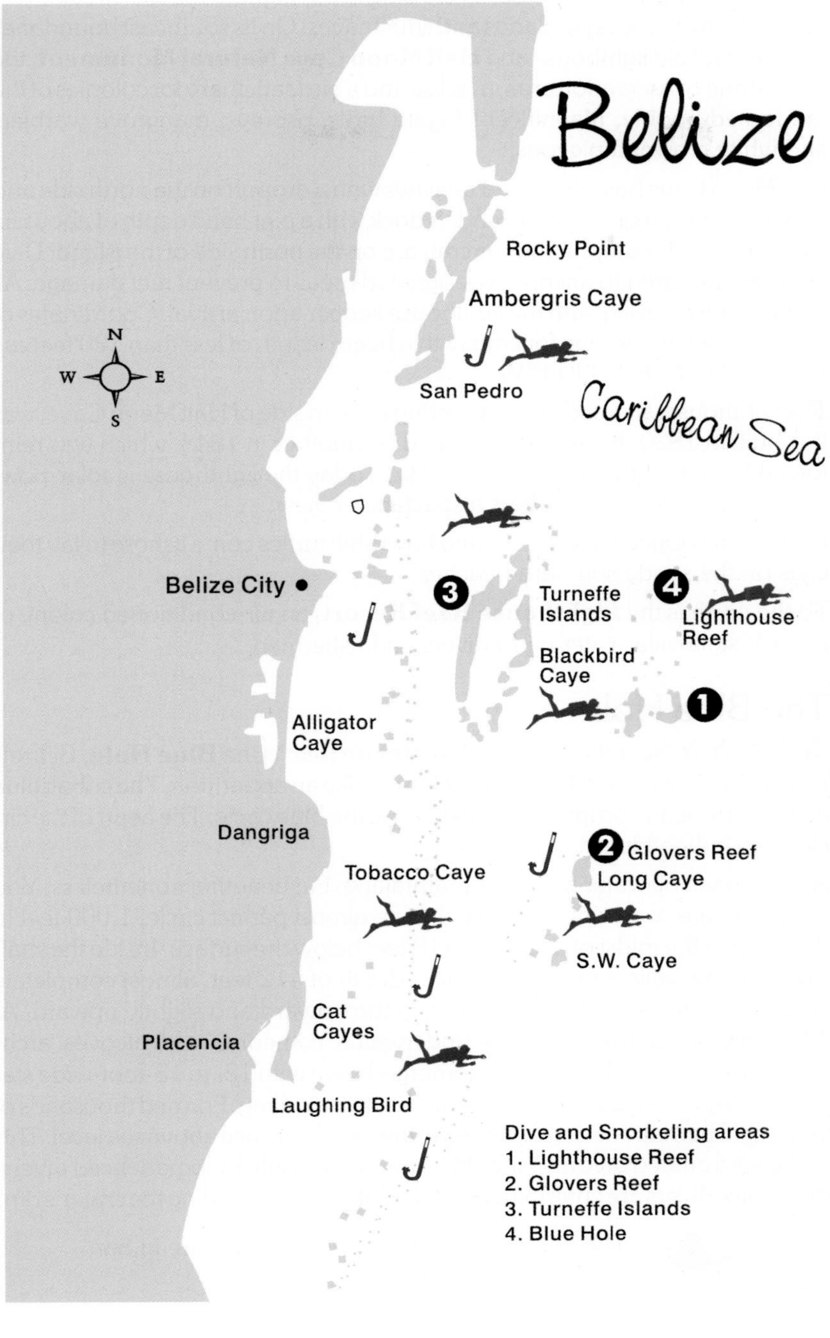

Belize

Rocky Point

Ambergris Caye

San Pedro

Caribbean Sea

Belize City ●

3

Turneffe
Islands

4

Lighthouse
Reef

Blackbird
Caye

1

Alligator
Caye

N
W ◆ E
S

Dangriga

Tobacco Caye

2 Glovers Reef
Long Caye

S.W. Caye

Cat
Cayes

Placencia

Laughing Bird

Dive and Snorkeling areas
1. Lighthouse Reef
2. Glovers Reef
3. Turneffe Islands
4. Blue Hole

offshore islands within the Belize cruising area. Lighthouse is a circular reef system featuring several islands and small cayes. On its southeast boundaries is a beautiful old lighthouse and **Half Moon Caye Natural Monument**, the first marine conservation area in Belize and a bird sanctuary for colonies of the red-footed boobie, Magnificent frigate birds, ospreys, mangrove warblers and white crowned pigeons.

Half Moon Caye has white sand beaches with a dropoff on the north side and a shallow lagoon on the south end. A dock with a pier head depth of about six ft and an area for amphibious aircraft are on the north side of the island. Dive boats are required to anchor in designated areas to prevent reef damage. All boaters must register with the lighthouse keeper upon arrival. Coordinates of an approved anchorage for craft with a beam length of less than 120 feet are 17° 12' 25'' N, 87° 33'11''W.

The lighthouse, situated on the tapering eastern side of Half Moon Caye, was first built in 1820. It was later replaced by another in 1848, which was reinforced by a steel-framed tower in 1931. Today the lighthouse is solar-powered. A climb to the top offers a spectacular view.

Endangered loggerhead turtles and hawksbill turtles come ashore to lay their eggs on the sandy southern beaches.

To the north is the **Lighthouse Reef Resort**, an air-conditioned colony of English-style villas catering to divers and fishermen.

The Blue Hole

☆☆☆☆☆ Near the center of Lighthouse Reef is the **Blue Hole**, Belize's most famous dive spot. From the air it looks like an apparition. The cobalt blue of the Caribbean abruptly changes to an azure blue circle. The heart of the circle is an indigo blue.

An approach by water is not as breathtaking, but beautiful nonetheless. You know you are somewhere special. It is an almost perfect circle, 1,000 feet in diameter in the midst of a reef six to 18 feet below the surface. Inside the shallow reef, the walls drop suddenly to a depth of 412 feet, almost completely vertical for the first 125 feet. Here they turn inward and slightly upward. At 140 feet you reach an awesome underwater "cathedral" with alcoves, archways and columns. It is a huge submerged cave with 12- to 15-foot-wide stalactites suspended 20 to 60 feet from the cavern ceiling. Formed thousands of years ago, perhaps during the Ice Age, the cave was once above sea level. This is always a guided dive and should be attempted only by experienced divers, but novice divers are entertained by the shallows surrounding the crater's rim.

 The nearest recompression chambers are in San Pedro and Belize City.

Travel time to and from the Blue Hole and the cost of your trip will vary according to the location of your accommodations. If you are staying on Ambergris Caye the trip will take an entire day and cost about $150. From the Turneffe Islands, travel time to and from is about half a day and the cost is included. If you are on a live-aboard, one of your stops will surely be the Blue Hole.

☆☆☆☆ South of the Turneffe Islands and Lighthouse Reef is the third and most remote atoll, **Glover's Reef**. It is a reef system formed by coral growing around the edges of a steep limestone plateau. An almost continuous barrier reef encloses an 80-square-mile lagoon that reaches depths of 50 feet. The lagoon is an outstanding snorkeling spot, with over 700 coral heads. Outside, the reef starts at 30 feet and drops to more than 2,000 feet. Visibility exceeds 150 feet. Grouper, queen triggerfish and parrotfish are in abundance. Mantas, pods of dolphins, spotted eagle rays and sea turtles are occasionally seen on the reefs. It is a spectacular diving and snorkeling spot, with more than 25 coral species to be explored and thousands of sheltered spots. The reefs remain largely unexplored and are seldom visited by live-aboards. Two dive/fishing resorts, **Glovers Reef Resort** and **Manta Reef Resort**, offer experienced guides and services.

Gladden Spit Marine Preserve, off Belize's south coast, directly east of Placencia appeals to divers and snorkelers who want to interact with BIG marine critters. Fifty-foot-long whale sharks arrive each spring to feed on tiny fish eggs during the annual spawning season. The reserve attracts over 25 species of reef fish that congregate to deposit their eggs. This happens during the first full moon of each spring. The Nature Conservancy conducts intensive scientific research in the Gladden Spit Marine Reserve in an effort to maintain the continued health of these dramatic whale sharks and fish aggregations. More and more divers and snorkelers flock to Placencia to interact with the gentle 50-foot-long whale sharks.

Where to Stay

Rates listed are for winter, in US dollars, and are subject to change. Most resorts and restaurants accept US dollars, travelers checks, and major credit cards. Note: Direct-dial service is available between Belize and the US and Canada. To call Belize, dial ☎ 011-501 before the local number. E-mail, widely available, may be used to book direct.

Ambergris Caye

There are flights between Belize City and San Pedro, the main town on Ambergris Cay, every 30 minutes from sunrise to sunset. Ferries depart Belize City for Ambergris Caye from the Swinging Bridge, a 20-minute taxi ride from the airport.

Ambergris Caye is twenty-five miles long; its width ranges from a few hundred feet to over four miles. Ferries connect resorts on the north end of Ambergris Caye to San Pedro for $20 US round-trip (one to four passengers). The cost from San Pedro to The Caye Resort, Mata Chica, Green Parrot & Casa Caribe and in-between destinations runs $30 US round-trip. Pick-up and drop-off is at docks in the area from Ramon's Village to Hustler Tours. Other pick-up and drop-off locations can be negotiated before the trip.

The Blue Tang Inn, formerly the Rocks Inn, has newly renovated air-conditioned suites that can be packaged with dive trips from $890 for six nights, four dive days, breakfast and dinner. Accommodation-only rates run from $110 to $175 per night. ☎ 866-881-1020, www.bluetanginn.com.

Ramon's Village in San Pedro offers 20 lovely air-conditioned, thatched-roof bungalows with double beds and full baths. The resort has a nice pool side bar, saltwater pool, restaurant, and fully equipped dive shop offering reef trips and basic rentals. Relaxed atmosphere. Daily room rates start at $125 daily for a double, to $245 for a suite. ☎ 800-MAGIC 15 or 601-649-1990, fax 601-425-2411; or write PO Drawer 4407, Laurel MS 39441, www.ramons.com.

Victoria House, on its own nine-acre beach, features 31 casually elegant rooms, suites, apartments and villas and on-site Fantasea PADI dive shop. The barrier reef lies three quarters of a mile out, directly in front of the hotel. Day rates for standard air-conditioned rooms are from $155 to $325 in summer; $195 to $485 in winter. Seven-night all-inclusive dive packages include a welcome cocktail, three to four full days of diving (a daily two-tank dive), continental breakfast, lunch and dinner, round-trip air transfers between Belize City and San Pedro, transfers between Victoria House and San Pedro Airstrip, all hotel taxes and gratuities at the resort Package rates range from $2,490 for a couple in summer; from $3,144 to $4,750 in winter. ☎ 800-247-5159 or 504-865-0717, fax 504-865-0718. Local 026-2067, fax 026-2429, www.victoria-house.com, or write to Victoria House, Ambergris Caye, Belize, Central America.

Belize Yacht Club, within easy walking distance of San Pedro Town and restaurants, features modern, Spanish-style, air-conditioned, one- and two-bedroom suites with fully equipped kitchens, cable TV and phones. Light meals are served at the resorts' **Splash Bar**. Internet access in some suites.

Dive packages for seven nights include accommodation in a garden-view, one-bedroom suite, five days of local two-tank boat dives, plus weights, belt and tanks, for US$662 per person based on a double (summer, or May 1 to December 14). US$392 per non-diver accompanying a diver. Add $135 per diver for day-trip to the Blue Hole; add $100 per diver for nitrox. Add $93.75 for round-trip air transfer from Belize International to San Pedro Airport.

The resort has its own dive shop and boasts the highest safety standards. ☎ 800-688-0402 or write to PO Box 62, San Pedro, Ambergris Caye, Belize, Central America, www.belizeyachtclub.com.

Coral Beach Hotel and Dive Club, situated on the main street of town, is a dive shop with 19 adjacent rooms. Rooms, with reef views, are plain and simple, some with air conditioning, some with fans. The hotel's **Jambel Jerk Pit Restaurant** serves Jamaican and Belizean cuisine. Dive packages, snorkel-sail trips, airport pick-up. Room rates per day, per person start at $75. Diving extra. ☎ 011-501-226-2013, fax 011-501-226-2864, www.coral-beachhotel.com, coralbeach@btl.net.

Caribbean Villas Hotel, three quarters of a mile from San Pedro, features 10 recently updated air-conditioned beachfront studios and suites with ocean views. Nice pier and beach. Hot tubs, elevated perch for bird watching. Winter rates range from $85 for a studio to $295 for a six-person suite. Dive shops pick you up at the dock. Dives are $55 for a two-tank local excursion. ☎ 800-633-4734 or direct, 011-501-226-2715, fax 011-501-226-2885, www.caribbeanvillashotel.com, info@caribbeanvillashotel.com.

Paradise Resort Hotel, located a stone's throw away from the center of San Pedro, offers divers a rustic, Caribbean environment. Guests choose from 25 oceanfront, thatched-roof cabanas cooled by air conditioning or fans. Coconut palms shade a broad, white-sand beach. An on-site dive shop offers daily reef trips, night dives, Blue Hole trips, snorkeling trips, open-water certification, and gear rental. Divers swap tales over sumptuous, barbecued pizza, burgers, fish, shrimp, and lobster at the resort's beach bar and deli. Rates are from $90 for an air-conditioned room in summer, $120 in winter. ☎ 800-451-8017, direct ☎ 501-226-2083, www.ambergriscaye.com, paradise@btl.net.

Paradise Villas Beachfront Resort Condos offer one- and two-bedroom, oceanfront townhouses with ceiling fans, air conditioning, TV and kitchenettes. An artificial reef off the compound's long pier attracts hordes of fish. Diving is arranged with Reef Adventures. Pool, restaurant. Rates are $155 to $175 per night in winter, $125 to $135 in summer, plus 7% tax. Resort folks will meet you at the Belize airport. Dive packages are offered by Reef Adventures. Accommodation for seven nights including 16 dives costs $588 in summer, $642 in winter. US ☎ 503-452-9257; nellie@btl.net, direct phone 501-226-2087, cell phone 501-614-5298, fax 501-226-2400.

Captain Morgan's Retreat, a thatched-hut village, offers air-conditioned beachfront cabanas with ceiling fans and solid mahogany floors. Modern baths. Roomy. The resort, 3½ miles north of San Pedro, is reached by water taxi. Vacation packages for seven nights include five days of two-tank dives, a night dive, round-trip transfers from Belize City, tax and gratuity. From June 6 to May 31, $1,587 per person; from June 7 to December 19, $1,232 per person. ☎ 888-653-9090. Write to 1408 Meadow Lane, Cody, Wyoming 82414, belizevacation@yahoo.com, www.belizevacation.com.

Journey's End, is an outstanding, PADI resort hotel just 500 yards from the barrier reef. The 50-acre resort is accessible by water taxi – 10 minutes from the airstrip. Guests stay in luxurious beach cabanas, poolside villas, or waterfront rooms. All have been recently renovated. Amenities include a gourmet restaurant, tennis courts, beach bar, and freshwater Olympic pool with swim-up bar and grill. All watersports are offered. The 125-member staff caters to guests' *every* whim. Seven-night dive package includes a lagoon-view guest room, daily breakfast, welcome drink, round-trip air transfers from Belize City to San Pedro including water taxi to the resort, five days of two-tank reef diving plus one night dive. Package is per-person, based on double occupancy, two divers or one diver and one non-diver. Non-diver receives equal value dive rate resort package. Package price does not include 17% tax and service charge. Rates are from $974 to $1,465. ☎ 800-460-5665, www.journeysendresort.com. info@journeysendresort.com.

Portofino Resort, north of San Pedro, accommodates guests in either beach cabanas with Caribbean views, or in one of the very luxurious Tree Top suites that are on 10-foot stilts, offering great views over the Caribbean and the barrier reef. All have air conditioning. There is also a honeymoon suite with a spacious balcony overlooking the sea, four-poster bed, Jacuzzi, double sink and spacious jungle rain shower.

Eight-day/seven-night dive packages include three days of reef diving, one night dive, and one full-day atoll dive, with a choice between the Blue Hole and Turneffe Islands; breakfast and three-course dinner daily.

Package includes a welcome cocktail, round-trip airfare from Belize city to San Pedro, boat transfer to the resort, use of all resort watersports facilities. Low-season rates per person are from $1,400 ; peak season, $1,800; Tree Top suite $1,650 to $2,050. Taxes and service charge included. ☎ 501-220-5096, fax 501-226-4272, www.portofinobelize.com.

Banyan Bay Villas houses guests in two-bedroom suites, with full kitchen, air conditioning, Jacuzzi tub, cable TV, pool, alfresco dining, full dive shop and dive tours, snorkeling tours, fishing guides, jungle trips, Mayan ruin tours, Hobbie Cat sailing school, windsurfing school and rentals. Located on Ambergris Caye. Summer rates from $195 per suite; winter rates from $275. ☎ 501-226-3739, www.banyanbay.com, banyanbay@btl.net.

Sunbreeze Beach Hotel, a U-shaped, 39-room air-conditioned beach-front inn has a PADI dive shop on premises, restaurant, wide sandy beach and pool. Spacious guest rooms have private bath, ocean views, two double beds, balconies, phone, cable TV. Summer room rates for a double start at $130 per night; winter from $160. US & Canada ☎ 800-688-0191 or 501-226-2191, www.sunbreeze.com, sunbreeze@btl.net.

Caye Caulker

Iguana Reef Inn on Caye Caulker, on the water's edge, offers upscale accommodations and the "Old Caribbean" island lifestyle. The inn is just minutes away from great diving, restaurants and the "Split" beach – a popular place to chill out. **Paradise Down Diving** is nearby.

Spacious guest rooms feature tiled floors, refrigerators, air conditioning, ceiling fans and bright furniture and artwork by local artists. Choose between junior suites with two queen-size beds or a single queen-size bed and a futon, or deluxe suites with a semi-private veranda. The inn's lounge features more than 20 different rums, and a diverse selection of classic Caribbean and jazz CDs. ☎ 501-226-0213, fax 501-226-0087, www.iguanareefinn.com, iguanareef@btl.net; Paradise Down Diving, www.paradisedown.com.

St. George's Caye

St. George's Lodge is the only commercial establishment on Saint George's Caye. The lodge, which is beautifully hand-crafted of exquisite local hardwoods, houses a dining room, rosewood bar, secluded sun deck and 12 private rooms cooled by trade winds. In addition, there are four new thatched-roof cottages, each with a private veranda overlooking the sea. All rooms and cottages feature private bath with shower, and windmill-powered electricity. (A 110-V AC converter is located in the lodge for recharging strobes, etc.) Gourmet meals featuring fresh lobster, broiled native fish, and outstanding conch chowder, followed by fabulous desserts created with local fruits, are the fare of the day. Diving takes place on a shallow wall with depths ranging from 40 to 100 feet, where there is a wide variety of corals and endless schools of fish. Visibility exceeds 100 feet. Rates include round-trip ground and boat transportation from Belize International Airport, private bath, all meals, tanks, weights, full diving privileges with two trips, and maid service; Per person-per day rates based on a double are $409 (cottages)

or $359(lodge). Non-divers rates are $279 (lodge), $409 (cottage). Non-divers may swim from dive boats on a space-available basis. Nitrox diving available. Instruction extra. In the US ☎ 800-678-6871 or 941-488-3788, direct 501-226-4444, info@gooddiving.com.

South Water Caye

 Escape the masses on this private 18-acre island off **Dangriga**, 35 miles south of Belize City. Transfers from the mainland are by the Blue Marlin Lodge launch or by charter flight. By boat, the trip takes about 90 minutes. Driving from Belize City to Dangriga takes about 2½ hours, or 20 minutes by air.

The big plus for this pristine spot is easy beach diving and snorkeling on the barrier reef that sits 120 feet offshore. Sounds like a short swim, but actually the water is so shallow between the shore and the dropoff that it's a short walk. Despite Belize's current trend towards marine conservation, spear fishing is allowed here.

The Blue Marlin Lodge is spread over six acres. Catering primarily to divers and fishermen, the all-inclusive, oceanfront, rustic lodge features five beach cabanas, three dome-shaped cabins and nine guest rooms with private baths. Five of the guest rooms are quite small. All rooms have a private bath with hot and cold running water. The lodge produces its own 110-volt, 60-cycle power and has a desalinization plant to produce pure water. The restaurant and bar serve three sumptuous meals daily. Fresh fish, shrimp and lobster are nicely prepared. Snacks and beverages are served all day. The bar is always stocked with fine Caribbean rums and an assortment of other liquors and beers. No phones or TV in the rooms or cottages, but there is a phone in the office that guests may use, and the bar has one satellite TV and a VCR. The lodge's dive office has an air compressor, tanks, weights and a small supply of gear. Bring your own personal equipment and snorkeling gear.

Dive/snorkel trips are aboard a fast Pro 42 dive boat or one of two 26-foot power boats. Fishing trips are aboard a 28-foot Mako.

All-inclusive dive packages for $1,475 per person, based on a double, from Saturday to Saturday, include pick-up in Dangriga, standard accommodations, three meals daily plus snacks, two boat dives daily (on six days), and unlimited shore dives. Add $180 for an air-conditioned cottage. ☎ 800-798-1558, 501-522-2243 or 501-522-2296, Belize direct: 501-522-2243, www.bluemarlinlodge.com, marlin@direcway.com.

The Turneffe Islands

Turneffe Island Lodge accommodates guests in one of their 12 air-conditioned beachfront cottage rooms with private bath or at the main lodge. Cellular and fax service (no phones). American-owned and -operated, this delightful outpost lies approximately 30 miles from Belize City, via a two-hour boat trip supplied by the lodge. Lodge rooms feature tropical décor and screened porches facing the Caribbean. Specialties from the gourmet dining room include local fish dishes, conch, and island-grown fruits and vegetables.

A sheer coral wall that starts at 40 feet and drops to more than 2,000 feet surrounds the entire island. Outstanding snorkeling reefs lie about 350 yards off the resort beach. Get there by either paddling one of the resort's four sea kayaks, sailing a Sunfish or taking the skiff. Rates (per person based on a double) during the high season run $1,843 for seven nights, seven days, including round-trip transfers from the Belize City airport, three meals daily, 17 single-tank dives, day-trip to the Blue Hole, Half Moon Wall and Long Caye Wall, use of sea kayaks, windsurfer, sailboat, volleyball, horsehoes and lodging. Off season costs $1,760. To upgrade to a single room or cabana add $633. Non-divers pay $1,395. Tanks and weights supplied. Bring your own personal gear. ☎ 800-874-0118, fax 713-236-7739, www.turneffelodge.com, info@turneffelodge.com.

Blackbird Caye Resort, located 35 miles from Belize City within the Turneffe Reef Atoll on Blackbird Cay, defines "ecotourist paradise." Unique and exciting, with miles of deserted beaches and jungle trails, the island sits close to 70 impressive dive sites with depths from 20 to 80 feet. Reefs are spectacular, with huge tube and barrel sponges, dramatic overhangs, large loggerhead turtles, dolphins, perfect coral formations. Abundant groupers and reef fish, frequent manatee sightings. The resort's crystal clear lagoon is terrific for snorkeling and swimming. Calm waters inside the reef make it a safe spot for novices. Per-person rates based on a double for an all-inclusive dive package are $1,695 for seven nights. Children between ages seven and 11 stay for $100 per day. Ages six and under stay free. Children who are certified divers pay standard rates. Accommodations are in thatched-roof cabanas with ceiling fans and private baths. Packages include airport reception, boat transfers, lodging, all meals (excellent buffet-style), trails, three dives per day, air, tanks and weights. Dive shop on property. Morning and afternoon snorkeling excursions. Boat to the island departs from Belize City. Travel time is four to five hours. ☎ 888-271-DIVE (3483) or 305-969-7947, fax 305-969-7946. dive@blackbirdresort.com, http://dive.blackbirdresort. com.

Lighthouse Reef

Lighthouse Reef Resort on **Northern Cay**, a private island at the northern end of the Lighthouse Reef Reserve, boasts a protected lagoon perfect for snorkelers of all ages. For experienced divers, the resort's custom-built cruiser takes off for the best of Belizean adventure dives, including the fabulous Blue Hole and Lighthouse Reef where 15- by 10-foot basket sponges, kelp-like gorgonians and sea fans up to nine feet across, thrive.

The resort offers luxury air-conditioned rooms and villas. **Tropic Air** meets incoming flights at Belize International Airport and transports guests to the resort's private airstrip. Flight time is 20 minutes. Diving packages cost $1,200 (non-divers $1,050) and run from Saturday to Saturday; they include air-conditioned room with bath, three meals per day and snacks, three boat dives per day, night dives, tanks and weights. A fish-and-dive package may be combined for $1,400. ☎ 800-423-3114. Write PO Box 26, Belize City, CA.

Placencia

Placencia is a great spot for divers seeking off-the-beaten-track adventures and especially for those on a low budget. Forty cayes between the mainland and the barrier reef offer pristine diving and snorkeling. During the first full moon of every spring when 25 species of reef fish come together to spawn, **Gladden Spit Marine Preserve**, just east of Placencia, is prime whale shark watching territory. **Placencia Village** has guest rooms for as low as $35 per night. Affordable open-air bars serve pizza, chili and Creole fish dishes. Camping is available in **Seine Bight Village**. For complete listings contact the **Belize Tourist Board**, ☎ 800-844-3688, www.placencia.com. Mosquitos and other stinging insects make their presence known on Mainland Belize. Many travelers find that taking tasteless garlic pills before and during a trip to Placencia repels pesky bugs nicely. Avon Skin-So-Soft helps, too.

Rum Point Inn, a NAUI and PADI Dream Resort three miles from Placencia Village, comprises 10 seaside cabanas, a main house and a small sandy swimming beach. E-6 film processing. High-season rates per person, per day, for a double are $165 for accommodations, add $56 for three meals prepaid; children under 12 are $35, $50 with meals. Add 7% hotel tax and 15% service charge on meals. Pro-42 dive boat, the *Auriga*. **Rum Point Divers** offer open-water referral certification, refresher and advanced courses. Snorkelers join the dive boats for shallow reef exploration. ☎ 888-235-4031, 501-523-3239, www.rumpoint.com, rupel@direcway.com, dbevier@cox .net.

Turtle Inn, a mile north of Placencia Village, offers six beautiful, thatched-roof cabanas along 500 feet of Caribbean beachfront. Romantic, Balinese-inspired cabanas have private baths, solar-generated lighting and kerosene lanterns. Guests are offered a number of dive, snorkeling, and mainland jungle expeditions. ☎ 800-746-3743, direct 501-523-3244, info@blancaneaux.com, www.turtleinn.com.

Nautical Inn, a modern, clean resort on the Placencia peninsula in Seine Bight Village, features air-conditioned beachfront rooms with private baths and airy, tropical décor, the Oar House Restaurant, a gift shop, salon, scooter rentals, canoeing, scuba, snorkeling and jungle tours. Rooms that sleep two are $165 per day. Seven night packages with five dive days include two-tank boat dives with a PADI dive master, three meals daily, round-trip air transfer from Belize airport to Placencia, round-trip transfers from Placencia's air strip to the inn. ☎ (reservations only) 800-688-0377 or 501-523-3595, fax 501-523-3594, www.nauticalinnbelize.com, nautical@btl.net.

Singing Sands Inn features private, individual thatched-roof cabanas, modern on the inside, with private bathrooms, ceiling fans and gentle ocean breezes. Excursions for diving, snorkeling and day-trip visits to Maya ruins and the Cockscomb Jaguar Preserve are offered. Room rates are from $110 to $135 per day and include maid service and continental breakfast. ☎ 501-520-8022 or 501-523-8017, www.singingsands.com, singingsands @direcway.com.

Soulshine Resort dive tours take off to Laughing Bird Caye, Ranguana Caye and Little Caye. This small dive resort offers rustic, wood-paneled, thatched-roof cabanas, breakfast and dinner, four two-tank dives, transfers for rates starting at $1,200 per person, double occupancy. ☎ 800-890-6082, www.soulshine.com.

The Placencia Dive Shop specializes in friendly service, dive and snorkeling trips such as their Creole seafood feast and snorkel trip to nearby French Louis Cay. ☎ 501-62-3313 or 501 62-3227, fax 501-62-3226.

Sightseeing

Day-trips to Belize's archaeological sites, the rain forest, and Belize Zoo are offered by local tour companies in Belize City and Ambergris Caye or can be arranged as part of your trip in advance. Day rates are from $100 to about $250 from Ambergris Caye or Placencia to inland sites, depending on where you are headed.

Altun Ha is the most popular Mayan ruin and least expensive from Ambergris Caye. Tours include a picnic lunch, ground and sea transportation.

Xunantunich (Maiden of the Rock) is on the west coast about 80 miles from Belize City. This is the largest ruin unearthed in Belize. Impressive views are had from the top of **El Castillo**, the main pyramid. Xunantunich is accessible only by ferry, which runs from San Jose Succotz daily from 8 am to 5 pm. Trips often include a tour of the Belize Zoo and a drive around Belmopan, Belize's capital.

Animals at the **Belize Zoo** are housed in naturalistic mesh-and wood-enclosures. The animals – jaguars, pumas, toucans, spider and howler monkeys, and the "mountain cow" – are all indigenous to Belize. They were originally gathered for a wildlife film. The zoo is 30 miles west of Belize City.

From Belize City, driving up the Western Highway to Mile Marker 21 will bring you to **Gracie Rock**, one of the sites used in the movie *Mosquito Coast*, where you'll find the remains of the huge icemaker blown up by Harrison Ford.

Guanacaste Park, about 50 miles southwest of Belize City, is a 50-acre parcel of tropical forest located in the Cayo District at the junction of Western Highway and Hummingbird Highway. It is named for the huge Guanacaste tree, which can reach a height of 130 feet with a trunk diameter in excess of six feet. More than a hundred species of birds have been spotted here.

Blue Hole National Park & **St. Hermans Cave** are 12 miles southeast of Belmopan. This inland "blue hole" is popular as a recreational spot. Water, on its way to the Sibun River, emerges into the base of a collapsed sinkhole about 100 feet deep and 300 feet in diameter. **St. Hermans Cave** is 500 yards from the Hummingbird Highway and is accessible via a hiking trail from the blue hole. The nearest of the three known entrances is impressive – a large sinkhole funneling to a 65-foot entrance. Mayan pottery, spears and torches have been found here.

Dining

 Divers staying on Ambergris Caye will find restaurants in the village of **San Pedro** offering fresh seafood and local dishes such as conch chowder, conch fritters, broiled snapper, shrimp, lobsters, and rice dishes, often accompanied by home-baked breads or soups. Chinese food is also extremely popular. **Jerry's Crab Shack & Pizza** cooks up crispy pizzas, crab cakes and steaks. It's across from Ramon's Village on Coconut Drive. ☎ 06-2552. **Ramon's Village Restaurant**, ☎ 226-2071, offers a variety of fresh seafood in Chinese, Cajun and island dishes (breakfast, lunch and dinner). Or try the **Celi's Diner & Deli**, ☎ 226-2014, next to the Holiday Hotel for fabulous fish in beer batter and Key lime pie (beach barbecue on Wednesdays), or **Elvi's Kitchen**, ☎ 226-2176, for fabulous lobster, conch and shrimp (open for lunch and dinner).

Located on the beach, in the heart of San Pedro at the Spindrift Hotel, **Caliente** guarantees great views of the Caribbean Sea, whether you dine inside or out. Specialties are conch fritters, tortillas, chicken, beef and seafood dishes with a Mexican or Caribbean spin.

If you are staying at an out-island resort, meals are included in the price of the stay. Local fish, conch and chicken dishes are the usual.

Shopping

Small shops at the airport and resorts offer T-shirts, straw crafts and carvings from native woods including mahogany, rosewood and ziricote, a two-toned wood indigenous to Belize.

Major credit card companies from the US and Canada charge an additional two to five percent for charges made in Belize. Use cash or traveler's checks.

Live-aboards

Belize live-aboards offer access to these pristine diving areas and are popular among those who thrive on 24-hour diving.

Peter Hughes Diving operates the 138-foot *Sun Dancer II*, ☎ 800-932-6237 or 305-669-9391; in the US, 5723 Northwest 158th Street, Miami Lakes, FL 33014, www.peterhughes.com, ☎ 800-525-3833.

Belize Aggressor II is a 110-foot luxury yacht that carries 18 passengers. It offers all the amenities of a dive resort: air-conditioned private rooms, photo shop, film processing, mini movie theater, plus fast cruising speeds. ☎ 800-348-2628, or write Aggressor Fleet Ltd., PO Drawer K, Morgan City, LA 70381. Week tours start at $2,195 and depart from Belize City. Port fees are extra. ☎ 800-525-3833.

Facts

Helpful Phone Numbers: Police and ambulance: Belize City, ☎ 90; San Pedro, ☎ 02-82095; Placencia, ☎ 06-23129. ☎ 911 works in some areas; if you try and it doesn't work, dial 90. Hospital, Belize City, ☎ 02-77251 or 90. Tourist board, ☎ 800-422-3435 or 501-26-2012, fax 501-26-2338. Coast Guard, ☎ 02-35312.

Nearest Recompression Chamber: San Pedro, Ambergris Caye. Emergency helicopter service from atolls. Dial ☎ 90 for assistance.

Health: Anti-malaria tablets are recommended for stays in the jungle.

Airlines: Belize's major airport is ***Philip S.W. Goldson International Airport*** in Belize City (Ladyville), ☎ 02-52014. Scheduled commercial service from the US and Canada is by **American Airlines** (☎ 800-433-7300), **Continental**, and **TACA**. **Tropic Air** services major cities, Ambergris Caye and the out islands. Calling from Cancun, Mexico, ☎ 800-422-3435 or 501-26-2012, fax 501-26-2338; Belize, ☎ 2302; San Pedro, 2012 or 2439. Additional Belize cities are served by **Island Air**, ☎ 2219.

Private Aircraft may enter Belize only through the Phillip Goldson International Airport in Belize City. Belizean airspace is open during daylight hours. Pilots are required to file a flight plan and will be briefed on local conditions. Landing fee for all aircraft.

By Car: Belize can reached from the US and Canada via Mexico, though reports of hold-ups and fees totaling at least $250 on the roads deter most motorists. You must possess a valid driver's license and registration papers for the vehicle. A temporary permit will enable use of your vehicle without payment of fees going through customs. A temporary insurance policy must be purchased at the frontier to cover the length of stay in Belize. After three days, visitors must obtain a Belize driving permit, for which they need to complete a medical form, provide two recent photos and pay $20.

Private Boats must report to the police or immigration immediately. No permits are required. Boaters need documents for the vessel, clearance from last port of call, four copies of the crew and passenger manifest and list of stores and cargo.

Documents: Visitors are permitted to stay up to one month, provided they have a valid passport and have a ticket to their onward destination. For stays longer than 30 days an extension must be obtained from the Immigration Office, 115 Barrack Road, Belize City.

Transportation: Bus service around Belize City is readily available via **Batty Brothers**, ☎ 02-72025; or **Z-Line**, ☎ 02-73937/06-22211. Since few cars are available on the islands, transportation is usually arranged by the resorts. On the mainland, reservations for car rental can be made through **National** (☎ 800-CAR-RENT; in Belize, 2-31650) or **Budget** (☎ 800-927-0700; in Belize, ☎ 2-32435 or 33986). Reserve prior to trip. Jeeps and 4WD vehicles are mandatory on back roads. Avoid local car rental companies or carefully check vehicles for scratches or dents and have them documented by the rental company beforehand.

Internet Access & Telecommunications: Direct-dial phones, fax, telex, and cable are available, but calls from Belize are much higher than an equivalent call to Belize. The country code for Belize is (501) and there are currently 17 area codes within Belize. Remote jungle lodges usually have short-wave radio communications linked to cellular service. If you are business visitor planning to spend some time in Belize and want a temporary Internet account, you can make arrangements by contacting Belize Telecommunications, Inc. (BTL), Belize's sole Internet access provider, at sales@btl.net.

Visitors on Ambergris Caye can check e-mail or browse the Internet for about $7.50 per hour across from **Elvi's** or at the **Caribbean Connection Internet Café** on Front Street next to the Coral Beach Hotel in San Pedro Town, carconcafe@hotmail.com; or at **Coconet**, coconetbelize@hotmail.com, on Front Street next to Manleys Ice Cream.

Ferries: Several fast boats ferry passengers back and forth between Belize City and San Pedro, including *Thunderbolt, Andrea* and *Triple J*. Probably the most accessible boats are those that belong to the **Caye Caulker Water Taxi Association**. These leave from the Marine Terminal near the Swing Bridge in Belize City, which has a waiting area and two small museums to visit while you wait. Boats to San Pedro leave at 9 am, noon and 3 pm, with a brief stop at Caye Caulker. Fares are US$12.50 one-way to Ambergris Caye. You disembark at Sharks pier in the middle of town. Fares just to Caye Caulker are US$7.50, and boats depart at 9 am, 10:30 am, noon, 1:30, 3 and 5 pm. Children ages five to 10 go at half price; under five free. You can make reservations, but service is more likely to be first-come, first-served. A cab to down Belize City from the International Airport is about 20 minutes and costs US$17.50 for up to five people. The ferry is is first come first served. The *Andrea* leaves at 3 pm. It is the latest ferry.

To get to the ferry from the airport, take a taxi from International Airport to Belize City (rates are generally not posted in taxis). The airport is located nine miles from the city and is about a 15-20 minute ride. Taxis are available from the airport and in all towns.

Departure Tax: US$20.

Customs: Personal effects can be brought in without difficulty, but it is best to register cameras, videos and electronic gear with customs before leaving home. American citizens can bring home $400 worth of duty-free goods after a 48-hour visit. Over that, purchases are dutied at 10%. Import allowances include 200 cigarettes or a half pound of tobacco; 20 fluid oz of alcoholic beverages and one bottle of perfume for personal use.

 Removing and exporting coral or archaeological artifacts is prohibited. Also, picking orchids in forest reserves is illegal.

Taxes: Belize's sales tax is set at 8%, and is applied to all goods and services except hotel accommodations. There is a 7% hotel tax. Some hotels also add a 10-15% "service charge" to the bill; inquire about this when checking hotel prices.

Currency: Belize dollar; BZ$1=US50¢.

Climate: Belize has a subtropical, humid climate. Average temperature 79°F. The rainy season is from April to December. Hurricanes form during late summer. Best time to visit is February through May, though summer diving when weather permits (mid August) is often done in calm seas with excellent visibility.

Clothing: Lightweight clothing with long sleeves to protect against sunburn and a light sweater for evening wear. The dive resorts are extremely casual. Leave dress wear at home. Those who want to combine an expedition into the jungle with their diving vacation should check with the tour company about additional clothing needs. Bring mosquito repellent.

Dive Gear: Rental equipment is available but limited in Belize, so be sure to bring all of your own personal equipment. The resorts do supply weights and tanks, but little else.

Electricity: 110/220V 60 cycles. Most island resorts run on generators, which are out of service for at least part of the day. Air conditioning is limited on the out islands.

Time: Central Standard Time.

Language: English.

Additional Information: *Belize Tourism*, ☎ 800-624-0686 , fax 800-563-6033. In Belize, 83 North Front Street, PO Box 325, Belize City, Belize, C.A. ☎ 501-2231913, www.travelbelize.org, www.ambergriscaye.com.

Bonaire

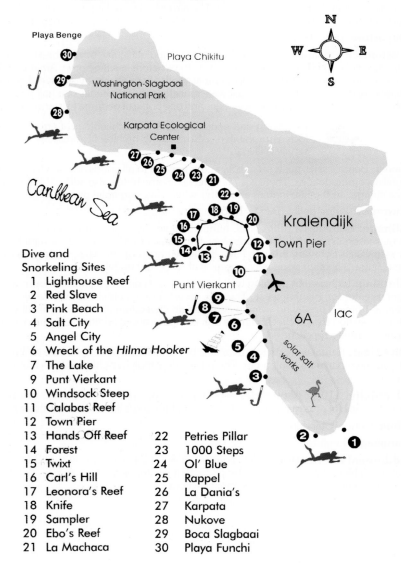

Playa Benge

Playa Chikitu

Washington-Slagbaai
National Park

Karpata Ecological
Center

Caribbean Sea

Kralendijk

Town Pier

Punt Vierkant

lac

6A

solar salt
works

Dive and Snorkeling Sites

1 Lighthouse Reef
2 Red Slave
3 Pink Beach
4 Salt City
5 Angel City
6 Wreck of the *Hilma Hooker*
7 The Lake
9 Punt Vierkant
10 Windsock Steep
11 Calabas Reef
12 Town Pier
13 Hands Off Reef
14 Forest
15 Twixt
16 Carl's Hill
17 Leonora's Reef
18 Knife
19 Sampler
20 Ebo's Reef
21 La Machaca
22 Petries Pillar
23 1000 Steps
24 Ol' Blue
25 Rappel
26 La Dania's
27 Karpata
28 Nukove
29 Boca Slagbaai
30 Playa Funchi

Note: Bonaire sites are periodically closed down for rejuvenation.
Check with local dive shops for availability before diving on your own.

Bonaire

Both above and beneath the sea, Bonaire is a colorful island. The south is flat, blessed with 15,000 resident flamingos and miles of pink coral-rock beaches. **Kralendijk**, its capital, sparkles with bright, pastel buildings. To the north, narrow roads wind through green mountains and cactus-laden deserts where more than 190 species of tropical birds reside. Rare species include bright green Amazona parrots, ruby-topaz hummingbirds, pearly-eyed thrashers, and Caribbean parakeets. At the island's southern tip, home of the **Antilles International Salt Company**, mountains of glistening white salt offer a striking contrast to the blue Caribbean. At day's end a green flash follows the setting sun.

Beneath the sea a brilliant rainbow of marine life has earned Bonaire a reputation as a world-class dive location. Strict conservation laws together with calm waters protected by the crescent shape of the island have preserved Bonaire's bountiful coral reefs and marine animals.

The second-largest of the islands of the Netherlands Antilles, Bonaire sits well out of the hurricane belt – 1,720 miles south of New York, 50 miles north of Venezuela – and is therefore protected from reef damage. It has dependably dry weather and calm seas most of the year, though changing global weather patterns bring an occasional midwinter storm and water-temperature drop.

With only 22 inches of rain annually, there is no freshwater runoff, so water visibility is typically 100 feet or more. Because sites are close to shore, visitors can pick up a tank and dive anytime day or night. Bright yellow painted rocks along the beach road mark dive and snorkeling sites. Excellent snorkeling exists off all the south-coast beaches.

Less than a mile from the west coast is **Klein Bonaire** (Little Bonaire), an islet surrounded by beautiful coral reefs. The sheltered waters between Bonaire's western shores and Klein Bonaire are always smooth – perfect for diving and snorkeling anytime. Bonaire's north coast, by contrast, is battered by strong waves that pound against rocky, coral cliffs.

History

Arawak Indians inhabited Bonaire for centuries before Amerigo Vespucci claimed discovery in 1499. The word Bonaire comes from the Arawak "bo-nah," which means "low country."

Spain attempted to colonize the island between 1527 and 1633, but in 1634 the Dutch claimed it and established a military base for defense against Spain. In 1639 the Dutch West India Company developed Bonaire for salt production, corn planting and livestock breeding. The company imported 100 African slaves and ran the island for the next 160 years.

The British occupied Bonaire briefly during the early 1800s, but the Dutch regained control in 1816 and established a government plantation system based on commercial crops. With the abolition of slavery in 1863, the operations became unprofitable and the island was divided and sold.

Over the next 90 years a severe economic recession forced many Bonaireans to migrate to Curaçao and Aruba seeking work in the oil industry. By the 1950s, however, Bonaire's economy recovered. The salt pans were modified to use solar energy and became the most successful such plants in the world. Tourism was introduced and divers have since come from around the globe.

Bonaire Marine Park

In 1979, the **Netherlands Antilles National Parks Foundation** (**STINAPA**) received a grant from the World Wildlife Fund for the creation of the Bonaire Marine Park. The park was created to maintain the coral reef eco-system and ensure continuing returns from scuba diving, fishing and other recreational activities.

The park incorporates the entire coastline of Bonaire and neighboring Klein Bonaire. The protected area is defined as the "sea bottom and the overlying waters from the high-water tidemark down to 200 feet (60 meters)."

All visitors are asked to respect the marine park rules – no sitting on corals; no fishing or collecting of fish while scuba diving; no collecting of shells or corals, dead or alive. Spearfishing is forbidden. Anchoring is not permitted except in the harbor area of town (from the yacht club to the new pier). All craft must use permanent moorings, except for emergency anchoring. Boats of less than 12 feet may use a stone anchor.

Popular dive sites are periodically shut down to rejuvenate the corals. Moorings are periodically removed and placed on different sites.

Best Dive & Snorkeling Sites

Hotels and dive shops offer daily trips to nearby offshore sites. Most are less than a 10-minute boat ride, but you don't need a boat or even a mask to see Bonaire's reefs. They grow to the surface in many areas and are visible from the shore. Excellent beach dives exist along the shores on the leeward side where channels have been cut allowing access to deeper water. These reefs slope down to a narrow ledge at 30 feet, then drop off to between 100 and 200 feet. Expect to pay a $10 "annual"

fee for using the marine park. Most of the resorts and dive shops offer guided snorkeling trips that include a map and instructional text materials.

☆☆☆ **Lighthouse Reef** takes its name from the nearby **Willemstoren Lighthouse** and is at the southernmost point of the island. It is a shore-dive, which can be entered at the lighthouse or at most any point west. Owing to the surf, this dive is only recommended for experienced open-water divers. During calm seas, however, the site can also be dived by the novice if accompanied by a qualified dive master or instructor.

Lighthouse sparkles with sea plumes, sea fans, star, yellow-pencil, and brain corals. Marine life tends to be larger than at most other sites and includes parrotfish, schoolmasters, snappers, and sea turtles. Old anchors and chains rest in this area, remains of ships wrecked prior to the opening of the lighthouse in 1838.

☆☆☆☆ To reach **Red Slave**, drive south from Kralendijk, past the Solar Salt Works beyond the second set of slave huts. Strong currents and surf limit this site to experienced open-water divers.

The size and number of fish at Red Slave is spectacular. It is not unusual to spot four-foot tiger, yellowfin, or Nassau groupers. Gorgonians, orange crinoids, and black corals are found on the southern slope. Artifacts from pre-lighthouse wrecks rest on the slope, such as anchors and ballast stones from the 1829 shipwreck HMS *Barham*.

☆☆☆☆ **Pink Beach**, named for the unusual pinkish tint of the sand, is either a boat- or shore-dive. Drive south from Kralendijk, past the Solar Salt Works, to the rock marked "Pink Beach." Park along the road and walk north to the beach. The mooring offshore marks the start of the dive.

Seaward of the mooring are clumps of staghorn coral and gorgonians. Schools of goatfish, porgies and horse-eye jacks feed in this area, with many large barracudas.

☆☆☆☆☆ One of the favorite boat-dive areas is **Alice in Wonderland**, a double-reef complex, separated by a sand channel and extending from Pt. Vierkant south toward Salt Pier. A number of good dive sites exist within this reef system, all marked by dive buoys. **Angel City**, the most popular, starts at about 30 feet, then drops off to a deep channel. Swim down the first reef slope to a narrow sand channel, keeping right. One of the largest purple tube sponges you will ever see is at the channel's northern end.

Scattered throughout the shallow terrace are stands of staghorn, star, giant brain, and flower corals – home to goatfish, jacks, groupers and trunkfish. Farther down is a garden-eel colony, queen conchs, and swarms of fish. Initially, the garden eels look like a bed of grass, but will retract into the sand if you wave your arm over them.

☆☆☆ Boat dives in Bonaire are inexpensive ($16 and up) and very convenient but, if you miss the boat, **Angel City** can be reached by swimming from shore. Drive to the Trans World Radio transmitting station, south of Kralendijk – its huge tower is easy to spot. Follow a track before the station entrance, which leads to the shore. From there, enter opposite the Angel City buoy.

☆☆☆☆ **Salt City** is a boat- or shore-dive at the southern end of "Alice in Wonderland." To reach Salt City, drive south from Kralendijk past the salt-loading pier (very visible). You'll spot a large buoy south of the pier. Enter along the left "bank" formed by the large "sand river," a wide sand stretch that eventually drops off the shallow terrace into a short, reef slope "island."

The terrace is landscaped with star, fire, elkhorn and staghorn corals. Sea life is superb, featuring scad, palometa, big groupers, snappers, garden eels, tilefish and French angelfish.

☆☆☆ The **Hilma Hooker**, a 250-foot freighter, lies right offshore just north of Angel City Reef. Reached from the beach or by boat, this is Bonaire's most spectacular and notorious shipwreck. The ship was seized during a drug raid when a member of the Antillean Coast Guard discovered a false bulkhead. The crew abandoned the freighter and fled the island. Because of an unmanageable leak, Bonaire law enforcement agents were afraid that the ship would sink and damage the reefs, so they towed her out to where she now lies, creating an intriguing dive site. The wreck rests on a sandy bottom at 91 feet. Divers should stay outside the wreck and monitor bottom time.

☆☆☆☆ **The Lake** is yet another part of the "Alice in Wonderland" complex. Sea plumes, purple tube sponges and a profusion of groupers, coneys, rock hinds and moray eels are in residence.

☆☆☆ **Punt Vierkant** is marked by the first buoy past the small lighthouse north of the "Alice in Wonderland" complex. To reach the site, drive south from Kralendijk past the Belnam residential area and toward the lighthouse. On the swim out you'll be joined by trunkfish, groupers and snappers. As you descend, the fish are larger and the rays more numerous. Pastel gorgonians and sponges decorate the wall.

☆☆☆ **Windsock Steep** is known for great snorkeling. This dive is off the small sand beach opposite the airport runway. Watch out for fire coral as you explore the shallow terrace. The bottom is sandy, but stacked up with sergeant majors, angelfish, snappers, trumpetfish and barracudas.

☆☆☆☆ **Calabas Reef**, just off the beach in front of the Divi Flamingo Resort, is reached by swimming over a sand shelf. Giant brain and star corals grow from the slope. Old anchors are scattered about. To the north is a small sailboat wreck. The hotel pier is well lit after dusk, making it an easily accessible and attractive night-dive spot.

Reef inhabitants are parrotfish, French angels, damsels, Spanish hogfish and yellow snappers. Spotted, goldentail and chain morays peek out from the crevices.

☆☆☆☆☆ **Town Pier** refers to the "old pier" in the center of town, between the customs office and the fish market. Both the Town Pier and the neighboring, new cruise-ship pier are popular for moonlit dives, though recent security restrictions require divers to obtain special permission before entering the area. Bright sponge crabs and several species of decorator crabs materialize with darkness, then disappear with daylight. Because water entry and finding one's way around the maze of pilings gets tricky, we find this site more interesting, and much more fun as a guided tour, with Bonaire's "Touch-the-Sea" guru, Dee Scarr. She knows where to find all the good stuff. For details, contact Dee from the US at ☎ 599-717-8529 or dee@touchthesea.com.

Check with your dive shop or the Harbormaster for current restrictions. The Harbormaster's office is at the old fort with the cannon, next to the main government building, ☎ 599-717-8151.

☆☆☆ Off the main road, in front of the Habitat dive shop, is **La Machaca**. Ideal for night and warm-up dives, this site is named after a small, wrecked fishing boat. Every variety of fish found in Bonaire's waters can be seen here by divers and snorkelers. Mr. Roger, a huge green moray, an old tiger grouper, friendly rock beauties, and two black margates inhabit the wreck.

☆☆☆ **Petries Pillar** gets its name from the colony of pillar coral that grows on the reef face. To reach this site travel north toward Gotomeer, turn left just short of half a mile past the last house onto an unpaved road. Follow that road down to the sea. Fine for boat or shore entry.

☆☆☆☆☆ **1,000 Steps (Piedra Haltu)** may be either a boat- or a shore-dive, though a boat-dive may be easier and will definitely save you carrying your gear down 67 (by actual count) steps. To reach 1,000 Steps, drive north from town along the scenic road towards Gotomeer until you reach the entrance of the Radio Nederland transmitting station. On your left are steep concrete steps leading down the mountainside to a sandy beach and the dive site.

Swim through the marked channel to a sandy shallow terrace. Gorgonians and flower corals are abundant. Lavender shrimp, barracudas, black durgons, yellowtail snappers, horse-eye jacks and schoolmasters populate the reef.

☆☆☆☆ **Ol' Blue**, a favorite with snorkelers for its walls of reef fish, cleaning stations and calm waters, may get choppy when the wind kicks up. Get there by driving north along the scenic road to Gotomeer past the transmitting station to the white coral-rubble beach. The dive site is at the point where the road descends to the ocean and the cliff bends away from the road.

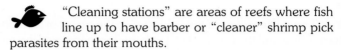 "Cleaning stations" are areas of reefs where fish line up to have barber or "cleaner" shrimp pick parasites from their mouths.

☆☆☆☆☆ **Rappel**, one of the best dives on the island, was named for its sheer cliff face. Divers have been known to "rappel" down the wall. Usually a boat-dive, it can also be reached by swimming out from Karpata.

Rappel's exceptional marine life includes orange seahorses, green moray eels, spiny lobsters, squid, marbled groupers, orange tube coral, shrimp, encrusting sponges, black coral and dense pink-tipped anemones.

☆☆☆☆☆ **Nukove** lies off a little road between Boca Dreifi and Playa Frans. It is a particularly nice shore-dive with a channel cut through the jungle of elkhorn coral that grows to the surface.

Numerous juveniles, shrimp and anemones may be seen in the cut. To the south are huge sponges, black coral, crinoids and sheet and scroll corals. Scrawled filefish, black durgons, groupers, wrasses and barracudas are in residence.

☆☆☆☆ **Boca Slagbaai** provides an opportunity to see the best examples of buttress formations in Bonaire water. In addition, green morays, white spotted filefish, tarpon and barracudas are in abundance. Slagbaai boasts six concrete cannon replicas, halved and buried for the 1974 film, *Shark Treasure*.

To reach this dive, drive through the village of Rincon into Washington Slagbaai National Park, where you follow the green arrows to Slagbaai. The center of the bay is sand, but a swim to the north brings you across ridges and valleys of coral. Excellent snorkeling is to the south, where two real cannons can be seen at the southernmost point of the bay.

☆☆☆☆ **Playa Funchi**, in Washington Slagbaai National Park, is another popular snorkeling area. From Rincon, follow the green or yellow signs. Enter next to the man-made pier and swim north for the best snorkeling. Rays, parrotfish, rock hinds, jacks, groupers and angels swim through fields of staghorn coral. On shore, picnickers are greeted by hoards of fearless lizards in search of scraps.

Klein Bonaire

The dive sites surrounding Klein Bonaire are great for both diving and snorkeling. Some may be closed down at various times for rejuvenation.

☆☆☆☆☆ **Leonora's Reef**, on the north side, is a snorkeler's paradise heavily covered with yellow pencil coral, fire coral, star coral and elkhorn stands on a narrow, shallow terrace. West of the mooring are pillar coral formations. Expect to be greeted by masses of fish. "Attack" yellowtail snappers and tiny royal-blue fish are joined at cleaning stations by tiger, yellowmount and rare yellowfin groupers.

☆☆☆☆ **Hands Off Reef** was named in 1981 when an experiment was conducted to determine whether inexperienced and camera-carrying divers do more damage to the corals than others. "Hands Off," as the name implies, was not to be dived by photographers or resort course classes, designated solely as a control for later comparison to unlimited-access dives.

The reef slope is alive with black margates, groupers, rockhinds, parrots. Some of the narrow valleys of the dropoff zone contain the remains of coral-head "avalanches" worth exploring.

☆☆☆☆ Nearby is **Forest**, another fabulous snorkeling and diving spot. The reef starts at 15 feet, dropping off to undiveable depths. This site is named for the abundant black coral "trees" growing from the wall at 60 feet. Two-foot queen triggerfish, morays, filefish, black durgons, puffers and an abundance of small critters roam the "forest."

☆☆☆☆☆ **Twixt** is just north of Forest, around the southwest bend of Klein Bonaire. It provides excellent opportunities for wide-angle photography, with huge basket sponges, sea whips, black coral, enormous pastel fans, tube sponges and star corals. Depths range from 15 to 100 feet. The coral wall slopes down to a sandy bottom. Seas are almost always calm and flat here.

☆☆☆☆☆ Large groupers frequent the pillar coral cleaning station at the upper edge of **Carl's Hill**. Named after photographer Carl Roessler, this spot is great for snorkeling and diving. The sharp dropoff begins at 15 feet and continues to 80 feet, creating a narrow precipice called **Venus Mound**. An occasional strong current cleanses the huge purple finger sponges on the slope. West of the mooring, divers will find a buttress and sand valley lined with coral rocks and cleaning stations.

☆☆☆☆ **Ebo's Reef** (aka Jerry's Jam) is superb for video and still photography. Shallow enough for snorkeling, the dropoff starts at 20 feet and slopes off to a sandy bottom at 150 feet. Dramatic overhangs of black coral grow in less than 30 feet of water. Masses of grunts, Spanish hogfish, groupers, sergeant majors, parrotfish and yellowtails swarm the shelf. Small tunnels along the shelf are good hiding places for juvenile fish and small critters.

☆☆☆☆ **Knife Reef** is excellent for snorkeling and diving. A shallow half-circle of elkhorn coral creates a mini "lagoon," protecting star coral heads, gorgonians, and a multitude of fish. Bermuda chubs, peacock flounders, lizardfish and yellowhead jawfish rove the shallow terrace. The dropoff zone is fairly barren (the result of reef slides), but gorgonians, stinging coral, and yellow pencils thrive.

☆☆☆☆ Another snorkeler's delight is **Sampler**. Resident spotted eels and hordes of tamed, friendly fish will charm you as you investigate the lovely pillar- and staghorn-coral formations.

Touch the Sea

 Learn to pet moray eels, tickle sea anemones, get a manicure from a cleaner shrimp, massage the tummy of a "deadly" scorpionfish and befriend marine animals you would normally keep at a safe distance. Diving with Touch the Sea creator, Dee Scarr, is an experience divers won't soon forget.

Ms. Scarr recommends that divers not try these antics without first participating in her program, which includes classroom and underwater time. Bring or rent a camera; you'll enjoy shooting these normally hard-to-get-close-to creatures.

Arrangements to dive with Dee Scarr must be made prior to your trip to Bonaire by e-mailing her at dee@touchthesea.com, or writing her c/o Touch the Sea, PO Box 369, Bonaire, Netherlands Antilles, www.touchthesea.com. From the US, ☎ 599-717-8529. A maximum of four divers can participate in one dive. Touch the Sea programs close from March to October. In the US, specialized land programs are offered for universities and groups.

"Touch the Sea" is a PADI Specialty Certification available to all certified divers. Environmentalist Dee Scarr is author of *Touch the Sea*; *Coral's Reef*, a children's book; and *The Gentle Sea*.

Dive Operators

 Expect to pay a marine park use fee of $10. Purchase of the Bonaire Marine Park tag entitles you to one year's unlimited access to the sea surrounding Bonaire for diving, snorkeling, windsurfing and boating. The fees pay for the upkeep of the park.

Black Durgon Scuba Center, at the Black Durgon Inn, mixes personalized reef and wreck boat-dives with guided beach diving. The shop teaches PADI, NAUI Resort and certification courses in English, Dutch, Spanish and German. ☎ 599-717-5736, fax 599-717-8846, bkdurgon@bonairelive.com. Write to PO Box 200 Bonaire, NA.

Bon Bini Divers at the Lions Diver Resort features Nitrox, guided diving and snorkeling trips by boat or off the beach. Also PADI and underwater photo instruction in English, Dutch, Spanish, German, Italian, and French. ☎ 599-717-5425, info@bonbinidivers.com, www.bonbinidivers.com.

Buddy Dive Resort's drive-through air-fill station is a terrific service for shore-divers. They offer Nitrox too. The shop has varied PADI courses, including rebreathers, guided boat- and shore-diving and underwater photo instruction. Six days of shore-diving run $110; with six boat-dives, $210. One-tank boat dive is $34. Snorkelers welcome. Guides speak English, Dutch, Spanish, German and French. ☎ 866-GO-BUDDY or 599-717-5080, fax 599-717-8647, diveshop@buddydive.com, www.buddydive.com.

Carib Inn Dive Shop, a full-service PADI shop at the Carib Inn, offers reef trips, resort, certification and advanced courses. Owner Bruce Bowker has been diving Bonaire since the early '70s and knows all the best spots. Equipment sales, rental and repair. Tank, weight and belt rental for shore-diving runs $12 per day or $99 for six days. Six boat-dives over six days with unlimited air fills and use of tank cost $189. ☎ 599-717-8819, fax 599-717-5295, info@caribinn.com, www.caribinn.com.

 The area code for Bonaire is 599.

Dee Scarr's "Touch the Sea" meets at the town pier and features personalized dives with an opportunity to interact with reef fish and moray eels. Super photo opportunities. Closed from July through October. Dee gives a terrific slide show and talk at 8:30 pm on Monday evenings in the Habitat Resort, ☎ 599-717-8529, www.touchthesea.com, dee@touchthesea.com.

Dive Inn, on the waterfront in Kralendijk, offers scuba packages, PADI courses, reef trips, picnic trips. Six days of unlimited shore-diving cost $99; six boat-dives are $205. ☎ 599-717-8761, fax 599-717-8513, www.diveinn-bonaire.com. Or write Kaya C.E.B. Hellmund 27, Bonaire, NA.

Dive Bonaire, at the Divi Flamingo Resort (see page 87), specializes in reef trips; resort, certification and advanced courses; underwater photo and video courses. Daily E-6 and color-print processing. Equipment sales, rental, and repair. Dive/hotel packages with Divi Resort start at about $1,200 for seven days. ☎ 599-717-8285, www.divebonaire.com, divibon@bonairelive.com.

Bonaire Dive and Adventure, adjacent to the Sand Dollar Resort Condos, features a brand new pier and PADI shop. They offer certification courses, boat trips, kayaking and nature hikes. Non-refundable dive packages run $105 for a six-day shore package that includes use of tanks, weights and belts, plus unlimited air fills. If you prefer Nitrox, add $8 per fill. Their six boat dive package, with tanks, weights and unlimited air fills costs $220, with Nitrox $300. If you buy the package, you can use the unlimited air fills and tanks for shore diving in-between the boat dives. For kids ages 6-15, there are the PADI Bubblemaker program and snorkeling trips. Equipment sales, rental and repair. ☎ 599-717-2227, fax 599-717-2229, www.bonairediveandadventure.com.

Great Adventures Bonaire, at the Harbour Village Beach Club, offers certification, PADI and NAUI referrals, with underwater photography programs, boat- and shore-dives, night-dives and equipment rental. If you're diving à la carte you'll pay $12 for a tank, weights and belt for a shore-dive. A one-tank boat-dive costs $40. A six-day package including unlimited shore-diving with weights, belt, tanks and air runs $225. Add $10 per fill for Nitrox. ☎ 800-424-0004 or 305-567-9509, direct 599-717-7500, www.harbourvillage.com.

Bon Photo Tours specializes in underwater photography with boat and shore-diving, scuba, and photo courses, kayak, gear and camera rentals. Six boat-dives and unlimited shore-diving costs $189 per week, shore-diving alone is $99 per week. ☎ 599-717-5353 ext 328, fax 599-717-8060, www.bonphototours.com, info@bonphototours.com.

Captain Don's Habitat Dive Center at Captain Don's Habitat, a NAUI Dream Resort, is a PADI Five Star facility offering resort, certification and advanced courses, reef trips and 24-hour shore-diving, rebreathers and tri-mix. Guides speak English, Dutch, Spanish and German. Certification for PADI, NAUI, SSI referral and TDI. ☎ 800-327-6709, in Bonaire 717-8290, www.habitatdiveresorts.com, info@habitatdiveresorts.com. Or write PO Box 88, Bonaire, NA.

Snorkeling Specialties

FreeDive Bonaire: CMAS dive master and owner/operator Dominique Serafini worked for more than 20 years as a member of the Cousteau team, participating in many expeditions around the world on board the *Calypso*. Dominique has studied free-diving and yoga respiration control techniques with world champion free-divers Jacques Mayol and Umberto Pellizari, and offers workshops for $150 per person in aqua yoga and controlled respiration techniques. After the five-day intensive workshop, beginners typically descend to 65 feet and hold their breath for over two minutes. FreeDive offers boat trips to both the leeward side of Bonaire ($30) and the windward side ($50), where **wild dolphins** are frequently at play. ☎ 599-785-9959 or 599-717-2050, www.freedivebonaire@aol.com.

Sea & Discover offers marine-environment learning and discovery programs for children and adults. Their half-day snorkeling course for $40 combines classroom instruction and one hour of ocean time. ☎ 717-5322, www.bonairenature.com/seandiscover, info@seandiscover.com.

Where to Stay

 Bonaire's entire tourist trade revolves around its beautiful reefs. All but a couple of the island's hotels were built in the last 20 years to accommodate divers. All have dive shops attached or nearby. Money-saving dive/accommodation packages can be arranged through any hotel listed below. Rates listed are winter prices.

The Black Durgon Inn, north of town, offers 10 rooms from $85 per night, including breakfast. Good for divers on a budget, and they have a beach and dive shop. ☎ 599-717-5735, fax 599-717-8846, www.blackdurgon.com, blackdurgon@bonairelive.com.

Buddy Beach & Dive Resort sits just north of Kralendijk, offering 40 luxury oceanfront apartments with TV, air conditioning, fully equipped kitchens and nicely furnished living rooms. Restaurant and PADI Five Star training facility on premises. Drive & Dive packages range from $984 per person in summer to $1,119 per person in winter for seven nights in a one-bedroom, fully equipped apartment, with six boat-dives, unlimited airfills for six days, vehicle rental (often a pickup truck). Larger apartments house up to six divers. Non-divers can opt for the Adventure Package, with kayaking, cave and ocean snorkeling, biking, touring and hiking. ☎ 717-5080, fax 717-8647, www.buddydive.com.

Bruce Bowker's Carib Inn is one of Bonaire's first dive resorts. Clean and comfortable, oceanfront apartments have air conditioning and cable TV, maid service, pool. An on-premise, full-service PADI scuba facility provides advanced and beginner scuba courses, boat- and shore-dives. A six-boat-dive package with unlimited air fills and use of tank, weights and weight belt for six days costs $189. Open-water certification referrals welcome. Apartment rates (*not* per person) go from $99 for a one-bedroom that houses two people to $159 for a three-bedroom, two-bath house that sleeps six. ☎ 599-717-8819, fax 599-717-5295, www.caribinn.com, info@caribinn.com. Or write PO Box 68, Bonaire, NA.

Divi Flamingo Resort (recently renovated) offers deluxe oceanfront guest rooms with full ocean views and private balconies. Standard rooms have tropical garden views, and are located on the first floor of the two-story hotel block, or in casual summer camp-style villas with private patios. Each room includes one or two double beds, color television, air conditioning, and in-room safe. A few have balconies directly over the water where you can view the reef and see fish swimming by. The resort features a PADI dive shop, two freshwater swimming pools, two fine restaurants, Hertz car rental, casino, activities desk, salon, grocery mart, gift shop, fitness center and Internet kiosk at the front desk.

The Divi Flamingo also has spacious studio units perfect for families. Children under the age of 15 can stay free when sharing a room with an adult.

Divi Flamingo participates in the Bonaire Marine Education Center's Sea and Discover Programs. Children may join the center's Reef Explorers program – exciting mornings of supervised sea explorations with a marine biologist. Special need divers are offered both wheelchair-accessible custom dive boats and accommodations.

Dive package includes seven nights' accommodation, six days of two-tank morning boat-dives, breakfast and lunch daily, taxes and service charges and airport/hotel transfers, starting at $899 per person based on double occupancy. ☎ 800-367-3484 or write Divi Hotels, 6340 Quadrangle Drive, Suite 300, Chapel Hill, NC 27514.

Lions Dive Hotel Bonaire features 31 magnificent ocean-view, one- and two-bedroom apartments with patio or balcony, each with a fully equipped kitchen. Amenities include a freshwater pool with sun deck, waterfront restaurant, and dive shop, diving and fitness school. Rates for a one-bedroom suite are from $150 to $220 per day, a two-bedroom suite from $159 to 250. RCI timeshare members pay from $700 per week. ☎ toll-free 866-LIONSDIVE (866-546-6734), fax 954-217-9980, www.lionsdivebonaire.com, info@lionsdivebonaire.com.

Plaza Resort Bonaire, a 224-unit luxury hotel, offers divers PADI, and NAUI instruction, custom dive boats and rental equipment through the on-premises **Toucan Diving**. The resort's "3-D" (drive, dive, deluxe) package features seven nights in an air-conditioned one- or two-bedroom villa (complete with living room, cable TV and telephone, full kitchen and dishwasher), six days unlimited shore-diving (including tanks and weights) plus seven-day car rental with unlimited mileage, all tax and service charges. Winter rates based on a double for seven nights run $1,159 per person plus $121 for diving. From April 16 to December 19 it drops to $922, plus $101 for diving. Add $89 for the daily continental breakfast buffet.

Other resort amenities include three restaurants offering everything from fine French cuisine to beach barbecues, a salon, gift shop, fitness center, pool, tennis courts and a white sand beach. ☎ 800-766-6016 or direct 599-717-2500, www.plazaresortbonaire.com, reservations@plazaresortbonaire.com.

Harbour Village Beach Club sits opposite Klein Bonaire on a powdery sand beach close to town. Diving is available with **Great Adventure**. The resort offers 72 air-conditioned rooms, one- and two-bedroom suites with French doors leading to patios or terraces, cable TV, telephones, hair dryers.

Pool, three restaurants (including the Lighthouse Bar & Grill; *see* page 91), bar, marina, and dive shop, plus meeting and banquet facilities. Rooms are $275 to $470; one-bedroom suites run $445 to $545 per night, two-bedrooms from $625 to $780. Villas start at $5,565 per week. ☎ 800-424-0004 or 305-567-9509, fax 305-567-9659, in Bonaire, 599-717-7500, fax 599-717-7507, www.harbourvillage.com.

Captain Don's Habitat offers deluxe oceanfront cottages, cabanas, villas, and studios. Package rates, per diver, start at $840 for seven nights in a junior suite, including 12 boat-dives. Non-divers pay $570. Per-day rates for accommodation only start at $176 to $235 for a cottage for two, or $230 to $246 for a four-person cottage. Entire villas cost from $420 to $485 daily. Dive shop, open-air restaurant, bar, pool, gift shop. Credit cards accepted. ☎ 800-327-6709 or 599-7-8290, fax 305-438-4220 or 599-717-8240, www.habitatdiveresorts.com, captaindon@maduro.com, bonaire@habitat diveresorts.com. Or write PO Box 115, Bonaire NA. Guests who are certified divers can take out tanks and dive the reef off the beach 24 hours a day.

Sand Dollar Condominium Resort features contemporary oceanfront condos – all air-conditioned – with kitchens, private baths, cable TV, balcony or terrace and decent diving and snorkeling off the shore, which is flanked by a wide sun deck. Dive trips are arranged with **Bonaire Dive and Adventure**, conveniently located next door. Sand Dollar also has a pool, tennis court, grocery store and adjacent restaurant. Rates go from $155 to $360 per night. ☎ 800-288-4773, direct 599-717-8080, fax 599-717-8760, www.sanddol-larbonarie.com, info@sanddollarbonaire.com.

Happy Holiday Homes rents 14 one-, two-, or three-bedroom homes with air conditioning; living room with cable TV and radio, dining room; fully equipped kitchen; patio and barbecue area. All are close to southern beaches. Bungalow rates are from $65 to $130 per day. Call for brochure: ☎ 599-717-8405, hhh@bonairelive.com.

Caribbean Club Bonaire features comfy low-budget digs. Guests choose between apartments or cottages with tropical décor, all perched on a hillside with ocean views. Air conditioning is in the bedrooms only – uncomfortable during the summer months. Their on-site dive shop is run by **Yellow Sub-marine**, a PADI Five Star/Gold Palm operation. Divers and snorkelers are offered boat and guided shore dives, PADI courses, underwater photo courses, tec diving, and cave snorkeling. There are kayaks for eco tours. At the center of the resort are a swimming pool and sun deck. The on-site **Hilltop** restaurant is open for breakfast, lunch and dinner. High-season rates start at $75 per night (for two people), including taxes. ☎ 800-550-1869, direct 599-717-7901, fax 599-717-7900, www.caribbeanclubbonaire.com, info@caribbeanclubbonaire.com.

Other Activities

A day-trip to explore **Washington Slagbaai National Park** is a fun alternative to diving. One of the first national parks in the Caribbean, it is home to over 190 species of birds, thousands of towering candle cacti, herds of goats, stray donkeys, lizards and more lizards. The park covers the entire northern portion of the island. Its terrain is varied and those who are ambitious enough to climb some of the steep hills are rewarded with sweeping views.

Cars can be taken through the park, and the two driving trails offer visitors the choice of a thorough tour of the park or a shorter excursion. A map, available at the entrance gate, indicates points of interest. The park is open from 8 am to 5 pm, though no one is permitted to enter after 3:30 pm. Small entrance fee. Visitors are advised to bring a picnic lunch, binoculars, a camera, sunscreen and plenty of drinking water. Opportunities for exotic bird photography are outstanding; www.washingtonpark.org.

Driving south from the park you'll pass roadside cliffs with 500-year-old Arawak Indian inscriptions. Just beyond is **Rincon**, the island's oldest village. A drive to the southern tip of the island will bring you past primitive stone huts that were once homes to slaves working the salt flats. It is hard to imagine how six slaves shared one hut when you see the small size of them. Nearby, 30-foot obelisks were built in 1838 to help mariners locate their anchorages. Farther down is the island's oldest lighthouse, **Willemstoren**, built in 1837.

The **salt ponds at Gotomeer** are always occupied by resident flamingos, but flamingo watching is best at the solar salt flats on the southern end of the island. You can watch from the road only, as the area is a sanctuary, but the huge bird population en masse makes a spectacular display. Every day at sunset, the entire flock (10,000 to 15,000 birds) makes the short trip to Venezuela. During spring, a highlight is seeing the fluffy gray young. It is only after months of consuming brine shrimp that they attain their characteristic pink color. Since the birds are extremely shy, bring binoculars.

Guided bus tours of the national park or entire island are available through **Bonaire Sightseeing Tours**, ☎ 717-8778.

Ernest van Vliet's Windsurfing Bonaire features top-of-the-line equipment and classes for beginners to advanced board sailors. Production or custom boards can be rented by the hour, day or week. He even provides transportation to and from island resorts twice a day.

Tours through the tiny capital city of **Kralendijk** ("coral dike" in Dutch) are highlighted by the colorful, well-preserved buildings such as **Fort Oranje**, **Queen Wilhelmina Park**, **Government House** and the miniature Greek temple-style **fish market**. The town pier makes for an interesting stop, as do any one of Kralendijk's open-air bars and restaurants. Sunset- watching is best from Pink Beach in the southeastern part of the island.

Dining

Restaurants in Bonaire offer a unique selection of local, Creole and seafood dishes. Enjoy a delicious Cantonese, Bonairean or Indonesian dinner at **China Nobo**, Kaya Andres A. Emerenciana 4, ☎ 717-8981; or Caribbean seafood and steak dishes at the **Chibi Chibi**, an open-air restaurant at the Divi Flamingo Resort (☎ 717-8285); or **Banana Tree Restaurant** at the Plaza Resort (☎ 717-2500). **Kon Tiki**, at the Kon Tiki Beachclub on Kaminda Sorobon 64 (☎ 717-5369), will prepare a banquet of Argentinean steaks, beer batter fish, vegetarian dishes, fresh salads and homemade desserts. Vegetarian favorites are found at the **Garden Café**, Kaya Grandi 59 (☎ 717-3410).

Dine under the stars at the **Lighthouse Bar & Grill**, at the Harbour Village Beach Club (see page 88); conch fritters, grilled ribeye with chimichurri sauce, baby back ribs with guava sauce and local seafood favorites are featured. **Mona Lisa**, a sweet Dutch bar and restaurant on Kaya Grandi 15, the main street in Kralendijk, serves French cuisine with pizzazz; a favorite treat here are warm chocolate muffins with ice cream (☎ 717-8718). Carry-out and sit-down pizza and salads are offered by the **Pasa Bon Pizza & Bar**, Kaya Gob N Debrot 42 (☎ 790-1111).

Local foods include *juwana*, a stew or soup made from local iguana; *piska hasa*, a fried fish dish served with funchi and fried plantains; *tutu*, funchi with frills – cornmeal mush with black-eyed peas; and goat stew made with onions, peppers, tomato, soy sauce and spices.

In Kralendijk, sumptuous local dishes are served at **Gibi's Terrace** on Kaya Andres A. Emerenciana, **Eden Garden** at the Great Escape Hotel on EEG Boulevard (☎ 717-7488), and the **Rose Inn** on Kaya Guyaba 4 (☎ 717-6420). Fast-food lovers will delight in finding **Kentucky Fried Chicken** in the Harborside Mall and **Subway** at Les Galeries shopping mall (☎ 717-2110).

Facts

Helpful Phone Numbers: Police, ☎ 717-8000; **ambulance,** ☎ 717-8000/114; **taxi,** ☎ 717-8100; **airport,** ☎ 717-5600; **San Francisco Hospital,** ☎ 717-8900; **tourist information,** ☎ 717-8322.

Nearest Recompression Chamber: San Francisco Hospital on the island, ☎ 717-8900. ☎ 717-8000/114 for an ambulance.

Getting Here: American Eagle, ☎ 800-433-7300, flies nonstop from San Juan, Puerto Rico to Bonaire four times weekly, Friday to Monday, with return flights on Saturday to Tuesday. **Air Jamaica** flies to Bonaire via Montego Bay on Wednesday, Thursday, Saturday, Sunday. Gateway cities from the US include Boston, New York, Newark, Philadelphia, Baltimore, Chicago, Atlanta, Ft. Lauderdale, Miami and Los Angeles. **Air Jamaica** can be reached at ☎ 800-523-5585.

American Airlines flies direct/non-stop to Curaçao from Miami, and **Delta** flies here from Atlanta. Passengers may use either **BonairExel** (see below for schedule) or **Dutch Caribbean Airline** (DCA) to connect to Bonaire. Flying time between Curaçao and Bonaire is approximately 15-30 minutes. Another inter-island (Curaçao/Bonaire) option is a private air charter by **Divi Divi**, which flies numerous times daily, ☎ 599-9-888-1050.

Driving: On the right. Foreign and international licenses accepted.

Language: The official language for Bonaire is Dutch, but residents speak Papiamento – a blend of Dutch, African and English. English and Spanish are widely spoken.

Documents: US and Canadian citizens may stay up to three months, providing they prove citizenship with a passport, state birth certificate with raised seal or a voter's registration card accompanied by a photo identification.

All visitors must have a confirmed room reservation before arriving and a return ticket. A visa is required for visits over 90 days.

Customs: US citizens may bring home $400 worth of articles, including one quart of liquor and 200 cigarettes. Canadian citizens may bring home C$300 of goods once each calendar year.

Currency: Netherlands Antilles florin or guilder, but US dollars are widely accepted. US$1=NAf 1.77 (variable).

Credit Cards: Widely accepted.

Climate: Mean temperature 82°F year-round; water temperature 80°; rainfall 22 inches annually.

Clothing: Casual lightweight. A wetsuit is not necessary most of the year, but water temperatures occasionally drop down in midwinter. A lycra wetskin or 1/8th shortie wetsuit is advisable for late January and February diving.

Electricity: 127 volts, 50 cycles. Adapters are necessary.

Time: Atlantic (EST + 1 hr).

Tax: Airport departure tax $20 international flights; $5.75 inter-island.

Religious Services: Roman Catholic, Seventh Day Adventist, Jehovah's Witnesses.

Additional Information: *USA,* ☎ 800-BONAIRE (800-266-2473), 10 Rockefeller Plaza, Ste. 900, NY, NY 10020, www.infobonaire.com, tcb@infobonaire.com; *Europe,* ☎ 31-70-395-4444, europe@tourismbonaire.com.

Cayman Islands

Dubbed "The Islands that Time Forgot" by *the Saturday Evening Post* in the early 1950s, the Caymans today – **Grand Cayman**, **Cayman Brac** and **Little Cayman** – have become one of the world's top dive-travel destinations. Some 480 miles and an hour's flying time south of Miami, this Caribbean trio entertains more than 200,000 visitors each year.

Physically beautiful, each island is blessed with an extraordinary fringing reef, superb marine life and sparkling, palm-lined beaches.

Underwater Cayman is a submerged mountain range complete with cliffs, dropoffs, gullies, caverns, sink holes and forests of coral. The islands are the visible above-the-sea tips of the mountains. At its deepest, the **Cayman Trench** drops off to more than 23,000 feet. Storms in recent years have swept the reefs clean of debris and dead matter, making them prettier than ever.

 Grand Cayman, the largest and the most developed of the three islands, boasts world-class dive operations, restaurants and scores of luxury hotels and condominiums. The islands' no-tax status – granted by Britain in the 1700s because of the heroic action of Caymanians in saving the lives of passengers and crews of 10 sailing ships – has attracted numerous corporations and banks. Its capital, **Georgetown**, ranks as the fifth-largest financial center in the world, with nearly 600 international banks.

Cayman Brac and **Little Cayman** lie 89 miles northeast of the big island and are separated by a seven-mile-wide channel. Both are wildly beautiful, and each has its own special personality.

Little Cayman is *very quiet* – virtually untouched by developers. The smallest of the three islands – only 10 square miles – it has about 35 permanent residents. There are no shops, restaurants, movie theaters or traffic. Phones are few and far between. Small resorts cater almost exclusively to divers and fishermen.

With daily direct flights from North America and easy access from many other parts of the globe, most divers head first for **Grand Cayman**. Its famed **Seven Mile Beach** is headquarters for dive activity. More adventurous divers seeking a unique wilderness experience flock to the Brac and Little Cayman for superlative wall dives. Little Cayman is also noted for unsurpassed flats fishing.

When To Go

Late summer and fall bring the chance of a hurricane, but diving is possible year-round. Conditions are generally mild, although steady winds can kick up some chop. When this happens, dive boats simply move to the leeward side of the island and calmer waters. Air temperature averages 77°F. Water temperature averages 80°.

History

As with many other Caribbean islands, the discovery of the Caymans is attributed to Christopher Columbus, who first saw them on his second voyage while en route from Panama to Cuba in 1503. Amazingly, his primitive ships were able to negotiate the coral reefs with little trouble. He named these islands "Las Tortugas" for the countless marine turtles who came to Cayman beaches to breed. The turtles, which could live in captivity for long periods, became a source of fresh meat for the sailors, and the Cayman Islands became a regular stop for exploring ships.

Marine Regulations

With a dramatic growth in tourism and an increase in cruise ship arrivals, the islands have enacted comprehensive legislation to protect the fragile marine environment. Marine areas are divided into three types: Marine Park Zones, Replenishment Zones and Environmental Zones.

The **Marine Park Zones** outlaw the taking of any marine life, living or dead, and only line fishing from shore and beyond the dropoff is permitted. Anchoring is allowed only at fixed moorings, of which there are more than 200 around the islands.

It is an offense for any vessel to cause reef damage with anchors or chains anywhere in Cayman waters. In a **Replenishment Zone**, the taking of conch or lobster is prohibited, and spear guns, pole spears, fish traps and nets are prohibited. Line fishing and anchoring (at fixed moorings) are permitted.

Environmental Zones are the most strictly regulated. There is an absolute ban on the taking of any kind of marine life, alive or dead; anchoring is prohibited and no in-water activities of any kind are tolerated. These areas are a breeding ground and nursery for the fish and other creatures that will later populate the reef and other waters.

Spear guns and Hawaiian slings may not be brought into the country. The **Marine Conservation Board** employs full-time officers who may search any vessel or vehicle thought to contain marine life taken illegally. Penalties may include a maximum fine of CI $5,000 (US$6,125) or imprisonment, or both.

Grand Cayman

Best Dive & Snorkeling Sites

Grand Cayman, noted for its fabulous wall-diving, has steep dropoffs on all sides. The **West Wall**, a dropoff that runs parallel to Seven Mile Beach, offers the most convenient diving on the island. Most dive operators are in this area, and many hotels offer dive and snorkeling trips to the sites – all are five- to 10-minute boat rides. Flat-bottom dive boats attest to the calm seas. Several beach dives are possible. More sites along the **South Wall** have recently opened, particularly for experienced divers and photographers. This area is defined by a barrier reef that breaks the surface and serves as a coral fence. Conditions here are more demanding.

The **North Wall** also lays claim to some of the most spectacular dive sites because of its unusual coral formations and frequent pelagic sightings.

Least explored is the **East End Wall**, often referred to as the last frontier.

Water temperature holds steady at 82°F; visibility ranges from 100 to 150 feet. The coral reefs are exceptionally healthy, largely due to the conservancy measures enforced by the dive shops.

☆☆☆☆☆ **Stingray City** is the most photographed dive site in the Caymans, if not the entire Caribbean. Pictured in all the tourist board ads, the subject of endless travel articles and an Emmy-award film by Stan Waterman, this gathering of southern stingrays in the shallow area of North Sound is a marine phenomenon that has thrilled scuba divers and snorkelers since their discovery by two dive instructors, Pat Kinney and Jay Ireland, early in 1986.

After observing the normally solitary and shy rays gathering regularly at a shallow site where boats cleaned their conch and fish, Kinney and Ireland began hand-taming exercises – carefully avoiding the razor-sharp, venomous spines in their whip-like tails. When safe hand-feeding became a predictable event, they invited small groups of divers and snorkelers out to watch.

Today, the 20 rays are big celebrities, luring curious visitors – as many as 150-200 per day – from across the globe. The location is shallow, 12 to 20 feet, ideal for snorkelers as well as divers. Feeding time occurs whenever a dive or snorkeling boat shows up.

☆☆☆☆☆ **Trinity Caves**, off the north end of Seven Mile Beach (see page 101), winds into a maze of canyon trails between 60 and 100 feet. Reef features consist of gigantic barrel sponges, black coral, towering sea whips,

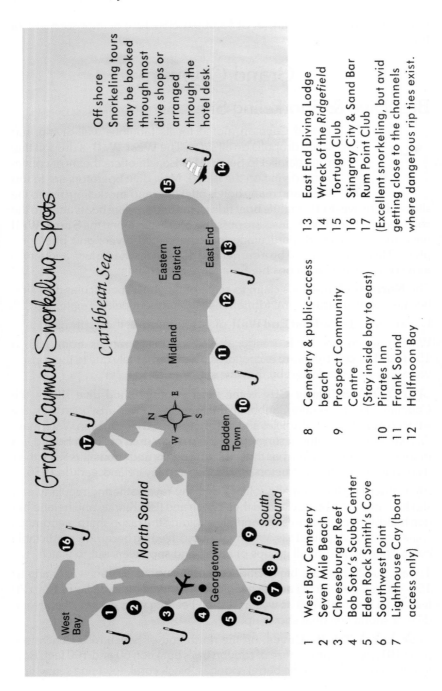

Grand Cayman Snorkeling Spots

1 West Bay Cemetery
2 Seven Mile Beach
3 Cheeseburger Reef
4 Bob Soto's Scuba Center
5 Eden Rock Smith's Cove
6 Southwest Point
7 Lighthouse Cay (boat access only)

8 Cemetery & public-access beach
9 Prospect Community Centre (Stay inside bay to east)
10 Pirates Inn
11 Frank Sound
12 Halfmoon Bay

13 East End Diving Lodge
14 Wreck of the *Ridgefield*
15 Tortuga Club
16 Stingray City & Sand Bar
17 Rum Point Club
(Excellent snorkeling, but avid getting close to the channels where dangerous rip ties exist.

Off shore Snorkeling tours may be booked through most dive shops or arranged through the hotel desk.

sea fans, and a host of critters. Huge groupers and turtles, lobsters, squirrelfish, and schooling reef fish inhabit three cathedral-like caves for which the site is named. Their walls grasp clusters of pink anemones, vase sponges, and star corals. Sea conditions are generally calm, with an occasional light current. Exceptional visibility. Suggested for experienced divers.

☆☆☆☆ **Orange Canyon**, north of Trinity Caves, glows with vibrant orange elephant-ear sponges. The reef starts at 45 feet, the edge of a deep wall adorned with sea plumes, lavender sea fans and bushy corals – cover for shrimp, sea cucumbers, brittle stars, arrow crabs, filefish, turtles and small octopi. Calm seas.

☆☆☆☆ **Big Tunnels**, north of the Seven Mile Beach area, feature a 50-foot coral archway linked to several tunnels and ledges bursting with rainbow gorgonians, sea fans, basket sponges, tube sponges, and branching corals. Eagle rays drift by walls of sea urchins, anemones, grunts, pufferfish, bigeyes, and shrimp. Big morays peek from the ledges. An occasional nurse shark appears. Depths average 110 feet, with excellent visibility. Experience recommended.

☆☆☆☆ **The Wreck of the *Balboa***, a 375-foot freighter, rests at 30 feet in George Town Harbor – 200 yards off the town pier. A favorite night-dive, its twisted wreckage creates interesting video and still opportunities. Seas are calm with good visibility, though several divers visiting the wreck at one time may kick up silt. Schools of sergeant majors, groupers, queen and French angels mingle about the hull.

☆☆☆ **Aquarium** sits close to shore off the center of Seven Mile Beach. As the name implies, this spot serves as a grand meeting center for most every species of fish in the Caribbean. Count-and-name-the-fish is the favorite sport *du jour* at this 35-foot-deep coral grotto. Be sure to tote a waterproof fish ID card or book.

Spotted trunkfish, parrotfish, snappers, filefish, spotted morays, butterflyfish, queen angels, queen triggerfish, puffers and schooling barracudas inhabit Aquarium. Though hard to see through the crowds of fish, the reef is very pretty with nice stands of staghorn coral, sponges and soft corals. Visibility superb. Calm seas make this a good choice for new divers.

☆☆☆ **The Wreck of the *Oro Verde*** lies 30 to 50 feet beneath the surface, straight out from the Holiday Inn on Seven Mile Beach. After this 180-foot freighter ran aground in 1976, local dive operators scuttled the wreck to create an artificial reef. The hull, intact, is very photogenic. Divers are warmly greeted by its inhabitants – Spanish hogfish, French angels, snappers, butterflyfish, blue tangs, rock beauties. Seas are calm.

☆☆☆ **Tarpon Alley**, a coral canyon, mirrors schools of giant silvery tarpon, mammoth groupers and stingrays. Large pelagics flash by too. The "alley," south of Orange Canyon, lies partially in the Seven Mile Beach replenishment zone. Top of the canyon walls are at 60 feet. Outside dropoffs plunge to several thousand feet. Surface conditions are occasionally choppy.

☆☆☆☆ **Grand Canyon**, an enormous channel enclosed by jagged, perpendicular mountains off Rum Point, is the favored North Shore dive. The walls display a cornucopia of sponges, sea whips, sea fans, hard corals and critters. Depths start at 60 feet and drop off. Experience a must. Excellent visibility.

☆☆☆ **Japanese Gardens**, a series of long coral ridges off the island's south tip, blossom with elkhorn and antler corals, vase sponges and schooling fish. Depths start at 50 feet.

Snorkeling

Patch reefs and coral heads teeming with reef fish lie just a few yards off several of the island's swimming beaches. The best shore spots are off West Bay Cemetery, Seven Mile Beach, the Eden Rock Dive Center in Georgetown, Smith Cove, Treasure Island Resort beach, Rum Point Club, Parrots Landing, Seaview Hotel, Coconut Harbour, Sunset House, Pirate's Inn, Frank Sound, Half Moon Bay, East End Diving Lodge and Morritt's Tortuga Club. Depths range from three to 20 feet. Clearer water and more dramatic coral formations are found farther offshore and may be reached by boat. Snorkeling cruises, some with dinner or lunch, are offered by the hotels and dive shops. Snorkelers are urged to inquire about currents and local conditions in unfamiliar areas before attempting to explore on their own.

Swimmers off the Rum Point Club beach should stay clear of the channels, which have rip tides. Grand Cayman's Southwest Point shows a good variety of juvenile reef fish and invertebrates on a rocky bottom close to shore. Currents beyond 100 yards are dangerous.

A trail marked by a round blue and white sign with a swimmer outline denotes access through private property to the beach. All Cayman beaches are free for public use.

☆☆ **Smiths Cove**, south of George Town, shelters a shallow reef whiskered with pastel sea fans and plumes. Trumpetfish, squirrelfish, schools of grunts, sergeant majors, butterflyfish, parrotfish and angels offer constant entertainment. The reef sits 150 feet from the beach at Southwest Point. Depths are from 15 to 45 feet.

☆☆ **Eden Rocks**, favored by cruise ship groups, lies less than 200 yards offshore from the Eden Rock Diving Center. Depths range from five to 40 feet. The reef features beautiful coral grottoes, walls, caves and tunnels and tame fish. If you've yet to befriend a fish, this area offers the proper social climate. Good visibility and light currents are the norm here.

☆☆ **Sand Bar** at Stingray City in North Sound is home to several tame stingrays. Depths are shallow to 12 feet. Boat access. Trips departing from Georgetown or Seven Mile Beach are either a half- or full-day tour.

East End Diving

Grand Cayman's rural East End, 20 miles across the island from Seven Mile Beach, offers an entirely different dive-vacation setting. Devoid of shopping centers, traffic jams and commercial establishments, this wilderness region lures divers who relish a slower, laid-back pace, uncrowded beaches and un-charted dive sites. Underwater terrain is similar to West Wall sites, with fabu-lous walls, overhangs, caves, tunnels, grottos and remnants of shipwrecks. There are no moorings.

Strong currents sometimes rule out a number of the sites in this area, but they greatly benefit the marine life by carrying nutrients that encourage the growth of gigantic, brilliantly colored sponges and soft corals. Fish life is outstanding, with passing pelagics, walls of tarpon, gigantic jewfish, eagle rays, green and hawksbill turtles. Whale sharks have been spotted here during winter.

Dive Operators

Costs for a two-tank dive average $60; one-tank dives, $45. Snorkeling trips range from $25 to $65, with the average about $30. All the dive shops that offer boat tours have Stingray City tours. These average $55 from the west coast.
Most shops rent photo, video, dive and snorkeling gear. Trips include tanks and weights. Resort and certification courses are offered everywhere. Unless otherwise noted, shops accept American Express, MasterCard or Visa credit cards.

Ambassador Divers, a PADI shop located at Ambassadors Inn in George Town, offers computer diving, resort and full certification courses, snorkeling trips, dive equipment and photographic rentals. Trips to Stingray City. ☎ 345-949-8839, fax 345-949-8838, www.ambassadordivers.com, jason @ambassadordivers.com.

Bob Soto's Diving Ltd is a PADI Five Star facility with Seven Mile Beach locations at the Treasure Island Hotel and the Scuba Centre, near Soto's Reef. The operation offers dive and snorkeling trips, underwater photo and video services, camera and gear rentals, open-water PADI certifications, completion dives, and comfortable custom dive boats. Complete dive-accom-modation packages with Grand Cayman hotels and condos available.

☎ 800-BOB-SOTO or 345-949-2871, www.bobsotos@candw.ky, bobsotos@candw.ky. Write to PO Box 11800 APO, Grand Cayman, BWI.

Cayman Diving School, a PADI Five Star center, in the Greenery Plaza, George Town, offers courses from Resort to Dive Master. ☎ 345-949-4729, www.caymandivingschool.com, info@caymandivingschool.com. Write to PO Box 1308, Grand Cayman, BWI.

Divetech now offers full-service diving, quality training available, both recreational and technical, along with some decent dive-and-room packages through **Cobalt Coast Resort & Suites** and **Turtle Reef Resort**. Dive/hotel packages include unlimited shore-diving. Turtle Reef and Colbolt Coast feature courses from learn-to-dive through trimix, rebreather diving and scooter wall flying to extended range on the walls and wrecks of Cayman. Both shops offer videos of your dive and private photo lessons. At Cobalt Coast Resort, ☎ 888-946-5656, 345-946-5658, www.divetech.com, www.cobaltcoast.com, divetech@candw.ky. At the Turtle Reef Resort, 857 NW Point Road, ☎ 345-949-1700, fax 345-949-1701.

Divers Down, on Coconut Place, Seven Mile Beach, specializes in PADI Nitrox certification courses and Nitrox diving. Their custom, eight-passenger boat takes off for two one- or two-tank dive trips daily. Stingray City trips. Dive/hotel packages. Dive and snorkeling gear rentals. ☎ 345-916-3751, www.diversdown.net.

Don Foster's Dive Cayman, a full-service facility on Seven Mile Beach, offers certification and resort courses, daily dives, rental and a photo center. Plus snorkeling excursions, WaveRunners and sailboats. ☎ 800-833-4837, 345-945-5132, fax 945-5133, www.donfosters.com.

Eden Rock Diving Center, favored by cruise-ship visitors, touts unlimited shore-diving on GeorgeTown's waterfront, with guided tours of Eden Rocks Reef and Devil's Grotto. Boat tours, gear rentals. Certification courses. Photo, video, dive and snorkel gear rentals. ☎ 345-949-7243, fax 345-949-0842, www.edenrockdive.com, edenrock@candw.ky.

Fisheye of Cayman offers scuba tours aboard three custom dive boats to the north, west and south sides of the island, including Stingray City. Snorkelers may join dive trips to Stingray City and North Wall, based on space availability. Trips include free use of underwater cameras. Accommodation packages. ☎ 800-887-8569, 345-945-4209, fax 345-945-4208, www.fisheye.com, fisheye@candw.ky.

Off the Wall Divers offer personalized dive tours. No credit cards. ☎ 345-945-7525, www.otwdivers.com, info@otwdivers.com.

Red Sail Sports, across from the **Hyatt Regency** and at the **Westin Casuarina** on Seven Mile Beach, offers dive and snorkeling trips, PADI certification courses and daily resort courses. Snorkel and dive trips, dinner sails and cocktail cruises. Water-skiing and parasailing. ☎ 345-947-5965, fax 345-947-5808, www.redsailcayman.com.

Sunset Divers at **Sunset House** has snorkeling, scuba instruction, and dive-accommodation packages, but is best known for its **Underwater Photo Centre**, operated by Cathy Church. The Centre offers still and video camera rental. Photo instruction for all levels. Informal and friendly. ☎ 800-854-4767 or 345-949-7111, fax 345-854-7101, www.sunsethouse.com/dive. Write PO Box 479, Grand Cayman, BWI. Resort-dive packages start at $931 per person, based on a double for three days of diving and four nights accommodation.

Soto's Cruises, for snorkelers, features Stingray City tours from $30. ☎ 345-945-4576, fax 945-1527, www.sotoscruises.com, scruises@candw.ky. Free pick-up from the cruises ship pier and designated spots along Seven Mile Beach.Write to PO Box 30192, Seven Mile Beach, Grand Cayman, BWI.

Atlantis Submarines takes up to 48 adventurous passengers wall diving in completely dry, air-conditioned, surface-pressure comfort. The 65-foot submarine plummets to depths of 150 feet as it explores the reef, with divers outside that feed fish. Children must be at least four years old. Cost is $82 per person with the accompanying divers, $72 without. half price for children up to 12 years old. ☎ 345-949-7700, www.atlantisadventures.com.

Dive Resorts & Accommodations

Grand Cayman has accommodations and packages for every budget and every need. Every dive shop listed above offers a money-saving dive/accommodation package, some with air. For a complete list of guest houses, cottages and condos, contact the **Cayman Islands Department of Tourism**, 6100 Blue Lagoon Drive, Suite 150, Miami, FL 33126, ☎ 800-346-3313 or 305-266-2300, fax 305-267-2932. New York, ☎ 212-682-5582, fax 212-986-5123. United Kingdom, ☎ 071-491-7771, fax 071-017-1409. Canada, ☎ 800-263-5805 or 416-485-1550, fax 416-485-7578. Grand Cayman, ☎ 345-949-0623, fax 345-949-4053, www.caymans.com.

Seven Mile Beach

The Avalon, the most luxurious Seven Mile Beach condo resort, offers 14 spacious units with air conditioning, barbecue, cable TV, ceiling fans, cribs, dishwashers, hair dryers, irons, Jacuzzi, kitchen, microwave oven, phone, porch or patio, radio, stereo, tropical décor. Wheelchair accessible, eight miles from George Town (taxi $18), laundry, maid services, washer/dryer.

Deluxe units sleep up to six. The complex sits near central George Town, near local restaurants, shops, supermarkets, and entertainment. An 18-hole golf course is five minutes away. Winter rates are $740 to $815. ☎ 345-945-4171 ext. 100, fax 345-945-4189, www.cayman.org/avalon.

The Courtyard Hotel by Marriott sits five miles from GeorgeTown (taxi fare $20) across from Seven Mile Beach at 590 West Bay Road. It features 231 air-conditioned rooms (smoking and non-smoking) with cable TV, coffee makers, cribs, fax machines, hair dryers, high-speed Internet access, mini bar, phones, radio/stereo, refrigerators, safes, rollaways and VCRs. The property has a gift shop, ocean views, pool, laundry, restaurant, and is wheelchair accessible. An on-site dive shop offers scuba and snorkeling tours, as well as ocean kayaks. Ocean-view rooms in summer run from $169, winter, from $280 per day. Garden-view rooms are from $149 in summer, from $240 in winter. Address: PO Box 30364 SMB Grand Cayman, BWI. ☎ 345-946-4433, fax 345-946-4434. US and Canada, ☎ 800-321-2211.

Coral Sands Resort, on the outskirts of George Town and the Seven Mile Beach (taxi fare $15), features 12 all-suite air-conditioned two-bedroom units that can sleep up to six, with spacious living areas and fully equipped kitchens. Rooms are poolside with ocean views; two are oceanfront. Snorkeling off the beach. Summer rates are $235 for standard rooms, $260 deluxe; winter $290 for a standard, $325 deluxe. ☎ 345-949-4400, fax 345-949-4005, www.coralsands.ky, coralsan@candw.ky. Write PO Box 30610 SMB, Grand Cayman, BWI.

Cobalt Coast Resort & Suites, Grand Cayman's newest, small oceanfront resort is sits on West Bay's north shore on Sea Fan Drive – 10 miles from George Town (US$25 taxi fare), just past the Turtle Farm. Built like a Caribbean Great House from days past, the resort combines the laid-back island ambiance with modern comfort in 18 lovely rooms. Units have air conditioning, cable, satellite TV, ceiling fans, coffee makers, cribs, fax machines, hair dryers, irons, Jacuzzi, kitchen, phones, porch or patio and refrigerators. Snorkel or dive from the resort dock or sign up for a North Wall trip with on-site dive-center, **DiveTech**, for a real underwater experience! Gift shop, beach, restaurant, meal plans, maid services, voice mail, oceanfront pool. Non-smoking rooms. Garden-view room are from $155 per day in summer; from $190 in winter. ☎ 888-946-5656 or 345-946-5656, fax 345-946-5657, cobalt@candw.ky, www.cobaltcoast.

The Grand Caymanian Resort at North Sound offers 98 luxurious one- and two-bedroom villas and deluxe rooms that have air conditioning, satellite TV, ceiling fans, coffee makers, cribs, phones and hair dryers. Villas feature fully equipped kitchens, Jacuzzi, and a porch or patio. Laundry and maid service available. Dive shop on site. Located 1.5 miles from Seven Mile Beach Road and 3.5 miles from George Town (taxi fare $25), the resort is fairly convenient to shops and restaurants. Summer rates start at $120 per day for a room that sleeps two; $185 in winter; from $175 for a suite for two in summer; from $330 for a superior room. A two-bedroom villa starts at $275 in summer; $385 in winter. ☎ 345-949-3100, fax 345-949-3161, reservations@grandcaymanian.ky, www.grandcaymanian.ky. Write to 31495 SMB, Grand Cayman, BWI.

Comfort Suites and Resort, across the road from Seven Mile Beach, features 108 spacious air-conditioned suites; 16 studios, 46 deluxe studios, 25 one-bedroom suites, 18 two-bedroom suites and one king suite. Studios have an efficiency kitchen with fridge and microwave as well as toaster and coffee machine. Larger suites have full kitchens. Two units are equipped for the physically handicapped. All are non-smoking and have two phone lines for data ports, satellite TV, hair dryer, iron and ironing board. Restaurants, shopping, cinema, supermarket and banking are within walking distance.

They offer dive packages with **Don Foster's Scuba Center**, which is on the property. All dive packages include accommodation, a two-tank boat dive daily, including tanks and weights, plus daily continental breakfast. Summer per-day dive-package rates for a room and one dive start at $172 for a studio suite; in winter, from $205. Add $60 per day for an additional diver in the room, $15 for a non-diver. One-bedroom suites start at $180 in summer, $225 in winter. To book dive packages, call ☎ 800-4CHOICE, 800-424-6423 or e-mail diving@caymancomfort.com.

Hyatt Regency Grand Cayman sits on Seven Mile Beach two miles from George Town (taxi $14) in the center of **Britannia Golf & Beach Resort** and offers 236 luxurious guest rooms with every amenity, 53 beachfront suites, tropical gardens, swimming pools, gazebo-style swim-up bar and private marina. Dive shop and watersports operation on site. Camp Hyatt House available for children ages 3 to 12. Restaurants range from casual to fine dining. Smoking and non-smoking rooms. Wheelchair-accessible. Babysitting, maid, laundry. Summer rates from $220; winter from $415. ☎ 800-233-1234 or 345-949-1234, www.hyattregencygrandcayman.com, zrochez@caymapo.hyatt.com. Write Hyatt Regency Grand Cayman, Seven Mile Beach, PO Box 1588GT, Grand Cayman, BWI. Dive/hotel packages are available with **Red Sail Watersports**, ☎ 877-REDSAIL (877-733-7245), infocayman@redsailcayman.com, www.redsailcayman.com.

Wyndham Sunshine Suites Resort, central to Seven Mile Beach diving and snorkeling activities, welcomes divers with fully equipped studio and one-bedroom suites, wireless high-speed Internet access, and terrific diving and snorkeling packages with **Red Sail Watersports**.

Air-conditioned guest rooms are equipped with barbecue, cable, satellite TV, ceiling fans, coffee maker, crib, hair dryer, iron, microwave oven, phone, stereo, refrigerator, toaster and washer. Pool, laundry, maid service and babysitting available. Beach access, beach chairs, conference rooms, smoking and non-smoking rooms, rollaways, safes, wheelchair accessible The resort's casual, veranda-style beach bar and restaurant serves guests a complimentary breakfast daily. Suites are steps away from a sandy beach, supermarket and shopping. Discounts at the Safehaven Golf Course and on-property Budget Car Rentals. George Town is 3.5 miles away (taxi fare $15-20). Summer rates for studios start at $185; winter rates from $260. One-bedroom suites that can sleep up to four start at $205 in summer and $250 in winter. ☎ 877-786-1110 or 615-269-9044, fax 615-269-9044, www.sunshine-suites.com, mail@sunshinesuites.com. To book with Red Sail Watersports, ☎ 877-733-7245, www.redsailcayman.com, infocayman@redsailcayman.com.

Sunset House, a 59-room resort owned and operated by divers for divers, sits south of Seven Mile Beach. Good diving and snorkeling can be done from the shoreline. Room rates start at $175 per day. Dive packages are from $809 per person for five nights, four days of two-tank diving and unlimited shore-diving. Rooms and suites are air conditioned, with cable TV, and telephone with data port. Dive packages include a full "made to order" breakfast and daily two-tank boat trips, except day of arrival and departure. Complimentary off-shore diving every day except the day of departure, tanks, weights and belt, use of dive gear locker, welcome rum punch, taxi transfers from and to the airport. Free resort course plus an afternoon review and instructor-guided dive for a non-diving partner on a five-night or longer package. Discounts on catamaran sails. Items not included are 10% government room tax, 10% service charge and dive shop gratuities.

All rates are quoted in US dollars unless otherwise stated, and are subject to change without notice. Three-night minimum deposit required within seven days of booking. Additional for groups. Cancellations must be made 21 days prior to arrival, 45 days for groups, or deposit will be forfeited. Reservations may not be shortened. No refunds or exchanges on unused portions. Rates are per person.

Indies Suites, a beachfront 41-suite hotel, features a pool, Jacuzzi, bar, and handicap access. Apartments rent from $170 per day in summer, $225 in winter. **Indies Divers** on premises offers dive and snorkeling trips to Stingray City, the North and West Walls, plus gear rental. ☎ 800-654-3130 or 345-947-5025, fax 345-947-5024.

Sunset House, a 59-room resort owned and operated by divers for divers, sits south of Seven Mile Beach. Good diving from the beach! Room rates for a standard start at $110 in summer, $135 in winter. Packages for five nights, four days of two-tank diving and unlimited shore-diving start at $662.50.

☎ 800-854-4767 or 345-949-7111, fax 345-949-7101. Write PO Box 479, George Town, Grand Cayman, BWI.

Turtle Nest Inn, in the village of Bodden Town on Grand Cayman's south shore, is a lovely alternative to the higher priced resorts. The inn offers studios and one-bedroom suites, gorgeous beaches and good snorkeling on coral heads off the beach in a calm lagoon.

 Outside the lagoon there is a strong current and surges.

North Side

Cayman Kai Resort Ltd features luxurious cottages, villas, and townhouses, some air conditioned, on the north side of Grand Cayman. Lodges have a living-dining area, kitchen and patio. One bedroom with one bath for two divers rents for $190 per day in winter, $150 in summer. Two bedrooms are $240 in winter, $190 in summer. A dive shop on the premises offers gear rentals and reef trips to North Walls sites. ☎ 800-223-5427 or 345-947-7722.

East End

Morritt's Tortuga Club caters to those seeking luxurious oceanfront accommodations in a very private setting. The resort, with 121 air-conditioned, newly renovated suites, offers a freshwater pool, Jacuzzi, restaurant, bar, laundry facilities. **Tortugas Divers** shop on premises An RCI timeshare resort. ☎ 800-447-0309 or 345-947-7449.

Other Activities

 An 18-hole course, a nine-hole course and a special Cayman golf course are located next to the **Hyatt Regency Grand Cayman**. On the latter, you use special lightweight balls that travel about half the distance of a normal ball. Grand Cayman's nightclubs and larger hotels offer live entertainment and dancing. The **Cayman National Theater** presents live performances of drama, comedy and musicals. Fishing, windsurfing, parasailing, and tennis are offered at most condos and resorts.

Sightseeing

The capital city, **George Town**, has a well-scrubbed look not always found in the Caribbean. Visitors can tour the area by foot, taxi, moped or rental car. Courtesy phones at the airport connect to the car rental dealers. Driving is on the left. Along George Town's waterfront several historic clapboard buildings have been lovingly restored and converted into souvenir shops, galleries and boutiques.

Heading north along the famed **Seven Mile Beach**, you come to the largest congregation of hotels, condos, shopping malls and restaurants. Each morning dive boats line up here and offer door-to-reef service to resort and condo guests.

 A side-trip to the **Cayman Turtle Farm** is always fun, as is a visit to **Hell**, the town where visitors delight in having mail postmarked to send back home.

Dining

 Grand Cayman offers visitors an enormous variety of choices in dining. For more formal dining – all seafood – try the **Wharf**, waterfront on West Bay Road; **Seaharvest Restaurant** in front of Sunset House; or **The Lobster Pot**, above Bob Soto's Dive Shop.

Shopping centers along West Bay Road and downtown George Town house several fast-food eateries such as **Burger King**, **Pizza Hut** and **Arthur Treachers**. On Seven Mile Beach try **The Wharf**, **Treasure Island** (previously Hook's), or **Treats**. George Town features a **Wendy's**, two **Subways**, **Coffee & Bites** or **Al La Kebab**, the Marquee Shopping Plaza. For superb local specialties such as conch stew, curried chicken and native fish try the **Cracked Conch by the Sea** on West Bay Road or **Myrtle's** on North Church Street.

Cayman Brac

 Often called the loveliest of the islands, this 12-mile strip of land is rumored to be the resting place of pirates' treasure. Lying some 87 miles east of Grand Cayman, Cayman Brac's most striking feature is a 140-foot-high limestone formation (*brac* is Gaelic for bluff) covered by unusual foliage, including flowering cactus, orchids and tropical fruits such as mango and papaya. Rare species of birds, including the endangered green, blue and red Caymanian parrot, inhabit the island, which is a major flyway for migratory birds. Resident brown booby birds soar the cliffs. Cayman Brac is also known for its many caves where pirates, in earlier centuries, took refuge and, according to legend, buried their treasures. In fact, a peg-legged turtle pirate is the country's national symbol. Native fir, palm and papaya trees shade the narrow streets. Fragrant thickets of bougainvilleas, hibiscus, periwinkle, and oleander surround the islanders' houses, many of which were built with wood salvaged from the wreckage of ships that crashed on the reefs. A visit to the **Cayman Brac Museum** in Stake Bay offers a look at the history of ship building on the island.

Activities other than diving and snorkeling are limited. There are a few restaurants scattered along the main road that also feature elevated caves with ladders for the tourists; Nims gift shop offers local crafts and post cards; and the main town area has a convenience store, post office, gift shops and the island museum.

Best Dive & Snorkeling Sites

☆☆☆☆ **Wreck of the *Tibbetts***, a 330-foot Russian destroyer originally built for the Cuban navy, was renamed the *Captain Keith Tibbets* and deliberately sunk off the northwest coast of Cayman Brac on September 17, 1996. The vessel, the most exciting new dive attraction in the Cayman Islands, is easily accessible from shore, if you don't mind a 200-yard swim, but it's favored as a boat-dive. All levels of divers can explore several swim-throughs, including the bridge and upper deck. Fore and aft cannons, a missile launcher and machine gun turrets remain on the ship. Snorkelers can easily view the top of the radar tower at 12 feet and the bridge at 32 feet below the surface.

☆☆☆☆ **The Hobbit**, off the Brac's southeast tip, presents divers with a fairy tale setting of giant barrel sponges and dazzling corals inhabited by chubs, turtles, queen angels, octopi, grunts and queen triggerfish. Average depth runs 70 feet. Suggested for intermediate to advanced divers. Excellent visibility. Boat access.

☆☆☆☆ **Radar Reef** encompasses a series of coral pinnacles and canyons, each home to a splendid variety of elkhorn, star, and brain corals, lavender sea fans, tube and barrel sponges, feather dusters, and sea whips. Inhabitants of this lively community include turtles, stingrays, octopi, and swirls of tropicals. A normally calm surface and shallow depths – from 30 to 60 feet – make this a good choice for new divers. Boat access or you can swim out from the beach adjacent to Island Dock.

Snorkeling

Several excellent shore-entry points exist off the north and south shores. Wind conditions determine which area is calm. Usually, if the north shore spots are choppy, the south shore is calm. Check with area dive shops for daily conditions.

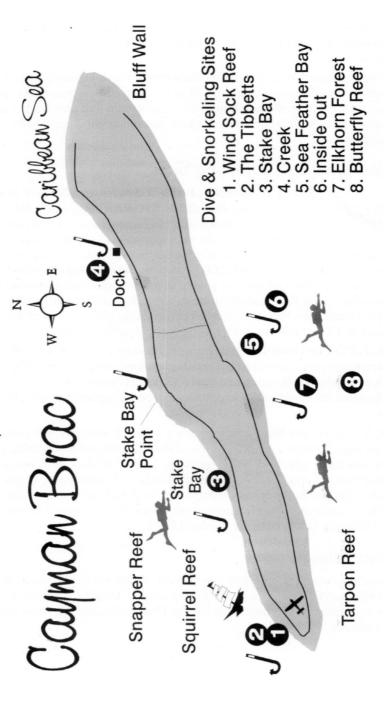

Cayman Brac

Caribbean Sea

Bluff Wall

N
W ─── E
S

Dock

Stake Bay
Point

Snapper Reef

Squirrel Reef

Stake
Bay

Tarpon Reef

Dive & Snorkeling Sites
1. Wind Sock Reef
2. The Tibbetts
3. Stake Bay
4. Creek
5. Sea Feather Bay
6. Inside out
7. Elkhorn Forest
8. Butterfly Reef

North Shore

 ☆☆☆☆ **WindSock Reef and the Wreck of the *Tibbetts***, in White Bay off the northwest coast is the Brac's most popular snorkeling spot. The reef, which lies close to the shoreline, shelters elkhorn and brain coral patches while providing haven for a good variety of juveniles and tropicals. This spur and groove reef encircles gardens of elkhorn, pillar corals, sea fans, orange sponges and gorgonians. Angels, barracudas, butterflyfish, filefish, trumpetfish and critters hide in the ledges and crevices. Expect good visibility and usually calm seas. Typical inhabitants are stoplight parrotfish, blue tangs, midnight parrotfish, sergeant majors, turtles, grey angels, grunts, and triggerfish. Shore area depths range from four to 20 feet.

The mast of the *Tibbetts'* wreck breaks the surface and is easily spotted from the beach. Some prefer snorkeling the wreck, which lies 200 yards offshore, from a boat; but if you're in superior physical shape, you can swim out. The top of the wreck lies 12 feet below the surface. See scuba section for details. Check with area dive shops before venturing out. Visibility usually 100 feet or better.

To reach White Bay, travel the North Shore Road (A6) west from the airport to Promise Lane. Turn left. The beach entry point is behind the closed Buccaneer Inn Hotel.

☆☆ **Stake Bay**. Find this spot by turning off the North Shore Road at the Cayman Brac Museum. Reef terrain, depths and fish life are similar to White Bay. Sea conditions usually calm, but will kick up when the wind is out of the North.

☆☆ **Creek** lies off the north shore. A turn toward the shore from Cliff's Store on the North Shore Rd (A6) will lead to the Island Dock. Enter from the beach area left of the dock, facing seaward. Dense patches of elkhorn predominate. Depths are shallow to 30 feet. Angels, small turtles, and sergeant majors swarm the reef. Wind speed and direction determines the conditions, though seas are usually calm, with a light current.

Additional entry points are found at the boat launching areas where cuts through the dense coral have been blasted. Parking is available along the north road.

South Shore

☆☆ **Sea Feather Bay**, off the South Shore Road at the Bluff Road crossing, provides a haven for pretty wrasses, turtles, blue parrotfish, groupers, indigo hamlets, squirrelfish, porkfish, blue tangs, and rockfish. Reef terrain comprises long stretches of dense elkhorn interspersed with tube sponges, fire coral, rose coral and gorgonians. After a big storm, this area becomes a wash-up zone for some strange cargo, such as rubber doll parts and unusual bottles that may come from Cuba. Expect some surge and shallow breakers. Visibility is good, though silt may churn up the shallows following a storm.

Experienced snorkelers may want to dive the barrier reef at the southwestern tip of the island. Water entry is best by boat, but if you enjoy a long swim you can get out to the reef from either the public beach or one of the hotel beaches.

Dive Operators & Accommodations

 Brac Aquatics offers courses, reef tours and gear rentals. ☎ 345-948-1429, fax 345-948-1527, bracdive@candw.ky.

Brac Reef Beach Resort and Reef Divers has comfortable air-conditioned rooms with satellite TV, a great beach, freshwater pool, whirlpool, beach bar and restaurant. Complete dive/accommodation packages start at $449 per person for three nights, five boat-dives and breakfast daily. Nitrox diving available. Rates are higher during holiday periods. Unlimited beach dives. ☎ 800-594-0843 or 345-948-1323, fax 948-1207, www.bracreef.com. Write to PO Box 56, Cayman Brac, BWI.

Brac Haven Villas has six one-bedroom condos that rent from $180 per day. ☎ 345-948-2478, fax 345-948-2329. Write to PO Box 89, Stake Bay, Cayman Brac, BWI.

Divi Tiara Beach Hotel and Dive Tiara cater to divers and snorkelers. This first-class resort features a freshwater pool, Jacuzzi, tennis, 71 spacious air-conditioned rooms, auto rentals, sailboards, bicycles and paddleboats. Snorkeling is done off the resort's palm-lined beach. Divi Tiara spares no effort to make every dive trip relaxing, safe and fun aboard any one of six custom-designed dive boats. The shop offers daily tours to the best dives of Cayman Brac, as well as Little Cayman. A seasoned boat crew readily assists divers with gear set-ups and getting in and out of the water. There's no need to lug your gear back and forth to your room; it stays overnight in a gear storage room on Tiara's dive pier. Room rates based on a double are $95 in summer, $125 in winter. One-tank dives are $25, two-tank, $50. Package rates available. ☎ 800-367-3484 or 919-419-3484, fax 919-419-2075. Write to Divi Resorts, 6340 Quadrangle Drive, Suite 300, Chapel Hill, NC 27514.

Brac Caribbean offers a three-story condo resort with one-, two-, three- and four-bedroom suites that start at $220 per night. Suites are nicely decorated and have balconies overlooking the beach. Diving and snorkeling must be arranged separately. ☎ 866-843-2722, www.866thebrac.com, info@866-thebrac.com.

Carib Sands Beach Resort, a sister resort to Brac Caribbean and one of Cayman Brac's newest condo resorts, also features one-, two-, three- and

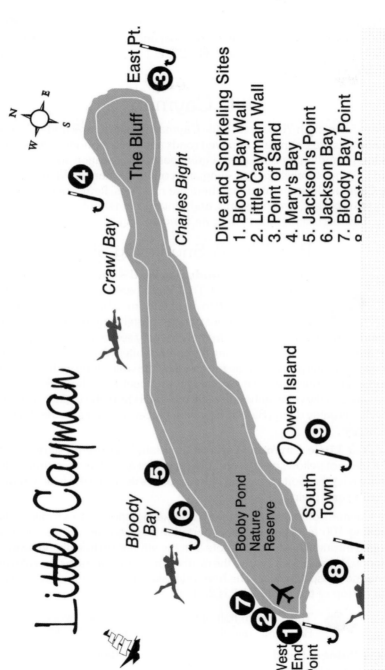

Little Cayman

Dive and Snorkeling Sites
1. Bloody Bay Wall
2. Little Cayman Wall
3. Point of Sand
4. Mary's Bay
5. Jackson's Point
6. Jackson Bay
7. Bloody Bay Point
8. Preston Bay

four-bedroom suites starting at $220 per night. Beautiful. From $825 to $1,950 per week. Dive operation on site. Bar and restaurant 100 yards from the resort. ☎ 866-843-2722, www.866thebrac.com, info@866thebrac.com.

Little Cayman

Home to fewer than 70 people, Little Cayman retains a rural and unhurried ambiance. Its grass runway, unpaved roads and limited phone service attest to its long-standing reputation as a great get-away vacation spot. Activities include diving, snorkeling, fly fishing and counting iguanas. When you visit Little Cayman, keep in mind that there are no stores. Items such as aspirin, mosquito repellent, decongestants, and suntan lotion should be packed from home. Few accommodations offer air conditioning.

Best Dive & Snorkeling Sites

☆☆☆☆☆ **Bloody Bay Wall** is one of the top five dives in all the Caymans. The "Wall" peaks as a shallow reef at 15 feet and drops off to an unfathomed bottom. Bright orange and lavender tube sponges, pastel gorgonians and soft corals flourish in the shallows. An extremely friendly six-foot barracuda named Snort may join your dive – flashing his pearly whites while cheerfully posing for videos and still photos. Eagle rays blast by the wall, along with slow-moving turtles and huge parrotfish. Spotted morays peek from the walls. Sea conditions are usually calm, although a stiff wind will churn the surface. Divers of all levels will enjoy diving Bloody Bay Wall. Super snorkeling in the shallows. Boat access.

☆☆☆☆ **Little Cayman Wall**, off the island's west end, starts shallow with a blaze of yellow, orange and blue sponges at 15 feet then drops off to unknown depths. Soft corals, big barrel sponges decorate the wall. Great for snorkeling and diving. Boat access.

Little Cayman offers several superb snorkeling spots with visibility often exceeding 100 feet. Ground transportation to beach-access sites is easily arranged through the dive operators. For the ultimate in free diving head out to Bloody Bay and Spot Bay off the north shore, where the seas are calm and the marine life spectacular. The boat ride takes about 25 minutes. Average depth on top of the North Wall is 25 feet.

 The Western half of the wall is called the "Bloody Bay Wall" and the eastern half "Jackson Wall."

☆☆☆ **Point of Sand**, off the southeast end of Little Cayman, is excellent for experienced and beginning snorkelers. A gentle current flowing from west to east maintains very good visibility. The bottom is sandy, with many coral heads scattered about. Marine life is fine and the site is accessible from the shore. Ground transportation can be arranged from the resorts.

☆☆☆ Good snorkeling for beginners at **Mary's Bay** starts 50 yards from the beach – inside the barrier reef. There is no current and visibility runs about 30 to 50 feet. A host of fish and invertebrates are found in the shallows. Depth averages three to eight feet. The bottom is turtle grass, requiring booties or other submersible footwear. An old shack on an otherwise deserted shore marks the spot.

☆☆ **Jackson Point**, aka **School Bus**, is for experienced snorkelers only. Swim out about 75 yards from the beach, where you'll see a small wall towering from a sandy bottom at 40 feet to 15 feet. Hundreds of fish, rays and turtles congregate in the shallows. Corals and sponges carpet the area. Swimming another 50 to 60 feet brings you to a much larger wall that drops off to extraordinary depths.

☆☆ **Jackson Bay** resembles Jackson Point, except for the bottom of the mini-wall, which drops off to a depth of 50 to 60 feet. Beach access.

☆☆☆ **Bloody Bay Point**, recommended for seasoned snorkelers, requires a 100-yard swim out to the reef. The bottom eases down to about 30 feet before the dropoff to The Great Wall begins. Well worth a visit for the spectacular coral and marine life.

☆ **Preston Bay**, just east of the lighthouse, provides another good shore-entry choice for beginning snorkelers. Maximum shoreline depth is six feet, and visibility 30 to 50 feet. Swarming fish and a white sandy bottom offer endless photo opportunities.

☆☆ **Blossom Village**, a lovely, shallow reef, displays crowds of reef fish and critters amidst staghorn and brain corals at depths from four to eight feet. Boat access. A light current maintains 50- to 100-foot visibility.

Dive Operators & Accommodations

Little Cayman dive operations are smaller than those on Cayman Brac and Grand Cayman.

Little Cayman Beach Resort features air-conditioned rooms, freshwater pool, Jacuzzi, cabana bar, tennis, restaurant, and a full-service dive/photo operation. Board surfers, sailboats and bicycles are available. Rates per-person for a double for three nights with breakfast and dinner and five dives run $663; for seven nights, $1,654 in winter. Lower rates for non-divers. ☎ 800-327-3835 or 345-948-1033, www.reefseas.com.

Paradise Villas Resort (also home to Paradise Divers and the Hungry Iguana Restaurant) sits on a wide stretch of beach. Each of the 12 one-bedroom villas are a stone's throw from the ocean. Villas have a kitchenette, ceiling fans, air conditioning, cable TV, and large front and back porches. ☎ 877-3CAYMAN (877-329-9626), www.paradisevillas.com.

Southern Cross Club, a fishing and dive resort with 11 beachfront cottages, warmly welcomes divers. Repeat visitors will appreciate the new docks. Dive guides tour the top dive and snorkel sites on Bloody Bay Wall or the South Shore. Snorkelers mix with scuba groups. IANTD Nitrox facility. Dive courses are available. Packages include three meals daily, a two-tank daily dive, r/t transfers, beachfront room, service charge and room tax. For six nights, cost is $1,930 per person in the high season, $1,700 in the summer. Add $120 per day for children aged five to nine in the room with their parents. No children under five. ☎ 800-899-2582 or 345-948-1098, www.southerncrossclub.com, info@southerncrossclub.com. Write to Southern Cross Club, Little Cayman, Cayman Islands, BWI.

Sam McCoy's Diving & Fishing Lodge, on the north side of Little Cayman, offers fully air-conditioned rooms with private bathrooms. Meals are served family-style in the main lodge. Rates include accommodations, three home-cooked, Caymanian meals per day, and diving (two-tank morning boat-dive and unlimited afternoon/night shore-diving). Winter (October 16-May 31) per-day room rates run $170 per person, single-occupancy, $145 per person, double-occupancy, $125 per person, triple-occupancy, $85 per child, (ages four-12). Rates drop in summer and fall and for non-diving companions. Rates exclude the 10% government tax, airport transfers and gratuities. ☎ 800-626-0496, 345-948-0026, fax 345-945-3617, www.mccoyslodge.com. Write to Carl McCoy, PO Box 711, Georgetown, Grand Cayman, BWI.

Pirate's Point Resort features rustic guest cottages and a guest house on seven acres of secluded white beach. Owner Gladys Howard offers friendly service, all-inclusive dive packages from $195 per person per day in summer, $215 in winter. ☎ 800-327-8777 or 345-948-1010, fax 345-948-1011.

Facts

Nearest Recompression Chamber: George Town. This chamber is operated and staffed 24 hours a day by the British Sub-Aqua Club. ☎ 555 for help.

Getting Here: There are more than 55 weekly flights into the Cayman Islands, including 28 flights each week between Miami and Grand Cayman with connections to Cayman Brac and Little Cayman. **Cayman Airways** connects Grand Cayman and the US with service from Miami, Tampa, Fort Lauderdale, Chicago, Houston and Boston. Cayman Airways also connects to Cayman Brac, Little Cayman, Kingston and Montego Bay, Jamaica and Havana, Cuba, plus a weekly non-stop flight from Miami to Cayman Brac. ☎ 800 4-CAYMAN (US/Canada toll-free), ☎ 171-491-7771 (UK), or visit Cayman Airways at www.caymanairways.com.

Island Air flies from Grand Cayman to Cayman Brac and Little Cayman four times each day. Book on their Website, www.islandaircayman.com, or contact them at ☎ 345-949-5252, atiair@candw.ky.

American Airlines provides non-stop daily flights from Miami to Grand Cayman, www.aa.com. **Continental Airlines** departs from Newark International Airport, www.continental.com. **Delta Airlines** flies from Atlanta to Grand Cayman daily, www.delta.com. **Northwest** connects Detroit to Grand Cayman, www.nwa.com. **US Airways** flies from Charlotte, North Carolina, www.usairways.com. **Air Canada** provides a direct twice-weekly service to Grand Cayman from Toronto on Sunday and Wednesday, www.aircanada.com. **British Airways** offers service to Grand Cayman from Heathrow Airport, London, www.britishairways.com. Flight time from Miami is 70 minutes. Grand Cayman is a regular stop on many cruise lines.

Island Transportation: Rental cars, motorbikes, and bicycles are available on Grand Cayman and Cayman Brac. Friendly and informative taxi drivers are stationed at hotels and other convenient locations.

Driving: As in England, driving is on the left. A temporary license is issued for a few dollars to persons holding US, Canadian or international licenses.

Documents: Proof of citizenship (birth certificate, voter registration) plus photo ID and an outbound ticket are required from US, British, or Canadian citizens. No vaccinations are required unless you are coming from an epidemic area.

Customs: The penalties for trying to bring drugs into the Cayman Islands are stiff fines and, frequently, prison terms. No spearguns or Hawaiian slings permitted into the country.

Currency: The Cayman Island dollar (KYD), $1=US82¢.

Climate: Temperatures average about 80°F year-round. The islands are subject to some rainy periods, but generally are sunny and diveable.

Clothing: Casual, lightweight clothing. Some nightclubs require that men wear a jacket. Wetskins or shorty wetsuits are useful to avoid abrasions, as are light gloves for protection against the stinging corals. Snorkelers should wear protective clothing against sunburn.

Electricity: 110 volts AC, 60 cycles. Same as US.

Time: Eastern Standard Time year-round.

Tax: There is a 6% government tax on accommodations. A service charge of 10-15% is added to hotel and restaurant bills. Departure tax is US$25.

Religious Services: Catholic, Protestant, Baptist, Mormon and non-denominational churches are found on Grand Cayman.

Additional Information: The Cayman Islands have six regional offices in the US, Canada, and UK. *Miami*, Doral Centre, 8300 NW 53rd Street, Suite 103 Miami, Florida 33166, ☎ 305-599-9033, fax 305-599-3766. *New York*, 3 Park Avenue, 39th Floor, New York, NY 10016, ☎ 212-889-9009, fax 212-889-9125. *Houston*, Two Memorial City Plaza, 820 Gessner, Suite 1335,

Houston, Texas 77024, ☎ 713-461-1317, fax 713-461-7409. **Chicago**, One Lincoln Centre, 18 W 140 Butterfield Road, Suite 920, Oakbrook Terrace, IL 60181, ☎ 630-705-0650, fax 630-705-1383. **Canada**, 234 Eglinton Avenue East, Suite 306, Toronto, Ontario, Canada M4P 1K5, ☎ 416-485-1550, fax 416-485-7578, in Canada, 800-263-5805. **United Kingdom & Continental Europe**, 6 Arlington Street, London, SW1 1RE, ☎ 0207-491-7771, fax 0207-409-7773, www.caymanislands.co.uk.

Or you can contact the *Cayman Islands Department of Tourism* headquarters at The Pavilion, Cricket Square, Elgin Avenue, George Town, PO Box 67 GT, Grand Cayman, BWI, ☎ 345-949-0623, fax 345-949-4053.

Sea anemones, Aruba

Above: Oranjestad, Aruba
Below: Catamarans at sunset, Aruba

Above: Angelfish and red coral
Below: The Blue Hole, Belize

Above: Moray eel, St. Lucia (© Dennis Sabo, Landfall Productions)
Below: Pedersen shrimp, Bonaire (© Charles Seaborne)

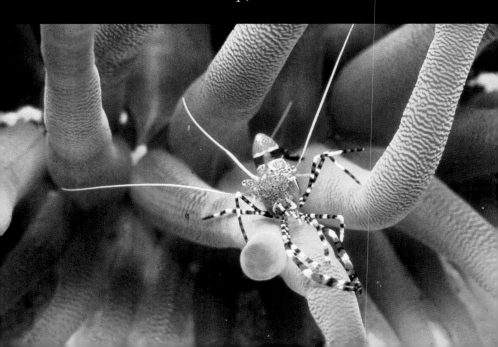

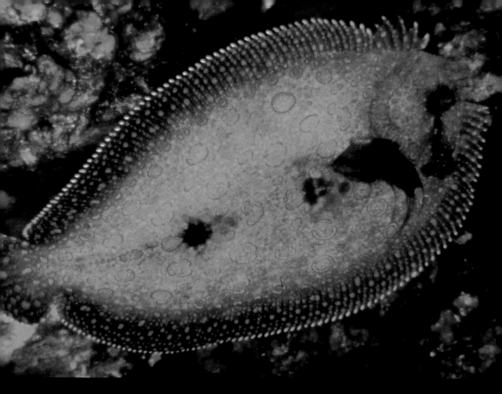

Above: Peacock flounder (© Karen Sabo, Landfall Productions)
Below: Marble grouper (© Jon Huber)

Above: Seascape, Bonaire (© Jon Huber)

Below: Seven Mile Beach, Grand Cayman (courtesy CI Tourist Board)

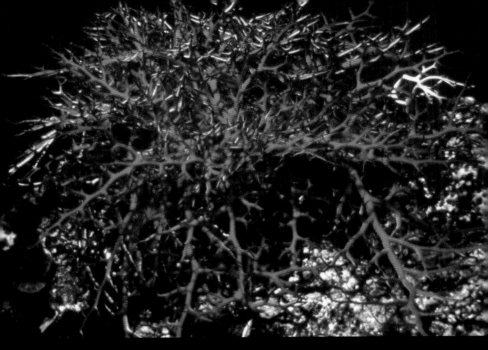

Above: Basket star, Bonaire: resembles a leafless bush during the day, and roams at night

Below: Rock beauty (photos © Jon Huber)

Hawksbill turtle & grey angelfish,
Palancar Pinnacles, Cozumel (© Randy Hodge)

Myrea bush, Akumal, Cozumel

Above: Cenote diving, Cancun
Below: Stingrays and snorkelers, Cayman Islands

Above: Blue tang & crab, Marine Park, Cozumel
Below: Palancar reef (photos © Jon Huber)

Above: Daboои Beach, Curaçao
Below: Knip Bay, Curaçao (photos © Jon Huber)

Above: Willemstedt, Curaçao (© Jon Huber)

Below: Orange sponge (courtesy Curaçao Tourist Board)

Above: **Fishing village, Soufriere, Dominica** *(© Dennis Sabo)*
Below: **Turtle Bay Beach, Dominica** *(courtesy Dominica Tourist Board)*

Above: Misty Mountain View, Dominica (Dominica Tourist Bd)
Below: Diver at Scotts Head, Dominica (© Karen Sabo)

Above: Grenada's scenic topside

Below: Marketplace (photos courtesy Grenada Tourist Bd)

Cozumel & Akumal

Cozumel

Mexico's largest island and top Caribbean dive destination lies 12 miles off the Yucatán Peninsula, separated by a 3,000-foot-deep channel. Dense jungle foliage covers most of this island's interior, but its surrounding coast welcomes visitors with miles of luxuriant, white sand beaches.

Topside tourist activity centers around San Miguel, the island's cultural and commercial center, which boasts an impressive seaside maze of shops, cantinas and restaurants. An ultra-modern cruise-ship terminal accommodates the ocean liners and ferries arriving daily from the mainland. Most dive resorts are scattered along the west coast, where calm waters prevail.

A 1961 visit by **Jacques Cousteau** first brought attention to Cozumel's spectacular diving and its incredible water clarity. Its fringing reef system is fed by warm, fast-moving Yucatán currents (a part of the Gulf Stream) as they sweep through the deep channel on the west side of the island. These currents bring a constant wash of plankton and other nutrients that support thousands of exotic fish. Immense rays and jewfish populate the spectacular dropoffs and wrecks on the outer reefs; sea turtles nest along the beaches from May to September. And visibility remains a constant 100 to 150 feet year-round, except during and after major storms.

Despite a continuous onslaught of divers and a few direct hurricane hits, Cozumel's reefs and marine life are better than ever. Conservation efforts have made dramatic improvements since reefs surrounding the island were given marine park status by the Mexican government. Safety is improved too, with a functional, free-to-divers recompression chamber now in operation.

When to Go

The best time to visit Cozumel is from December to June. Water and air temperatures average 80°F year-round, with hotter conditions in summer. Summer and fall often bring heavy rains or hurricanes.

History

 Cozumel was first inhabited by the Maya Indians, who settled as early as 300 AD. They named it *Ah-Cuzamil-Peten*, place of the swallows. Remains of their temples and shrines still can be found.

During the 1800s Cozumel was a busy seaport stopover for ships carrying chicle (used to make gum) from Central America to North America.

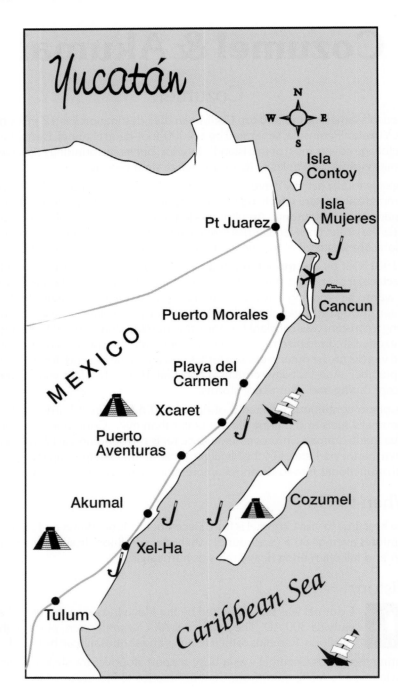

Cozumel

Lighthouse

Isla de la Pasion

El Castillo

Golf Course

San Gervasio

Los Cocos

Airport

N
W — E
S

Downtown Pier

Punta Langosta Pier

San Miguel

International Pier

Puerta Maya Pier

Chankanaab National Park

San Francisco Beach

El Cedro

Ecological Reserve

Lighthouse

Dive and Snorkeling Areas
1 **Palancar Reef**
2 **San Francisco Reef**
3 **Paraiso Reef**
4 **Chankanaab Lagoon**
5   **Colombia Reef**

Marine Park

Best Dives

Most tours include a shallow dive on the inner reef and a drift dive along the outer wall. Currents on the drift dives vary with the weather from very mild to too-strong-to-stop-for-a-photograph. The dive boat drops you off at one end of the reef, then follows your bubbles as you drift with the current to a predetermined point where you surface to rendezvous with the boat.

A maximum depth of 120 feet is enforced by the dive operators. Novice divers may wish to avoid the strong currents associated with drift diving and stick to the inner reefs. National marine park status protects all of Cozumel's reefs.

★★★★★ The **Palancar National Marine Park** (*Marine Parque Arricefes De Cozumel*) reef complex, off the southwestern tip of the island, encompasses more than three miles of winding tunnels and coral canyons. Depths on the inner reef range from 30 to 60 feet. Visibility exceeds 100 feet. The dropoff on the reef's outer wall is laced with immense coral arches and tunnels – shelter for huge crabs, lobsters and all types of morays. Vibrant growths of tree-sized sea fans, yellow and lavender tube sponges, barrel sponges, giant sea whips and pink-tipped anemones adorn the walls.

Huge towering coral pinnacles on the south end of Palancar provide excellent photo and video opportunities. Fish are abundant, with gigantic parrotfish and groupers, schools of porkfish and grunts everywhere. Many of the groupers are tame and may be hand-fed. At greater depths you'll find a profusion of black coral. There is a $2 fee for diving in the marine park.

★★★★ **San Francisco Reef** offers underwater photographers a kaleidoscope of seascapes, with an array of pastel gorgonians and sea fans, vase and barrel sponges, coral arches, caves and tunnels. Usually a drift dive, with huge angels, rays, groupers, and sea turtles greeting you along the way. Depths along the reef ledge are from 20 to 70 feet. The wall then drops off to channel depths. Visibility is excellent – usually 150 feet.

★★★ **Paraiso Reef North** is a popular shallow dive just north of the cruise ship pier in San Miguel. The reef is accessible by swimming straight out 200 yards from the beach at the Hotel Sol Caribe or by dive boat. The remains of a twin engine airplane, sunk intentionally as part of a movie set, rest at 30 feet, creating a home for a vast array of fish. Huge green morays, eagle rays, turtles, yellowtails, French angels, schools of porkfish, butterflyfish, and queen triggerfish can be found. The reef is a good choice for novice divers.

Snorkeling

 Cozumel's east-coast beaches make terrific entry spots for easy snorkeling. The reefs are too far out for easy shore-entry snorkeling, but you'll find varied tropical fish inhabiting the rocky areas. The shallows off the beaches at both the **Scuba Club Resort** and **San Francisco Beach** have a constant show of juvenile tropicals and invertebrates.

☆☆☆ **Chancanaab Lagoon**, south of the cruise-ship pier at Laguna Beach, is protected from wind and waves. Ideal for beginning snorkelers, depths range from very shallow to about 30 feet. Its most prominent feature is a 12-foot bronze statue of Christ, created by sculptor Enrique Miralda to commemorate the first Catholic Mass said on the island.

Schools of grunts, angelfish, damselfish, trumpetfish, turtles, and snappers dart between the clumps of coral. Sea fans and soft corals adorn the reef. Visibility runs about 75 feet, sometimes better. Snorkeling gear can be rented from shops on the beach. Changing rooms, freshwater showers and lockers are available. Small admission fee. A botanical garden and restaurant are on the premises.

A pretty snorkeling-depth reef aprons the south end of neighboring **Isla Mujeres**. Enter from the shore at **Playa Garrafon**, four miles from town. This spot – *El Garrafon* (the carafe) – is one of the most populated (by fish and swimmers) in the Caribbean. Just wade out from the beach with some cracker crumbs and you'll immediately be surrounded by crowds of friendly fish. Ideal for first-time snorkelers. The beach has a dive shop, showers, refreshment stands and shops.

 To telephone or fax any Mexican number from the US, dial ☎ 011-52 + 987 + the five-digit number. In Mexico just dial the last five digits. Prices are in US dollars, subject to change.

Dive Operators

 Most of the dive shops offer three- to seven-day, reduced-rate dive packages. Before forking over your money, ask if refunds are given for missed dives and whether you can get that in writing. Some divers prefer to pay each day rather than risk missing the boat and losing the price of a trip.

Aquatic Sports aka **Scuba Cozumel**, a PADI Five Star Dive Center and first-class operation, visits Palancar National Marine Park, Maracaibo Reef, Chankanaab Bolones and more, aboard comfortable custom boats carrying six to eight divers. Aquatic Sports has had 30 years of diving on the reefs without an accident. Rates for a two-tank dive are $75. ☎ 52-987-20640, www.scubacozumel.com and www.cozumelsafediving.com.

Aqua Safari, a PADI Five Star facility on the ocean at 5th Street South, offers drift dives on Palancar Reef, night-dives, rentals and repairs. Custom dive boats can accommodate up to 20 divers. Multilingual dive guides offer resort and PADI certification courses. A boat trip with all scuba equipment costs $65 and includes two tanks, weights and belt. Snorkelers may join the trip for $20. Expect a crowd during high season. ☎ 52-987-872-0662, fax 52-987-872-0101, www.aquasafari.com, info@aquasafari.com. Write PO Box 41, Cozumel, Quintana Roo, Mexico 77600.

Blue Bubble Divers offers wreck and reef dives, with a certified Captain and dive master. Dive/accommodation packages from $660. Guides are friendly and helpful. Good briefings. Punctual. Five two-tank dive trips run $290, one two-tank reef trip costs $68 plus tax. Dive trips include tanks, weights, belts, fresh bottled water, fruit, snacks, clean towels. Dive packages include equipment locker, pick-up, rinse and delivery. ☎ 866-405-5749, 52-987-872 1865, www.bluebubble.com, info@bluebubble.com. Write PO Box 334, Cozumel, Quintana Roo, Mexico 77600.

Caribbean Divers International has relocated to Calle 3 between the waterfront and Avenida 5. As with most large dive shops, they enable you to complete the open-water dive part of your scuba certification course in Cozumel with a referral form or letter from your dive instructor. They will also assist divers who wish to use dive computers to calculate bottom time (RBT) or adavnced computers that calculate remaining Nitrox, decompression stops and ascent time. The shop visits Palancar, Santa Rosa and Maracaibo reefs, plus *cenote* diving (cenotes are sunken limestone caverns with dazzling sta- lagmites and stalactites). NAUI, PADI and PDIC courses. Equipment rental. ☎ 52-987-872-1080, www.cozumel-diving.net/caribbean~divers, cdi- vers@prodigy.net.mx. Write PO Box 191, Cozumel, Quintana Roo, Mexico 77600.

Dive Palancar, operting out of both the **Occidental Allegro Cozumel** and **Occidental Grand Cozumel** resorts, offers dive trips to Palancar and Santa Rosa, plus inland cenote dives. Beach diving tours. Dive and snorkeling courses. English-speaking guides. One-tank dive costs $36; add $8 for Nitrox. Ten-dive package costs $300. Open-water referrals, $200. Boats on time. Fine service. ☎ US 866-385-0256, international 435-627-0503; Occidental Allegro Resort, ☎ 52-987-9770; Occidental Grand Resort, ☎ 872-9730; www.divepalancarcozumel.com.

Liquid Blue Divers offer PADI instruction, fast, small boats, dive trips and courses. The shop is on Avenida 5 between Rosado Salas and Calle 3. The store opens nightly from 6:30 to 8 pm. ☎ 869-7794 (on-island), www.liquidbluedivers.com.

Scuba Cozumel Repair has relocated to 1st Street, between 85th and 90th Avenues. Maintenance and repair for all brands of regulators, BCDs, and scuba equipment. Equipment storage facility available. Open Mon-Fri 9 am-5 pm, Sat 9 am-1 pm. ☎ 987-872-3567 or 987-872-6727, cell 044-987-876-1831 or 044-987-876-0674.

Scuba-Cozumel, the in-house dive operation for Scuba Club Cozumel (see below), whisks divers to Palancar Marine Park in seven custom-designed boats. The training center offers all levels of certification and specialty courses. See Scuba Club Cozumel's accommodation listing. ☎ 800-847-5708 or 713-783-3305, www.scubaclubcozumel.com.

Scuba Du at the Presidente Inter-Continental offers personalized dive tours, small groups, Nitrox and fast custom boats. PADI and NAUI courses. Dive/hotel packages. ☎ 52-987-21379, fax 52-987-24130. Write PO Box 137, Cozumel, Quintana Roo, Mexico 77600, www.scubadu.com.

 To telephone or fax any Mexican number from the US, dial ☎ 01152 + 987 + the five-digit number.

Where to Stay

 **Scuba Club Cozumel**, on the waterfront one mile south of the downtown ferry dock, accommodates divers in a modern Spanish-colonial waterfront complex. Spacious guest rooms are all tile and stucco, ready for dripping-wet suits with a drying rack on each terrace. All have A/C, ceiling fans, hair dryers, alarm clocks, and a small refrigerator. But no TV or telephone. Most rooms have an ocean view. King-size beds are available, as well as rooms with two doubles. Larger family rooms have two doubles and an additional sitting area with a twin-size bed. A few rooms have been remodeled to accommodate the needs of handicapped divers. Ground-floor rooms edge the the beach.

Meals, included in your package at Scuba Club Cozumel, are served at the resort's two restaurants. Their weekly beach party features a full buffet of Mexican dishes.

Hotel Presidente Inter-Continental features plush guest rooms from $330 per night, oceanfront from $430. Located two miles south of San Miguel at the Chancanab Lagoon, the resort property has a large pool, tennis court, restaurants, entertainment and dive packages. Rates for hotel and a daily two-tank dive for two start at $650 per person for three nights, with breakfast buffet. Other dive packages available. Good snorkeling off the beach. ☎ 888-424-6835, 800-327-0200, www.ichotelsgroup.com.

Fiesta Americana Dive Resort features 172 deluxe ocean- and reef-view rooms and four parlor suites with satellite TV, private terraces, room service. On-site scuba shop, **Dive House Cozumel**, visits all the best southwest sites. Amenities include two lighted tennis courts, fax service, equipment storage lockers, custom charters, gym and jogging trail, two restaurants, gift shop, poolside snack bar car, bike and moped rentals and purified water. Night-dives and snorkeling trips. ☎ 800-FIESTA-1 or 52-987-87-29600, fax 52-987-22666, rinternet@posadas.com, www.fiestamericana.com.

Hotel Cozumel, one mile south of downtown San Miguel, has sparkling, newly renovated rooms, the largest pool on the island, lovely Mexican architecture, open-air restaurant, dive shop, gear lockers, boat dock, ocean or pool view rooms with private balcony or terrace. Friendly staff.

All-inclusive seven-night dive packages start at $1,189 per person based on two in a room, including all meals and beverages, five two-tank morning dives, five one-tank afternoon divers. Same package without meals costs $849. ☎ 888-599-3483, www.bayadventures.com/cozumel.

Occidental Allegro Cozumel, a five-star all-inclusive resort is just five minutes from Palancar Reef. Guests unwind in a choice of 300 charming rooms housed in two-story, Polynesian-style, thatched-roof villas with eight rooms per villa. Package rates cover all taxes and gratuities, meals and snacks, unlimited domestic and international beverages, juices and soft drinks – plus non-motorized watersports. Diving is extra.

The property has two swimming pools and a children's pool, four lighted, hard-surface tennis courts, and a Jacuzzi. Kid's Club offers supervised activities. ☎ 866-385-0256 (US toll-free) or 435-627-0503 (international).

The Melia Cozumel is a five-star, all-inclusive, luxury resort located on the largest section of sandy beach on the north side of Cozumel. Daily activities include basketball, tennis and non-motorized watersports. Also included are the Children's Club and bi-weekly nightly activities. Relax and enjoy the view from one of the open-air bars, including a popular swim-up bar.

All of the guest rooms are newly decorated in vibrant colors, with Caribbean furniture. The all-inclusive plan features fine dining and drinks at a variety of food and beverage outlets on the premises. Guests start their day with a buffet-style breakfast. A beachside bar and grill serves sandwiches. There are two restaurants. Guest rooms have air conditioning with individual climate control, private balcony or terrace, electronic safety deposit box, marble bathroom with shower, bathtub, hair dryer and deluxe toiletries, satellite TV, and direct-dial telephone. For two people, rates start at $244 per day, which includes taxes, all meals, drinks and gratuities. Scuba and snorkeling are arranged through **Carib Divers**, their on-site shop. ☎ 888-95-MELIA (63542), www.solmelia.com.

Cozumel Palace, built in 2005, features spacious colonial design with touches of contemporary Mexican décor. It has two restaurants, a pool with a fabulous swim-up bar, a kids' club, unequalled watersports, and 24-hour room service. Every suite has a Jacuzzi and balcony with a hammock, and most have ocean views. Ten-minute walk to San Miguel. Diving arranged at desk. ☎ 800-346-8225, www.palaceresorts.com.

Guests at **Reef Club Cozumel** climb into luxurious thatched-roof "huts." The resort is 10 miles south of San Miguel on a gorgeous stretch of beach. All-inclusive rates start at $145 per person, based on a double, cover food, drinks, tips, activities and entertainment. Amenities include on-site car rental, disco, **Sand Dollar Dive Shop**, a water sport center that rents Wave-Runners, board surfers, parasailing, banana boats and surf mats. Plus nightly entertainment, a gift shop, health club, two restaurants, three lounges and medical services, with a doctor on call 24 hours a day. ☎ 888-773-4349, direct 52-987-872-93-00, fax 52-987-872-93-15, www.reefclubcozumel.com, reef-clubcozumel@prodigy.net.mx.

Villablanca Garden Beach Hotel is less than four miles from Cozumel International Airport and about a mile and a half from downtown San Miguel. Diving or snorkeling is easily arranged with either of the dive shops on the premises – **Dive Paradise** and **Papa Hogs**. The hotel offers 50 guest rooms, comprising 25 standard and 25 superior rooms. Standard guest room ameni-ties include marble bathrooms with sunken tubs, air conditioning, ceiling fan, satellite TV with remote control, mini-refrigerator and telephone. In addition to standard room amenities, superior rooms feature king-size bed and sofa bed plus a balcony or terrace. Hotel amenities include a swimming pool, pool-side bar, tennis court, restaurant, and volleyball court.

A short swim from the Villablanca beach brings you over the first reef south of the island, home to an abundance of marine delights. Dive packages for five days, four nights range from $325 to $365 per person for a standard room to $605 per person for a superior room. Divers enjoy a welcome tank on arrival for a shore-dive. Pick-up from hotel pier for all dives, use of tanks, belt, and weights. ☎ 888-790-5264, 52-987-872-0730, www.villablanca.net.

The **Barracuda Hotel** is locally owned and considerably cheaper than the full-service dive resorts. It's conveniently located within walking distance of the plaza in San Miguel. Few frills, but the entire 52-room property has been completely renovated and now touts a couple of shops, private docks, a fewwform pool, air-conditioned guest rooms with private bath, a refirgerator, email and phone. Most rooms have ocean views. A double with two double beds costs $100 per night during the high season. Dive packages available with **Dive Paradise**. ☎ 866-327-1389, direct 011 52-987-1389, www.cozumel-hotels.net/barracuda, barracudahotelczm@prodigy.net.mx.

Sightseeing & Other Activities

Diving and sport fishing are the main activities on Cozumel, followed by wind surfing, JetSkiing, and water-skiing, which are offered by the resorts. The widest range of watersports rentals are at **Playa San Francisco**.

San Miguel's main tourist areas are **Plaza del Sol** – where you'll find cafés, craft shops, jewelry stores, restaurants and fast-food joints – and the *malecón*, Cozumel's seaside boardwalk. While touring the town, stop in at the **Museum of the Island of Cozumel**, a two-story former turn-of-the-century hotel that features displays of island wildlife and anthropological and cultural history. Between May and September the museum offers marine-biologist-led tours to witness the sea turtles lay eggs on the eastern shore.

Farther south you'll come to the **Celarain Lighthouse**, which you can climb for a spectacular view of the area. Be sure to clear your visit first with the resident caretaker.

Rent a jeep to explore the windward east coast of Cozumel. You'll find pounding surf and marvelous stretches of uninhabited beaches lined with mangroves and coconut palms. It may be wise to avoid swimming here because of the dangerous currents and strong undertow, except at **Playa Chiquero**, a protected crescent-shaped cove, and **Playa Chen Rio**, which is protected by a rock breakwater.

Remains of Mayan temples and pyramids can be found at the northern end of the island. Guided tours to explore **San Gervasio** (once the Mayan capital), also on the north end, may be booked through most large hotels. Ferry trips to the larger, more impressive Mayan ruins on the mainland can be booked in town at the **International Pier**. Most dive packages include a side-trip to **Tulum**, a Mayan walled city built in the late 13th century, or to **Isla Mujeres**, a fabulous nearby snorkeling island.

The **Chankanaab Lagoon Botanical Gardens**, two miles south of town, were under reconstruction at press time. They feature 300 species of tropical plants and trees and an interesting Mayan museum.

Sightseeing flights around Cozumel, to neighboring islands or to the mainland, can be arranged at the airport.

Dining

Local lobster, native grilled fish and a variety of Mexican dishes such as tacos, enchiladas or *caracol* (a giant conch) predominate at Cozumel's restaurants and roadside stands. Several superb native eateries within a few blocks of the pier offer island specialties such as grilled turtle, grilled fish in banana leaves, conch cocktail and spicy steak strips. All in all, dining is quite good in Cozumel, whether you choose romantic garden dining with strolling serenaders or a fast snack at one of the many stands.

Carlo's and Charlie's, on the waterfront at Punta Langosta shopping mall, serves barbecued ribs, shrimp, lobster chowder and fine fajitas. If you can stomach something HOT, try *diabla* – a deviled oyster dish with ham and bacon. Their quesadillas are magic, with melted cheese and guacamole grilled inside a flour tortilla.

Casa Denis is the island's oldest restaurant, favored for a big selection of steaks, ribs, fajitas, soups, salads and melts. Bring your appetite! Owners Denis and Juanita Angulao boast visits to the eatery by Jackie Onassis and Placido Domingo. ☎ 52 987-872-2267 (locally just dial 2-22-67).

La Laguna, on the beach at Chankanaab National Park, serves up tasty shrimp, crabs and fish. ☎ 52 987-872-0584 (2-05-84).

Naturalia, at 20 Avenida 1132, dishes out organic veggie omelettes, smoked fish snacks and salads for breakfast and lunch. Coffees and desserts all day. Try Chaya – a spinach, onion, tomato and trout combo. Naturalia's integral health-food shop sells a variety of natural products and foods. ☎ 52 987-872-1862 (2-18-62).

Guido's Pizza, on Avenida Melgar 23, specializes in Italian favorites, www.guidoscozumel.com.

Akumal

Akumal ("place of the turtle") lies 60 miles south of Cancun on Mexico's Yucatán Peninsula in an area known as the Tulum Corridor. Laid-back and off the beaten track, this tiny resort community originated as a section of a large coconut plantation. It wasn't until 1958 that Mexican treasure divers salvaging a sunken Spanish galleon discovered great sport-diving opportunities along the off-shore barrier reef. Pristine corals and sponges, frequent turtle sightings, silky white sand beaches and terrific beach snorkeling have popularized Akumal with local divers and a discriminating group of visitors. Three dive operators serve the area.

Drawbacks exist for those who like "pampered" diving – Akumal dive guides are friendly and helpful, but they *do not* carry, store or wash your gear. The diving is not easy in terms of services. Divers "schlepp" their own tanks, weights and equipment to and from the boats. The boats are open, with ladders – no platforms, no sun canopies. On the other hand, most sites lie close to shore, a five- to 10-minute boat ride. Spear fishing is prohibited.

Akumal dive operators also offer tours to freshwater jungle pools, or cenotes. These inland adventures include a jungle trek through nature's most exotic gardens.

When to Go

The best time to dive Akumal is October through April. Weather is very hot in May and June and rain is heavy during July, August, and September.

Best Dives

 Akumal's ocean scuba sites are gentle drift dives over the **Great Mayan Reef**, which runs parallel to the shoreline and continues along most of the Yucatán coastline. The dive boat follows your bubbles and picks you up when you surface. For snorkeling, there are good beach-entry points to the reef at neighboring Half Moon Bay and nearby Yalku Lagoon.

The reef structure comprises three distinct systems running parallel to one another at progressively greater depths. The inner reef, a network of patch reefs, ranges from three to 35 feet, with huge stands of elkhorn and formations of boulder, brain and plate corals. An expanse of white sand separates the inner reef from the middle reef, which is three miles long at depths from 40 to 55 feet. Several reef areas are shot through with coral caves and tunnels. Farther out, a well-developed outer reef from 60 to 125 feet. features more outstanding caverns and canyons. Abundant tropicals inhabit the patch reefs and the middle reef. Larger fish and turtles roam the outer reef.

Frequent sightings of loggerhead, green and hawksbill turtles that nest along Yucatán beaches highlight many dives. Currents normally run less than one knot.

Snorkelers exploring from the beach can swim up to the breakers on the reef. Conditions inside are normally calm, with depths from three to 20 feet.

☆☆☆ **Akumal Shark Caves**, at 40 feet, shelter six or more nurse sharks and walls of porkfish, grunts, and snappers. Cavern walls blossom with rose gorgonians, lettuce corals, yellow sea fans, flower and brush corals. Orange vase sponges and soft corals proliferate in the gently moving current. Drift dive. Expect some surge. Experience suggested.

☆☆☆☆ **La Tortuga**, named for the big turtles that paddle by, slopes from 70 to 80 feet. Located outside the reef, this site has a slightly more challenging current. Surface can get rough at times. Good to excellent visibility.

☆☆☆ **The Nets**, at 45-foot depths, and **El Mero**, at 75 feet, both adjacent to Shark Caves, offer normally excellent visibility, vibrant red sponges, star corals, sea feathers, and soft corals. Terrain slopes into a labyrinth of canyons, tunnels and overhangs. Both spots provide habitat to arrow crabs, sea cucumbers, lobster and shrimp. Lots of tunnels and small caves. French and queen angels, sergeant majors, trigger- and parrotfish bob with the current. Gentle drift dive.

The Cenotes

Cenotes are freshwater pools with submerged limestone caverns. "Gin-clear" best describes the visibility, though you may pass through a thermal layer of "soup" as you drop down to more crystal-clear water. Scuba depths average 40 to 60 feet. You'll see fish, but the magnificence of these limestone caverns lies in the fantastic stalagmites and stalactites. Lights make the colors stand out and your dive more exciting.

Akumal, Cozumel and Cancun dive shops offer guided cenote tours to certified divers. Unlike cave diving, you stay within close sight of the entrance. No special certification required. Before signing up for a cenote trip make sure your guide is cave-certified by either the **National Association for Cave Diving** (NACD), **National Speleological Society Cave Diving Section**, or **International Assocation of Nitrox and Technical Divers** (IANTD). The guide should also be wearing doubles with octopus rigs and using a continuous guideline (a rope to lead you back to the surface should one of you kick up the silt and decrease the visibility to zero). Groups should be very small. A thorough briefing on emergency procedures should precede the dive.

Be sure to maintain neutral bouyancy to avoid kicking up the silty bottoms and smashing the flowstones. Keep a close watch on your air supply. Don't explore passageways on your own. You'll need a wet suit; water temperatures in the cenotes average 70°F. Cenote dives cost about $45 per tank.

☆☆☆ **The Car Wash**, **Gran Cenote**, **Temple of Doom** and **Dos Ojos** are favorite cavern dives in Akumal. All average 50- to 60-foot depths. Temple of Doom requires jumping from a ledge 15 feet above the pool.

Some of these caverns are partially above water and shallow enough for snorkelers, who are offered specialty tours.

☆☆☆☆ **Nohoch Nah Chich**, listed in the *Guinness Book of World Records* as the world's longest underwater cave system, was also featured in the PBS TV series, *The New Explorers*, as one of Yucatán's most exciting caverns. Visitors snorkel in the shallow freshwater amidst brilliant white stalactites and stalagmites. Unlimited visibility and an openness to the caverns offer breathtaking views.

Joining a jungle walk and snorkeling expedition to Nohoch Nah Chich involves a mile-and-a-half trek through impressive flora. Horses or donkeys carry your gear. Be sure to apply sun protective lotions and bug repellent and wear a hat that will shade your face. Not suitable for young children or people with severe disabilities or medical problems.

Snorkeling

Uncrowded beaches, secluded bays and a healthy marine population make Akumal delightful for family snorkeling vacations.

☆☆☆ **Akumal Bay's** best snorkeling is off the beach in front of the **Club Akumal Caribe**. Depths range from three to 20 feet, with coral heads leading out to the breakers at the barrier reef. A variety of corals, sea fans, sponges, reef fish, occasional moray eels, barracudas, jacks, groupers,stingrays, parrotfish and turtles inhabit the bay. Bottom terrain is sandy, with coral heads scattered about. Bay conditions inside the barrier reef are almost always tranquil.

☆☆☆ Half Moon Bay is about three minutes down the interior road from Akumal Bay, and resembles Akumal Bay in terrain and marine life. This is a residential area, but anyone can use the beach.

☆☆☆☆ **Yalcu Lagoon**, at the end of the interior road, a short drive from Half Moon Bay, features partially submerged caves, throngs of fish and crystal-clear, tranquil water. Fresh water mixing with sea water provides nutrients for aquatic plants that attract rich marine life. Big parrotfish, angels, Spanish hogfish, rays, juvenile turtles and spotted eels nibble on the plants around the rocks. A natural entrance from the sea ensures a constant mix of nutrients. The outlying barrier reef protects this magnificent natural aquarium from wind-driven waves and rough seas. Enter the lagoon from the head of the bay or climb down the big rocks anywhere along the shore. Guided boat and beach-entry snorkeling tours are offered by the dive shop at **Club Akumal Caribe**.

Snorkeling Up & Down the Coast

Several sheltered bays and secluded beaches with good shore-entry snorkeling exist along the coast. About six miles south of Akumal, the dirt road turn-off at KM 249 leads to ☆☆ **Chemuyil**, a quiet, horseshoe-shaped cove of tranquil water edged by a lovely, powder-white beach. A shallow snorkeling reef crosses the mouth of the bay. A small beach bar (the Marco Polo) serves fresh seafood, cold beer and soft drinks. Full camping facilities and a few tented "palapas" for overnight rental are available.

☆☆ **Xel-Ha** (pronounced shell ha), the world's largest natural aquarium, with 10 acres of lagoons, coves and inlets teeming with exotic fish, lies about 20 miles south of Akumal. Platforms above the rocky limestone shore offer sea-life viewing for non-swimmers. Unlike Akumal, this spot is packed with tourists and avid snorkelers who arrive regularly by the busload in season. Admission fee.

Amenities on-site include showers, shops, a maritime museum, seafood restaurant and Subway sandwich shop. Snorkeling gear is available for rent. Despite the crowds, most snorkelers, especially those touring with children, immensely enjoy it. Venture across Highway 307 to visit some small ruins.

☆☆ **Xcaret** (*"scaret"*), Mayan for "little inlet," about 40 miles north of Akumal, is a private ranch turned aquatic theme park. Once a Mayan port, this novel playground now features dolphin swims and snorkeling in "the underground river," which flows through a series of open-ended caves. A mix of fresh and saltwater nourishes sea plants, which in turn feed armies of fish that entertain between 400 and 500 snorkelers per day. The effect is like drifting through a very big, very pretty, shaded pool stocked with fish. Holes in the "roof" of the river caves filter light into a spectrum of colors.

Topside features include a wild-bird aviary, butterfly pavilion, saltwater aquarium, botanical garden, a couple of Mayan temple ruins, and the **Museum of Mayan Archaeological Sites**, with scale models of 26 Mayan ceremonial sites found on the Yucatán peninsula. There are three restaurants, two snack bars, one cafeteria, showers, lockers, photo center, horse shows, gift shops and a sun deck with spectacular ocean views. Crowded, but very user-friendly.

The open-air restaurant, **La Peninsula**, offers a good selection of entrées and remains open at night. **La Caleta**, another alfresco restaurant near the inlet, specializes in spicy seafood.

 The Maya prized Xcaret, believing that its waters could purify bodies and souls. Thus it became important as a place to take a "sacred bath" before crossing the sea to Cozumel to worship Ixchel, Goddess of Fertility.

We can't guarantee the soul-purifying properties, but most snorkelers find Xcaret a fun half- or full-day diversion. One of our snorkeling researchers returning from Xcaret claims relief from back pain!

Dive Operators

 Akumal Dive Center at Club Akumal offers cenote, jungle, cave and open-water diving with top-notch dive masters. Groups are small and tours are personalized. C-cards a must. Cave dives only to certified cave divers. Dive/hotel packages with Hotel Akumal Carib (see above). Call or e-mail for rates,

☎ 800-351-1622, 011-52987-59025, www.akumaldivecenter.com, dive@akumaldivecenter.com.

Aquatech Villas DeRosa in Aventuras Akumal features technical training, Nitrox, rebreathers, cave and cavern diving, reef diving for all skill levels and snorkeling/fishing, as well as picnic excursions. ☎ phone/fax 866-619-9050, local 87-59020 or 87-59021, www.cenotes.com, e-mail dive@cenotes.com.

Dive Aventuras is a PADI full-service shop at the lovely **Puerto Aventuras Beach, Marina and Golf Resort**, an Omni Hotel complex. The shop offers reef dives at $40 for a one-tank, $84 for two-tanks, snorkeling for $35, cenote snorkeling for $60, cenote diving from $70 and terrific hotel/dive packages. Scuba dive rates include weights and tanks. ☎ 52-984-873-5031 or 5129, www.diveaventuras.com, info@diveaventuras.com (for the dive shop) and omnipave@sybcom.com (for resort information).

Where to Stay

Hotel Club Akumal Caribe features a variety of air-conditioned accommodations and an on-site dive shop. On the main beach choose from spacious Maya bungalows with garden views or first-class hotel rooms facing the pool and ocean. All are clean and modern with full baths, air conditioning, ceiling fans and compact refrigerators. Also on the main beach is the **Cannon House Suite**, with two bedrooms, two baths, living room and kitchen.

Two-bedroom condos on Half Moon Bay have one king-size bed, two twins, kitchens and living rooms. Winter rates range from $99 per night for a bungalow, from $125 for a hotel room, and from $420 per night for a three-bedroom villa. Contact the reservation desk for additional accommodation rates and information, including dive package rates. In the US, ☎ 800-351-1622; in Canada, ☎ 800-343-1440; from Texas, 915-584-3552; from Mexico, 984-875-9010; clubakumal@aol.com, www.hotelakumalcaribe.com.

Facts

Additional Information: ☎ 800-446-3942, contact@visitmexico.com, www.visitmexico.com, info@islacozumel.com, www.islacozumel.com.mx, www.rivieramaya.com, ☎ 877-746-6292.

Helpful Phone Numbers: Police (Cozumel), ☎ 872-0409 hospital (Cozumel), ☎ 872-0103.

Nearest Recompression Chamber: When you dive in Cozumel, be sure to check with your dive operator to know if they are associated with a recompression chamber service. Each diver pays $1 dollar per day to have full coverage against diving accidents. A form is completed and you sign it. Do not assume the shop participates. Be sure you are covered.

There are two hyperbaric chambers staffed with hyperbaric-certified physicians waiting to respond to the medical needs of divers.

- **Cozumel Recompression Chamber**, Radio VHF 16, ☎ 872-2387, 872-1430 Calle 5 Sur #21B.
- **Cozumel Hyperbarics Chamber**, Radio VHF 65, ☎ 872-3070. Located in the San Miguel Clinic at Calle 6 between Ave 5 and Ave 10.

Cozumel Recompression Center is supported in part by visiting divers who pay $1 per dive day to affiliated dive operators. For this dollar, CRC provides treatment for pressure/dive related problems and works with primary insurance carriers (DAN) to try to ensure that divers have no out-of-pocket expense for the treatment.

On the Yucatán mainland there is a recompression chamber run by doctors trained in hyperbaric medicine in Playa del Carmen on 10th Ave, ☎ 984-873-1755 or 873-1365; from outside Mexico 011-52-984-873-1755, playa@sssnetwork.com.

Getting Here: Direct flights to Cozumel and Cancun from the US are offered by **American Airlines**, ☎ 800-733-4300; **Continental**, ☎ 800-231-0856; **United**, ☎ 800-003-0777; **Delta**, ☎ 800-241-4141; **Mexicana**, ☎ 800-531-7921; and **Aero Mexico**. There are additional domestic flights from Acapulco, Cancun, Guadalajara, Mexico City, Merida, Monterrey, and Veracruz. Cruise ships from Miami: **Norwegian Caribbean Lines**, **Holland America**, **Carnival**. Cozumel island also can be reached by bus ferry, car ferry and hydrofoil from Cancun. Isla Mujeres is reached by bus ferry, car ferry and air taxi from Cancun. **AeroCozumel** and **Aerocaribe** fly between the islands. Cozumel is a 40- to 60-minute boat trip from Cancun.

Island Transportation: Taxi service is inexpensive and readily available. Mopeds, cars and Jeeps may be rented in town or at the airport. Book rental cars in advance of your trip.

Departure tax: US$21.

Driving: On the right.

Language: Spanish is the official language and Mayan is the local language, but English, French, Italian and German are also widely spoken.

Measurements: Speed limits are posted in kilometers. Dive operators generally use both feet/psi and meters/bars when communicating dive data.

Entry Requirements: Proof of citizenship is necessary to cross the border into Mexico. Either a current passport, birth certificate or voter's registration will suffice (for citizens not arriving from USA and Canada please check with your local consulate or embassy). Minors traveling alone or with one parent need notarized consent from both parents indicating that the parent who has legal custody knowingly approves of the child's visit to Mexico. Upon arrival, visitors are given a Tourist Card that must be turned in upon departure at the airport. At that time, a departure tax of US$10 is charged; it may be included with your airline ticket, or payable in US dollars or Mexican pesos.

Taxes & Service Charges: A 10% value-added tax called IVA is added to all goods and services within the State, including hotel rooms and rental cars. Be sure to ask if the tax is included in the quoted price on the menu in restaurants.

Tips: It's customary to leave 10 to 20% in tips, depending on service.

Customs: Plants, flowers and fruits may not be brought into Cozumel. Persons carrying illegal drugs will be jailed. You may bring three bottles of liquor and one carton of cigarettes. Dogs and cats should have a current vaccination certificate. Divers carrying a lot of electronic or camera gear, especially video equipment, should register it with US Customs in advance of the trip.

Water: Drink only bottled or filtered water to avoid diarrheal intestinal ailment. Also avoid raw vegetables and the skin of fruit and foods that sit out for any length of time.

Currency: The exchange rate of the Mexican peso fluctuates a great deal. At this writing US$1=11.32 Mexican pesos (variable). Banks are open weekday mornings. Major credit cards and traveler's checks are widely accepted in Akumal, Cancun and Cozumel.

Climate: Temperatures range from the low 70s in winter to the high 90s in summer, with an average of about 80°F. Winter months bring cooler weather; summer and fall can sometimes bring heavy rain.

Clothing: Lightweight, casual. Wetsuits are not needed, but lightweight (1/8-inch) short suits or wetskins are comfortable on deep wall dives.

Electricity: 110 volts; 60 cycles (same as US).

Time: Central Standard Time.

Language: Spanish; English widely spoken.

For Additional Information: For any further information in USA and Canada, ☎ 800-44-MEXICO (800-446-3942), www.visitmexico.com, www.allmexicohotels.com, www.mexico-travel.com, www.caribemexicano.mx.

Tourist Boards: *New York:* Director, Marisa Lopez, 375 Park Avenue, #1905, New York, NY 10152 , ☎ 212-308-2110, fax 212-308-9060, newyork@visitmexico.com.

Florida: Director, Teresa Villareal, 5975 Sunset Dr., Suite 305, So. Miami, FL 33143, ☎ 786-621-2909, fax 786-621-2907, miami@visitmexico.com.

Texas: (US Headquarters) Director, Dr. Jorge Davila Garcia, 4507 San Jacinto, Suite 308, Houston, TX 77004, ☎ 713-772-2581, fax 713-772-6058, texas@visitmexico.com.

Illinois: Director, Marta Varela, 225 N. Michigan Ave., #1850, Chicago, IL 60601, ☎ 312-228-0517, fax 312-228-0515, chicago@visitmexico.com.

California: Director, Alejandro Cruz Serrano, 1880 Centry Park East, #511, Los Angeles, CA 90067, ☎ 310-282-9112, fax 310-282-9116, losangeles@visitmexico.com.

United Kingdom: Mexican Ministry of Tourism (SECTUR), London Wakefield House 41, Trinity Square EC3 N4DT, London, UK, ☎ 0207-488-9392, fax 0207-265- 0704, info@mexicotravel.co.uk.

Curaçao

Curaçao, the largest of five islands that make up the Netherlands Antilles, which include Bonaire, Saba, Saint Maarten and St. Eustatius (Statia), is a dry and hilly island completely surrounded with rich coral reefs – many within a stone's throw of shore. Its coastline sparkles with beautiful sand beaches, secluded lagoons and snorkeling coves.

Willemstad, its capital, is delightfully Dutch, with open-air markets, narrow streets and rows of shops offering imports from all over the world. It is best known for its colorful Dutch Colonial architecture. According to legend, the first governor of Curaçao suffered from migraine headaches due to glare from the white houses and ordered all residents to paint their homes pastel. The rows of pastel-colored town houses with gabled roofs, red tile and rococo-style façades in downtown Willemstad probably are the most photographed sights on the island.

St. Anna Bay, like an Amsterdam canal, divides the capital city in two parts – the **Punda** and the **Otrabanda**. A pontoon walking bridge, which opens several times a day to allow cruise ships to dock in town, connects the two sides of the city.

Christoffel Park, in the northwestern sector of Curaçao, is marked by the island's highest peak. The volcanic crest of **Mt. Christoffel** dominates the landscape, rising 1,250 feet above the sea. Undulating hills are punctuated with the evergreen wayaca and cacti, reaching as much as 10 feet from the parched land like outstretched fingers.

History

 Curaçao's heritage and history is long and multi-faceted. The Caiquetio Indians, a tribe of which were the "Indios Curaçao," were the original inhabitants of Curaçao. In 1499, when Alonso de Ojeda, a Spanish navigator who sailed with Columbus, discovered the island and the Indians, he named it for them.

Later, in 1634, the Dutch captured Curaçao, forcing evacuation by the Spaniards and the Indian natives. By 1635, only 50 of the 462 inhabitants were native Indians and approximately 350 of the rest were Dutch soldiers. The island became one of the leading slave and salt trade centers for the Dutch West Indies Company.

For many years, England and France tried to conquer the island. The English were successful in 1800, but were defeated two years later by the Dutch.

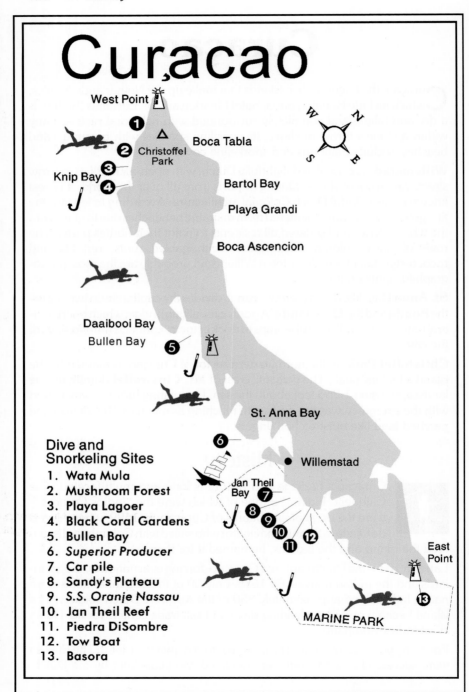

Curaçao

West Point

1

Christoffel Park

Boca Tabla

2

3

Knip Bay

4

Bartol Bay

Playa Grandi

Boca Ascencion

Daaibooi Bay

Bullen Bay

5

St. Anna Bay

6

Willemstad

Dive and Snorkeling Sites

1. **Wata Mula**
2. **Mushroom Forest**
3. **Playa Lagoer**
4. **Black Coral Gardens**
5. **Bullen Bay**
6. *Superior Producer*
7. **Car pile**
8. **Sandy's Plateau**
9. *S.S. Oranje Nassau*
10. **Jan Theil Reef**
11. **Piedra DiSombre**
12. **Tow Boat**
13. **Basora**

Jan Theil Bay

7

8

9

10

11

12

East Point

13

MARINE PARK

England eventually recaptured the island, only to give it back as a result of the Treaty of Paris in 1815.

By the mid 1800s, Curaçao's population was as varied as any in the world. One-time soldiers married Curaçaoan women and established a livelihood on the island. Merchants from Europe stayed. Others were freed slaves who chose to remain on the island. All carried a part of their culture and tradition to this tropical paradise.

Curaçao's harbor became the site of one of the world's largest oil refineries in 1914, following the discovery of oil in Venezuela.

Best Dive & Snorkeling Sites

Like its sister "ABC" islands, Aruba and Bonaire, Curaçao lies far south of the hurricane belt and offers clear skies and good diving year-round. Most dives require a boat. The reefs and wrecks are "a stone's throw from shore," but the "shore" adjacent to the best reefs is often formed of jagged, razor-like, ironshore cliffs. Seas along the south coast – locale of the underwater park – are usually dead calm in the morning, but may kick up a three- or four-foot surge in midafternoon.

The **Curaçao Underwater Park**, established in 1983 by the Netherlands Antilles National Park Foundation (STINAPA), stretches 12½ miles from the Princess Beach Hotel to East Point and features 20 dive sites marked by numbered mooring buoys and another 10 unmarked sites. Within the park, divers and snorkelers find crystal-clear water and spectacular subsea landscapes. The reefs are in pristine condition, with many yet to be explored. Diving did not become popular in Curaçao until the 1980s when officials realized the potential for additional tourist growth. Before then, the island was promoted solely for honeymoons, sport fishing and sailing.

Although the park's terrain features dramatic coral walls with deep dropoffs, there is excellent diving in the shallow waters, with 50-foot brain coral, gigantic sponges, huge, perfectly formed trees of elkhorn and enormous, lush sea fan gardens. Visibility is a dependable 100 feet.

To the west is the **Banda Abao Underwater Park**, with more than 21 outstanding dive and snorkeling sites.

For the very adventurous, the westernmost dive site, **Wata Mula**, features a sloping reef and cave frequented by huge moray eels, groupers, nurse sharks and rays. This area is diveable only on very calm days and only with an experienced dive guide. Seas at this end of the island are often very rough, with strong currents. Yet, visibility and marine life is outstanding. Suggested for experienced divers in top physical condition.

South of Wata Mula is **Mushroom Forest**, the most beautiful of the Banda Abao Underwater Park. This gently sloping reef is highlighted by giant mushroom-shaped elkhorn corals at 50 feet. It is located offshore from Sanu Pretu.

At the end of Mushroom Forest is **Playa Lagoen,** a snorkeling beach nestled between two massive rock formations. Snorkelers will find some juvenile fish and small coral heads along the rocks. Be sure to tote a floating dive flag as small fishing boats weave in and out of the area. Energetic divers can swim out about 150 yards to the dropoff.

South of Playa Lagoen, sea turtles and occasional mantas are sighted at the **Black Coral Gardens** off Boca St. Martha. Steep dropoffs, 60 to 130 feet, support a colossal black coral forest. Nearby is **Mike's Place**, known for a giant sponge locally called the "double bed."

☆☆☆☆ **Sandy's Plateau** (aka *Boka di Sorsaka*), is part of the marked trail. It can be reached by swimming out from Jan Thiel Bay. It is an excellent spot for novice divers and snorkelers. The terrain is a combination of walls and steep slopes colored with lavender and pink star corals, yellow pencil corals and orange tube sponges. Lush stands of elkhorn coral grow to within 10 feet of the surface. Dense coral flows around an undercut ledge from 10 to 30 feet. Soldierfish, trumpetfish and schools of sergeant majors hover at the ledge.

The wreck of the ☆☆☆☆ **SS *Oranje Nassau*** (also known as *Bopor Kibra*, Papiamento for broken ship), a Dutch steamer that ran aground here on the Koraal Specht over 80 years ago, lies offshore from the **Curaçao Seaquarium** in Jan Thiel Bay. This is a shallow dive and a favorite spot for free diving. The seas are always choppy over the wreck. Entry is best from the dive-shop docks adjacent to the Seaquarium. Check with the dive master for the day's conditions.

This area is known for outstanding corals. Depths start shallow with large pillar and star corals, sea fans, huge brain coral, and gorgeous stands of elkhorn. It then terraces off to a wall starting at 50 feet. Fish life includes swarms of blue chromis and Creole wrasses, French angels, barracuda and jacks. Sea conditions are choppy and recommended for divers and snorkelers with some ocean experience.

☆☆☆☆ **Jan Thiel Reef**, just outside of Jan Thiel Bay is a fabulous snorkeling site. Lush, shallow gardens at 15 feet are alive with a mass of gorgonians, two-foot lavender sea anemones, sea fans, long, purple tube sponges, pastel star, leaf, fire, pencil and brain corals. Fishlife is superb, with walls of grunts, trumpetfish, parrotfish, angels and small rays. Added buoyancy from a snorkeling vest or shorty wetsuit will help you to stay clear of the fire coral. You can swim from Playa Jan Thiel, just east of the Princess Beach Hotel. The beach has changing facilities and is a favorite for picnics. Admission fee.

☆☆☆ **Piedra Di Sombre** is located between Caracas Bay and Jan Thiel Bay. Ideal for snorkeling and diving, the site is a steep wall covered with abundant sea fans, sea whips, wire coral, star coral, club finger coral, and rows of gorgonians. Depths are from 30 to 125 feet. Numerous black corals grow on the wall. Reef residents are lizardfish, black durgons, angelfish and barracuda.

☆☆☆☆ **The *Superior Producer*** is Curaçao's favorite wreck dive. The 100-foot freighter sank in 1977 when her heavy cargo of clothing shifted. The ship is intact and stands upright on a sandy plain at the foot of a steep, coral-covered slope. The wreck is encrusted with orange, red, purple, green and yellow corals and sponges. Clouds of silversides command the wheel house; rays and porpoises are frequently sighted. The site has a mooring buoy and is most conveniently reached from a boat, but can also be reached by a rugged swim from shore. The closest water-entry point is from the Curaçao public swimming pool at the **Rif Recreation Area**. Top of the wreck is at 90 feet, with sections of the mainmast reaching up to within 40 feet of the surface. Divers are advised to watch the tables or dive computer as several bounty hunters have ended up in the island's recompression chamber.

☆☆☆ **Car Pile**, off the Breezes Resort shoreline, is an artificial reef constructed from piles of old car and truck wrecks. Depth is 60 to 125 feet. Watch out for jagged pieces of metal and avoid getting under the heaps as the mass is not dependably stable. The wrecks are covered over with corals, algae and sponges with resident lobster, crabs and fish. You can reach it by swimming out from the hotel beach. Expect a light to moderate current.

☆☆☆ **Tow Boat**, the favorite shallow dive in the Curaçao Underwater Park, is intact, sitting upright on a sandy shelf, and can be explored at 15 feet. Tube corals, Christmas tree worms, sponges and sheet corals cover the wheelhouse. Schools of reef fish frolic around the bow. Great for wide-angle photography. Divers can continue down a steep dropoff to explore black corals, vase and basket sponges. The wreck is accessible only by boat, a short ride from Caracas Bay.

☆☆☆☆ **Piedra Pretu**, near the easternmost corner of the coast, can present a choppy approach, but the effort is paid back with exposure to one of the most spectacular reefs in the Caribbean. Massive black-coral trees, huge barrel sponges and dense beds of staghorn and elkhorn adorn a shallow terrace which drops off to a vertical wall. Depths are from 20 to 150 feet. Boat access only.

☆☆☆☆ **Basora** is the easternmost dive site on Curaçao. Much like Piedra Pretu, the area is rich with huge brain and star corals and towering pillar formations. Sheets of star corals drape the wall. Fish include monster grouper, stingrays and morays.

☆☆☆ **Bullen Bay**, just north of the park, is an outstanding dive with a protected shallow area for snorkeling and a nice dropoff for diving. Yellow pencil corals and pretty white sea plumes highlight the reef. Average depth is 40 feet.

☆☆☆☆☆ **Klein Curaçao** (little Curaçao) is an uninhabited island about a two-hour boat ride east of Curaçao. It is a rugged strip of desolate volcanic rock which plunges into a most spectacular reef. A constant parade of scorpionfish, red-legged hermit crabs, yellow stingrays, spotted morays, yellow frogfish, eagle rays and huge turtles whistle by the wall. The shelf drops 100 feet into a blaze of orange elephant-ear sponges, purple tube and rope sponges, black corals, huge sea fans and massive boulder corals.

Beaches

Curaçao is surrounded by beautiful beaches, from popular hotel beaches to intimate secluded coves. Along the southern coast, there are free public beaches at **West Point Bay**, **Knip Bay**, **Klein Knip**, **Santa Cruz**, **Jeremi Bay** and **Daaibooi Bay**. Knip Bay is the largest and loveliest swimming beach on the island. Snorkeling is good along the adjacent cliffs.

The main private beaches, which charge a small fee per car, are **Blauw Bay**, **Jan Thiel**, **Cas Abao**, **Barbara Beach** and **Port Marie**.

Be careful of the tree with small green apples that borders some beaches. This is the *manzanilla*; its sap will cause burns and blisters on wet exposed skin. Its fruit is poisonous.

Dive Operators

Reef and wreck diving and snorkeling trips may be booked through the following operators. Most offer certification courses.

The Dolphin Academy at the **Curaçao Sea Aquarium** is the place for those who can't get enough of dolphins. They offer diving, snorkeling, swimming and just watching encounters with dolphins, www.dolphin-academy.com.

All West Diving & Adventures Curaçao at West Point Beach. Contact Hans & Bernardien v/d Eeden. ☎ 864-0102, fax 864-0107.

Aqua Diving, Grote Berg. Contact Arjan v/d Meule. ☎ 011-5999-864-9700, fax 864-9288.

Atlantis Diving, Drielstraat 6. Roland de Kneg, Manager. ☎ 465-8288, fax 465-8288.

Caribbean Sea Sports at the Curaçao Marriott beach on JFK Boulevard. ☎599-9-462-2620, wwwcaribseasports.com, ss@cura.net at the Marriott.

Seascape Curaçao , on the beach at the Curaçao Hilton Resor, has fast, comfortable, custom dive boats and friendly service. Snorkelers welcome. Manager, Eva Van Dalen. ☎ 462-5000, fax 462-5846.

Habitat Curaçao Dive Resort, Rif St. Marie. Albert Romijn, Manager. ☎ 800-327-6709 local 864-8800, www.habitatdiveresorts.com, cura-cao@madura.com, reservations@habitatcuracaoresort.com.

Scuba Do Dive Center, at Jan Thiel Beach & Sports Resorts. Contact H. Ferwerda. ☎ 767-9300, fax 767-9300.

Toucan diving Curaçao, a full-service PADI shop, sits on one of Curaçao's most beautiful beaches, at the Kontiki Beach Club next to "Mambo Beach". ☎ 465-3790, www.curacao-toucandiving.com.

Where to Stay

 All prices in US dollars

Breezes Curaçao, adjacent to the Undersea National Park and Sea Aquarium, features 341 rooms and suites. This all-inclusive resort boasts the largest casino on the island, three restaurants. **Pastafari** (Italian style), **Jimmy's Buffet** (continental & island dishes) and **Munahana** (Japanese cuisine), plus a beach grill and a children's snack bar. Besides on-site **Scuba One Dive Shop**, facilities include tennis courts, three swimming pools and beach volleyball, shuffleboard, bicycles, fitness center, Jacuzzis, and a spa.

Winter per-person rates for seven nights, based on a double, for an oceanview room start at $1,106; summer for a garden-view room from $988, oceanview, from 1057. Everything is included in the price except diving (add $35 per day, or $25 and up for shore diving); tipping is not allowed. Nitrox and helium are available. ☎ 877-467-8737, on island 925-0925, fax 954-925-0334, www.breezes.com.

Curaçao Marriott equips its 237 guest rooms with an in-room safe suitable for storing a laptop, high-speed Internet, air conditioning, alarm clock, coffee maker, individual climate control, iron and ironing board, down pillows, pull-out sofa bed, roll away bed, safe, bathroom with hair dryer, separate tub and shower room, cable/satellite TV, pay-per-view movies, wet bar and refrigerator. Amenities include restaurant, watersports center, casino, Winter room rates from $249; summer from $139. Diving and snorkeling excursions are with **Caribbean Sea Sports** on the resort's beach. All-inclusive rates available. ☎ 800-223-6388, local 736-8800 or 599-9-433-7753. http://marriott.com.

Habitat Curaçao, on the southwest coast in St. Marie, offers a pool, restaurant, satellite TV, tennis courts and a variety of watersports. Twenty-four-hour-a-day unlimited diving.

The resort sprawls over a private estate on Curaçao's southwest coast. Guest accommodations feature two queen beds, full air conditioning in bedroom, cable television, in-room safe, kitchenette, coffee-maker, toaster, bathroom and an outdoor balcony or lanai. In addition to the PADI Five Star IDC Dive Center, the resort has a beautiful pool, coral and sand beach where you can swim and snorkel. Internet access in the game room.

Porto Marie and Daaibooi beaches are next door. A complimentary shuttle bus runs into Willemstad three times per day or drops you at nearby **Blue Bay Golf Club**. On-site car rental. Bikers can rent a Harley Davidson, moped or bicycle and explore.

Habitat's house reef, **Nos Kas**, lies a few yards out from shore in front of the resort. Decent visibility and marine life on the reef make for terrific night diving. During September and October the reef blooms with spawning coral.

Easy Divers, a full-service PADI facility at Habitat, offers weekly dive/hotel packages in a garden- or ocean-view room, choice of three or six two-tank boat dives and six days of 24-hour unlimited shore diving, plus tanks and weights and weight belt, from $931 per person based on a double. ☎ 800-327-6709, ☎ 864-8800, reservations@habitatcuracao.com, www.habitatcuracao.com, info@maduro.com.

Hilton Curaçao, ten minutes from the airport and four miles from the sights of Willemstad, offers two private beaches, one with a shoreline walkway, a casino, an on-site PADI/SSI dive shop, free-form swimming pool, 196 guest rooms – many with ocean views – two restaurants, two bars, spa and fitness center, mini-golf course and adjacent casino.

Deluxe rooms feature 180° door viewer, air conditioning, alarm radio, balcony, bathroom, coffee maker, connecting rooms (on request), electronic locks, electronic smoke detector, hair dryer, iron and ironing board, safe deposit box, shower, telephone with auto wakeup, voice mail, and dataport, thumb, dead-bolt lock, cable TV. Dive/hotel package rates start at $175 per day, per person, three night minimum. ☎ 877-GO-HILTON, 599-9-462-5000, www.hiltoncaribbean.com/Curacao/index.htm.

The **Holiday Beach Hotel**, located on Coconut Beach facing Curaçao Underwater Park, is blessed with two coral reef sites off it's beach alive with sea rods, yellow sea plumes and lavendar sea fans. Marine life includes butterflyfish, surgeon, grunts, damsel and parrotfish. The 200-room hotel has a complete PADI dive shop, beach, casino, two restaurants, open-air bar, pool, satellite TV, tennis courts and meeting rooms. Handicapped facilities. Rooms are spacious and modern with air conditioning, wireless internet and safes. Room rates based on a double start at $200 per day including tax and service charges. PO Box 2178, Curaçao, N.A. US & Canada, ☎ 800-444-5244. Curaçao, 011-462-5400, fax 462-5409; dive shop, www.holidaybeachdivecenter.com.

The new **Lodge Kura Hulanda and Beach Club**, located on the Western End of of Curaçao near West Punt, features 74 villas, suites and guest rooms, most with kitchens. All suites and studios are luxuriously furnished with tile floors, remote-controlled air conditioning, large bath rooms with tubs and showers, remote-controlled cable TV, entertainment system with DVD player, in-room high-speed Internet access, personal safe and patio or balcony.

Resort amenities include a dive shop on premises, an open-air restaurant serving breakfast, lunch and dinner, cocktail bar overlooking the ocean, and a beach bar open for lunch, beautiful beach with soft white sand, a large pool and sun tan area. Located 30 minutes from the Curaçao Hato International Airport. Non-smoking and all-inclusive packages available. USA and Canada ☎ 877-264-3106, lodge direct 011-5999 434-7700, www.kurahulanda.com.

Lions Dive Hotel & Marina is a comfortable, 72-room, oceanfront dive complex adjacent to the Curaçao Seaquarium. Rooms overlook the Curaçao Marine Park and the *Oranje Nassau* shipwreck Rooms are air conditioned and have an ocean-view balcony or terrace. The resort features three restaurants, fitness center and dive shop.

Dive packages include daily two-tank boat dives and unlimited air for shore diving, and use of tank, weights, belt and locker for the days booked. Certification required. Note: Dive packages are non-transferable and non-refundable. Rooms can be garden-view, pool-view, street-view or ocean-view and are assigned on a first come first serve basis. For guaranteed ocean-view rooms, contact the resort. Meal plans available. ☎ 599 9-434-8888, fax 434-8889, www.lionsdive.com, info@lionsdive.com.

The Papagayo Beach Resort on Jan Thiel Bay on the south side of the island, features 75 spacious stand-alone bungalows in villa style with all the luxury you can stand. **Scuba Do Dive Center** is on the beach, in a colorful terraced building and a great view of the turquoise Caribbean Sea. The shop offers a variety of gear.

Just a stone's throw from the villas lies the white sandy beach and the crystal clear waters of Jan Thiel Bay. There is an open-air Moroccan-style restaurant on the beach serving fine meals and exotic drinks. The Jan Thiel Beach is free of charge for all the visitors of Papagayo Beach Resort. Rates per bungalow start at $240 per day for two, from $275 for three, $290 for four, $315 for five. US and Canada, ☎ 800-652-2962 or 954-919-0191, fax 954-919-0196, www.papagayo-beach.com.

Sunset Waters Beach Resort, on Curaçao's northwestern coastline sits 25 minutes from the airport and 35 minutes from downtown. The resort is known for its lovely snorkeling reef just offshore.

The resort features 70 guest rooms with one king-size or queen-size or two double beds, air conditioning, satellite color TV, and a full, private bathroom with shower. Most offer private balconies and superb ocean views. All but 16 rooms overlook the ocean. Adjoining rooms, one- and two-bedroom suites are available. **Sunset Divers**, on premises, is a PADI Five Star IDC training center and scuba tour company.

A seven-night dive package including six days of two-tank boat dives, unlimited shore diving, use of tanks and weights, meals, beverages, taxes, shuttle bus to Willemstad and airport transfers starts at $1,700 per person in winter. ☎ 866-578-6738, 599-9-864-1233 www.sunsetwaters.com, cory@sunsetwaters.com.

Other Activities

 The **Curaçao Golf and Squash Club**, near the office for the refinery, has a 9-hole golf course with unique and unusual oiled-sand greens. Stiff winds add to the challenge. Two squash courts are open all week. ☎ 737-3590.

Wherever there is wind and water you are sure to find windsurfing – a cross between sailing and surfing. The area of the **Spanish Water Bay** at the southeast end of the island is *the* spot for testing your board skills. If you haven't tried it before take a lesson from a pro. The basics can be learned within a few hours from a certified instructor. Experienced board sailors should head for the **Marie Pompoen Area** near the Seaquarium. The winds average 12-18 knots, and blow from left to right when facing the water. Check with your hotel's front desk for more information. Sailboards, Sunfish sailboats, and JetSkis are rented at most of the hotels' watersports centers.

Horseback riding the beach trails or through the *Kunucu* (countryside) can be arranged through the **Ashari Ranch** (☎ 869-0315) or **Rancho Alegre** (☎ 868-1181).

In addition to horseback riding, active travelers can jog along the special paved path at the Rif Recreation Area *Koredor*, a two-mile stretch of palm-lined beachfront about a mile from Willemstad's pontoon bridge.

Deep-sea-fishing charters complete with bait and tackle can be arranged for about $50 an hour for a party of four through the marinas at Spanish Water Bay or through the hotel watersports centers. Sport fishing is for marlin, tuna, wahoo and sailfish. Hook-and-line fishing is allowed in the underwater parks.

Sightseeing

Architecture is the big topside attraction in Curaçao. Walking tours of Willemstad and the surrounding countryside are offered by **Old City Tours**. Scheduled departures are on Tuesdays and Saturday at 9 am, with pick-up by jeep at your hotel. A variety of escorted tours for groups of four or more are offered by **Casper Tours**, **Blueangel Tours** and **Taber Tours**. Arrangements may be booked through most hotels. Taxi tours are about $15 per hour and take up to four passengers. Casper Tours, ☎ 465-3010; Blueangel Tours, ☎ 567-6770, www.blueangeltours.com; Taber Tours, ☎ 737-6673.

Many of the hotels offer a free shuttle van to and from Willemstad every half hour until evening. Traffic in town is busy and walking is the best way to see the town. The main town area (Punda) is safe for tourists, but there are occasional robberies. Avoid the long, narrow streets on the outskirts of town. One area is a government-sanctioned red-light district established to serve transient seamen and is best left unexplored.

In the 1700s, lavish homes and plantations, known as *landhuisen* or landhouses (estates), were built in the countryside. Government and private funds have assisted in the restoration of many of these homes, which now serve as museums, shops, restaurants and even the famous **Senior & Co. Curaçao Liqueur** factory.

Landhuis Jan Kock, built in 1650, on the road to Westpunt (near Daaibooi Bay), is one of the oldest buildings on the island. Said to be haunted, the *landhuis* was restored as a museum in 1960. On Sundays from 11 am to 6 pm, Dutch-style pancakes and local specialties are served. Nice gift shop.

Landhuis Brievengat, a Dutch version of the 18th-century West Indian plantation, was torn down and rebuilt. It now operates as a museum and cultural center, open daily from 9:30 am to 12:30 pm. It is located just north of Willemstad.

The beautifully restored 1700 ***Landhuis Ascension***, originally a plantation house, is a recreation center for Dutch marines stationed on the island. An open house featuring local music, handicrafts and refreshments is held on the first Sunday of the month.

Landhuis Habaai is the only remaining "Jewish Quarter" home built by early Sephardic settlers. Located in Otrobanda (St. Helena), the plantation home has an authentic cobbled courtyard.

Landhuis Chobolobois (Choboloba Estate) is home to the Senior & Co. Curaçao Liqueur factory, which distills and distributes the world-famous Curaçao liqueur using the original recipe and distilling equipment from the early 1900s.

The popular drink is the result of an agricultural mistake. When Spaniards landed on the island in the early 1500s, they planted hundreds of orange trees. The arid climate and sparse rainfall did not provide appropriate growing conditions for the citrus crop, and inedible, bitter fruit was produced. The settlers were not dismayed. They discovered that the orange peel, when dried in the sun, produced an aromatic oil which could be used to prepare a variety of drinks and foods. Today, the fruit is used to produce Curaçao liqueur. Visitors can tour the factory weekdays from 8 am to noon and 1 to 5 pm to view the process and sample the liqueur.

 The island's **Amstel Brewery** manufactures Amstel Beer – the only beer in the world brewed from distilled sea water. Tours available on Tuesday and Thursday at 10 am.

In downtown Willemstad, just a few minutes walk from the pontoon bridge, is a colorful floating market. Scores of schooners tie up alongside the canal offering fresh fish, tropical fruits, produce, and spices. Docked vessels arrive daily from Venezuela, Colombia and other West Indian islands. Park where you can and walk, as traffic is heavy and stopping on the narrow street is tough.

At the western end of the island is **Christoffel National Park** and Mt. Christoffel. A protected wildlife preserve and garden covering 4,500 acres of land, the park has been open to the public since 1978 and features 20 miles of one-way trails through fields of cactus, divi divi trees and exotic flowers. Wild iguanas, rabbits, donkeys, deer and more than 100 species of birds inhabit the preserve. If you love roller coasters, you will love the big rolling hills of this park. Drive slowly. Hiking trails are very rugged and should be traveled in the cool morning hours. The park is open Monday through Saturday.

Walking tours are popular and may be arranged, in advance, through most hotels. Jeeps and four-wheel-drive vehicles are available for rent.

 Boca Tabla is the site of a wonderful cave which opens to the sea. You walk the sand path to the cave entrance (signs lead the way) and climb down a path of huge boulders for a spectacular view of crashing waves into the cave entrance. Very photogenic! Because Curaçaons believe women make the ocean angry or more active, a woman may be asked to stay in the cave to liven up the attraction.

So strong is this belief that during a rescue operation off the north shore in 1992, a woman reporter was asked to leave the area so that male divers might do their job more easily.

An even more spectacular natural wonder is **Wata Mula**, a 30-foot-wide crater that tunnels to the open sea. Huge waves crash and recede rhythmically while spewing fountains of froth and rainbows high into the air. Both dramatic and mesmerising, it is a photo buff's delight. Take care if you are driving. The ground is sharp ironshore. The land meets the sea quite abruptly and without warning shoots straight down jagged cliffs into crashing waves. Plus, the area is badly littered with broken beer bottles.

You'll see 20-foot sharks, turtles as big as manhole covers, giant moray eels and more than 400 species of fish, crabs, turtles, anemones, sponges, corals and marine life at the **Curaçao Seaquarium**. A touch tank allows children to pick up starfish, sea urchins and other small sea animals. All species in the 75 hexagonal aquariums are native to the surrounding waters.

The Seaquarium complex also has two restaurants, a magnificent beach and gift shop. It's open daily from 10 am to 10 pm. Admission fee.

Other attractions include the **Arawak Clay Factory**, the **Curaçao Museum**, the **Hato Caves** near the Hotel Holland, the **Botanical Garden and Zoo**, and numerous old fortresses such as **Rif Fort**, **Fort Amsterdam** and **Fort Nassau.**

Dining

 With culinary influences from more than 40 countries, Curaçao offers a wide and wonderful variety of restaurant choices, including Dutch, Indonesian, Creole, Swiss, Chinese, French, South American, Indian, Italian and American cuisine. They range from casual eateries to gourmet restaurants, many with spectacular views. Popular fast-food eateries are scattered about the island. Local food is usually chicken, fish or meat in a thin sauce made of onions, peppers and tomatoes, with French fries or a biscuit-like pancake.

The **Golden Star Bar and Restaurant**, in town at Socratesstraat 2, is *the* place for goat stew and fungi or other local cuisine at low prices. Hamburgers, sate (skewered meat or fish), bacon and egg sandwiches, sailfish cakes, and fried chicken are on the menu too. Open for lunch and dinner. ☎ 54795 or 54865.

La Pergola, at Waterfort Arches in the Punda section of Willemstad, is a fine Italian restaurant with lovely views and excellent food. Local seafood, pasta, and steaks. Expensive, but a definite memorable treat. Reservations a must. ☎ 4613482. Ask for Simone.

Rumours at the Lion's Dive Hotel is open daily for breakfast, lunch and dinner and features meat dishes and fresh catches of the day. ☎461-7555.

For the charm of a typical Dutch coffee house with Creole and international dishes, try the **Bon Appetit Lunchroom** in the heart of Willemstad's shopping center, at Hanchi Snoa. ☎ 461-6916.

The Landuis Groot Davelaar houses the 18th-century **De Taveerne Restaurant & Wine Cellar**. An international lunch and dinner menu also features fine wine and cheeses. Closed Sunday. Reservations. ☎ 737-0669.

History buffs and romantics will love candlelight dining at the **Fort Nassau Restaurant**. The fort sits high over Willemstad with a 360° panoramic view of St. Anna Bay. Both the food and view are spectacular! Open daily from 7 to 11 pm and for lunch Monday to Friday from noon to 2 pm. Prices for lunch average $15 per person. Dinner entrées (à la carte) are from $22. ☎ 461-3086 or 461-3450.

Fine seafood, from Creole red snapper to Spanish specialties, such as paella mariner, are offered by **El Marinero Seafood** in Biesheuvel, at Schottergatweg Noord 87B. Reservations, ☎ 79833.

Fort Waakzaamheid Bistro is known for its BBQ salad bar and fresh seafood. In Otrobanda, at Berg Domi. ☎ 462-3633.

For downhome Antillean dishes, there is the **March** – an open-air restaurant where you can choose your lunch from dozens of Curaçaoan delicacies cooked up in giant pots. Low, low prices.

In West Punt, stop in at **Jaanchie's Restaurant** for conch stew, goat stew and fried or broiled fish. Located at Westpunt 15. ☎ 864-0126. This is a beautiful, open-air restaurant with a garden atmosphere. The work of local folk artists decorates the columns. Very casual, very charming, very special. Excellent local dishes. Average prices.

Fincamar at Lagoen K-27 at West Point is marked by a huge horse sculpture outside. This seafood restaurant is one of Curaçao's finest. The back wall is open to scenic views of West Point's towering cliffs. European atmosphere. Prices for dinner entrées start at $18 sans service charges. ☎ 864-1377.

Fast-food fans will find their fill at **Breedestraate** in Willemstad.

Facts

Helpful Phone Numbers: Police, ☎ 114. Taxi Service, ☎ 616711. Island Bus Service, ☎ 684733.

Nearest Recompression Chamber: St. Elisabeth Hospital, ☎ 624900 or 625100.

Getting Here: *Curaçao Hato International Airport* is served by **American Airlines**, **Delta**, **Air Jamaica**, **Continental**, **US Air** and **ATA** fly to Curaçao daily from Miami with connecting flights from major cities.

Driving: On the right. A US driver's license is accepted.

Car rentals: Budget, ☎ 683198; National, ☎ 683489 or 611644; Jeep Car Rental, ☎ 379044; Love Car Rental, ☎ 690444; 24-Hour Car Rental, ☎ 689410 or 617568. Curaçao also has an excellent bus system to transport visitors around the island.

Language: The official language is Dutch, but English and Spanish are spoken as well. Most residents speak Papiamento, a blend of Portuguese, Dutch, African, English, French and some Arawak Indian.

Entry Requirements: US and Canadian citizens need either a valid passport, or proof of citizenship in the form of an original birth certificate accompanied by photo ID, and an onward or return ticket. Most other nationals need only a passport. Visitors from the Dominican Republic, Colombia and Haiti require a visa. You will need to apply for a resident permit if you plan to stay for longer than three months. You are not allowed to work or live on Curaçao without a work permit. A passport or birth certificate and photo ID is necessary for reentering the US.

Customs: Arriving passengers may bring in 400 cigarettes, 50 cigars, 100 cigarillos, 2 liters of liquor. There is a duty-free shop at the airport.

Visitors should generally not have a problem bringing items for personal use and gifts into Curaçao. Prescription drugs, particularly if they contain narcotics, should be clearly marked. Possession of even a small amount of marijuana or other illegal drug is a serious offense. If you are traveling with expensive jewelry, cameras or electronics you may want to bring proof of purchase to avoid paying duties on it when you return home.

US residents may bring home, free of duty, $400 worth of articles, including 200 cigarettes, and 1 quart of liquor per person over 21 years of age plus $25 worth of Edam or Gouda cheese for personal use.

Airport Tax: For international flights, $22; for inter-island flights, $6.65.

Currency: The florin, or guilder, is the Netherlands Antilles' unit of money. The official rate of exchange is US$1=NAf 1.77 (variable). However, US dollars and major credit cards are accepted throughout the island.

Climate: Curaçao's tropical climate remains fairly constant year round. The average temperature is 80°F and less than 23 inches of rain fall annually. The island is outside of the hurricane belt and its cooling trade winds average 15 mph.

Clothing: Snorkelers should bring wetskins or long-sleeve shirts to protect from the sun. Wetsuits are comfortable when making several deep dives, but warm ocean temperatures make them unnecessary baggage for the average sport diver. Topside dress is casual, lightweight. Topless sunbathing is practiced on some beaches. Jackets are required for a few restaurants.

Cruise Lines: Air Tours/Sun Cruise, Deutsche Sectouristik, Carnival Cruises, Holland America, Princess Cruises, Norwegian Cruise Line, Royal Caribbean Cruise Line, Royal Cruise Line.

Electricity: 110-128 volts, AC (50 HZ), which is compatible with American electric razors and blow dryers. Adaptors are not needed.

Religious Services: Protestant, Catholic, Jewish, Episcopal.

Additional Information: *Curaçao Tourist Board*, www.curacao.com. *In US*, 3361 SW Third Avenue, Suite 102, Miami FL 33145, ☎ 800-3-CURACAO (800-328-7222), northamerica@curacao.com. *In Curaçao*, Curaçao Tourism Board Curaçao, Pietermaai 19, PO Box 3266, Curaçao, Netherlands Antilles; ☎ 599-9-434-8200, fax 599-9-461-2305, info@ctdb.com.

Dominica

Dominica, (pronounced Dom-in-ee-ka) is located in the Eastern Caribbean, north of Martinique and south of Guadeloupe, 375 miles southeast of San Juan, Puerto Rico. It lies between the Caribbean Sea and the North Atlantic Ocean. Covering 290 square miles, it is the largest island in the Windward chain, mountainous with sheer cliffs on the coasts and volcanic peaks inland. Narrow strips of grey sand skirt much of its perimeter. It's ideal for the diver who craves a wilderness adventure – there are no casinos, and no duty-free shopping.

Intrepid travelers are lured by the island's sensuous environment and dramatic scenery, both topside and beneath the sea. Its mountainside trails throb with the colors and scents of wild orchids and teas, heliconias, giant ferns, and fruit trees. Cascading waterfalls and wild rivers harmonize with the sounds of exotic parrots and seabirds. Mountain pools simmer from the volcanos seething beneath them. Hillsides, dotted with tiny villages and the ruins of forts and former plantations, climb toward **Morne Diablotin**, the island's tallest peak, with an elevation of 4,747 feet.

Subsea terrain, too, is spectacular, with hot springs bubbling up through the sea floor, and shallow wrecks, caves, ledges and walls of critters. Black coral "trees" thrive in water as shallow as 50 feet.

The island's economic mainstay is agriculture, with abundant banana and coconut crops. But the island's most outstanding feature is water. There are more than 365 rivers, thermal springs, pools, and waterfalls fed by 350 inches of rainfall per year in the interior and 50 inches on the drier west coast. Thankfully, all of the resorts and dive sites lie off the "dry" western shores.

Most of the 84,000 inhabitants live on the coasts, but 3,700 acres in the northeastern section of Dominica are set aside for the Carib Indian, the island's original inhabitants. The Caribs are fishermen and farmers, canoe builders, basket makers and carvers.

Roseau, the capital and main city, is built on a flat plain of the Roseau River. It is a busy area which may be seen in its entirety by way of a half-hour walk. Most interesting are some old French-colonial buildings, botanical gardens at the south end and the Old Market on the waterfront where island crafts are offered.

Visitors arriving by cruise ship at the **Cabrits National Park**, on the northwest tip of Dominica, step off the 300-foot pier and are immediately surrounded by twin waterfalls and a lush garden.

When to Go

The best time to dive Dominica is during the driest season, February through April, though expect the possibility of "liquid sunshine" (rain) all year. Whenever you go, plan on doing combat with a ferocious mosquito population, especially at dawn and dusk.

History

 Dominica means Sunday in Latin (*Dies Dominica*, day of the Lord). The island was named by Columbus for the Sunday he discovered it, November 3, 1493. It is also called *Waitukubuli* by the Carib Indians, which is translated by some to mean "tall is her body," and by others to mean "land of many battles."

Dominica as first assigned to the Carib Indians in 1660 by an Anglo-French treaty, but later French settlers moved in and established sugar plantations worked by imported black labor, which stirred friction between the Caribs, the Brits and the French. Hence, possession passed back and forth between France and Britain during the 18th century. The island gained independence in 1978.

Best Dive & Snorkeling Sites

 In Dominica, underwater tunnels teaming with schooling fish lead to vertical walls and lava pinnacles are found side-by-side with rich shallow reefs. Offering one of the healthiest reefs in the Caribbean, a diversity of coral and marine life, underwater visibility ranging up to 100 feet, a varied underwater terrain, and a number of full-service dive operators offering equipment and excursions for divers of all skill levels, it's easy to see why Dominica can usually be found at or near the top of lists of the world's top dive destinations.

Underwater terrain is made up of solid rock encrusted with corals, sponges and other forms of marine life. Because the bottom terrain is dense, little space is left for fish to hide, making Dominica one of the best fish-watching locations (seahorses and frogfish can be spotted on a daily basis!).

Most sites are close to shore, on the southwest, central west and northwest coasts. Located at the southwest tip of the island is the **Soufriere-Scott's Head Marine Reserve** (SSMR), which was established in the late 1990s to ensure conservation of the surrounding area, and has some of the island's most dramatic dive sites. It is a picturesque bay, and it's home to **Scott's Head**, a peninsula that separates the calmer Caribbean Sea from the more

Dominica

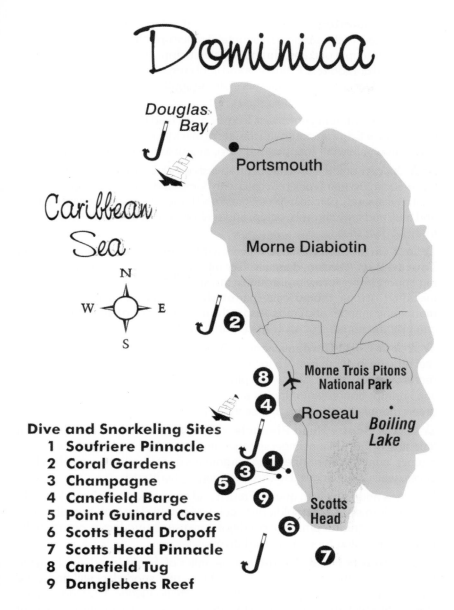

Douglas Bay

Portsmouth

Caribbean Sea

Morne Diabiotin

N

W ──◇── E

S

Morne Trois Pitons National Park

Roseau

Boiling Lake

Scotts Head

Dive and Snorkeling Sites
1 **Soufriere Pinnacle**
2 **Coral Gardens**
3 **Champagne**
4 **Canefield Barge**
5 **Point Guinard Caves**
6 **Scotts Head Dropoff**
7 **Scotts Head Pinnacle**
8 **Canefield Tug**
9 **Danglebens Reef**

turbulent Atlantic Ocean. A gigantic and extinct volcanic crater, at points plummeting to depths immeasurable while at other points falling just below the surface of the water, is located northwest of Scott's Head; here, divers will find mooring bouys for dive boats marking the sites.

☆☆☆☆ **Soufriere Pinnacle** rises from the depths of Soufriere Bay to within five feet of the surface. A favorite of macro-photographers, the pinnacle is a cornucopia of crabs, shrimp, lobster, octopi, anemones, starfish, tree worms, and gorgonians. Calm seas and light currents invite all levels of divers and snorkelers. The site is four miles off the southwest shore – a 15-minute boat ride.

☆☆☆☆ Continuing northwest from Scott's Head Pinnacle divers will find the **Crater's Edge** teaming with masses of black jack, bar jacks, rainbow runners, tuna, yellowtail snapper and cero, all pursuing schools of baitfish.

☆☆☆☆ A notable site on the central west coast is **Rodney's Rock.** A shallow dive amidst giant rocks covered with corals and sponges, divers will find mini caves, sandy patches with seagrass and large schools of sergeant majors, and blue and grey chromis, octopi and seahorses. In this area there are more than 12 dive sites.

☆☆☆ On the northwest coast divers will find more than 10 sites including **Toucari Bay.** A secluded area with coral covered rocks and tunnels providing opportunities for swim-throughs; this site boasts a wide variety of sea life including octopi, moray eels, parrotfish and schools of French grunts, mahogany snapper and crabs. Also in the northwest at **Cottage Point** divers can visit the remains of an 18th-century wreck.

☆☆☆☆ **Coral Gardens**, a short trip from Castaways Beach, is a shallow reef ranging in depth from 15 to 90 feet. Good for diving and snorkeling, the reef is vibrant with corkscrew and pink anemones, arrow crabs, violet Peterson shrimp, flourescent crinoids and flamingo tongue snails. Spotted and green moray eels,stingrays and scorpionfish hide in the shadows.

☆☆☆☆ **Scotts Head Pinnacle,** off the southwest tip of the island, is a kaleidoscope of brilliant finger sponges, nudibranches, bushy wire corals, sea plumes, crinoids, anemones, and gorgonians over a vertical maze of arches, caves, walls, and ledges. Beware the stinging hydroids!

Fish life is abundant with queen, French and gray angels, mackerel, kingfish, spotted drums, blackbar soldierfish, eels and octopi. The reef starts at 15 feet and drops to great depths. Sea conditions are usually moderate, occasionally rough. Suggested for experienced divers.

☆☆☆ **Scotts Head Dropoff** lies five miles off Scotts Head, a fishing village at the southern tip of the island. Divers and snorkelers will find large sponges and lavish soft corals along the reef's shallow ledge. The ledge, which starts at five feet, runs along a wall that drops to 140 feet. Conditions are light to moderate. Good visibility.

☆☆ **Champagne** is a shallow site highlighted by sub-aquatic freshwater hot springs that emit a continuous profusion of hot bubbles. A fun dive, it's like jumping into a giant glass of club soda. Near shore with dependably calm conditions, the site covers an area of about 300 square feet. Depths range from near the surface to 80 feet, with 10 feet the average. The bottom is uninspiring brown weeds ruffled by schools of tiny sprat, reef fish and lobster. Dive or snorkel.

☆☆☆ **Canefield Tug** is a 60-foot wreck lying upright on a sandy bottom. The wreck is intact and acts as an artificial reef attracting colonies of hydroids, anemones, schools of squirrelfish, soldierfish and sergeant majors. The site is four miles from shore at Rivermouth. Visibility and sea conditions vary. Depths are from 55 to 90 feet.

☆☆☆ **Canefield Barge** is an overturned barge over patches of shallow reef. Depths of five to 40 feet and calm seas make this a good choice for snorkelers and divers. A bevy of small reef fish hover about the wreck. The bottom is vibrant with basket stars, anemones, hydroids and iridescent sponges.

☆☆☆ **Point Guinard Caves**, an area of shallow reefs, grottoes and caves, are fun for all level divers and snorkelers. The Caves at 50 feet may be penetrated at 30 feet, but there is rich coral growth in the shallows. It is a great spot for night dives and macro-photography, with seahorses, blood stars, octopi, crabs, lobster and hordes of sponges.

☆☆☆☆ **Danglebens Reef**, named for one of the dive master's ancestors, is a complex of small pinnacles and canyons ending in a deep wall. Average reef depths are 40 to 120 feet. Large barrel and tube sponges, healthy corals, black coral bushes, big grouper and morays delight all level of divers. Excellent visibility. Sea conditions are light.

Shore Snorkeling

The best shore-entry snorkeling spots are **Scotts Head** on Soufriere Bay in the southwest, and **Douglas Bay** in the northwest, which has a reef less than 200 feet from the shore. **Point Guignard** off the southwest coast is another popular spot. On the north and northeast coasts try **Woodford Hill Bay**, **Hodges Bay**, **Grand Baptiste Bay** and **Hampstead Beach**. Check with dive shops for wind and water conditions before snorkeling.

Dive Operators

Dive Dominica at Castle Comfort Lodge is a full-service dive center. Boats depart at 9:30 for a two-tank trip. Refreshments on board. Friendly staff will wash, rinse and store all of your gear and return it to the boat for the next dive. Shore diving in front of the lodge. ☎ 767-448-7188, fax 767-448-6088, www.castlecomfortdivelodge.dm. divr@cwdom.dm.

Dive Castaways features personal tours to their own special sites. ☎ 767-449-6244. Dive/hotel packages from $925, www.castawaysdominica.com, divecastaways@cwdom.dm.

East Carib Dive sits on the beach at Salibury, about 12.5 miles (20 kms) from Roseau, center of the west coast. The shop offers PADI courses, daily trips to Scott's Head, night dives, two-tank boat dives am or pm, and snorkeling trips to Rodney's Rocks. **Howard's Deco Bar**, on the premises sells snacks. ☎ 767-449-6575, http://eastcaribdive.free.fr/en/ecd/index.php Write PO Box 375, Roseau, Dominica.

Nature Island Dive caters to small groups with a variety of water and landsports including kayaking and mountain biking. Dive boats visit Soufriere, Scotts Head Reserve and local reefs. The shop is located in the heart of the Soufriere-Scotts Head Marine Reserve, on Soufriere Bay. Boats trips to 20 terrific dive sites in the bay take less than 10 minutes. The bay also offers a calm and beautiful setting for various kayaking excursions. ☎ 767-449-8181, fax 767-449-8182, www.natureislanddive.com, natureidive@cwdom.dm.

Where to Stay

 Castle Comfort Diving Lodge is a cozy 15-room dive hotel. Five rooms have ocean-view balconies. All are air conditioned and have ceiling fans. Great meals! Friendly service. Six-night dive packages with **Dive Dominica** run from $930 and include breakfast and dinner daily, service charge and taxes, four days of two-tank boat dives, round-trip airport transfers, unlimited shore dives 24/7 (off dock), tanks, weights and weight belt and a welcome rum punch upon arrival. Oceanfront pool, hot tub, bar and grill. Sites are about 25 minutes from the lodge. Boats depart at 9:30 am. ☎ 888-414-7626 or on island 767-448-2188, www.castlecomfortdive.com, dive@cwdom.dm.www.

The **Fort Young Hotel** is a lovely hotel within the walls of the original fort built in 1770. High on a cliff overlooking the Caribbean, the hotel features 53 air-conditioned guest rooms and suites with sweeping views of the sea via terrace or balcony, cable TV, direct-dial phones. Property has a restaurant and bar, pool and is in walking proximity of the city. Nice atmosphere. Dive packages are offered with **Dive Dominica** from $950 per person, based on a double. Dive package includes room, full breakfast daily, all taxes and service charges, round-trip airport transfers, two-tank boat-dive per day, site user fees and welcome rum punch. ☎ 800-525-3833 or 767-448-5000, fax 767-448-5006, www.fortyounghotel.com.

The Castaways Beach Hotel, a clean and updated 27-room waterfront resort surrounded by awesome botanical gardens. Choose from Caribbean-style cottages or a deluxe beachfront room with ceiling fan and air condition-ing. Adjacent **Dive Castaways** dive shop offers personalized service with six or fewer divers per boat. Room rates start at $160 per day. Cottages from $1,500 per week including maid service (two days), utilities and water. Creole snacks, drinks and international cuisine are served at the resort's **Almond Tree** restaurant, **Rhum Barrel Bar** and **Castaways Beach Bar**. The Almond Tree and Rhum Barrel offer spectacular views of the ocean and sun-set, and tropical drinks blended with spices and flavors of produce grown in Dominica. Dive and snorkeling sites in the west-central coastal area of Domi-nica lie directly off Castaways, less than a 10-minute boat ride from the jetty. These sites are pristine with hordes of fish and critters, and frequented only by small groups. Opposite the beachfront of the hotel lie three dive sites: **Maggie's Point**, a spot overflowing with bright yellow pencil coral; **Castaways Reef**; and **Berry's Dream**. US and Canada ☎ 888-CASTAWAYS, 767-449-6245, www.castaways-dominica.com, enquirys@castaways-dominica.com.

Dining

Local specialties include frog's legs (mountain chicken), stuffed land crab backs, callaloo soup – made from dasheen leaves and coconut cream – and spicy freshwater shrimps. Manicou, a rodent similar to an opossum, is a local favorite that sometimes turns up on restaurant menus. Restaurants in Roseau serve more familiar dishes, too.

Corner House, in Roseau, offers homemade bagels, locally roasted coffee, local dishes and Internet access. Casual. Open for breakfast, lunch & dinner. Monday, 8 am-3:30 pm; Tuesday-Friday, 8 am-4 pm; closed Saturday and Sunday. ☎ 767-449-9000.

Coconut Beach Hotel Restaurant on the beach near Portsmouth over-looks the Caribbean Sea and the twin peaks of Cabrits National Park across Prince Rupert Bay. Specializing in tasty local Creole cooking. $10-$35. 8 am-11 pm, ☎ 767-445-5393/5415, fax 767-445-5693, www.coconut-beachhotel.com.

Cartwheel Café, a popular breakfast and lunch eatery sits bay-front in downtown Roseau. ☎ 767-448-5353.

Calalloo Restaurant in Roseau serves calalloo soup and other specials including lobster, crayfish and mountain chicken. Bananas flambé is one of their delicious desserts. ☎ 767-448-3386.

Perky's Pizza serves tasty pies daily, Monday-Thursday 9 am-11 pm, Friday-Saturday 9 am-midnight, Sunday 10 am-11 pm. ☎ 767-448-1268.

Sightseeing & Other Activities

As in all high-altitude areas, be sure to figure strenuous and high-altitude climbs into your dive tables. More than one person has suffered decompression sickness from the combination.

Besides diving, activities include hiking, canoeing, guided jungle-river tours and rain forest tours. A new coastal road rings the island. Resorts offer wind-surfing, water-skiing, sailing and tennis.

 To get an "overview" of the island, take a trip on the island's 4,600-foot-long **Rainforest Aerial Tram**, which offers a breathtaking and scenic 70-minute journey over the dense rain forest.

The favorite topside wonder is **Trafalgar Falls**, just north of Roseau. You can drive to within a 15-minute walk of the 100-foot falls, which converge into a lovely pool of granite boulders.

Scotts Head, at the southwest tip of the island, is a picturesque fishing village offering scenic views of the Atlantic Ocean and Caribbean Sea. It is also the site of the region's first aloe farm.

Heading north, turn left at the village of Soufriere to reach **Sulfur Springs**, where you can see bubbling hot springs of grey mud. Or if you enjoy long hikes, head for **Valley of Desolation** and **Boiling Lake**, east of Roseau, where the scenery is absolutely intoxicating.

 Emerald Pool in the **Central Forest Reserve** is a short hike from the road on the northeast side of **Morne Trois Pitons National Park.** Located in the rain forest, the pool is fed by a lovely waterfall.

Boat tours of **Indian River** will bring you close up to exotic birds and plants. Or take the cross-island road to the **Carib Reserve** on the central eastern coast. Native craft shops pave the way. Tours in this region take off from **The Floral Gardens**, ☎ 445-7636, situated at the base of the tropical rain forest bordering the Carib Reserve.

Souvenir shoppers seeking island crafts should head for the craft stalls in **Roseau's Old Market**, located in the courtyard behind the post.

Facts

Helpful Phone Numbers: Police, ☎ 999; ambulance, ☎ 999; Tourist Board, ☎ 767-448-2351/82186; Canefield Airport ☎ 767-449-1199.

Nearest Recompression Chamber: None within a reasonable distance.

Airlines: Dominica has two airports: *Melville Hall* and *Canefield*. Melville Hall is located in the northeast, 32 miles from Roseau, the capital city; Canefield

Airport is located in the southwest, three miles from Roseau. Flights from the US with connections on international and local carriers are readily available via Puerto Rico, St. Maarten, St. Lucia, Antigua, Barbados, Guadeloupe and Martinique. Dominica is served by **American Airlines/American Eagle, Caribbean Star, LIAT** and **Coastal**. There are no direct flights.

Baggage: Only one carry-on bag is permitted and it must fit under your seat. International baggage allowances prevail on flights to Dominica and may not exceed a total of 44 pounds. Baggage in excess of 44 pounds will be charged (depending upon the carrier) around US$1 per pound and flown on a "space available" basis.

Ferries: Passengers can get to Dominica daily by ferry from neighboring Guadeloupe and Martinique. The ferries dock at the Ferry Terminal in Roseau.

Island Transportation: is readily available in the form of local buses that run regularly along the coast between Roseau and both Scott's Head and Portsmouth. Fares are set by the government. Taxis are also readily available (look for license plates that begin with H). Fares are not set (except from the airports to Roseau), so negotiate before departing.

Car Rental/Driving: Driving is on the left side of the road. For a small fee (US$12) drivers can get the required local driver's license from immigration at the airports or at the Traffic Department, High Street, Roseau (Monday to Friday). Must be between ages 25 to 65 and show a valid driver's license with at least two years experience. Car rental companies include Avis, Budget, and a number of local agencies. Primary roads are well paved and clearly marked with signs.

Documents: A valid passport and onward/return ticket are required for stays of up to 21 days.

Customs: Banana, coconut, plants and straw materials cannot be brought in. Citrus, coffee, avocado, plants and soil are forbidden.

Currency: The currency is the Eastern Caribbean Dollar: EC$2.67=US$1 (variable). US dollars are widely accepted by shops, restaurants and taxi drivers. Most hotels, car rental agencies, dive shops, tour operators and restaurants accept MasterCard, Visa and American Express cards.

Language: English is the official language; French-based Creole (kwéyòl) is widely spoken, especially in outlying villages.

Climate: Temperatures drop and the chance of showers rises with the elevation. The coolest months are December through March. Temperatures can vary widely depending on location. On the coast high temperatures range from 85 to 90°F (29 to 32°C), while the lows range from 68 to 72°F (20 to 22°C). Conditions in the mountains tend to be cooler and wetter. Rainfall patterns vary and are dependent on location as well. Rainfall in the interior, in the rain forests, can be as high as 300 inches per year with the wettest months being July to November and the driest being February to May. Inland rainfall is more moderate with February to June being the driest months.

Clothing: Lightweight casual cottons are best. Visitors should *not* wear swim suits or short shorts in the streets or stores. A light sweater is suggested for cooler evenings. Pack light, the island is not dressy.

For hiking, bring comfortable hiking shoes, light weight raincoat, camera and film, knapsack and shoulder bag, bottled water, hat, sunglasses, sun screen and mosquito repellent.

The water temperature on a deep dive may drop as low as 72°F. Baggage permitting, a shorty or wetsuit jacket is recommended.

Electricity: 220/240 volts, 50 cycles. A converter is necessary for US appliances.

Time: Atlantic Standard Time, one hour ahead of Eastern Standard Time and four hours behind GMT.

Valuables: Lock everything up as you would at home. Avoid taking valuables to the beach.

Departure Tax: US$12.

Religious Services: Roman Catholic, Anglican, Methodist, Pentecostal, Berean Bible, Baptist, Seventh Day Adventist and Baha'i Faith.

Additional Information: contact the *Dominica Tourist Office* in New York, ☎ 888-645-5637, or visit Dominica's official Website at www.dominica.dm.

Dominican Republic

The Dominican Republic shares the Caribbean's second-largest island, **Hispaniola** (between Cuba and Puerto Rico), with Haiti. Located on the eastern half of the island, the Dominican Republic, with an area of 19,376 square miles, is flanked by the Atlantic Ocean to the north and the Caribbean Sea to the south. Its central portion is sculpted by four great mountain ranges with peaks over 10,000 feet. Its coastline varies from rocky cliffs to sandy beaches. Reefs and ancient wrecks surround much of the shoreline.

Santo Domingo, on the south Caribbean coast and eastern bank of the Ozama River, is the main port and capital city. Home to more than one million people, it is the oldest city of the New World and professed burial place of its founder, Christopher Columbus. Built in the early 1500s, the city was the first hub of Spanish culture and commerce in the western hemisphere.

One section of the capital, about 15 city blocks, has been restored as "Old Santo Domingo," and includes the castle of **Diego Colon**, Columbus' son and the island's first viceroy. The 22-room castle has been tastefully refurbished with paintings and tapestries to reflect the 16th century. Colonial-style shops, galleries and restaurants surround the old city's central plaza. When touring Santo Domingo expect solicitations from countless beggars and youthful entrepreneurs pushing shoe shines and other services.

The main city area is very cosmopolitan and tourist-oriented, with 3,498 hotel rooms, several casinos, shopping malls, nightclubs and restaurants. The city boasts the New World's first cathedral, first university (**Santo Tomás de Aquino**), first hospital (**San Nicolas de Bari**), the **Monastery of San Francisco**, the **Ozama Fortress** and the world's largest open-air discotheque along its shoreline drive, the **Malecón**.

Boca Chica, 31 miles east of Santo Domingo; **La Romana**, 110 miles east of Santo Domingo; and **Bayahibe**, 125 miles east of Santo Domingo, are the jumping-off points for the country's best Caribbean dive and snorkeling sites, including **La Caleta National Park** and the **Eastern National Park** (***Parque Nacional del Este***), which encompasses the islands of **Saona** and **Catalina**. The marine portion of the parks is a sanctuary for manatees, turtles and pods of passing dolphins. Dependably calm seas and miles of virgin reefs prevail.

Dive-material contributor: Walter Frischbutter, Treasure Divers.

Costa Caribe, just west of Boca Chica, is the chief weekend playground for Santo Domingo's million residents. Formerly known as the fishing villages of **Juan Dolio** and **Guayacanes**, this beautiful stretch has more than 15 miles of uninterrupted beaches shaded by coconut palms and serviced by first class hotels. It is a half-hour drive from the Las Americas International Airport and under an hour from Santo Domingo. Given the proximity to the capital this area draws crowds on weekends.

On the north coast, the main tourist area stretches from **Puerto Plata**, a large city and deep-water port, to **Cabrera**, where impressive beaches and coconut groves have lured Europeans for more than 500 years. This area is also a prime whale-watching spot. During winter months (December to March) thousands of humpback whales migrate to an offshore breeding ground. The breeding ground is 50 miles north of the coast, but the herds are spotted en route as they pass the Samana Peninsula, which forms the northeast corner of the Dominican Republic. Reefs and wrecks dot the northern shores, but rough seas frequently rule out diving except during summer. Large, modern, upscale resorts skyline the area.

The country's southwest region is the least developed. It is the locale of the largest lake in the Caribbean, **Lake Enriquillo**, which has water three times more saline than the ocean, and where the largest **American crocodile** colony of the New World resides.

Mosquitos readily announce their presence throughout the coastal areas. Bring and use repellent. We find Autan (sold in the Caribbean) and Off Deep Woods useful. Autan, if you can find it, is the best defense against the tiny gnats or no-see-ums that come out after a rainfall.

The best weather and the fewest mosquitos exist from mid December through April, but divers may prefer the summer months when the water is warmer and calmer seas prevail on the north and east coasts. When the skies cooperate, diving along the Caribbean's southeast coast is good year-round.

History

Christopher Columbus discovered the island of Hispaniola in December, 1492 when his flagship, *Santa Maria*, ran aground on what is now Haiti's north coast. Thirty-nine crewmen who were left behind started the first Spanish settlement in the New World, La Navidad. But, when Columbus returned a year later, the settlement had been destroyed and all the crewmen killed.

Late in 1493, Columbus established a new colony at Isabela, near Puerto Plata, but abandoned the site for a better harbor on the south coast, now known as Santo Domingo (originally Santiago de Guzman). Columbus' son Diego was appointed viceroy, and Hispaniola became the hub of Spanish culture and commerce in the New World. From there the Spanish colonizers moved on to exploit Mexico and Peru.

French, Dutch and English explorers settled various parts of Hispaniola during the 1500s and 1600s. As the Spanish settlers congregated around Santo Domingo, the north and west coasts were left to buccaneers and foreign settlers who eventually came under the protection of France. In 1697 Spain recognized France's claims to the western third of the island.

The French colony, first known as Saint Domingue, and later as **Haiti**, prospered while the Spanish colony declined. By 1795, Spanish Hispaniola was ceded to France. By 1844, Juan Pablo Duarte established the Dominican Republic as an independent nation, but the nation, under constant Haitian threat, asked Spain to reinstate its sovereignty. Fighting between Spain and Haiti continued until 1865 when a strong-willed military dictator, Ulises Heureaux, took over. Heureaux was in power until 1897 when he was assassinated.

The early 1900s brought intercession by the US. American occupation brought military rule and economic exploitation by US businesses. The Dominicans resented the US military troops and forced their evacuation in 1924.

From 1930 to 1961, the island was ruled by Dominican military dictator **Rafael Leonidas Trujillo Molina**. Trujillo's corrupt form of government left no citizen safe from arrest or degradation by his secret police. Despite the misery he brought upon the people, Trujillo modernized and rebuilt highways, sugar, coffee and cocoa plantations, and by 1947, paid off all of the nation's foreign debts. On May 30, 1961, he was assassinated by his army.

With Trujillo's death, the Dominican Republic attempted to establish a democracy. In 1962, the country held its first free election in 38 years and elected **Juan Bosch**, a writer and professor. The new government, plagued by unrest and agitation from the upper class and military, fell to national unrest in a bloodless coup. The US, alarmed at reports of communist influence, stepped in. Military command was then turned over to an Inter-American Peace Force.

Since then, the Dominican Republic struggled through the 1970s' worldwide recession, which touched off a crisis in the sugar industry; then a 1979 hurricane, which devastated much of the island; and social unrest fueled by crowded cities. The 1980s brought rising foreign debt and inflation.

With its continued struggle for a better quality of life, the Dominican Republic remains at peace; its golden beaches flaunt the promise of a new era of tourism.

Dive and Snorkeling Sites
1 Wreck of the *Hickory*
2 Wreck of the *Capitan Alcina*
3 Isla Catalina
4 Isla Saona
5 Punta Cana reefs
6 Puerto Plata reefs

Best Dive & Snorkeling Sites

The best dive and snorkeling sights are off **Boca Chica**, 30 miles east of Santa Domingo, and the marine portion of the **Eastern National Park** (***Parque Nacional del Este***) off Bayahibe, 110 miles east of Santo Domingo. Both marine parks, less than a mile from the shore, display healthy corals in all but the extreme shallows. Large fish are rare, but on the return as sport fishing is big and reef preservation is new to Santo Domingo. New laws prohibiting spear fishing and coral collecting in the sanctuary have brought back a decent population of tropicals. Visibility runs 60 to 100 feet.

Parque Nacional del Este was declared a protected area in September 1975. Its protected areas include coral reefs, sea grass beds, mangrove forests, beaches, moist and dry subtropical forests and salt-tolerant plant areas.

There are also several good dive sites in **La Caleta** and along the reefs that start 1½ miles out from **La Romana** and follow the coast past Bayahibe, a small fishing village, to **Isla Catalina** and **Isla Saona**. Reef depths range from the shallows to 150 feet, with most dives taking place between 30 and

100 feet. Dive and snorkeling boats leave from the marinas at Boca Chica, La Romana and Bayahibe.

Another highlight in front of Bayahibe is the wreck of the **Saint George**, a freighter resting at 120 feet, scuttled to create an artificial reef.

 ☆☆☆☆ **Isla Catalina** is an uninhabited islet, 2½ miles off La Romana, which was once used as a zoo. Exotic wild birds and monkeys are often sighted along its beaches. The island, surrounded by beautiful reefs that start at 15 feet and drop to 110, is ideal for snorkelers and all levels of divers. The reef, protected from spear fishing and coral collecting, flourishes with walls of tropicals, lobster, sea fans, sea rods, big barrel sponges and black corals at depth. Seas are calm with an occasional light current. Visibility is excellent, though the shallows get kicked up when several snorkeling boats anchor at the same time. Scuttled to give an artificial reef the 240 ft steel freighter stands upright in the sand providing a new home for the marine life. Depths to 120 feet.

The best spot off Catalina Island for diving and snorkeling is **The Wall**, a reef area that starts shallow and drops to 300-foot depths. Expect to see black corals at about 75 feet. Hordes of fish dart in and around stands of elkhorn and staghorn. Terrific snorkeling lies between six and 15 feet.

There are no facilities or fresh water on the island but, for the adventurous among you, camping is possible if permission is obtained from La Romana Naval Station in advance. You need to bring everything with you. At dusk you will be joined by a ferocious mosquito population. Wear and carry as much bug repellent as you can.

☆☆☆ **The Hickory** is a 140-foot wreck intentionally scuttled in the shallows of **La Caleta National Marine Park** off La Caleta Beach. Remains of the wreck are found between three and 60 feet. The wreck is covered with anemones, hydroids, and lots of reef fis, including squirrelfish, sergeant majors, and spotted drums. It is surrounded by a pretty reef. Calm seas and 100-foot-plus visibility make this spot good for divers and snorkelers.

☆☆☆ **Wreck of the *Capitan Alcina*** is another ship purposely sunk in La Caleta National Park to attract fish. The wreck sits in a ravine between canyons of the reef. You can reach the top at 75 feet, the bottom at 126 feet. Expect a good reef-fish population, with pillar corals, big brain corals, sea rods, plumes, sea fans and deep-water gorgonians. The water here is always fairly calm and currents are mild. Suggested for experienced divers.

When the Atlantic seas are calm (usually in summer for a short period) there is additional diving off **Isla Punta Cana** on the southeast coast, and off **Sosua** and **Cabrera** on the north coast. Sport fishing and spear fishing in the northern coastal areas have taken a toll on the fish population, but some of the underwater terrain is pretty. Numerous dive shops exist in Puerto Plata.

Punta Cana Dive Sites

Pristine coral reefs and mini-walls off **Bavaro** and **Punta Cana** on the east coast are subject to wind and current patterns. When seas are calm this is a super diving area.

☆☆ **Pepe** features massive hard coral formations, groupers, rays and nurse sharks. Depths range from 45 to 60 feet. Good photo opportunities. Conditions vary with the wind.

☆☆ **Entrada de Las Cuevas**, from seven to 50 feet, starts inside of the barrier reef which is formed of caverns and overhangs covered with hard corals. Huge schools of silversides, lobsters and rays inhabit the caverns. Conditions vary.

☆ **El Acuario**, from seven to 35 feet, is a horseshoe-shaped area within the inner reef. Chutes, passages, overhangs and caverns shelter hordes of tropicals. On calm days this area is good for all level divers.

☆ **La Choza**, part of the barrier section of the reef, extends out to form high coral channels, and is a habitat for schooling fish and several stingrays. This spot is often calm with depths from 35 to 50 feet.

☆ **El Tiburon**, from 60- to 70-foot depths, is part of the outer reef, which is a series of eroded spur and groove formations and large coral heads. Reef sharks, large groupers and large schools of fish are often sighted around the coral heads. Conditions vary. Expect some surge on most days.

Dive Operators

 Stick with the dive shops associated with the resorts, as most of the Dominican dive shops cater to locals with Spanish the main language. Certification cards are required to dive in the Dominican Republic.

Treasure Divers at the Don Juan Beach Resort in Boca Chica has one of the finest English-speaking operations in the Dominican Republic. Instructor Walter Frishchbutter, a *Best Dives* panel member, offers reef and wreck trips and cave diving (experienced and properly equipped cave divers only) off Boca Chica and La Caleta. PADI certification courses. ☎ 809-523-5320, fax 809-523-4444, djuanbch@diveres.com.

Scubafun has two south-coast locations, one in Bayahibe and the other in La Romana. Both visit Saona Island, Catalina Island and Cove Dominicano via catamaran and three power boats. Staff members take pride in helping divers and snorkelers. They tote your gear and, on long trips to Catalina Island, and provide lunch and drinks.

The Bayahibe shop, halfway between Boca Chica and La Romana, is about a two-hour drive south from Punta Cana. Bayahibe is off the beaten path, but offers a few good restaurants, a small discotheque and Villa Iguana with simple rooms and apartments. The owners of "Villa Iguana" and two dive centers have been in Bayahibe for 10 years and know the area. Snorkelers join the dive boats. Two-tank boat dives cost $65, snorkelers pay $35. ☎ 809-833-0003. http://www.scubafun.info/.

Punta Cana Dive Center, at the Punta Cana Resort, visits reefs off Punta Cana on the east coast. Cost for a one-tank dive is $45; three dives for $115. Includes BCD, regulator, tank, weights, snorkel and mask. Resort course is $80. ☎ 800-972-2139, 809-541-2714, fax 809 541-2286.

If you are staying on the north coast, try **Caribbean Marine Puerto Plata**. This PADI center visits the northern wrecks and reefs. ☎ 809-320-2249, fax 809-320-2262.

The resorts listed below treat tourists well and either have dive shops or can arrange for dive and snorkeling trips.

Where to Stay

A complete list of resorts and rates is available from the Dominican Republic tourist office, PO Box 497, Santo Domingo, Dominican Republic. ☎ 809-689-3657, fax 809-682-3806, www.dominicanrepublic.com.

Coral Hamaca Beach Hotel, a Hilton resort, Boca Chica, features 460 deluxe rooms and suites, a PADI dive center, Four free-flow pools – two with swim-up bars – a gorgeous beach, spa, sauna, water sports, tennis, horseback riding, gym, five terrific restaurants, six bars, children's playground, gift shop, Internet access. All rooms have A/C, cable TV, private bathroom. All-inclusive rates per person for four nights start at $650. Costs includes all meals and snacks, activities and taxes. Scuba and snorkeling boat trips are not included. ☎ 877-GO-HILTON (877-464-4586), direct 809-526-4611, hamaca@coralhotels.com, http://coralbyhilton.com/hamaca.

Viva Wyndham Dominicus Beach Resort, on the southeast coast, 11 miles from Punta Cana Airport, has three pools, four restaurants, four bars, 500 standard or superior rooms and bungalows and a PADI Five Star dive center. The staff consists of English, French, Dutch, German, Spanish and Italian-speaking PADI certified Instructors and guides. Winter rates for an all inclusive dive vacation start at $350 per day. ☎ 1-800-WYNDHAM or direct 809-686-5658, viva.dominicusbeach@vivaresorts.com.

Don Juan Beach Resort in Boca Chica on the southern coast, features 224 air-conditioned suites, snack bar, restaurant, pool, disco, tennis, dive shop, sand beach, entertainment, baby sitting service, and free parking. The Don Juan is the oldest and smallest of the large all-inclusive hotels in Boca Chica, but it has a terrific location and layout and budget rates. There are no buildings over four stories and no elevators. Consider requesting a room on one of the lower floors if you carry a lot of personal dive equipment.

Guest rooms have queen-size beds, cable TV, direct-dial telephones, in-room safe deposit box, private bath with tub (the Captain's Club have whirlpools). Non-smoking and handicap access rooms available. Diving with **Treasure Divers**. All-inclusive rates start at US$100-130 per person/per day. ☎ 809-687-9157, h.donjuan@BocaChicaBeach.net.

On-site Treasure Divers visit La Caleta Underwater National Park, Catalina Island, Saona Island, a freshwater cave, and the wrecks of the *Hickory* and *Capitan Alcina*. Diving trips depart from the resort's beachfront Makey Pier in 21-foot open boats for small groups, the 38-foot *Robin Hood* equipped with 350 hp motor and the *Armen*, a 170-foot steel sailing vessel.

Breezes Punta Cana Resort Spa & Casino awaits you on **Arena Gorda Beach**. Ideal for families, couples and singles, this new four-star resort is the largest in the SuperClubs chain, and is situated on a super stretch of beach with an on-site dive shop. Guests unwind in beautiful rooms, dip into a spectacular free-form pool and feast in gourmet restaurants. Winter rates pp start at $1100 for seven nights; off season from $900 pp. Garden view. The resort's 735 air-conditioned guest rooms have direct-dial telephones, private bath and shower, iron and ironing board, hair dryer, coffee and tea maker, safes, stocked mini fridge, satellite TV, CD player and balcony. Book online at www.breezes.com or through your travel agent. ☎ 877-GoSuper, 877-467-8737.

Dining

Don't drink the water or eat the skins of raw fruit or vegetables! You might suffer *Caonabo's revenge*, aka "the tourist's disease." The cure, even worse to some than the disease, is mangu, a purée of green plantains.

 Menu prices are often in Dominican pesos. D$12.50=US$1.

Italian, Spanish, French and Jamaican restaurants are plastered along the beach roads and the cities. Full-course dinners in the tourist areas are about US$20. Much lower prices prevail in the small local restaurants. Several good restaurants and wonderful street vendors are found along the beach road (the Malecón) in Santo Domingo. The vendors' carts steam with sizzling fried pork rinds (chicharones) and meat-filled pastries (pastelitos). American sandwiches, snacks, pizza, and salads are offered at the Sheraton's coffee shop. Beer afficionados will enjoy a cold Presidente.

In **La Romana** you'll find a wide range of restaurants in the **Casa de Campo** complex.

Dominican menus typically offer a version of *La Bandera*, a compote of white rice, red beans and stewed meat, usually served with a salad and fried plantains. Regional dishes include fish in coconut milk, in Samana; and goat meat, in Azua, where the goats are fed a daily dish of wild oregano. In Puerto Plata and the south coast, crabs are the favored menu item. A breakfast favorite is *tortilla de jamon* – a hot ham omelet. *Sancocho* is a Dominican stew prepared differently in each region. *Sancocho prieto* is a black stew made with seven different meats (don't ask which seven meats).

Sightseeing & Other Activities

If you plan to tour Old Santo Domingo, include a stop at **El Alcazar**, Diego Columbus' Castle; **Casa del Cordon**, the first residential house built in Santo Domingo; the **Dominican Monastery**; and the ruins of **St. Nicolas De Bari Hospital**. The remains of Christopher Columbus are believed to be in the **Cathedral of Santa Maria la Menor**, the oldest cathedral in the New World.

In La Romana there is the **Museum of Archaeology at Altos de Chavon**, which features exhibits of the Taíno Indians, Hispaniola's first inhabitants.

Facts

Helpful Phone Numbers: Police or ambulance, ☎ 911. Doctor: Santo Domingo, Clinica Gomez Patino, Independencia, ☎ (701) 685-9131; La Romana, Centro Medico Oriental, Sta. Rosa, ☎ 556-2555. Tourist board, ☎ 689-3657.

Nearest Recompression Chamber: Santo Domingo. Dr. Edward Cano and Dr. Caro Newman treat divers in six monoplace chambers, and there is a multiplace Chamber in Bavaro, www.hospiten.es, ☎ 809-686-1414, fax 809-686-7869 bavaro@hospiten.es.

International Airports: *Las Americas*, Santo Domingo, ☎ 549-0450/80; *Herrera*, Santo Domingo, ☎ 567-3900; *Punta Aguila*, La Romana, ☎ 556-5565; *Punta Cana*, Higuey, ☎ 686-8790; *La Union*, Puerto Plata, ☎ 586-0219; *Cibao*, Santiago, ☎ 582-4894. See www.cdc.gov/travel for current travel advisories. Direct service is available from US gateway cities and most Canadian and European travel centers. **Airlines: American**, ☎ 800-433-7300; local 809-542-5151; **American Eagle**, ☎ 800-433-7300, local 809-542-5151. **US Airways** 809-540-0505.

When you need transportation to and from ports and airports, try to agree on a fare in advance to avoid problems and ask for the cab driver's identification *before* entering the car. Not all vehicles that serve these routes use meters, and the fares set by syndicates vary, based on distance and the number of passengers occupying the car.

Driving: On the right. Most hotels and tour operators have transportation to and from airports for their clients. Additionally, all airports have car rental offices that facilitate this service. Car rental agencies formalize rental contracts only on presentation of a credit card. Minimum age is 21, and you must present a valid driving license from your country of origin, or an international license. Gas stations measure fuel by American gallon. Toll is paid on expressways.

Rental Cars: Alamo, ☎ 549-8303; Hertz, ☎ 221-5333; Budget, ☎ 586-4433; Thrifty, ☎ 689-9000.

Documents: Citizens of the US, Canada and the Caribbean must have a valid passport and a Tourist Card, which costs $10 and may be purchased upon arrival at one of the international airports. Maximum stay is 60 days. Citizens of the United Kingdom may stay up to 90 days with a valid passport.

Customs: You are allowed to bring two liters of alcoholic liquor, 200 cigarettes, and gift articles to the value of US$1,000. Anyone entering the country with opium, cocaine, coca, cannabis or related drug-making herbs will be imprisoned without bail. You may not leave with more than US$5,000 in cash or travelers checks.

Currency: The Dominican Peso. US$1=DOP 16.90 (variable). Change only as much as you think you'll need as most banks won't change it back to US currency. It is easiest to change currency at the airport. Banks are closed on weekends. Major credit cards are accepted at large establishments; however, a surcharge of 3 to 5% is added on.

Language: Spanish is the official language. English is widely spoken at resorts.

Climate: Temperatures along the south coast are approximately 82°F in winter, slightly higher in summer with highs in the 90s.

Clothing: Lightweight. Carry a sweater or jacket for winter evenings. The seashore resorts are informal. Shorts and bare chests are not welcome in the churches. Divers should bring a shorty wetsuit, lightweight wetsuit or wetsuit jacket during winter months. In summer a wetskin or T-shirt suffices.

Electricity: American-style plugs are used; power is 110-120 volts, 60 cycles. Power cuts occur. However, all hotels and restaurants have back-up generators.

Time: Atlantic Standard (Eastern Standard + 1 hour).

Religious Services: Catholic, Evangelical Protestant, Assembly of God, Protestant Episcopal, Seventh-Day Adventist.

Additional Information: ☎ 809-541-5652, www.dominicanrepublic.com, travel@dominicanrepublic.com.

Grenada

Nestled in the eastern Caribbean, Grenada – the largest of a three-island nation that also includes **Carriacou** and **Petite Martinique** – is the most southerly of the Windward Islands and is the gateway to the Grenadines.

Renowned for its deep, sheltered harbors, the island has long been a favorite stopover for yachts and cruise ships. **St. George's**, the capital city, boasts a superb harbor, shaped like a horseshoe, that was formed partially out of the crater of an extinct volcano. The island's perimeter is blessed with 80 miles of white sand beaches. Its coastline stretches out in hundreds of small peninsulas that form numerous sheltered bays and lagoons. Offshore coral reefs are home to huge turtles, stingrays, and tropicals. Shipwrecks abound. Intriguing, too, is Grenada's mountainous terrain. Volcanic in origin, it is thickly wooded, and wildly tropical, with towering thickets of bamboo, banana plantations, orchids, bubbling hot springs and waterfalls – with butterflies, armadillos, monkeys and exotic cuckoo birds. Fertile soils produce a fragrant bounty of tropical fruits, cocoa, nutmeg, mace, ginger root, thyme, tonka bean, tamarind, turmeric, cinnamon and cloves. Red-roofed houses dot the hillside.

Carriacou and Petite Martinique retain the idyllic character of early life in the Caribbean. In Carriacou, boat builders still construct and launch sturdy, wooden schooners as they have for generations. The brightly colored boats ply between the islands, carrying passengers and cargo, their huge white sails billowing in the trade winds. Carriacou has great diving and snorkeling reefs off her south and west coasts around **White**, **Mabouya** and **Sandy Islands**.

History

History records Christopher Columbus as the first to sight Grenada in 1498. He named this island *Concepcion* for its egg-like shape. Peaceful tribes of Ciboneys and Arawaks were the first known inhabitants, followed by the more warlike Caribs, who called the island Camerhogne.

The Caribs stuck around until 1651, when French explorers drove the entire populace to mass suicide at a spot now known as "Carib's Leap," on the north end of the island where the town of **Sauteurs** (named after the event – French for "jumpers") now stands.

During 18th-century dynastic wars, Grenada went back and forth between the British and the French, until 1783 when British troops gained power. Grenada became independent on February 7, 1974.

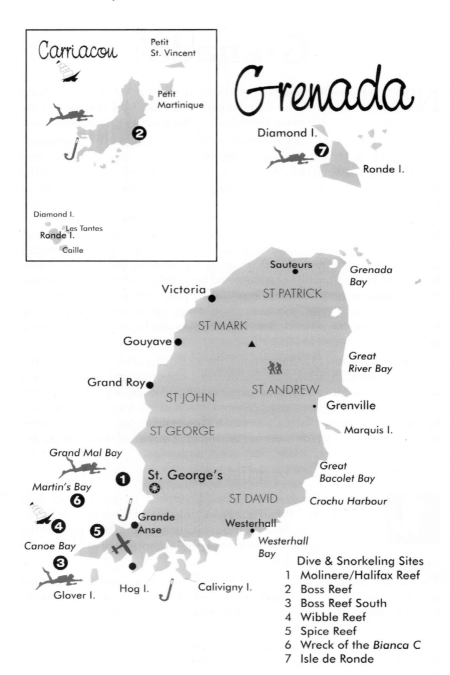

Carriacou

Petit
St. Vincent

Petit
Martinique

❷

Diamond I.

Grenada

❼

Ronde I.

Diamond I.
Les Tantes
Ronde I.
Caille

Sauteurs

Grenada
Bay

Victoria

ST PATRICK

ST MARK

Gouyave

Great
River Bay

Grand Roy

ST ANDREW

ST JOHN

Grenville

ST GEORGE

Marquis I.

Grand Mal Bay

Great
Bacolet Bay

Martin's Bay

❶ St. George's

ST DAVID

Crochu Harbour

❻

❹ ❺

Grande
Anse

Westerhall

Canoe Bay

Westerhall
Bay

❸

Hog I.

Calivigny I.

Glover I.

Dive & Snorkeling Sites
1 Molinere/Halifax Reef
2 Boss Reef
3 Boss Reef South
4 Wibble Reef
5 Spice Reef
6 Wreck of the Bianca C
7 Isle de Ronde

The late 1970s brought the reign of a Marxist government, which endorsed the establishment of a Cuban military runway and submarine base on Grenada. Tropical fields were being devastated, the tourist population dwindled and the deteriorating island was crawling with Soviet operatives. In 1984, terrorists took over an American medical school. President Reagan responded by sending in troops and replanting the seeds of democracy. Today, peace and tranquility reign and the island is rebuilding a healthy tourist trade.

Nicknamed the "Isle of Spice," Grenada is one of the last Caribbean islands that actively exports spices. Many of the islanders' homes are constructed of the ballast stones off-loaded by early merchant ships when they took on spices.

Best Dive & Snorkeling Sites

Grenada's primary dive and snorkeling sites are offshore from **Grand Anse Beach**, **Molinere Point** and **Dragon Bay**, all on the west (leeward) coast.

Diving and snorkeling is weather-dependent. During dry periods the visibility exceeds 100 feet. After a heavy rainfall, runoff from the rivers can lower visibility to 25 feet. Decompression dives are not recommended, as there are no chambers in the area.

Good snorkeling from Grenada's shore is possible at the southernmost headland of **Morne Rouge Bay** and the reef system of **Grand Anse**. The innermost reef has been destroyed, but a 100- to 200-foot swim will take you over huge sea fans and nice coral heads teaming with tropicals. Bring a floating dive flag and stay close to it as many small craft are in the area. A light surge should be expected.

Sandy Island, off the southwest coast of Carriacou, is surrounded by outstanding reefs and gorgeous beaches. It is one of the best snorkeling spots in the Caribbean. You need a boat to get there. Anchorage is south (leeward) of the island (yachtsmen need two anchors to avoid being washed ashore).

☆☆ The **Bianca C.**, a 600-foot cruise ship that sank on October 24, 1961, is possibly the largest wreck in the Caribbean, and this is certainly the most adventurous scuba trip in the area. The cruise liner, crippled by a boiler explosion, was at anchor for two days outside St. George's while it burned. It sank as it was being towed by the HMS *Londonderry* during an attempt to move it out of the shipping lane. The bottom rests on a sandy plain in 167 feet of water. The top decks at 90 to 120 feet are encrusted with hydroids and have collapsed since the sinking. Remains of the internal walls are badly rusted and crumble to the touch.

Because of the depth, you are down just 15 to 17 minutes. Most dives proceed around the stern of the boat, where you can "swim" in the pools with resident barracudas. Eagle rays, an occasional shark, hawksbill turtles or groupers shadow by. A scattering of corals are beginning to grow on the hull.

Strong currents do occur on the *Bianca*, but die out at 50 feet or so. All divers should have open-water experience before attempting this dive, and then only with a qualified local dive guide. **Dive Grenada's** dive master, David Macnaghten, fastens a safety line from the anchor line to the ship. Once everyone is back on the line, it is cast off and you begin your slow ascent to the surface.

 ☆☆☆ An easier dive, and also good for snorkeling, is **Boss Reef**, a six-mile-long reef that stretches from Grande Anse Bay to Canoe Bay off the southwestern tip of the island. Just a five-minute boat ride from the shore, it extends some 100 feet across and offers three main dive sites – **The Hole**, a fish hangout that slopes down to 50 feet; **Valleys of Whales** (named for one whale sighting), a coral canyon with walls of grunts, yellow tails and parrotfish; and **Forests of Dean**, an area dense with branching corals. All three range in depth from 20 to 40 feet with some dropoffs to 60 feet. Fish are abundant, with schools of sergeant majors, goatfish, rays, groupers, turtles and barracudas. Seas usually run a one- to two-foot chop.

☆☆☆ West of Boss Reef is **Wibble Reef**, where gentle (one-knot) currents take you through vast schools of Creole wrasses and chromis. The reef starts at 40 feet and slopes down to 167 feet toward the north, and gently to the south. Groves of black coral and gigantic sea fans adorn the wall, which displays a constantly changing panorama of fish. The bottom is sandy, with soft corals, lobsters and small critters.

☆☆☆ **Spice Island Reef**, just off Pt. Salines, the southwest tip of Grenada, is one of the best spots for snorkeling and shallow dives. The reef drops gradually from 20 to 80 feet. The shallows are home to a vast of array of juvenile fish, octopi, parrotfish, sea fans and finger corals.

☆☆☆ **Isle de Ronde**, a group of tiny, picturesque islands off the north coast of Grenada, drops off to pristine fringing reefs vibrant with soft corals, sea fans and gorgonians. Trips to these islands take about 1½ hours from St. George's. For experienced divers.

☆☆ **The Halifax-Molinere Wall** is close to shore, making it a favorite night-dive. The reef starts at 20 feet and drops down to a sandy bottom at 90 feet. Marine life is decent, with large vase sponges, sea whips, gorgonians, sea fans, finger corals, spotted morays, Spanish hogfish, large French angels, sergeant majors, turtles and rock beauties. Visibility varies with the weather. A day of rough seas and winds can kick up the silt and reduce visibility. Expect a light current. Previous open-water experience is suggested.

Dive Operators

 Aquanauts Grenada is a PADI Five Star Gold Palm Resort, SDI & TDI facility. It is on site at the **True Blue Bay Resort**, and in walking distance of the Allamanda Beach Resort, Coyaba Beach Resort, Flamboyant Hotel, GEM Holiday Beach, Grand Beach Resort, Grand View Inn, Mariposa Beach Hotel, Siesta Hotel and some small guest houses.

Aquanauts provides a courtesy shuttle from most beach hotels to and from the marina at True Blue Bay, where you board the dive boats. Dive gear can be stored at the dive shop for the duration of your vacation. Pick-up time from your hotel in the morning is around 8.30 am, noon and 1 pm.

Their boats visit the best sites around Grenada and offer Nitrox, scuba certification courses, snorkeling, scuba and underwater camera rentals. ☎ 888-446-9235, local 444-1126, 439-2500, www.Aquanautsgrenada.com, info@aquanautgrenada.com.

Dive Grenada, on Grand Anse Beach and at the **Flamboyant Hotel**, offers dive trips at 10 am and 2 pm. Night-dives at 6:30 pm, snorkeling on Molinere Reef at 2 pm. PADI courses for all skill levels. One-tank dives cost $45, two-tank dives, $80. Nitrox fills available. Trips to Isle de Ronde for diving and snorkeling run $120 (minimum four people). Dive Grenada also offers water-skiing, board surfing and offshore fishing. ☎ 473-444-1092, fax 473-444-5875, www.divegrenada.com, info@divegrenada.com.

Eco Dive and **Eco Trek**, on Grand Anse Beach, offer dive, snorkel and hiking tours of Grenada. They visit the wreck of the *Bianca C.*, sites around Isle de Ronde, Molinere Reef, Flamingo Bay and Dragon Bay. PADI certification, and beginner courses are offered. They cater to small groups aboard a nicely outfitted dive boat. Seven-day packages with the **Siesta Hotel**, including seven-night accommodations and 10 dives, cost from $750. All dive package rates are per-room, based on single or double occupancy. A full set of rental equipment is an additional $5/dive. To reserve at these rates all payments must be made in advance of arrival, and there will be no refund. For bookings and inquiries, ☎ 473-444-7777, www.ecodiveandtrek.com, dive@ecodiveandtrek.com.

ScubaTech, Grenada, at the **Calabash Hotel** on Prickly Bay, visits dive sites both on the Atlantic and Caribbean sides of the island – all less than a 20-minute boat trip. They offer PADI courses from Open Water to Dive Master, Nitrox Diving and Rebreather diving and training, plus Bubblemaker and Seal Team for the children. Other watersports activities are also available, including sailing, kayaking, snorkeling trips and dive/sail excursions on the luxury catamaran *Timshel*. ☎ 473-439-4346, hotel 473-444-4334, www.scubatech-grenada.com, robnkatie@caribsurf.com.

Sailing

Formerly Starwind Enterprises, **First Impressions** has a new power catamaran, *Starwind IV,* that accommodates up to 35 people. They offer whale- and dolphin-watch tours. ☎ 473-440-3678, fax 473-440-3678, starwindsailing@caribsurf.com, catamaranchartering.com.

Horizon Yacht Charters is based at the **True Blue Bay Resort** in Grenada, with a full-service marina facility. Snorkelers should carry their own gear. Divers wishing to visit the Grenadines can rent gear from neighboring **Aquanauts** or join one of the Grenadine dive shop tours upon arrival. Overnight mooring and stern-to dockage is available. Cruise on fully equipped yachts, bareboat or crewed. ☎ 473-439-1000, fax 473-439-1000, horizonyachts@caribsurf.com, www.horizonyachtcharters.com.

Trade Wind Yacht Charters, at the **Spice Island Marine Centre**, offers daily and weekly sailing charters – bareboat or skippered, with any of four different provisioning packages. ☎ 473-444-4924, fax 473-444-4924, twygnd@caribsurf.com, www.tradewindyachts.com.

Where to Stay

Grenada

Grenada is one of the Caribbean's best bargains. Guesthouse rooms rent for as low as $40 in summer and $50 in winter. More luxurious cottages are offered for $90 a night. Hotels average $150 for a double. Check the Website at www.grenadagrenadines.com.

True Blue Bay Resort and Marina teams up with on-site **Aquanauts Diving**, a PADI dive center, for convenient vacation planning. The resort features 31 rooms and cottages, two pools, a waterfront restaurant, boutique, marina, kayaks, catamaran sailing, snorkeling and a fitness room. Guest rooms comfort you with a private balcony or patio, air conditioning, ceiling fan, optional kitchenette, satellite TV with remote, international direct-dial phone, hair dryer, beach towels and safe. Connecting rooms available. Airports and shops are five minutes away. ☎ 866-3BLUEBAY, local 473-443-TRUE, www.truebluebay.com, info@truebluebay.com.

The Calabash Hotel has 30 plush suites stationed amidst acres of tropical gardens. Guest rooms have balconies or patios. All suites have air conditioning, ceiling fans, showers, whirlpool baths, hair dryers, CD player, clock radios, iron and ironing boards, mini-bars, wall safes and coffee makers. Cable TV is available upon request. The **Rhodes** restaurant at Calabash serves gourmet specialties with island spices and fruits, such as warm lobster salad with mango canonnaise, ribs on sticky pineapple plantain and wonderful desserts. Rates start at $235 per day plus a 10% service charge and 8% government tax for a double. Rates include an à la carte breakfast, welcome cocktail, fruit plate or fruit punch served on the beach each morning, afternoon tea, evening cocktail canapés delivered to your room. Diving with on-site **Scubatech**. ☎ 473-444-4334, fax 473-444-5050, US/Canada toll-free 800-528-5835, www.calabashhotel.com. For dive packages and specials, e-mail clive.barnes@caribsurf.com.

Coyaba Beach Resort on Grand Anse Beach, a low-rise, 70-room resort, offers a sea view from all rooms, which have balconies and air conditioning; tennis; palm-lined beach; phones; dive shop; two restaurants. Walking distance from shopping and restaurants. Winter room rates range from $125 for a single to $175 for a double. Summer rates from $80. **Grand Anse Aquatics** dive shop on premises. ☎ 473-444-4129, fax 473-444-4808. Write PO Box 336, St. George's, Grenada, West Indies.

Flamboyant Hotel & Cottages. If you want to stay on Grenada's renowned Grand Anse Beach without the hefty resort prices and don't mind a bit of hill climbing, this hillside enclave of cottages and suites can be just right. Recently renovated guest rooms offer island décor, air conditioning, satellite TV and great views of the sea. Studios and suites have fully equipped kitchens. There's a pool and a restaurant, and the beach is just a stone's roll down the hill. Dive packages with adjacent **Dive Grenada** (see www.divegrenada.com for rates). Meal plans are available for about $90 per adult, per day. Standard rooms run from $150 per night, suites from $200. ☎ 473-0444-4247, fax 473-444-1234, www.Flamboyant.com, flambo@caribsurf.com. PO Box 214, St. George's, Grenada, West Indies.

Spice Island Inn, on Grand Anse Beach, offers ultra-luxurious beachfront suites with whirlpool bath, spa, or private swimming pool. Dine on your own patio or enjoy sumptuous buffets in the beachside restaurant. All-inclusive rates (sans diving) range from $399 to $890 per room per day in summer; $478 to $1,040 in winter. Diving is arranged with nearby Aquanaut Dive Shop. ☎ 473-444-4258/4423, fax 473-444-4807, US 846-628-1701, www.spiceislandbeachresort.com, spiceisl@caribsurf.com.

Lance aux Epines offers comfortable, fully equipped beachfront cottages and apartments that are just a short walk to the ScubaTech Dive Centre.

Guests choose from 11 beachfront units scattered across three acres. Air-conditioned units are roomy (900+ sq. ft.) and clean, with from one to three bedrooms. Cooking, food shopping and housecleaning available weekdays. If you prefer eating out, there are five restaurants, all less than a 10-minute walk away. Cottages and apartments have been recently redecorated and renovated. Bedrooms have air conditioning. Child-friendly, with baby sitting services available. Per-day rates for a one-bedroom start at $150; two-bedroom from $822; three-bedroom, $1,254. ☎ 473-444-4565, fax 473-444-2802, US/Canada, ☎ 877-444-4565, www.laecottages.com, reservations @laecottages.com.

Siesta Hotel features 37 plain and simple units facing the Caribbean Sea. All guest rooms have air conditioning, a refrigerator, satellite TV, private bath, direct-dial phone. Studios are ground-level and have a mini-kitchenette with a two-burner stove, good for making a cup of tea or coffee. One-bedroom units are on upper floors and have a stove and oven, large refrigerator and cookware. Low-budget. ☎ 473-444-4646, fax 473-444-4647, www.siestahotel.com, siesta@caribsurf.com.

Boats leave Grenada for neighboring Carriacou from the **Carenage**, St. George's, and return from Hillsborough, Carriacou. Travel time is three to four hours. There are several low-key motels and a few dive shops on Carriacou.

Carriacou

Paradise Inn sits right on Paradise Beach, with a view of Sandy Island, and offers water-taxi service to nearby islets. Breakfast, lunch and dinner are available from the restaurant. Diving is with **Lumba Dive**, www.lumbadive.com. Room rates start and end at $60. Rooms are simple guesthouse-style. ☎ 473-443-8406, www.paradise-inn-carriacou.com, paradise_inn_carriacou@yahoo.com.

Silver Beach Resort is centrally located for watersports on Carriacou. Oceanfront rooms or cottages are between $85 and $105 per night in winter, from $60 to $95 in summer. The on-premises dive shop, **Karibik**, visits over 20 Carriacou sites. Guest rooms are "old Caribbean" – cooled by sea breezes and ceiling fans. They're fine in winter and throughout the high season, but stick with the oceanfront rooms any other time, They are ideally situated for that cooling sea breeze. Rooms are fairly unadorned, plain and outdated by American standards. However, the location is top notch and sunsets are spectacular. All the guest rooms have telephone and cable TV. Eight are ocean-view and two suites have kitchens. If you want a quiet stay, select one of the six fully equipped cottages set in tropical gardens. ☎ 473-443-7337, 473-443-7165, www.silverbeachhotel.net, silverbeach@caribsurf.com.

Other Activities

St. George's harbor shelters a number of sightseeing-tour boats that offer reef viewing, harbor tours, even moonlight cruises with barbecues, some with live electronic or steel-band music.

Sunfish sailing, water-skiing, JetSkiing and board-sailing can be arranged through your hotel. Or, for information, call the tourist board at ☎ 473-444-1353.

The **Grenada Golf and Country Club** has a nine-hole golf course. Concentration is key for this course, as the view of both the Atlantic and Caribbean waters can be distracting. **Cricket**, one of the most popular sports on the island, is played at 10 am on Saturday mornings from January to May near St. George's.

A less formal sport in Grenada is known as **hashing**. The sport is a run or walk – whichever one chooses. Participants are guided by special markers through the course, sometimes through Grenada's hilliest areas. Participants must be on the lookout for markers that are purposely put in place to take them off course. Those who make it to the end – and everyone does – enjoy a light-hearted celebration. It is held by the **Hash House Harriers' Club** in various parts of the island every other weekend.

St. George's

Most island tours include and take off from historic St. George's. It is known as one of the most picturesque and truly West-Indian towns in the Caribbean.

The center of activity in St. George's is the **Carenage**, or inner harbor. Fishing boats of all sizes and descriptions pull in and out continuously. The adventurous among you may want to bargain for a trip on one of the fishing boats out to Glover's or Hog Island for a day of snorkeling.

At the center of the Carenage stands **Christ of the Deep**, a statue given to Grenada by the Costa Cruise Line in remembrance of the hospitality shown the passengers of the *Bianca C.* when it burned in the harbor in 1961. Also at the harbor are the post office, public library and small shops selling perfumes, lotions, potpourri, and teas made from local flowers, spices and herbs. Nearby is the **Grenada National Museum**, which houses archaeological finds, Josephine Bonaparte's marble bathtub, the first telegraph installed on the island in 1871, a rum still, and memorabilia depicting the Indian cultures of Grenada.

The **Sendall Tunnel** takes you to the other side of St. George's, the Esplanade, the outer harbor with its fish and meat markets. In back is **Market Square**, where vendors sell brooms, baskets, fruits and vegetables. Early Saturday morning is the best time to see the market, when it overflows with exotic fruits, vegetables and spices.

Stop by **St. George's Anglican Church**, built on the site of a church originally constructed by monks. Its walls are lined with plaques relating the 18th- and 19th-century history of Grenada.

Forts surround the city. **Fort George**, which is the oldest, was built by the French in 1705 and **Fort Matthew** and **Fort Frederick** were started by the French and completed by the British in 1783. All can be visited. St. George's also has a **zoo**, **botanical gardens**, **Bay Gardens**, and **Tower House** – the Great House of a 1916 plantation filled with island relics, prints, paintings and historic family photos.

Island Tours

 Grenada is small enough to be toured in one day. Leaving St. George's, heading to the south coast, you come to **Westerhall**, a stunning peninsula known for its magnificent homes and gardens. Next, down a dirt road is **Bacolet Bay**, a wild peninsula on the Atlantic where high surf pounds against miles of uninhabited beaches. Continuing on, **La Sagesse Nature Center** offers hiking trails, wild birds, a banana plantation with guided nature walks, an extensive beach and a café. Next is **Marquis Village**, the center of a handicraft industry.

Nearby, also on the eastern shore, is the town of **Grenville**, Grenada's second city, which is the perfect spot to try the local seafood. Try a bit of barracuda or Iambi (conch) at the Seahaven, washed down with mauby – a local drink made from tree bark.

If you tour on a Saturday, be sure to stop by Grenville's large open-air market. This island "bread basket" offers fresh fish, fruits, vegetables, breads, pastries, spices and Grenadian delicacies prepared on the spot. While mingling with the Grenadians doing their weekly marketing, you can stop and watch the expert weavers from Marquis as they ply strips of wild palm into hats, baskets, bags and placemats.

Before leaving the east coast, you can see the old **Pearls Airport**, which was replaced by the Point Salines International Airport in 1984.

The half-hour ride back zigs and zags through the **Grand Etang National Park**. Dense tropical foliage, including bamboo, tree ferns, cocoa, bananas and elephant ears, mixed with vistas of the sea, make it one of the most beautiful drives in the Caribbean. Stop at the **Grand Etang Visitors Center** in the

Forest Reserve, which houses exhibits of the area's flora and fauna and video-tapes of the island. Nearby is **Grand Etang Lake**, the crater of an extinct volcano and, above that, the summit of **Mt. Qua Qua** (2,372 ft). There are boats for rowing and picnic facilities. Also in this area are hiking trails of varying difficulty, which wind through the tropical vegetation. Bring pants and a long-sleeved shirt.

The west-coast ride north from St. George's takes you past colorful fishing villages set at the foot of the mountains, where papaya and breadfruit trees abound. Not far up the coast, a turnoff leads to spectacular **Concord Falls**. For the adventurous, a half-hour hike into the interior tropical forest through spice and fruit plantations takes you to a more remote second falls, where the reward is a refreshing swim.

Continuing north along the coast road is **Dougaldston Estate**, where cloves, cinnamon, mace, nutmeg and cocoa are prepared and sorted. The employees will explain how the spices grow, their uses, and show you the large trays where the spices are set to dry before separating. Close by is **Gouyave**, a fishing village and the center of the nutmeg industry.

At the northernmost tip are the great cliffs of **Sauteurs**. Nearby is the deserted **Levera Beach**, ringed by seagrapes and palm trees and the meeting point of the Atlantic and the Caribbean. From here you can see the Grenadines.

If time permits, take a detour from the coast road to the **River Antoine Rum Distillery**, dating from the 18th century and one of the last enterprises still powered by a water wheel.

Tours encircling the island run six hours and hit all the high points. City tours run two hours. A special tour for photographers is **Photo Safari**, which includes a professional photographer-guide who will tailor a trip for you.

Dining

 Dining in Grenada is West Indian informal, characterized by open-air settings and views of the sea. In St. Andrews, **Rins** offers great seafood and island drinks; ☎ 442-1737. On the Carenage, try **Rudolf's** for a pub-like setting serving fish and lobster "as-you-like-it," ☎ 440-2241.

In **Belmont**, a five-minute drive south from St. George's, internationally praised **Mama's**, ☎ 440-1459, serves over 20 different dishes "family style." There is no menu – just the best and freshest offerings bought and prepared in the small kitchen. From lobster and callaloo soup to fresh fish, chicken, *manicou ortatou* (armadillo), and other entrées, to a wide variety of salads and vegetables. Exotic ice cream finishes the meal.

For those wanting a different ethnic cuisine, try **Coconuts Beach Restaurant**, ☎ 444-4644, a French Creole restaurant on Grand Anse Beach. For Chinese food, there's **Chopstix**, ☎ 444-7849, at Ross Point, or **Tropicana**, ☎ 440-1586, on Lagoon Road, for Grenadian/Chinese dishes.

Fast food can be found on the Carenage at **Kentucky Fried Chicken** or the **Creole Shack**. There's a second Kentucky Fried in the Grand Anse Shopping Center, and the **Tropicana Restaurant** features a takeout menu.

Grenada's **spice baskets**, filled with everything from whole nutmegs and cloves to saffron or bay leaves, make an ideal souvenir for as little as $15. You might even find a recipe book tucked among the spices so you can recreate a fête of your own.

Facts

Helpful Phone Numbers: Police, ☎ 911, 440-2244, 440-3999; **hospital,** ☎ 440-2052; **Coast Guard,** ☎ 440-2852, or on Marine channel 16 VHP.

Nearest Recompression Chamber: Barbados and Trinidad. Avoid decompression dives – no chambers are close enough for an emergency.

Airlines: American Airlines flies from US gateway cities through Puerto Rico. **BWIA** flies between Grenada and Aruba, Canada, Caracas, Curaçao, Frankfurt, London, New York, Miami (daily), as well as Stockholm and other European cities. **LIAT** connects with international airlines – British Airways, BWIA, Air Canada, American Airlines, Air France, Lufthansa, in Barbados, St. Lucia, Trinidad, Martinique, Carriacou and Antigua.

Airport: *Point Salines International Airport* is on the southwest tip of Grenada.

Driving: On the left. You must produce a bona fide drivers license for the local traffic department.

Documents: A valid passport is required.

Customs: There is no restriction on the amount of foreign currency brought into Grenada. Clothing and dive gear are also admitted freely, as long as they are for personal use.

Currency: Eastern Caribbean Dollar (EC$). US$1=EC$2.68 (variable).

Credit Cards: Major credit cards are accepted by most tourist-oriented businesses. Traveler's checks and US currency are accepted almost everywhere.

Language: English.

Climate: The year-round average temperature is 80°F and annual rainfall averages 78 inches. Peak rainfall is in summer and late fall.

Clothing: Bring a wetskin or shorty wetsuit in winter. For land, casual lightweight clothing. For hiking the rain forest, bring sturdy shoes with nonslip soles, a long-sleeved shirt and long pants – cotton or a coolweave fabric. Swimwear and very short shorts are not welcome in the city streets, stores or hotel restaurants.

Electricity: 220 volts, 50 cycles. AC transformers and adapters are needed.

Time: Eastern Standard.

Departure Tax: A departure tax of US$14 for adults; $6.50 for children over five. There is a $4 departure tax from Carriacou.

Religious Services: Catholic, Anglican, Presbyterian, Methodist, Scots Kirk, Seventh Day Adventist, Jehovah's Witness, Christian Scientist, Baha'i Faith.

Additional Information: *Grenada Board of Tourism*, Suite 900 D, 820 Second Avenue, NY, NY 10017. In the US, ☎ 800-927-9554, www.grenadagrenadines.com.

Guadeloupe

Touted by Jacques Cousteau as "one of the world's 10 best diving spots," Guadeloupe combines the cultural and cosmopolitan charm of a European vacation with fabulous diving on reefs untouched by all but a minimal group of discriminating dive-travelers. Named for Our Lady of Guadeloupe by Christopher Columbus in 1493, this charming French island is blessed with miles of beautiful white-sand beaches and spectacular subsea attractions. Guadeloupe is actually two main islands connected by a bridge across the **Rivière Salée** and several out islands. From the air it resembles the wings of a butterfly. **Basse Terre**, the western wing, is mountainous, highlighted by the still-active volcano, **Mt. Soufrière**. Travelers touring this portion of the islands will find tropical rain forests, bamboo trees, hot springs, postcard waterfalls, and a profusion of tropical flowers, fruits, almond and palm trees. **Grande Terre**, the eastern wing of Guadeloupe, is flat, dry, and home to modern resorts, beautiful swimming beaches, fields of sugar cane and unlimited topside tourist attractions.

The prime dive-vacation attraction is **Pigeon Island**, located just off the central western coast of Basse Terre. Pigeon Island, a mountain in the sea surrounded by miles of dense coral reefs, was the site for the film *The Silent World*.

Residents of Guadeloupe are extremely friendly and kind to tourists. Still, non-French-speaking divers visiting Guadeloupe should pick up a French phrase book and familiarize themselves with the language. English is *not* widely spoken; even the grunts grunt with a French accent. Also, divers and snorkelers must bring their own equipment, except for tanks and weights. European adapters, if needed, are widely available for a few dollars at any dive shop.

Topless sunbathing, snorkeling, scuba and swimming are *de rigueur* on Guadeloupe.

Best Dive & Snorkeling Sites

Pigeon Island, composed of volcanic stone and scrub trees, lies off the western coast of Basse Terre, the western wing of Guadeloupe. The area consists of two land masses, **North Pigeon** and **South Pigeon**. The waters surrounding it come under French Government protection as an **Underwater Natural Park – the Cousteau Marine Sanctuary**.

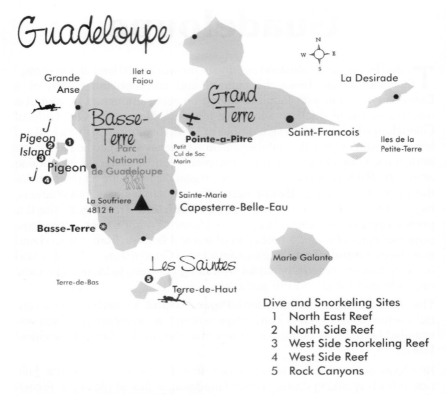

Guadeloupe

Grande
Anse

Ilet a
Fajou

La Desirade

Grand
Terre

Basse-
Terre

Pointe-a-Pitre

Saint-Francois

Pigeon
Island

Parc
National
de Guadeloupe

Petit
Cul de Sac
Marin

Iles de la
Petite-Terre

Pigeon

La Soufriere
4812 ft

Sainte-Marie
Capesterre-Belle-Eau

Basse-Terre

Les Saintes

Marie Galante

Terre-de-Bas

Terre-de-Haut

Dive and Snorkeling Sites
1   North East Reef
2   North Side Reef
3   West Side Snorkeling Reef
4   West Side Reef
5   Rock Canyons

☆☆☆☆☆ **North East Reef.** The northeast side of North Pigeon Island is a superb wall dive. Beginning at the surface, the wall drops 40 feet to a shelf, then slopes down to 70 feet and finally plunges steeply to 140 feet. The wall is carpeted with lacy soft corals, tube sponges, plate corals, and large pillar-coral formations. Residents include huge groupers, puffers, lobsters, big French angels and throngs of small critters – arrow crabs, feather dusters and tube sponges. The seas are usually calm, visibility more than 100 feet. Recommended for both novice and experienced divers.

☆☆☆☆☆ **North Side Reef.** You'll find superb seascapes for photography on the north side of North Pigeon Island. Huge clusters of tube sponges, some six feet tall, and enormous green and purple sea fans grow on the ledges and outcrops of the wall. The reef begins in the shallows and drops off to a maze of small canyons and outcrops. Divers are befriended by large gray snappers. They are tame and may be hand-fed. Large, curious barracuda circle overhead; trumpetfish and damsels adorn the lush thickets of coral. Star and brain corals abound. North Side Reef is a super dive for novices as well as experienced divers. Seas are calm, visibility excellent.

☆☆☆☆ **West Side Reef**, off North Pigeon Island, is everyone's favorite. The wall begins at the surface, drops to a shelf at 25 feet, slopes down to 40 feet, then drops off sharply to the bottom at 140 feet. As in all of the Cousteau Marine Sanctuary, the corals here are vibrantly alive with color and create a dramatic landscape. Large brain coral heads and gardens of soft corals thrive. Fish life is abundant. Inhabitants of the reef include large hog snappers, trumpetfish, and parrotfish. Photo enthusiasts are drawn to the gigantic orange sponges and teal sea fans. Calm seas invite divers of all experience levels to this site.

☆☆☆ **Rock Canyons**, located off **Iles des Saintes**, a small group of islands just south of Basse Terre, is a large maze of narrow rocky coral alleys and caves. Its walls, riddled with endless nooks and crannies, provide shelter for sea cumbers, bristle worms, tree worms, arrow crabs, seahorses, octopi, lobster, eels and an ever-present mob of grunts. Huge formations of rare pink corals color the area. The canyon entrance starts at 10 feet then drops to a sandy bottom at 45 feet. Tricky surface surges and currents make this a site for experienced divers.

☆☆☆☆☆ **Pigeon Island's West Side Reef** is the best snorkeling area in the Cousteau Marine Sanctuary. Its shallow walls ruffle with enormous feather dusters, sea plumes, sea rods, huge sea fans and sponges. Barrel sponges (large enough to camp in) thrive among clumps of elkhorn and enormous brain corals. Pufferfish and unusual golden moray eels are inhabitants. Expect calm seas and exceptional visibility.

Additional snorkeling and diving sites are found among the lagoons and bays of **Les Saintes**, the east coast of **Basse Terre**, and off-shore **Gosier** (the south coast of Grande Terre). Check out **Mouton Vert**, **Mouchoir Carré**, and **Cay Ismini**. They are close by the hotels in the bay of **Petit Cul de Sac Marin**, near Rivière Salée, the river separating the two halves of Guadeloupe. North of Salée is another marine reserve, **Grand Cul de Sac Marin**, where the small islets of **Fajou** and **Caret** also offer good diving. **St. François Reef** on the eastern end of the south shore of Grande Terre is a good snorkeling reef, as is **Ilet de Gosier**, off Gosier. Sport diving has grown enormously in the past ten years on Guadeloupe, yet every dive-explorer still can find a new "best dive" of his/her own.

Dive Operators

Scuba and snorkeling trips are easiest to arrange through your hotel. However, if you're fluent in French and must make your own arrangements, the following operators dive the best spots off Pigeon Island.

Archipel Plongée, Plage de Malendure, 97132 Pigeon, 97132 Bouillante, ☎ 590-98-93-93.

CIP Bouillante, Plage de Malendure, 97132 Pigeon, Bouillante, ☎590-98-81-72, fax590-98-16-23, www.cip-guadeloupe.com/coordonne.htm.

Les Heures Saines, Plage de Malendure, 97132 Pigeon, Bouillante, ☎ 590-98-86-63.

Tropicalys, 97180 Sainte-Anne, ☎ 590-54-49-26.

Ecole de Plongée Saint-François, 97118 Saint François, ☎ 590-85-81-18.

Blue Dive, 97117 Port Louis, ☎/fax 590-22-86-47.

Centre de Plongée Alavamas, 97115 Sainte Rose, ☎ 590-28-65-49, fax 590-28-43-69.

La Note Bleue, 97126 Deshaies, ☎ 590-28-53-74, fax 590-28-56-89.

Tropical Sub, 97126 Deshaies, ☎ 590-25-50-07, fax 590-28-53-48.

Anse Caraïbes Plongée, 97116 Pointe Noire, ☎ 590-99-90-95, fax 590-99-92-69.

Where to Stay

Rates are in US$. The country code and area code are both 590 (to dial direct, dial country code 590, then the number, which will begin with a second 590).

If your tongue doesn't curl comfortably around conversational French, head for one of the bigger hotels where English is spoken. Or if getting to know people is one of the reasons you travel, stay at a **Relais Créole**, a small family-owned inn. Most of the hotels are situated on Grande Terre (one-hour drive to Malendure).

Among the small hotels close to Pigeon Island on Basse Terre are Raphael Legrand's charming 12-room **Auberge De La Distillerie** at **Tabanon** near Petit-Bourg. This fully air-conditioned inn is a short ride from Pigeon Island dive operators. The adjacent bistro serves fine Creole dishes. Freshwater pool. ☎ 590-03-81-69-21-64, fax 590-63-81-69-16-22, www.auberge-distillerie.fr.

Hotel Paradis Créole, convenient to Pigeon, offers ten hotel rooms and two lovely bungalows with awesome views, A/C, direct-dial phones, pool. Good food. Weekly rates per person with diving run about $1,650. Website (French): www.paradis-tropical.gp. ☎ 590-81-21-62, fax 590-81-71-46, paradist@paradis-tropical.gp.

Le Domaine de Malendure, on Basse Terre overlooking Cousteau's Reserve, offers 45 spacious air-conditioned lofts or hillside cottages with terrific views of Pigeon Island and the Caribbean sea. Units include TV, A/C, showers, phones and mini-bars. Fine restaurant, superb pool and car rental on site. Dive and snorkeling tours to Pigeon Island. ☎ 590-98-92-12, fax 590-98-92-10, www.malendure@leaderhotels.gp.

La Créole Beach Hotel, located on the beach at Gosier, Grand Terre, offers 218 large, well appointed rooms, enormous swimming pool, kids club, kids pool, a good waterfront restaurant and pizza bar. The **Sea Cabin** on premises offers scuba and snorkeling tours to the coral reef surrounding Gosier Island, excursions to Pigeon Island as well as water-skiing, JetSkiing, board surfing and beach sports including *petanque* (like croquet with steel balls) and volleyball. Introductory dives. Rates for a double are $130 to $500. ☎ 590-90-4646, fax 590-90-1666, creolebeach@leaderhotels.gp. In the US, ☎ 800-742-4276.

La Sucrerie du Comte, Sainte Rose, spreads across seven acres on the site of an old rum distillery overlooking the sea. Guests pick from 26 bungalows divided into 52 modest rooms. All the rooms are air conditioned individually and equipped with ceiling fans, bathroom/shower, and private terrace on the garden (separating wall between the next terrace). In-room amenities are minibar, beverage maker, hair dryer, safe; no phone. Pool. ☎ 590-28-60-17, www.prime-invest.com, lasucrerie.reservation@wanadoo.fr.

The dive shop **Alavama** offers La Sucrerie guests excursions to the Grand Cul de Sac Marine Reserve. Included in rates are breakfast buffet, shuttle to marina three times daily, entry to beaches of the lagoon. Visitors' tax included in rates. Studios & villa rates include bed linens and towels. (one weekly provision per person). Beds are done upon arrival. Maid service once every seven days. Rates are from $134 for two people in a bungalow with breakfast buffet; $350 for a villa. Lower from January 6 to April 12. ☎ 590-28-60-17, fax 590-28-65-63, www.prime-invest-hotels.com.

L'Habitation de Lonvilliers, formerly the Meridien Guadeloupe, just east of Gosier at St. Francois, Grand Terre, features 265 four-star, beachfront suites. Bright and cheery Creole décor with very comfortable beds. Despite the boom in tourism, the town of St. François manages to retain its fishing-village look. To the east are any number of beachside bistros serving lobster and seafood. Rates are $203 to $350 for a double. Diving with **Scuba Fun**. Dive shops here offer daily trips to the offshore reefs of Grande Terre and excursions to Pigeon Island. ☎ 786-866-2864. Easiest to book through a travel agent.

Additional accommodations such as villas, bed and breakfasts, seaside bungalows are found at www.antilles-info-tourisme.com/guadeloupe.

Other Activities

Sailboats, crewed or bareboat, are plentiful. For rentals or tours stop by the **Marina Bas-du-Fort**, Pointe-A-Pitre. They also offer full-day picnic/snorkeling trips to Petite Terre, two beach-rimmed isles surrounded by the turquoise Caribbean.

Sightseeing

Hiking through Basse Terre's **Parc Naturel** takes you along well-marked trails through tropical rain forests to waterfalls, mountain pools, and **La Soufrière**, a 4,813-foot volcano and the park's most famous site. You'll also find exhibits on the volcano, coffee, the sea, and the forest. Hiking brochures are available from the Guadeloupe Tourist Office (address below). Local craft items, such as dolls, jewelry, furniture or souvenirs are made from fruit, wood, seashells, stone, and leather are available in town shops. Those who can dive all day and still party all night will find the cities of Guadeloupe alive with lights and loud with dancing and entertainment.

Dining

Guadeloupe is a gourmet's delight. Top restaurants and hotel dining rooms offer classic French and Caribbean cuisine. Though the island is French, it is also decidedly Creole, and Creole eateries are gaining enormously in popularity. Some are beachside cafés, some are in-town bistros, and several are little more than the front porch of the cook's home. On **Malendure Beach**, Basse Terre, check out **Chez Loulouse**, noted for Chef Loulouse's crayfish sauce Américaine. This is a small native seafood eatery in a simple setting. ☎ 98-7034. In **Gosier**, try the **Cybercafé** at Point Blanchard.

Facts

Helpful Phone Numbers: Police: ☎ 17 ; Fire department: 18; Ambulance: ☎ 87-65-43; Hospital: 89-10-10, Veterinary: 82-06-60, Weather Report: 08-92-68-08-08; Airport departure: 90-34-34; Airport arrival: 90-32-32.

Nearest Recompression Chamber: Located in Pointe-à-Pitre, Grande Terre.

Getting Here: Connections from Miami on **Air France**. From San Juan, take **American Eagle** (☎ 800-433-7300). Inter-island flights can be arranged at *Le Raizet Airport*. Water-ferries to Iles des Saintes are available from the city of Pointe-à-Pitre, Basse Terre, or Trois Rivières on the south coast.

Island Transportation: All major car rental agencies are at the airport. Reservations should be made before arriving in Guadeloupe to insure getting a car. Bus service in Mercedes vans is available between cities. The destination cities are clearly marked on the outside.

Driving: On the right. The main roads between major cities are clearly marked. A wonderful tourist map is available from the tourist office in Pointe-à-Pitre.

Documents: For stays of up to three months Canadian and US citizens require a return ticket and two forms of ID – either a passport or proof of citizenship such as a birth certificate or voter's registration card with some type of photo. A passport is recommended. British citizens require a passport.

Currency: Euro; €1=US$1.27 (variable).

Climate: Temperatures range from 75 to 85°F. Water temperatures are warm year-round so you won't need a wetsuit, although a wetskin or 18-inch shortie wetsuit is comfortable in midwinter.

Clothing: Casual light clothing. Most beaches are topless. Local women frequently dive topless.

Equipment Required: Bring all of your own scuba gear except for tanks and weights. Most operators have Scubapro tanks, which do not require any special regulator adaptor.

Electricity: European adaptors required.

Time: Atlantic Standard (EST + 1 hr).

Language: French, local Creole dialect.

Tax: A service charge of 10 to 15% is included on most hotel and restaurant tabs.

Religious Services: Catholic, Protestant, Jewish.

Additional Information: http://www.antilles-info-tourisme.com/guadeloupe.

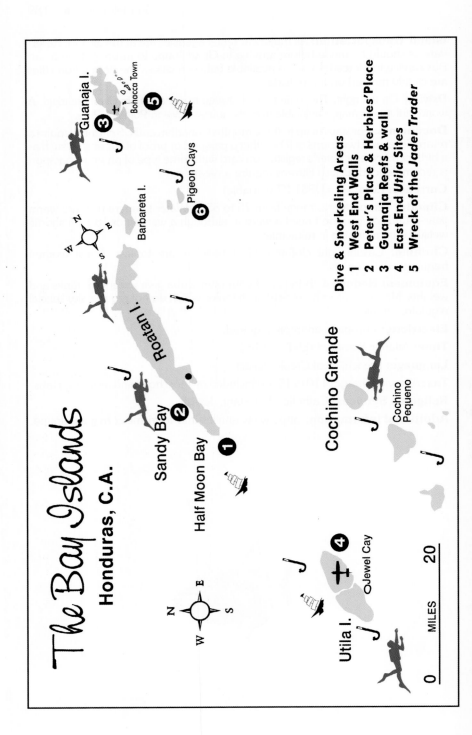

The Bay Islands
Honduras, C.A.

Dive & Snorkeling Areas
West End Walls
1. Peter's Place & Herbies'Place
2. Guanaja Reefs & wall
3. East End *Utila* Sites
4. Wreck of the *Jader Trader*

Guanaja I.
Bohacca Town
Barbareta I.
Pigeon Cays
Roatan I.
Sandy Bay
Half Moon Bay
Cochino Grande
Cochino Pequeno
Jewel Cay
Utila I.

0   MILES   20

Honduras

The Bay Islands

Located between 12 and 40 miles off the coast of Honduras, the Bay Islands (*Las Islas de la Bahia*) serve as a remote outpost set in the middle of the world's second-largest barrier reef. Geographically, the islands form the visible portion of the **Bonacca Ridge**, a subsea mountain range born of volcanic activity centuries ago. The islands, all mountainous jungle, slope down to postcard-perfect white sand beaches shaded by coconut palms. Inland, fragrant almond, mango, cashew, mandarin orange and breadfruit trees shade the cliffs and provide food and shelter to iguanas, parrots, snakes, deer and wild boar.

 Roatan, the largest of the 70-island chain, is the most populated, with 30,000 residents, and the most developed. It is where you'll find the most dive resorts and creature comforts. **Guanaja**, next in size, is surrounded by its own barrier reef. Third in size, and a newcomer to this "dedicated-dive-resort" group, is **Utila**. The **Cayos Cochinos**, a mini-cluster of small fishing-village islands, boasts one dive resort on their biggest island, **Cochino Grande**.

The smaller islands are uninhabited or sparsely populated. Most do not have roads. Phones, faxes and e-mail are newcomers. Surrounding reefs are impressive, with brilliantly colored sponges and corals, towering pinnacles, walls, tunnels, wrecks and caves. Visibility and water clarity are superb. Big turtles, grouper, rays, eels, and pelagics proliferate despite an active fishing industry. And snorkelers discover their own special paradise in the small patch-reefs that dot the shallow bays throughout the area.

And, while everyone in the Bay Islands speaks "dive" fluently, the predominant language is English. On the mainland, however, Spanish is spoken.

Plan on an entire day to reach the Bay Islands from the US. The islands are close to the Honduras coastline, but the mainland airport at **San Pedro Sula** is 160 miles away. Some flights use **La Ceiba**, which is closer. Connections are often erratic. Luggage sometimes arrives late. Sand fleas and no-see-ums are a nuisance and make their presence known as soon as you arrive. Apply repellent beforehand.

History

Evidence from shards of pottery and pre-Columbian remains indicate the early presence of Lanca, Maya and Payan Indians on the Bay Islands. Columbus is credited with their latter-day discovery in 1502.

During the early 1500s, the Spaniards, in their manic quest for gold and precious gems, brutally attacked and enslaved the Bay Island Indians. Finally, during the mid 1500s, the Indians revolted. One chief, Lempira, put up such a fierce offensive, it took thousands of Spanish troops to kill him. Lempira has since been declared a national hero and the currency of Honduras is named for him.

Following that conquest, word of Spanish treasure ships lured pirates from Jamaica and the Caymans to set up a base at Port Royal, Roatan. Tales of jewels and stashed treasures hidden on the island abound.

Best Dive & Snorkeling Sites

Roatan

☆☆☆☆☆ **West End Wall**, which encompasses **Peter's Place** and **Herbie's Place,** is great for diving and snorkeling. The reef starts at the shore and extends out 20 yards, where the wall drops off sharply from a ledge at 15 feet. Visibility often exceeds 100 feet. Fish life is superb, with schools of horse-eye jacks, permits, and schoolmaster. Seas are calm, with an occasional light current. No spearfishing.

The Natural Aquarium off the Bay Islands Beach Resort on Sandy Bay has several terrific snorkeling areas to explore. Shallow depths, calm surface and a marked snorkel trail entrance even diehard ocean explorers. Depths of the snorkel trail range from the surface down to 35+ feet with most interest between 10 and 20 feet.

Guanaja

☆☆☆☆☆ **The Bayman Drop and Pinnacle** are wall dives off the north shore. The top of the wall is between 10 and 40 feet. The Pinnacle rises from 135 to 50 feet at the top, where you'll find large barrel sponges, azure vase sponges, gorgonia and black coral. *Do not enter the crack at 70 feet.* Large black coral trees are found at 80 feet. Good for diving and snorkeling. No collecting or spearfishing.

☆☆☆☆ **Pavilions** is a series of blind tunnels, pillar corals and outcroppings between 30 and 60 feet. Soft corals and sponges dominate the shallows. *Beware of the fire coral, which seems hotter here than in other parts of the Caribbean.* The site is off Michael's Rock around the point next to the Bayman Bay Club. Good for diving and snorkeling.

☆☆☆ **Waterfall Reef**, the site of a huge black coral tree growing off the wall at 45 feet (top of the dive is five feet), takes its name from a series of overhangs with soft bushy corals which appear to cascade down the slope. Numerous anemones, big vase sponges and lots of fish make Waterfall a photographers' favorite. Good visibility.

☆☆☆☆ *Jader Trader* is a 200-foot wreck lying on its right side at 90 feet, off the southwest side of Guanaja. Big morays, schools of silversides, turtles and barracuda are in residence. Seas average two to four feet with a light current. Always good visibility. For experienced divers.

Additional dives along Guanaja's barrier reef are **Eel's Garden** off the Bayman Bay Club shore, **Black Rock Canyons**, a maze of tunnels and canyons, **Jim's Silverlode,** a sheer wall off southwest cay with huge sponges and soft corals. **The Cut** branches out into caverns and tunnels.

Cayos Cochinos

Cayos Cochinos are a group of 13 small islands deemed a **Biological Reserve** and managed, in part, by the Smithsonian Institution to conduct a scientific study of the reef. The reserve is patrolled by park rangers. Diving and snorkeling from the shore or by boat is outstanding.

Utila

Utila, fringed by virgin reefs, caves and canyons, offers some of the best shore diving and snorkeling in the Caribbean. Wildlife is exceptional, with turtles, eagle rays, southern stingrays and tropicals. Offshore sites are a 15 to 45 minute boat ride. The shore dives lie about 150 yards out.

Barbaretta

☆☆☆☆ **Barbaretta Wall** off Barbaretta island, a favorite snorkeling-picnic spot between Guanaja and Roatan, is a wonderland of barrel sponges and soft corals. The wall stretches for a mile.

Pigeon Cays

☆☆☆☆ Pigeon Cays are a small cluster of islands surrounded by shallow protected reefs, all perfect for snorkeling.

Where to Stay

Roatan

Each resort listed offers dive services. Add a 16% lodging tax to the rates. For additional resorts visit www.roatan.com and www.roatanonline.com.

Anthony's Key Resort was the first dedicated dive resort in the Bay Islands. The resort features beachside and reefside rustic cabins. Packages offered from $599 pp to $1125 per person, per week based on a double, include three meals daily, three boat dives daily, unlimited shore dives, kayaking and horseback riding. The **Institute for Marine Sciences** is on the grounds of the resort and features dolphin swims. ☎ 800-227-DIVE (3483), or 954-929-0090, www.anthonyskey.com.

Bay Islands Beach Resort on Sandy Bay, offers something for everyone from beginning swimmer to the most advanced diver. Guest rooms vary from an estate house to villas or a lodge along six acres of beachfront property on the northwest shore of Roatan. The property expands to 45 acres. Dive shop, good restaurant and bar. All rooms are air conditioned with private bath. Some are equipped with roll-in showers and grab-bars for disabled guests. Chair-friendly ramps and boardwalks connect the dive shop, room and bar/café. Dive shop staff offers personalized attention with no more than 12 divers on a boat.

They run three boat-dives and snorkel tours daily to the Marine Reserve on the leeward side of the island. Unlimited shore diving and snorkeling is available in **Spooky Channel** and **Natural Aquarium Buoyed Snorkel Trail** just off the resort's 450-foot sandy beach. The dive operation offers scuba diving, technical diving including nitrox, trimix and custom gas blending, snorkeling, fishing, kayaking and land packages. Family and children's programs available year round. Seven-night dive packages in winter start at $844 per person based on a double. Package includes five days of boat diving (two tanks in am, third tank in pm), one night-boat-dive, unlimited shore diving, accommodations, three meals daily, kayaks, airport transfers. ☎ 800-4-ROATAN, US agent 610-399-1884, fax 610-399-5265, bibrusa@yahoo.com.

Paya Bay Resort, sits on a cliff overlooking the sea and the Great Mayan Reef. Comfortable air-conditioned rooms have private balconies, high ceilings, queen-size beds, ceiling fans, refrigerators, and a private shower. Décor is simple – whitewashed walls, crisp linens, wood trim. A pristine section of the **Great Mayan Barrier Reef** lies less than a 100 yards from the shoreline. Walk down the cliffs to two white-sand beaches.

Paya Bay's restaurant features island-style fish, shrimp, lobster, conch, refreshing tropical drinks, wines and local Honduran brews. Beef, pork, and poultry dishes are also available.

On-site **Dive Roatan**, takes small groups of divers to the reefs off Roatan's **East End**, **Port Royal**, and the islands of **Santa Helena**, **Morat**, and **Barbareta**. Twenty-five miles of barrier reef lie on the north side of the island, plus another 20 miles of dropoff diving on the south side. Rooms are $125 per day. Boat-dive trips cost $30 each. ☎ 866-323-5414, direct 208-629-4251. Dive Roatan, ☎ 877-378-8078, www.payabay.com.

Tropical Beach Resort, on Roatan's East End houses divers in five wooden bungalows with private bath, fans, some with A/C. The ambience is very low key and laid back. The resort sports a PADI dive shop that offers every course, including fish identification, a nice stretch of white sand beach, sea pool, seafood restaurant. Seven night packages start at $700 and include lodging, five-days of two-tank boat dives, one-night dive, dive weights and belt, continental breakfast and lunch, one-private cabana on the beach, transfers to and from Roatan Island airport.

Room rates $65 per night 3rd person extra $10 per night. Children under 12 free. Add 16% tax. Divers add $30 per day for a one-tank boat dive or $50 for a two-tank boat dive. Includes: tank, weights and belt. ☎ 504-435-2725, www.bayislandtropicalbeachresort.com, rodjean123@yahoo.com.

Coco View Resort, on Roatan's southside peninsula, offers divers and snorkelers clean and spacious air-conditioned oceanside bungalows, two-story cottages, and cabanas built over the water. Each has a porch or balcony overlooking the Caribbean. Standard rooms each have one double and one twin bed. Bungalows have two rooms, each with a king-size bed.

Rates for a winter dive package start at $900 per person, double occupancy, for seven nights in either a cottage or cabana, and include three meals daily, beach barbecues, transfers from the airport, three two-tank boat dives, unlimited shore diving and night diving. Non-divers pay $800. Great wall dives are a stone's throw from the beach bar. Nearby is a 140-foot tanker wreck, *Prince Albert*, in 25 feet of water. Snorkelers enjoy extensive shallow reef formations and fish life right off the beach. Take a giant stride off your cabana or bungalow porch and you're on the reef. If you are new to snorkeling, instructors at **Dockside Dive Center** even provide free use of snorkel gear and an orientation! Disabled access. Decompression chamber with certified operator on site. Nitrox available. ☎ 800-510-8164, www.cocoviewresort.com, ccv@roatan.com.

Everything of vacation package plus three boat-dives daily, unlimited beach diving (9 am-6 pm), one night-dive (seven-night package only), tanks, air, weights, belt and boat trips with expert dive master.

Fantasy Island Beach Resort sprawls across its own 15-acre island off Roatan's south coast. A small bridge connects the resort to the main island. Built in 1989 by local entrepreneur Albert Jackson, the resort's 73 guest rooms are luxurious, with air conditioning, phones, refrigerators, full baths and cable TV. There is a full-service dive operation on premises with a fleet of 42-foot custom dive boats. Excellent shore diving and snorkeling. Package rates are from $920 per person (non-divers pay $750) for seven nights in a standard room with three boat dives and three meals daily, airport transfers in Roatan, unlimited snorkeling, unlimited shore diving, free use of kayaks, sailboats and Hobie Cats. Nitrox available; PADI courses. Rates drop in winter (September 15 to December 15). ☎ 800-676-2826, direct 504-455-7510, fax 817-579-2680, www.fantasyislandresort.com, npalandra@bonne-beach.com.

Inn of Last Resort, a spacious, hillside dive resort, features 30 large air-conditioned guest rooms using natural woods and tropical accents. Fine restaurant. Good shore diving and snorkeling off the resort's beach. Dive-vacation packages from $895 include six nights, three meals daily, three boat dives daily, unlimited shore diving, transfers. ☎ 888-238-8266, information@innoflastresort.com, www.innoflastresort.com.

Las Rocas Resort offers one- and two-story air-conditioned cabins on the beach in West Bay, each with a private porch and beautiful ocean views. Amenities include 24-hour hot water, private bath, minibar, ceiling fans and air conditioning. Prices are per cabin and include airport transfers, daily continental breakfast served in your room and scheduled boat service. One-story cabanas have one queen-size bed and one twin. Two-story bungalows have adjoining rooms with two queen-size beds and two double beds. Caribbean/Italian restaurant on premises. Rates for seven nights run about $1,000 per couple, with packages as low as $399 per person, including seven nights accommodations, transfers to and from the local airport, breakfast daily, two boat-dives a day (five days of diving), one night-dive, tanks and weight belts. If you need a complete diving equipment set up add $50 to the package. You can opt for a full meal plan for an extra charge of $175.

Price does not include 16% sales tax. On-site **Wet 'n Wild Dive Shop** is an authorized Padi Diving Center. Maximum nine divers per boat. US ☎ 877-379-8645, direct 504-403-8046, fax 504-403-8047, info@lasrocasresort.com.

The Reef House Resort touts 11 lovely cottages in two wings. All are furnished in tropical décor. Two are air conditioned, the rest have ceiling fans and the trade winds for cooling. Great shore diving and fine snorkeling off the jetty in front of the resort. Snorkeling trips to neighboring islands. Side trips to explore mainland Honduras Maya sites and hot springs are offered. Dive packages with round-trip transportation from the airport cost from $645 for five nights, $855 for seven nights, including room (double), welcome drink, three meals per day, unlimited shore diving, two boat-dives per day with an experienced guide, one night-dive, tanks, air, weight belts and weights. Non-divers pay $495 for five nights, $645 for seven nights. Nice wall dive from the pier. Dive shop offers equipment, camera housing rentals and courses. ☎ 866-478-4888, www.reefhouseresort.com, reefhouseresort@yahoo.com.

Guanaja

Posada Del Sol is a luxurious Spanish villa resort on 72 acres of oceanfront greenery and, except for two small villages, is the only developed area on the southeast shore. It has an excellent restaurant, bar, pool and tennis court. Rooms are luxurious and spacious. Three 42-foot dive boats whisk guests to 50 moored dive sites. Seven-night packages run $900 per diver for a double, and include three meals and two boat-dives daily, one night-dive, unlimited shore diving, weights, beach barbecue, and airport transfers on Guanaja. ☎ 800-642-3483, reservations@posadadelsol.com, www.posadadelsol. com. Handicapped access.

Utila

If diving is the only priority on your vacation, this is *the* place. Utila defines "hidden paradise." Diving and snorkeling are outstanding. Creature comforts are limited. Go anyway.

Utila sits about 18 miles from the mainland and can be easily reached from La Ceiba either by sea or air. The *Galaxy II* ferry operates daily, leaving from the municipal dock located east of La Ceiba. The trip takes only one hour on this fast motor vessel. Arrival in Utila is at the municipal dock, conveniently located in the central area of east harbor. Air service is available daily via **Sosa Airlines**, **IsleZa Airlines** and **Atlantic Airlines**. Sunday schedules are limited, plan on arriving and departing during the week.

Two story high **Utila Lodge** houses divers in eight air-conditioned rooms that overlook the sea. Dive shop on premises. Packages for seven nights, six days of diving are $750 per person. Included are three meals daily, three boat-dives per day, two night-dives, tanks and weights, belts, unlimited fills for shore dives and airport transfers. ☎ 504-45-3143.

Laguna Beach Resort, the most luxurious dive resort on Utila, has air-conditioned bungalows perched at the water's edge. Full-service dive operation offers three dives daily, night dives and unlimited beach diving on the spectacular fringing coral reef that lies about 150 yards offshore. Snorkelers find lots of fish in the turtle grass on the way out. The dock takes you halfway there. Kayaks for guests' use. Rates per day are $160 per person for a double; 190 for a single. Seven nights with diving average $1000 per person based on a double, $750 for a non-diver. ☎ 800-66-UTILA (88452) or 318-893-0013, fax 318-893-5024. Direct 011-504-45-3239, res@utila.com, http://www.utila.com.

Mango Inn located on Utila in the Bay Islands of Honduras Central America, is a A PADI Career Development Center and Gold Palm resort, offers all the adventures in diving from beginners to experienced divers. The inn is within walking distance of all amenities and beaches. A beautiful tropical garden surrounds the rooms and cabins. New deck and pool.

A seven-night dive package for $700 includes accommodations, two dives a day (six days of diving), one night-dive, local airport transfers, welcome cocktail, local taxes, and resort dive boat. For three dives per day add $50. Contact **Aquadream Travels** for packages. ☎ 888-322-DIVE, www.mango-inn.com, info@aquadreams.com.

Cayos Cochinos

The archipelago known as Cayos Cochinos, which is part of the Bay Islands of Honduras, is now officially a **protected biological reserve**, and its marine park status now protects the Cayos Cochinos rocks, surrounding waters, islets and reefs within a five-mile offshore buffer zone.

The **Smithsonian Institute** manages land and sea portions of the reserve. They have trained several Honduran Navy officers and civilians as park rangers at the Institute's permanent laboratory on **Cichino Pequeno**. Smithsonian scientists and personnel enforce fishing regulations, protect the turtle nesting areas and bird sanctuaries. Their laboratories are open to **Plantation Beach Resort** guests for special tours.

The coral-reef system in Cayos Cochinos has always been in excellent health with lots of competition for space among the invertebrates, hard and soft corals, algae and sponges. Since gaining park status in 1993 with the elimination of all nets, traps and long lines the fish population is spectacular. Enormous schools of fish, turtles, dolphins, rays and rare whale sharks are spotted more often.

A haven for micro photographers, Cayos Cochinos, shelters a myriad of critters and odd creatures such as tunicates, nudibranchs, seahorses, frogfish, batfish, flying gurnards and scorpionfish.

Plantation Beach Resort, formerly a pineapple plantation, on Cochinos Grand is a 10-room beachfront motel and an ecologists dream come true. Guest rooms feature solid Honduran mahogany construction, each with private bath, ceiling fans, and either one king or two twin beds. Rooms are clean and simple. Great diving and snorkeling is a giant stride off the beach. All-inclusive, seven-night packages are $895 per person. Transfers not included. ☎ 800-282-8932, res@roatan.com.

Facts

Nearest Recompression Chamber: Roatan. Bay Islands Air evacuation is possible from some other areas.

Getting Here: The best days to travel are Friday and Saturday. **Isleña Airlines** flies to the Bay Islands every day but Sunday from Tegucigalpa, San Pedro Sula and La Ceiba to Guanaja. *From Miami*: **American Airlines**, ☎ 800-433-7300, has daily flights to San Pedro Sula, Honduras. *From Houston:* **Continental Airlines** to San Pedro Sula with a stop in Tegucigalpa. Direct flights to Roatan from Miami, Houston and New Orleans are provided by **TACA** weekly. Water taxis are sent by the island resorts to pick you up.

Precautions: Register your cameras and electronic gear with customs before visiting Honduras. Do not bring drugs, plants or flowers into or out of the country.

Language: English on the Bay Islands, Spanish on mainland Honduras.

Documents: US citizens need a valid passport and return ticket. A tourist card will be issued on arrival. No health cards or shots are required for entry.

Departure tax: There is a ($2) entry fee and a ($25) departure fee.

Health: Vaccinations are not required. Check with your own doctor for health precautions. Ask about the water before drinking. Pack a diver's first-aid kit for sea stings and bug bites. Buy all your sundries and cosmetics before you leave home.

Currency: The lempira: L18.76=US$1 (variable).

Climate: Hot and humid. March and April are the hottest months. Rain clouds crop up most afternoons during summer and fall. Coolest months are January and February. Water temperature averages 80°F year-round.

Clothing: Shorts and T-shirts, jeans and sneakers. Long-sleeve shirts and long pants are good for mountain hikes and protection from bugs or sunburn. Snorkelers should wear protective clothing for the hot sun. Divers will find a lycra suit comfortable for deep wall dives.

Electricity: Most resorts have 110 volt current.

For Additional Information: Contact the resorts directly, the tour operators listed under *Where to Stay*, page 196, or the *Honduras Institute of Tourism*, ☎ 800-410-9608, www.letsgohonduras.com, www.roatan.com.

Jamaica

Jamaica's first tourists arrived in the late 1800s by banana boat, the result of a brainstorm by New England sea captain Lorenzo Down Baker, who fell in love with this mountainous island of delights. By the turn of the century banana exports had grown and Jamaica had become one of the trendiest vacation spots in the world.

Today most tourists arrive by jet and cruise ship. In all, 1.3 million tourists arrive each year to experience Jamaica's watersports, mountain vistas, night life and duty-free shopping.

 At 4,411 square miles, it is the third-largest island in the Caribbean after Cuba and Hispaniola. Geographically, it is a cornucopia of scenic wonders. Miles of soft sand beaches and lush greenery line the coasts, and high mountains loom inland. Overall, the terrain is very mountainous, with half of the land rising above 1,000 feet. The highest point, **Blue Mountain Peak**, soars to 7,402 feet. – higher than any other peak in the eastern half of North America. Hundreds of wild rivers and plunging waterfalls crisscross the mountains and moisten the fertile valleys, which produce some of the world's best coffee, fruits, flowers and vegetables. The flatter southern coast can look like the African savanna or the Indian plains and has alternating black and white sand beaches as well as mineral springs.

Offshore reef tracts provide a bounty of dive and snorkeling sites. Many are a short swim from the beach. Wall dives predominate as Jamaica's north stretch of reef edges the **Great Cayman Trench**. A ledge of shallow reefs stretches around the island's perimeter. Depths range from extreme shallows to awesome depths.

Almost everything imaginable grows in Jamaica's sensuous environment. Marine scientists have identified more than 50 species of sponges on the surrounding reefs. In the heyday of the British Empire, flowering and fruit trees were brought from Asia, the Pacific and Africa, evergreens from Canada, roses and nasturtiums from England. The breadfruit was sent from Tahiti, first by Captain Bligh on the *Bounty*. In return, Jamaica's native pineapple was sent to Hawaii and its mahogany to Central America. There are varieties of orchids, bromeliads and ferns in Jamaica that are native nowhere else and fruits like the Bombay mango that flourish only here.

The island's 2.4 million permanent residents are a mix of African, European, Afro-European, East Indian, Afro-East Indian, Chinese, Afro-Chinese – and seemingly every other combination of races. Most are black; many are shades of brown. Together they blend into a unique culture steeped in rituals, legends and customs.

Religion is an important force. The vast majority of Jamaicans are Christian, but there are communities of Jews, Hindus and Moslems. The Church of Jamaica, formerly the Church of England, has the largest membership. Rastafarianism commands a large following.

Jamaicans speak English and speak it eloquently, but with their own musical lilt and some words which are a survival from West African languages.

When Jamaicans speak the local patois, a blend of English and African, the discussion may be almost incomprehensible to the visitor at first, but after awhile you catch the rhythm and pick up some expressions – *Weh yuh ben deh* (Where've you been)? *Minuh hab nutten* (I don't have anything). *Yeh-mon* (Yes, man).

Proverbs and place names express the vitality of Jamaica talk. For "Mind your own business," there is "Cockroach no business inna fowl-yard"; for being corrupted by bad companions, "You lay down wid dawg, you get up wid fleas"; and for the pretentious, "The higher monkey climb, the more him expose."

Jamaica also boasts a broad variety of birds, both native and migratory, from the tiny bee hummingbird and its cousin the "doctor bird' (whose longer-tailed profile is the logo of Air Jamaica), to the mysterious solitaire with its mournful cry. Divers visiting the north coast will meet the kling-kling – a shiny black Antillian grackle who shares breakfast toast. A hike through the highest mountains may be rewarded by a sight of *papillio homerus*, one of the world's largest butterflies, also a native.

History

When Columbus sighted Jamaica on his second voyage in 1494, he recorded in his log: *"The fairest land ever eyes beheld... the mountains touch the sky."*

The Spanish never fully settled Jamaica, but they stayed long enough to kill off the peaceful resident Arawak Indians through forced labor, mass executions and European diseases.

Spanish colonists raised cattle on Jamaica and shipped lard, *manteca,* from a north-coast port today called **Montego Bay**. Jamaica became a provisions stop for ships headed to Central America in search of gold. In the century and a half of their rule, the Spaniards made two introductions that became pivotal to Jamaica's future. They brought in sugar cane and slaves from Africa to cultivate it.

In 1509 the Spaniards established New Seville as the capital, near the modern town of **Ocho Rios**. Today, the foundations of New Seville are being excavated and a search continues for the remains of two ships Columbus left beached nearby.

By 1655, the British conquered the island, driving the Spaniards from their new capital of **St. Jago de la Vega** (now **Spanish Town**) to Cuba.

 For nearly 200 years fortunes were built on sugar plantations with slave labor. Corruption became commonplace. Buccaneers were encouraged to operate from Jamaica, attack the treasure ships of Spain and France and capture territory. A young indentured laborer from Wales called Henry Morgan rose to become Jamaica's Lieutenant Governor and prospered as one of history's best-known pirates. His home base, **Port Royal**, on a peninsula outside today's capital, Kingston, was considered "the richest, wickedest city in Christendom," until one hot afternoon in 1692 when an earthquake tumbled most of it beneath the sea. Today, Port Royal and her treasures are covered by a dense reef. When winds are calm the site makes an interesting dive.

Magnificent plantation houses like **Rose Hall** and **Greenwood** rose above the cane fields. A spirit of independence among the planters and slaves took root during the early 1700s. There was the presence of the Maroons, descendants of slaves that had escaped from the Spaniards, called *cimarrones* (runaways). The Maroons lived in the mountains, defied the British troops, served as a magnet for other runaways and periodically staged rebellions, until a treaty in 1739 gave them some measure of local autonomy, which they still retain today.

The planters, too, were rebellious. When the 13 American colonies declared independence from Britain, the Jamaica House of Assembly voted to join them.

Slavery ended here in 1834. Economic chaos followed and Jamaica's Assembly voted away its traditional independence and became a full colony of England. Jamaica remained a British colony until August 6, 1962, when the Union Jack was lowered and the black, green and gold flag of the independent nation of Jamaica was raised.

Despite the loss of slave labor, Jamaica's rich farmlands prospered and indirectly launched its tourism industry when the banana-boat captains began carrying North American vacationers.

Jamaica also expanded citrus exports, including new hybrids like the *ortanique* and the "ugly fruit." Rum became the principal export and a new overseas market was found for Jamaican ginger in a product called ginger ale. Pimento was exported under the name "allspice," and Jamaica Blue Mountain coffee became a premium brand worldwide.

During the 1970s Jamaica supplied nearly two-thirds of the US needs for aluminum from the island's rich bauxite (alumina) deposits. With the current collapse of that market, Jamaica is building an economy where tourism and modern agriculture take a bigger place.

When to Go

The best months to dive Jamaica are December through May, the dry season. June through November brings the chance of a hurricane, though July and August are often dry.

Diving

Offshore diving is most popular along the north and west coasts of the island, particularly in **Negril** on the leeward western tip, which is sheltered from high winds and waves. **Montego Bay**, **Runaway Bay** and **Ocho Rios** follow in popularity. Despite many sites being a short swim from shore, diving on your own is prohibited. You must be accompanied by a guide from the Association of Dive Operators. Also, it is illegal to buy or possess coral and turtle products.

Marine Park regulations are as follows: 1) Always stay at least two feet above the reef. 2) Don't touch or stand on the coral and don't take souvenirs. 3) Don't wear gloves.

There is a closed lobster season from April through June 30.

Best Dive & Snorkeling Sites

Negril

Negril has three reef areas, with most interest between 50 and 70 feet. Seas are dependably calm and the visibility often exceeds 100 feet.

☆☆☆☆ **The Throne** is a 50-foot-wide cave at a depth of 65 feet, which you enter from the top at 40 feet. Its walls are carpeted with soft corals and huge yellow sponges hang from ceiling to floor. There is a chute at the back of the cave, 12 feet by three feet, with fine growths of black coral. Eels, octopi, turtles, stingrays, barracuda, reef fish, and an occasional nurse shark inhabit the cave.

☆☆☆ South of The Throne is a shallow reef area known as **Awee Moway**. Local dive guides have tamed resident stingrays, which you may pet if you approach them slowly. Eagle rays come by at night. Depths are 20 to 50 feet. Seas are calm.

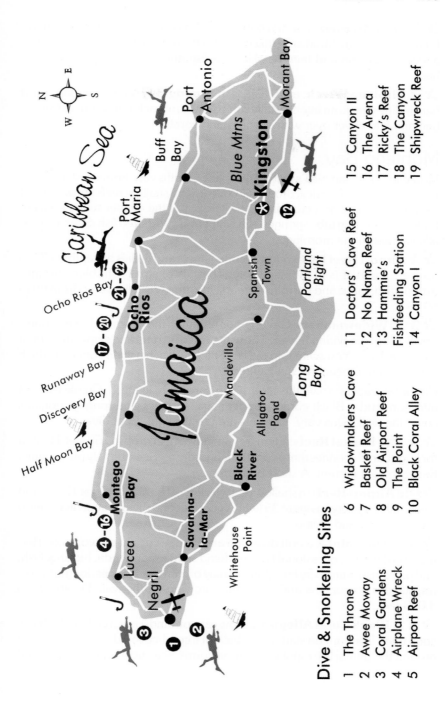

Dive & Snorkeling Sites

1 The Throne
2 Awee Moway
3 Coral Gardens
4 Airplane Wreck
5 Airport Reef

6 Widowmakers Cave
7 Basket Reef
8 Old Airport Reef
9 The Point
10 Black Coral Alley

11 Doctors' Cave Reef
12 No Name Reef
13 Hammie's Fishfeeding Station
14 Canyon I

15 Canyon II
16 The Arena
17 Ricky's Reef
18 The Canyon
19 Shipwreck Reef

☆☆ **Coral Gardens** is a shallow dive and snorkeling area near the shore. Elkhorn, staghorn, brain and star coral form the reef. Fish life includes filefish, angels, triggerfish and fairy basslets. Starfish and anemones are along the base.

☆☆ **Airplane Wreck**, at 70 feet, is in **Bloody Bay** off the Sandals resort beach. The wreck, an intentionally sunk Cessna, attracts numerous fish and is beginning to cover over with sponges and corals.

Montego Bay

Montego Bay is Jamaica's first marine park. Depths vary from waist deep to a ledge at 30 feet to vertical drops of 100 feet. The shallow reefs show signs of wear from storms and crowds of snorkelers, but the deeper scuba sites are fairly lush, with big tube sponges, sea whips and good sized fish. Seas are usually calmest in the morning.

☆☆ **Airport Reef** has expansive coral fingers and gullies at depths of 25 to 35 feet. The reef is in Montego Bay. Throngs of small fish, blue chromis, trumpetfish, tangs and parrotfish inhabit the area. Visibility varies from 60 to 80 feet.

☆☆☆ **Widowmakers Cave** is named after the cave in James Jones' novel, *Go to the Widowmaker*. The wall starts at 40 feet and slopes down to a cave at 80 feet. You swim into the cave till you reach a wide chimney which exits up onto a beautiful shallow reef.

Copper sweepers crowd the cave, as do parrotfish, kingfish, Creole wrasses and barracuda. Black corals, sea feathers, sponges and long gorgonians cover the wall. Seas vary. Currents are usually light. Boat dive.

☆☆☆☆ **Basket Reef** starts in 50 feet with a sheer drop to 150 feet. Named for huge barrel sponges that adorn the ledge, the reef is extremely photogenic. Expect a light current. A short boat trip.

☆ **Old Airport Reef** is a shallow reef with lots of fish and corals at 15 feet and small caves and crevasses at 35 feet. A good second dive. A boat dive. Good for snorkeling and diving.

☆☆☆ **The Point** is a drift dive with an average current of two knots. Bermuda chub, rays, occasional hammerhead sharks, barracuda, big angelfish, and parrotfish seem to fly by a static display of crimson sponges, long lacy corals, slender gorgonians and anemones growing on the wall. Depths go to 3,000 feet.

☆☆☆ **Black Coral Alley** is a narrow canyon landscaped with bushy black coral trees. The canyon starts at the base of a coral-covered seamount. Swim around the pinnacle to spot crabs, tubeworms, sea cucumbers, urchins and octopi hiding in the ledges and crevices. Depths are from 40 to 65 feet. Visibility about 80 feet.

☆☆ **Doctors Cave Reef** is a shallow dive opposite Doctors Cave Beach. Depths average 25 feet. This spot is ideal for beginners – completely sheltered from the afternoon wind and waves. The reef is mostly elkhorn clumps with some brain and star coral heads. Small, friendly reef fish scurry about. Visibility varies from 40 to 60 feet. Boat access.

☆☆☆☆ **No Name Reef** is straight out from Doctors Cave. The reef is pretty, with yellow and purple sea fans, tube and barrel sponges, lacy corals, gorgonians and patches of finger coral.

Shore Dives

The following sites are accessible from the jetty at **Chalet Caribe**, just west of Montego Bay. Currents are normally very light though winter storms blowing from the north will make entry difficult or impossible. Before entering the water check with the dive shop for rules on diving the Marine Park. Cave and tunnel dives should be attempted only by experienced cave divers.

☆ **Hammie's Fishfeeding Station** came about in 1981 when dive shop owners, Theo and Hammie Smit started a private marine sanctuary. The site is now part of the **Montego Bay Marine Park**. Friendly fish will pose for pictures. Check with dive guide for appropriate fish rewards. Depth is 25 feet.

☆☆ **Canyon I** is a cave/tunnel dive out past the fish-feeding station. There is an entrance to the cave at the edge of the reef 30 feet down. Exit at 70 feet. Rare orange sponges grow in the tunnel. Next to Canyon I is **Canyon II**, a hangout for spiny and rock lobsters, schoolmaster snappers and an occasional nurse shark.

☆☆ **The Arena** is about 250 yards from the jetty. This shallow reef is bowl-shaped, resembling an amphitheater with walls of coral. The walls slope to 70 feet, where two tunnels lead to more caverns with abundant black coral and big barrel sponges. There is a neat old anchor at the top of the reef. Turtles and eagle rays are common dive buddies.

Runaway Bay

☆☆☆ **Ricky's Reef** is a huge reef complex with gigantic lavender and yellow tube sponges, thick growths of lacy soft corals, bush corals, orange tube corals, cactus corals, lettuce corals, and stony corals. Most interest is at 90 feet. For experienced divers.

☆☆ **The Canyon** cuts between two walls covered with dense growths of sea rods, sea plumes, sea whips, tube sponges, feather corals, bush corals, and mesh sea fans. Depths are from 35 to 100 feet. Expect a rendezvous with curious angelfish, sergeant majors, trumpetfish, barracuda and an occasional nurse shark. For experienced divers.

⭐⭐ **Shipwreck Reef** is a shallow reef shot through with caves and crevices. The dive is in front of the **Ambience Jamaica** resort. An old freighter at 15 feet houses spotted morays, schooling fish and barracuda. An occasional visit by a turtle adds interest. Average depth is 30 feet. Nice for snorkeling or diving.

⭐⭐ **Silver Spray Reef** is another shallow garden with a good many of fish and nice soft corals.

Ocho Rios

⭐⭐⭐ **Wreck of *The Kathryn*** was a Canadian mine sweeper acquired by Jamaica many years ago and used as a cargo vessel and later as a fishing vessel. In 1991 it was acquired by **Fantasy Divers and Water Sports**, who sank it to create a new dive and fish-breeding spot. The ship sits in 50 feet of water. It's located a mile east of the mouth of the White River off the coast of St. Mary.

⭐⭐⭐ **Top of the Mountain** is a seamount at 60 feet, decorated with orange sponges, bushy corals, and gorgonians. At 75 feet a cave leads inside the pinnacle. Visibility averages 70 feet.

Dive Operators

Negril

Negril Scuba Centre at the **Negril Beach Club** on Norman Manley Boulevard offers reef and wreck trips, night dives, cave dives and underwater photography and equipment rentals and repairs. ☎ 867-957-9641 or for reservations: 888-634-7450, www.negriljamaica.com.

Sundivers Negril Ltd. is a PADI Five Star center at the **Point Village Hotel** offering reef trips and specialty courses, custom underwater videos. ☎ 876-957-4503 or 957-9943, www.sundiversnegril.com.

Bare Feet Ltd. located on Norman Manley Boulevard offers dive and scuba trips. ☎ 876-957-4944.

Scuba Jamaica offers PADI and NAU courses, dive and snorkeling trips, NITROX, ☎ 876-973-4910, www.scuba-jamaica.com.

Montego Bay

Captain's Watersports at the **Round Hill Hotel & Villas**, Hanover, west of Montego Bay, offers PADI Resort through Certification courses. Boat trips take off for the Jamaica Marine Park. A one-tank dive is $40, a two-tank dive $70. Add $20 for equipment rental. Open 8 am to 5 pm daily; every fifth dive is free. For kids they offer **SASY** (Supplied Air Snorkeling for Youth) and **Bubblemaker** programs. ☎ 876-956-7312, www.captainsdivecenter.com, captainswatersports@yahoo.com.

Scuba and snorkeling reef tours are offered by **North Coast Marine Sports**, at the Half Moon Hotel. ☎ 876-953-9266, fax 876-953-9266, busha201@yahoo.com.

Cool Aqua Divers Ltd., a full-service PADI Dive Facility offers wall and wreck dives daily along Jamaica's north coast. They offer free daily scuba clinics and dive classes from resort courses to dive master. Located at Rose Hall Beach Club, 12 miles East of Montego Bay. ☎ 876-680-0969, fax 876-953-8138, coolaqua@cwjamaica.com.

Jamaqua offers dive and snorkeling trips near Runaway Bay. The shop is on North Coast Highway, Runaway Bay. ☎ 876-973-4845.

Fisherman's Inn watersports center offers diving, snorkeling, fishing and sailing plus dockage for visiting yachts. It is located in Falmouth, a few miles east of Montego Bay. Handicapped divers program. ☎ 876-954-3427, fax 876-954-3427.

Ocho Rios

In Ocho Rios, all-inclusive resorts either have their own dive shops on premises or arange for beach and boat dives with local shops.

Where to Stay

The all-inclusive resorts following usually include airport transfers, all meals, drinks, dive trips, equipment, and tips. Scuba courses are extra and require a medical certificate from home. Rates change frequently, check Websites for specials.

Negril

Point Village oceanfront resort features 150 air-conditioned rooms and suites, all equipped with satellite television, kitchenette, phone, balcony or patio. Two sand beachs and spectacular cliffs with grottos. Property has a man-made pool and rock pools that are carved from ironshore and fill with salt water as the tide comes in. Jacuzzi. Winter rates per day from $320 for a double. Includes all meals, taxes and transfers. **Sundivers Dive Shop** on premises. Toll-free from US, ☎ 877-POINTJA (877-764-6852); local, 876-957-5170, www.pointvillage.com.

Rock Cliff Hotel is a charming resort with shore diving from the dock and Sundivers on premises. Packages. ☎ 876-957-4108. Write to **Sundivers**, Lighthouse Road, Negril, Jamaica.

Hedonism II is an all-inclusive resort for couples and singles only. Features include luxurious rooms and suites, five bars, a clothing-optional island with swim-up pool bar, laser karaoke, indoor game room with satellite TV, sauna, arts and crafts centers. Sports include scuba, water-skiing, snorkeling, windsurfing, sailing, kayaking, water trikes, tennis, fitness center, squash, bicycles, golf and horseback riding. ☎ 800-GO-SUPER (800-467-8737).

Grand Lido is an adults-only, all-inclusive resort scattered over 22 acres in Negril. Features include nine bars, clothing-optional beach, game room, tennis, 24-hour food-and-drink Club Houses. Sports include scuba, snorkeling, kayaking, Sunfish sailing, windsurfing, and water-skiing. ☎ 876-957-5517, www.superclubs.com.

Sandals Negril is yet another all-inclusive resort that caters to couples only. Facilities include two pools, swim-up bar, scuba center, satellite TV and disco. Rates for two for three nights range from $1,250 to $2,400 depending on type of accommodation and season. ☎ 800-SANDALS, www.sandals.com.

Those who prefer sleeping under the stars may pitch a tent at **Lighthouse Park** on the beach. Contact the Jamaica Tourist Board for details, ☎ 800-233-4582.

Montego Bay

Sandals Montego Bay is an all-inclusive resort for couples. See *Sandals Negril* above for contact information and resort details.

Falmouth

Fisherman's Inn & Dive Resort, a 30-minute drive east of Montego Bay, is a dedicated dive resort on a phosphorescent lagoon at **Oyster Bay**. Designed and built by divers for divers, the resort features modern, spacious, air-conditioned, waterfront rooms, a good restaurant, poolside bar. Dive sites are a five-minute ride from the resort dock. ☎ 876-954-4078.

Starfish Trelawny Beach Hotel is a beachfront family resort affiliated with the SuperClub resorts. With the exception of lunch and liquor, moderate rates include meals and watersports. Book through your travel agent or direct. ☎ 800-659-5436, www.starfishresorts.com or www.superclubs.com.

tagged below.

Ocho Rios

Boscobel Beach is an all-inclusive resort for families that offers scuba and snorkeling as part of the price. Guest rooms and suites have every imaginable amenity. A hurricane guarantee gives you another vacation at a Sandals or Beaches resort if a hurricane hits while you're there. ☎ 888-BEACHES, local 876-975-7330, www.beaches.com.

Sightseeing & Other Activities

Negril

Negril is the quietest area of Jamaica and one of the loveliest. Building codes have kept the highest structure "no higher than the highest palm tree." Most activities are water-related and can be arranged through the dive shops.

Getting around Negril is easy. You can rent a car, bicycle, or canoe, or just stroll along the beautiful seven-mile beach. Among the interesting buildings to visit is the 19th-century **Courthouse of Lucea**, and the **clock tower** modeled after the helmet once worn by the German Royal Guard. The clock itself was made in 1817; it keeps perfect time, and is tended by a family that has had the job for over a hundred years.

Montego Bay

This second-largest city in Jamaica offers many attractions, from architecture and museums to natural scenic beauty. **The Cage**, an 18th-century jail for slaves and runaway seamen, is in the center of the city and houses a small museum. **St. James Parish Church**, built in 1775-1782, is regarded as one of the finest churches in Jamaica. **The Bird Sanctuary** at Anchovy features "doctor bird" hummingbirds, one of 24 species found only in Jamaica. A trip into the interior on the **Hilton High Day Tour** gives a taste of country farm life and exposure to a different Jamaica: the mysterious cockpit country, and blond Jamaicans whose ancestors came long ago from Germany.

Montego Bay offers duty-free shopping for liquor, china, glassware, perfumes, cigars, English cashmeres and a variety of crafts. There are also several art galleries, including the **Gallery of West Indian Art**, that are worth a browse.

Montego Bay's nightlife is varied. Discos throughout the city play reggae and rock. A once-a-week event deserving special consideration is **An Evening on the Great River** – a torchlight ride in dugout canoes followed by dinner, dancing and entertainment.

Ocho Rios

Ocho Rios is the central point of a magnificent region that includes both deserted and developed beaches, fern-clad cliffs and breathtaking waterfalls. Tranquil, yet stimulating, it evolved from a center of Spanish cultural influence to a region of lush sugar and colorful fishing villages and finally to a modern Caribbean resort area.

Ocho Rios may well be the most-photographed area in the West Indies. **Shaw Park Gardens** on the high ground affords spectacular vistas of the coast. **Dunn's River Falls**, over 600 feet high and cascading in tiers onto the beach, is considered the Niagara of the Caribbean. **Fern Gully** offers a spectacular, curving three-mile journey through a world of tropical ferns, including the 30-foot-tall fern tree and more than 550 other native varieties.

Several excellent plantation tours give an introduction to Caribbean farming, and to strange and exotic vegetation. **"Firefly,"** the mountaintop house where Noel Coward lived and is buried, is open to visitors. There are the 16th-century Spanish ruins of **New Seville**, and, of course, there is **Discovery Bay**, which today features historic **Columbus Park**. The **Chukka Cove Equestrian Center** offers several scenic horseback trails as well as polo and dressage lessons (dressage refers to precision movements of a trained horse in response to barely perceptible signals from its rider).

Port Antonio

For many years, Port Antonio was the well-kept secret hideaway of people such as Clara Bow, Bette Davis, Errol Flynn, Ginger Rogers and J.P. Morgan. Today it is a playground of the world's elite – from royalty and movie stars to captains of industry, commerce and politics. It has also been the backdrop for several feature films.

Orchids, bananas, tree-ferns and palms grow along the roadside around this quiet port town. Elegant villas nestled in the hills and along the seacoast are a contrast to old abandoned mansions, historic forts, waterfalls, and caves.

Sightseeing in Port Antonio is relaxing. There is **Fort George**, overlooking the two harbors, with 10-foot-thick walls and cannons pointed out to sea. The once-glorious **Folly Mansion** is now a legendary ruin. In contrast, the **Errol Flynn Plantation** is well-tended and prosperous.

Water lovers can choose between an icy-cold dip in **Somerset Falls** and snorkeling, scuba diving and swimming in the "bottomless" **Blue Lagoon** (actually 180 feet deep). Or they can get carried away down the Rio Grande in a two-passenger 30-foot bamboo raft, guided by a licensed Jamaican raftsman. For those who like to explore, there are **Nonsuch Caves** with fossils, coral formations and remnants of an early Arawak Indian community. East of Port Antonio is **Reach Falls**, one of the most spectacular waterfalls in Jamaica.

Kingston

Kingston, Jamaica's capital, is the largest English-speaking city south of Miami.

Set against a backdrop of the Blue Mountain range, Kingston is a busy, well-populated, cosmopolitan city. It is the cultural center as well. The **National Gallery of Jamaica** and the **Institute of Jamaica** offer an exciting view of Jamaican culture, including the most complete collection of the country's art to be found anywhere.

Mandeville

The inland town of Mandeville is considered the most English town in Jamaica; many of its original buildings of early-1800s vintage remain. Outside Mandeville are bauxite mines and a production facility, which are open for touring. Nearby is the famous **Picakapeppa factory,** where the popular Jamaican hot sauce is produced. **Marshall's Pen**, located on a 300-acre cattle farm, is a well-kept 18th-century Great House with a hiking trail and bird sanctuary.

On the way from Mandeville to the south coast, **Bamboo Avenue** is a lovely two-mile drive covered by giant bamboos over a century old.

Facts

Helpful Phone Numbers: Police, ☎ 119; ambulance, ☎ 110. Hospital,Montego Bay, Cornwall Regional Hospital, ☎ 952-5100; Ocho Rios, St. Ann's Bay Hospital, ☎ 972-2272. Pharmacy, Montego Bay, McKenzie's, 16 Strand Street, ☎ 952-2467. US Embassy, ☎ 929-4850.

Nearest Recompression Chamber: The Marine Lab at Discovery Bay.

Getting Here: *Donald Sangster International Airport* in Montego Bay is the best entry point for the dive-resort areas. **American Airlines**, ☎ 800-433-7300, offers direct service from New York. **Air Jamaica**, ☎ 800-523-5585, flies from Atlanta, Baltimore, Chicago, Fort Lauderdale, Miami, Los Angeles, New York, Orlando and Philadelphia. **Continental**, ☎ 800-231-0856, flies from Newark; **BWIA** from San Juan; **Northwest**, ☎ 800-447-4747, has daily flights from Minneapolis and Tampa; **US Air** from Baltimore and Charlotte.

Precautions: Avoid touring the off-the-beaten-track areas of the cities, especially at night. Avoid Kingston completely. The dive-resort areas listed are fairly quiet, but ragged natives pandering *ganja* (marijuana) may approach you. Stick to resort restaurants and tourist shopping areas.

Driving: On the left. Rental cars are scarce in season. Be sure to arrange for a rental car in advance of your trip.

Language: English and Jamaican-Creole patois (dialect made up of particular words and speech patterns used by most of the population).

Documents: Visitors from the US or Canada must show a passport and a return ticket. British visitors must have a passport and a return ticket.

Customs: Visitors are prohibited from bringing in drugs, fresh fruit, flowers, meat or rum. Firearms or ammunition are prohibited.

Airport Tax: US$15.

Currency: The Jamaican dollar (JMD). The exchange rate fluctuates daily, depending on the foreign exchange markets. The current rate stands at US$1=JA$37.41.

Climate: Average temperature is 82°F. Water temperature ranges from 80° to 90°. Wetsuits are not necessary, but a lycra suit is comfortable in winter.

Clothing: Lightweight, casual. Hiking shoes for visiting the "mist forests."

Electricity: Varies with the hotel. Some have 110 volts/60 cycles and others 220. To be safe, carry a converter for your appliances.

Religious Services: Protestant, Catholic, Jewish, Rastafarian.

For Additional Information: *The Jamaica Tourist Board,* 3440 Wilshire Boulevard, Suite 805, Los Angeles, CA 90010; ☎ 800-233-4582 or 213-384-1123, fax 213-384-1780, http://www.jamaicatravel.com.

Puerto Rico

Puerto Rico's beautiful sand beaches, cosmopolitan cities and abundant man-made attractions pale in comparison to the pristine reefs that surround three quarters of its coastline. Coupled with first-class hotels, easy access from the United States, and a choice of rural or urban settings, it is gaining popularity as an all-around vacation spot for divers. At the eastern end of the Greater Antilles chain, this 110- by 35-mile island has the Atlantic Ocean to the north and the Caribbean to the south. **Vieques** and **Culebra** islands lie to the east, and **Mona Island** is to the west. There are 3½ million residents of Puerto Rico, with about one million in the San Juan metropolitan area.

The island's terrain ranges from palm-lined beaches on four coastlines, to rugged mountain ranges, gently rolling hills and deserts. There are 20 designated forest reserves in Puerto Rico and an additional six proposed. The most notable include the 28,000-acre **El Yunque** rain forest near San Juan, part of the **Caribbean National Forest** and the only tropical rain forest in the US Forest Service; the **Guajataca Forest,** with 25 miles of trails through karst reserves – an area of huge, moonscape craters and caves; and the **Guanica Forest Reserve**, a dry forest with the largest number of bird species on the island. There are also two **phosphorescent bays**, one off La Parguera on the southwest coast and one off the island of Vieques.

Diving and snorkeling is along the **Continental Shelf**, which surrounds the island on the east, south and west coasts. Underwater terrain is diverse, with shallow reefs off **Humacao** on the east coast, caves and wrecks off **Aguadilla** on the west coast, and dramatic walls at **The Great Trench**, which starts in the Virgin Islands, stretches the entire length of Puerto Rico's south coast and winds up at Cabo Rojo on the west coast. Marine life is exciting, with manatees in the brackish mangrove areas, pelagics at Mona Island (50 miles southwest), and all species of sea turtles at Culebra. In winter, migrating humpback whales travel the Mona Passage off the west coast. Dolphins frequent the eastern shores. Towering soft corals grow to 20 feet in some spots.

History

 Cave drawings indicate that people lived on Puerto Rico for more than 2,000 years before Christopher Columbus claimed it for Spain in 1493. Back then, it was known as *Borinquen* and inhabited by several Indian tribes, including the Taíno Indians. The Spaniards named it San Juan for St. John the Baptist, but later changed it to Puerto Rico, which means "Rich Port."

Ponce de Léon, seeker of the Fountain of Youth, was the first governor in 1508. During the next three centuries, settlers defended the island from the French, the Dutch and English – traditional enemies of the Spanish empire. Following the Spanish-American War in 1898, Spain ceded the island to the United States. Puerto Ricans became US citizens in 1917, held their first gubernatorial elections in 1948, and adopted Commonwealth status in 1952.

The Caribbean's most industrially developed island is a major producer and exporter of manufactured goods, pharmaceuticals and high-tech equipment. Since the 19th century, Puerto Rico has been a major exporter of rum and today 83% of the rum sold in the US comes from Puerto Rico.

East Coast

Best Dive & Snorkeling Sites

Diving off Puerto Rico's east coast centers around **Fajardo**, **Humacao** and the offshore islands of **Icacos**, **Palominos**, **Palminitos**, **Monkey Island**, **Vieques** and **Culebra**. Outstanding features are towering soft corals, walls, dramatic overhangs and abundance of fish. Many of the mainland dive sites are close to shore, but the best are about a 20-minute boat ride. Depths are from 35 to 100 feet. Shore diving and snorkeling is possible off Fajardo, but freshwater runoff near the shore clouds the water and lowers visibility. Spearfishing and coral collecting are prohibited.

☆☆☆☆**The Reserve**, a 20-minute boat ride from Humacao, appears like rivers of white sand between coral canyons. The spur and groove formations shelter towering pillar coral, large star and brain coral heads ruffled with sea rods, spiny sea fans and slender tube sponges. Nurse sharks, stingrays, spotted and green morays and tropicals inhabit the reef's ledges and overhangs. Seas average two to four feet. Depths average 50 to 80 feet. Water temperature ranges from 82° to 90°F. Divers should have some experience.

☆☆☆☆**Basslet Reef**, one mile from Humacao, is a small wall with overhangs, caves and swim-throughs. It is frequented by hawksbill turtles, nurse sharks, and enormous angelfish. Most of the reef is formed of mushrooming pillar corals rippled by a healthy display of sea plumes and sea rods. Dolphins visit the area during spring and early summer. Top of the wall is at 60 feet. Usually no current, but expect three- to five-foot surface swells. Basslet Reef is a 15-minute boat ride from Palmas Del Mar docks.

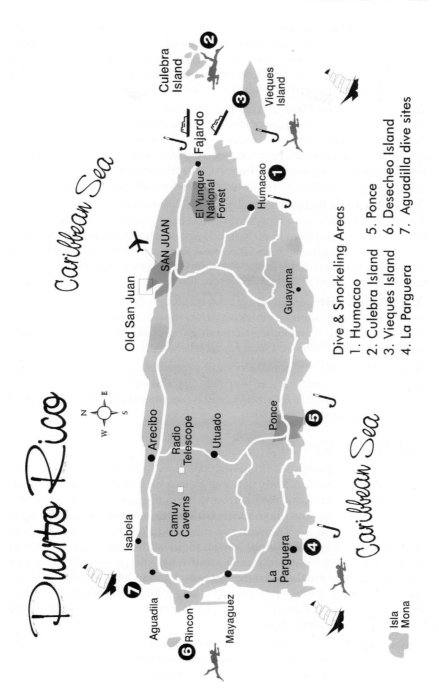

Puerto Rico

Caribbean Sea

N
W E
S

Old San Juan

SAN JUAN

El Yunque National Forest

Fajardo

Culebra Island

Vieques Island

Humacao

Desecheo Island

Aguadilla dive sites

Guayama

Ponce

Utuado

Radio Telescope

Arecibo

Camuy Caverns

Isabela

Aguadilla

Rincon

Mayaguez

La Parguera

Caribbean Sea

Isla Mona

Dive & Snorkeling Areas
1. Humacao
2. Culebra Island
3. Vieques Island
4. La Parguera
5. Ponce
6. Desecheo Island
7. Aguadilla dive sites

✮✮✮✮✮**The Cracks** is a section of subsea cliffs ripped apart by an earthquake. The result is an intriguing maze of chasms and fissures where throngs of fish and lobster hide out. Small caves and coral buttresses drop down to a sandy bottom. Dramatic photo opportunities. Depths are from 50 to 80 feet. For experienced divers only. Seas run three to five feet.

✮✮✮✮**Monkey Reef** is a 25-minute boat trip from Palmas Del Mar docks. The reef is an expanse of sloping hills covered over with acres of soft corals and sponges. One area slopes to a sandy bottom where you will find large, friendly southernstingrays, spotted eagle rays and thousands of shells. The other side is ledges and overhangs where you never know what to expect. Depths range from 20 to 50 ft. Excellent for novice and experienced divers.

✮✮✮ **La Jolla Ridge** is a small coral wall one mile from shore. A healthy display of soft corals, sea whips, sea fans and throngs of schooling fish starts at 40 feet and plunges down to 80 feet. Ledges, overhangs and swim-throughs are home to every imaginable sea creature. A spectacular dive at night, when the area becomes a ballet of basket stars. Recommended for novice and experienced divers. Seas average two to four feet.

✮✮✮ **The Grotto**, a spur and groove reef four miles from Palmas Del Mar docks, is a memorable dive experience. Small caves, overhangs and swim-thoughs are inhabited by crowds of copper sweepers, fairy tailed basslets and blue chromis. Good for all level divers.

✮✮✮ **The Drift** is a gently sloping hill covered on one side with giant sponges, sea rods and whips. As you glide over the top you approach a valley of swim-throughs and ledges frequented by moray eels, lobsters, queen and French angels, and nurse sharks.

Culebra & Vieques

Culebra is a mini-archipelago with 23 offshore islands, situated midway between Puerto Rico and St. Thomas. Shallow coral reefs surround the entire area. A favorite snorkeling and photo spot is **Culebrita**, where there is also a lighthouse. The main five-mile-long island, home to 2,000 people, is a National Wildlife Refuge known for its white sand beaches, seabird colonies – boobies, frigates, and gulls – and as a nesting ground for all species of Caribbean **sea turtles** – leatherback, green, hawksbill and loggerhead. The turtles nest from April through July. (National Wildlife Refuge, ☎ 787-742-0115.) Expeditions for turtle watching are conducted by Earthwatch, a nonprofit organization.

Vieques is a popular camping island for locals and a day-trip for east-coast divers and snorkelers. Known for its beautiful beaches, two thirds of the island is owned by the US Navy. Two towns, **Esperanza** and **Isabel Segunda**, serve Vieques' 8,000 residents. Accommodation is available in several guest houses and hotels, with rates from $70 per night near, Espernaza; www.vieques-island.com.

Shallow reefs and dropoffs lie within one mile of the shoreline. Many are less than 50 feet in depth, with some very shallow areas. Sea conditions, sometimes rough, vary with the wind. Swells on the leeward side average two to three feet. Vieques subsea highlights are walls, caves, giant barrel sponges, healthy fish populations, and a phosphorescent bay. Beach dives are possible off the West end at Green Beach, with reef depths from 10 to 25 feet.

Trips to Culebra and Vieques take off from **Humacao** or from **Puerto del Rey Marina** at Fajardo, north of Humacao (Puerto del Rey is the largest marina in the Caribbean, with 1,100 deepwater slips and service facilities). For low-cost ($3) public ferry schedules call ☎ 787-860-4560.

The **Puerto Rican Port Authority** ferry runs between the town of Fajardo and the island of Vieques several times a day, starting at 9:30 am weekdays amd 6:00 am weekends and holidays. The ride usually takes about an hour and 15 minutes. The car ferry takes about two hours. (Note: Rental cars are not allowed on the ferries.) The length of the trip varies with sea and weather conditions. ☎ 800-981-2005, 787-863-0705. Vieques office, ☎ 787-741-4761; Fajardo office, ☎ 800-981-2005, 787-863-0705 (or -0852, -4560, -3360). Reservations are not accepted for foot passengers but if you are in a vehicle a reservation is required. Arrive early. Fajardo is about a one-hour drive from San Juan International Airport (SJU); the ferry port is on Road 195 in sector Puerto Real. Round-trip fare $4.00.

Island High Speed Ferry out of Old San Juan also offers service to Culebra and Vieques. Their first trip of the day departs from the Pier 2 ferry terminal (Aquaexpresso Ferry Terminal), next to the cruise ship pier, at 8 am, and arrives at Culebra at 9:45, then departs for Vieques at 11 am. Reservations a must. Arrive early. ☎ 877-899-3993, www.islandhighspeedferry.com.

Culebra has daily flights arriving from SJU via **Isla Nena Air Service** (☎ 787-741-1577) and **Air Flamenco** (☎ 787-724-6464). Allow an hour for the taxi ride from San Juan to Fajardo.

A half-hour flight to Vieques from SJU costs about $165 round-trip. You can also fly to Vieques from San Juan Isla Grande airport, via **Vieques Air Link** or **MSN** for about $95 round-trip. A taxi from SJU to San Juan Isla Grande is about $20 – worth it if at least two people are traveling. Flights from Fajardo cost about $45 for the 10-minute trip.

Dive Operators

Caribbean School of Aquatics at the **Villa Marino** in Fajardo, visits the best sites aboard sleek power boats and catamarans, including the 51-foot

Fun Cat catamaran for 48 people; the 40-foot *Innovation*; and a custom 35-foot Pearson dive boat that carries 30 people. Diving lessons and certification. All-day boat trips, including transportation to vessel, diving and snorkeling equipment, lunch and refreshments. On the way back, rum punch is served and passengers are offered a cultural experience playing bongos, tambourines, maraca and guiro.

Two-tank dive trips cost $99 and include all equipment (same price without equipment). Referrals, PADI and NAUI courses. Snorkelers may join divers. US Coast Guard (USCG) certified. ☎ 787-728-6606, www.saildivepart.com. info@saildiveparty.com.

Caribe Aquatic Adventures at the **Park Plaza Normandie Hotel**, San Juan Metro Area, features shore dives off the resort beach, and snorkeling and scuba trips to the islands off Fajardo (Icacos for snorkeling, Palomino and Palominito for diving) aboard the 33-foot *Sea Horse Lady*. Lunch and transportation from San Juan are included. Equipment rentals available. ☎ 787-281-8858, www.diveguide.com, caribaqu@aol.com.

Where to Stay

Paradores are country inns throughout the island that offer quality lodging near historical monuments and points of interest.

Wyndham El Conquistador blends four luxury resorts into one – the **Grand Hotel** has panoramic views, spacious bathrooms and walk-in closets; **Las Casitas Village** offers a Spanish-style atmosphere with private check-in, pool and personal butler; the villas of **Las Olas Village** that are built into the side of a cliff; and **Marina Village**, where grand yachts tie up to the resort docks, and where the on-premise dive shop, Casa del Mar, picks up divers and snorkelers.

The resort amenities include an on-site dive shop that tours the best dive and snorkeling spots off the eastern shores, a golf course, and six swimming pools. Dive packages through Caradonna Tours offer the best prices that we have found. From July 31-October 6, dive packages for seven nights start at $1,142 per person; non-divers from $692. From July 31-October 6, five nights from $962, $692 for non-divers. The package includes accommodations, round-trip airport transfers from San Juan. Five night vacations include three two-tank dives, Seven night packages include five two-tank dives and all hotel taxes and service charges. Prices are per person based on double occupancy. ☎ 800-330-3322, www.caradonna.com.

South Coast

Best Dive & Snorkeling Sites

 Dive trips off the south coast originate in **Ponce**, Puerto Rico's second-largest city, or **La Parguera**, a sleepy fishing village known for its phosphorescent bay – one of four bio-luminescent bodies of water in the world. It is also home to the University of Puerto Rico's Marine Science Facility.

A 2½-hour drive from San Juan airport, La Parguera is not yet heavily populated by tourists. Accommodations are modest, local attractions and other activities are limited.

☆☆ **Ponce Caja de Muertos** (Coffin Island), **Cayo Ratones**, **Cayo Caribe** and **Cayo Cardon** form a crescent barrier reef from Ponce west to Tallaboa. All are a 20-minute boat ride from Ponce. Shore dives are possible off Coffin Island, a park administered by the Department of Natural Resources. Depths range from 15 to 40 feet.

☆☆☆ **La Parguera Wall Dives**

The best sites are along a 20-mile wall that edges the **Great Trench** from La Parguera to Ponce. Recommended for advanced divers; depths on the wall vary from 50 to over 100 feet. Visibility exceeds 150 feet. Currents, if any, are light. Seas average one to two feet. Boat trips are 45 minutes to an hour long; no wall dives are accessible from shore.

Black Wall starts at 60 feet and drops down vertically to great depths. Divers encounter lots of schooling fish, green morays, big crabs, deep-water black gorgonians, and good coral heads.

Hole in the Wall at 120 feet, as the name implies, is a hole where divers can swim through and come up in 100 feet of water.

Hai Lite is a group of deep-water trenches with valleys of schooling grunts and squirrelfish. Beautiful barrel and giant tube sponges. Lavender trumpetfish.

Grunts Valley, like Hai Lite, is a hangout for myriads of grunts, yellowtail, snapper, squirrelfish.

Cylinders is a sharp sloping wall named for huge gas cylinders dropped by a cargo ship 20 years ago. The cylinders are covered with corals and sponges.

Fallen Rock is an enormous rock in the middle of a Y-shaped trench. The walls are sheer, with lots of schooling fish, big barrel sponges and gorgonians. The adjacent trench is so conjested with traveling fish the locals nicknamed it "L.A. Highway." Expect the unexpected!

☆☆ La Parguera Inner-Reef Dives

The Playground is the site of the Parguera Divers Bubble Bell. You fill the bell with fresh air from your tank and experience an underwater habitat for two. You can talk, kiss, eat or just hang out under it. Two big French angelfish will hover close and play in your bubbles.

Barracuda City, at 50 feet, is a dense forest of staghorn and elkhorn corals packed with clouds of the silvery fish for which it was named. While encountering one or two barracuda on any Caribbean reef is scarcely noteworthy, this spot can be downright unnerving. Exciting photo possibilities for those who dare!

Hog Heaven I, II, III is a newly discovered triple-site reef off La Parguera with a fascinating complex of coral caves, holes and canyons. It was named by local dive master, Efra Figueroa. Upon first diving the area, he met a colossal hogfish. The big hogfish is gone, but sightings of nurse sharks are common.

The Pinnacles are coral formations estimated to be 5,000 years old. They appear like giant mushrooms with holes and caves. This is a spot for marine invertebrates – octopi, seahorses, arrow crabs, basket sponges and more.

The Forest is a mass of towering soft corals growing across rocky canyons. Many critters and fish. Expect a light surge.

Additional dive and snorkeling sites off the south coast are **1990, The Star, Aquarium, Manhattan, Coral Garden, Sponge Garden, The Chimney** and others.

Dive Operators

Parguera Divers Training Center, a PADI and NAUI instruction facility, offers basic certification, dive master, rescue and medic courses. Snorkeling, JetSkis, windsurfing, mangrove trail tours, phosphorescent bay trips, fishing and boat rentals can be arranged. Open-water referrals accepted for PADI and NAUI. Nitrox. Major credit cards and travelers checks accepted.

This English-, Spanish-, and German-speaking dive center takes small groups of up to 13 divers to all the best spots on the south coast. ☎ 787-899-4171, fax 787-899-5558, www.parguerdivers.com. Write Parguera Divers, PO Box 514, Lajas, Puerto Rico 00667.

Sea Ventures Dive Copamarina at the Copamarina Beach Resort offers two-tank dives aboard a sleek, custom dive boat for $95. The price drops a little after the first trip and continues dropping down to $70 the more you dive. Snorkelers enjoy special trips to **Gilligan's Island** and **Ballena Beach** where friendly angelfish, groupers, snappers, damsels, trunkfish, sergeant majors, hogfish, trumpetfish, puffers, bahama blue runners, seahorses, starfish, yellowtail, bonita tuna, fiddler crab, ballyhoo, eels, shrimp and lobster prevail in the calm shallows. ☎ 877-DIVE-COPA (877-348-3267), www.divecopamarina.com, info@divecopamarina.com.

Where to Stay

Copamarina Beach Resort in Guanica, a beautiful, 20-acre, dive resort halfway between Ponce and La Parguera, offers 106 deluxe air-conditioned rooms, tennis court, cable TV, direct-dial telephone, restaurant and pool. Diving and snorkeling off Gilligan's Island, less than a mile away, and along the offshore wall. All-inclusive rates most of the year run from $164 per person, based on a double and include three meals, house wines, most alcoholic beverages, soft drinks and non-motorized water sports. Wireless Internet connections in all rooms at no charge. Room-only rates start at $200 per night. Diving is extra. ☎ 800-468-4553 or 787-821-0505, toll free In Puerto Rico, 800-981-4676, fax 787-821-0070; www.divecopamarina.com, info@copamarina.com.

Parador Posada Porlamar is a family-run hotel with 40 modern air-conditioned guest rooms with TV and phone. Pool and ocean views. Rooms have been recently renovated with modern tiles and comfortable beds. The dive dock for Parguera Divers is directly in front of the hotel. Dive/accommodation packages start at $302 per person for three nights, four dives, and one dinner. ☎ 787-899-4343, www.pargueradivers.com.

Parador Villa Parguera in Lajas, is good for divers on a tight budget. This small hotel sits above the fishing village of La Parguera, high on a hillside, overlooking the Bay of La Parguera and phosphorescent bay. All 25 guest rooms have air conditioning, TV and private terraces. You'll need a rental car and get yourself down to the dive shop, but with room rates as low as $95 for three nights it may be a worthwhile option for some. ☎ 787-899-4265, villadelmar@isla.net, www.pinacolada.net/villadelmar.

West Coast

Best Dive & Snorkeling Sites

The hub of west-coast diving is **Aguadilla**, named for a natural spring which for centuries served as a watering place for Spanish sailors. Pretty beaches shaded by coconut palms stretch from **Rincon**, to the south of Aguadilla, to **Crash Boat Beach**, to the north. Visibility and water temperature along Puerto Rico's west-coast sites are best during spring and summer (March-November). Sea conditions are rough and suggested for advanced divers only.

Beach dives are possible at Crash Boat Beach, though visibility is often clouded by freshwater runoff.

☆☆☆ **Yellow Reef** is a pyramid-shaped seamount that starts at 15 feet and drops to 85 feet. Coral caverns, arches and a 10-ton anchor make it uniquely interesting. Average depth is 60 feet. The bottom is sandy and dotted with other pinnacles. Big schools of amberjacks (200+) are always about, as are queen angels, rock beauties and nurse sharks. Big star coral heads, orange cups and big barrel sponges prevail. This area is wind-dependent – wiped out for diving if swells exceed four feet.

☆☆☆☆☆ **South Gardens – Desecheo Island Marine Reserve**, 14 miles offshore, features a huge fish population, immense barrel sponges, giant sea fans (six feet across) and shallow depths. Stingrays and turtles are frequently sighted. Dives are off the protected southwest tip of the island, where you can explore an unknown wreck or a cave at 25 feet. Snorkelers will be followed by curious fish along the rocky shore. Star, brain and staghorn corals form the shallow reef. The depths at Desecheo Island range from shallow (beginning at 20-30 feet) to over 100 feet. Most sites are good for all levels of diving. Sites around the island encompass coral reef habitats, gardens of sea fans, rocky reefs and large swim-through arches and caverns.

☆☆☆ **Airplane Wreck** is a B-29 bomber that went down in 1949. Huge grouper patrol its coral-encrusted wings, propellers and landing gear. The wreck sits at 115 feet, on a sandy bottom surrounded by rocky ledges. Visibility is around 80 feet. Possible strong surface currents make line descent and ascents a must. Hordes of lobster hide in the surrounding rock ledges. This is a decompression dive with a mandatory (by the dive operator) stop at 15 feet. For advanced divers only.

Mona Island, a remote, uninhabited island 50 miles off the southwest tip of Puerto Rico, is a six-hour boat trip from the mainland across rough water or a half-hour flight from Mayaguez. The trip and stay are a rugged adventure, but intrepid nature lovers are rewarded with colonies of seabirds, colorful marine life, 200-foot cliffs and dazzling white beaches. Virgin dive sites average 80-foot depths.

Mona Island is managed by the **Department of National Resources**. Camping is allowed at **Sardinera Beach**. Other activities such as hiking, bird watching, snorkeling or scuba are allowed and coordinated by the resident biologist. Visitors are welcome, but no more than a hundred visitors can be on the island at any time. ☎ 787-722-1726.

Dive Operator

Aquatica Dive & Bike Adventures offers shore diving and snorkeling off Aguadilla and Isabella. Depths run from 30 to 75 feet. Calm during summer. C card and log book requested. Repairs and rentals. English-speaking dive master and captain. Nitrox available. They also offer cycling excursions with high-end mountain bikes, and bike-snorkel trips to the Aguadilla coastal forest trails, Cabo Rojo Lighthouse and bird reserve. ☎ 787-890-6071, www.aquatica.cjb.net, aquatica@caribe.net. Write Rd 110 Km. 10, Gate 5 Ramey Base, Aguadilla.

Where to Stay

 Joyuda Beach on Cabo Rojo is a quaint fishing and resort community with more than 20 terrific seafood restaurants. **Joyuda Beach Hotel**, Cabo Rojo, features 41 newly remodeled air conditioned rooms with cable TV, Internet, phone, private bath. Beachfront suites available. Pool, restaurant and bar. The dive-boat pier is a short walk away. Near shopping centers, theaters, zoo and a variety of tourist attractions. ☎ 787-851-5650 or 800-981-5464, www.joyudabeach.com, mail@joyudabeach.com.

Dining

Puerto Rico boasts some of the finest restaurants in the Caribbean, offering international dishes from Spain, France, Italy, Germany, Mexico, Argentina, and the Orient. Traditional Puerto Rican cuisine offers an interesting mix of Spanish, Creole and native Indian influences. Some of the island's best restaurants are *mesones gastronomicos* (gastronomic inns), located outside the San Juan urban area and featuring local cuisine at reasonable prices.

Sightseeing

 Visitors to Puerto Rico will find many attractions, especially in the capital city of San Juan. The seven-square-block area of **Old San Juan** (*Viejo San Juan*), named a National Historic Zone in the 1950s, is chock-a-block with interesting museums, churches, forts, restored homes, restaurants, boutiques, art galleries, sidewalk cafés and some of the most authentic examples of 16th- and 17th-century Spanish-colonial architecture in the western hemisphere. The peaceful countryside "out on the island" offers Spanish-colonial towns, 15 picturesque country inns (*paradores puertorriquenos*), great seaside restaurants, beautiful beaches, and dramatic mountain scenery.

OLD SAN JUAN. Founded in 1521, Old San Juan is the oldest capital city under the US flag. Among the many landmark sites are **El Morro,** constructed by the Spanish from 1540-1586 to protect the San Juan harbor from invasion by Sir Francis Drake; **La Fortaleza**, the official home and of the governor of Puerto Rico, built in 1540 and the oldest executive mansion in continuous use in the New World; **Casa Blanca**, built in 1523 as the residence of the family of Ponce de Léon, the first governor of the island and today housing a Taíno Indian museum and a Ponce de Léon family museum; the **Pablo Casals Museum**, which houses memorabilia of the famous cellist who lived in Puerto Rico for the last 20 years of his life; and the **San Juan Cathedral**, one of the oldest places of Christian worship in the Western Hemisphere.

PONCE. Puerto Rico's second-largest city is just 90 minutes by car south of San Juan. Since 1988, more than 500 historic buildings dating from the mid 1800s to the 1930s have been meticulously restored. The **Ponce Art Museum**, designed by Edward Durell Stone, is the most extensive in the Caribbean. Founded by former Governor Luis A. Ferre, the museum houses more than 1,000 paintings and 400 sculptures, and is noted for its late Renaissance and Baroque works. Ponce is also well known for its 1883 red-and-black firehouse, traditional town square, and pre-Columbian **Tibes Indian Ceremonial Park**, the oldest Indian burial ground in the Antilles. Nearby is **Hacienda Buena Vista**, a recently restored 19th-century coffee plantation and grain mill, now open to the public as a museum.

SAN GERMAN. This quaint Spanish town's **Porta Coeli Church**, built in 1606, is the oldest church still intact under the US flag. The town itself, located in the southwest corner of the island, still retains much of its original Spanish-colonial architecture and charm.

ARECIBO OBSERVATORY. Two hours from San Juan on the northwest coast, in the town of Arecibo, which dates to 1556, is the world's largest radio telescope, equal to the size of 13 football fields. Here scientists from Cornell University and the National Science Foundation study the planets and distant galaxies by gathering radio waves from space.

THE RIO CAMUY CAVE PARK. Opened in December 1986, this 300-acre park is one of Puerto Rico's most fascinating sightseeing attractions and is located near the Arecibo Observatory. The caves have been hailed by experts as one of the world's most spectacular cave systems with one of the largest underground rivers known.

EL YUNQUE, 35 miles east of San Juan, is a vast 28,000-acre rain forest in the Luquillo Mountains. Some 100 billion gallons of rain fall each year on over 240 varieties of trees and flowers. It is the only tropical rain forest in the US Forest Service.

LAS CABEZAS DE SAN JUAN NATURE RESERVE. Opened in March 1991, this 316-acre nature reserve encompasses seven different ecological systems, including: forest, mangroves, lagoons, beaches, cliffs, offshore islets and coral reefs. Visitors may tour the reserve's nature center and 19th-century working lighthouse, *El Faro*, which offers views of distant Caribbean islands. Contact The Conservation Trust, ☎ 787-722-5834. Las Cabezas is a 45-minute drive from San Juan.

 INDIAN CEREMONIAL PARKS. Two sites on the island showcase Puerto Rico's Indian heritage. Located near Ponce, **Tibes Indian Ceremonial Park** is the oldest Indian burial ground uncovered in the Antilles. The site has seven ceremonial ball courts, two dance grounds and a re-created Taíno Indian village. A museum displays Indian ceremonial objects, jewelry and pottery.

In the center of the island, near Utuado, is another Taíno site, the **Caguana Indian Ceremonial Park**, with 30 ball courts as well as carved monoliths and petroglyphs. *La Mujer de Caguana* is one of the best known of these petroglyphs – a figure of a woman with an elaborate headdress and the legs of a frog.

FESTIVALS. Each town honors its patron saint during the year. Catholic in origin, the festivities have incorporated many African and Spanish customs. The fiestas usually take place at the town's central square and can last up to 10 days. They include processions, games, local food, music and dance. Folkloric festivals are held year-round in many of Puerto Rico's cities and towns. Some celebrate the coffee harvest. Others showcase flower exhibitions, musical competitions and local crafts displays.

Other Activities

Fishing. Puerto Rico hosts many deep-sea fishing tournaments, in which 30 world records have been broken. The island's annual Billfish Tournament is the world's largest consecutively held tournament of its kind. Deep-sea fishing boats can be chartered in San Juan, Fajardo, Humacao, Mayaguez and other towns. Lake fishing for largemouth bass, peacock bass, sunfish, catfish and tilapia is also popular. For more details, contact the Department of Natural Resources at ☎ 787-722-5938.

Camping. Several camping facilities exist on Puerto Rico. For information, contact the Parks Association in San Juan at ☎ 787-721-2800.

Tennis courts and **golf** courses proliferate.

Shopping. Puerto Rico has duty-free shopping at the Luis Munoz Marin International Airport and several factory outlets in Old San Juan.

Facts

Nearest Recompression Chamber: San Juan Medical Center Doctor Juan Nazatrio. ☎ 787-777-3535 ext 6475 or 3827.

Getting Here: Major airlines including **American**, ☎ 800-433-7300, **United** and **USAir** fly into San Juan from most major US cities. American has service to Aguadilla from Miami. American has made the **Luis Munoz Marin International Airport** its hub for all flights from the US to other Caribbean destinations, Europe and Latin America. International carriers include **Air Portugal**, **British Airways**, **BWIA**, **Iberia**, **LACSA**, **LIAT**, **Lufthansa** and **Mexicana**.

Island Transportation: *By Road* – Taxis, buses and rental cars are available at the airport and major hotels. All taxi cabs are metered, but they may be rented unmetered for an hourly rate. *Publicos* (public cars) run on frequent schedules to all island towns (usually during daytime hours) and depart from main squares. They have fixed rates. The "Ruta Panoramica" is a scenic road meandering across the island and offering stunning vistas.

By Water: Ferries shuttle passengers to and from Culebra and Vieques at reasonable rates. ☎ 787-860-4560. Car transport is available on some. San Juan's harbor can also be crossed by the Catano ferry to the Bacardi Rum plant's free tours.

Driving: On the right. Distance markers are in kilometers. Signs in Spanish.

Customs: US citizens do not need to clear customs or immigration (other citizens do). On departure, luggage must be inspected by the US Agriculture Department, as laws prohibit taking certain fruits and plants out of the country.

Entry Requirements: Since Puerto Rico is a Commonwealth of the United States, no passports are required for US citizens. Visitors do need a valid driver's license to rent a car. If you are a citizen of any other country, a passport is required. Vaccinations are not necessary.

Pets: Dogs and cats may be brought to Puerto Rico from the US with two documents: a health certificate dated not more than 10 days prior to departure showing that the animal is disease-free and certified by an official or registered veterinarian; a certificate of rabies vaccination, dated not more than 30 days prior to departure, authenticated by the proper authorities.

Currency: The US dollar is legal tender and credit cards are widely accepted. Several exchange bureaus are available in San Juan and at the airport for the benefit of international travelers.

Climate: Temperatures average mid 80s on land and underwater. During winter and on deep dives a light wetsuit is recommended. The rainy season is April to November, but most days have some sunshine. The south coast receives much less rainfall than the north.

Clothing: Lightweight, casual. Bring a light jacket for mountain hikes in winter.

Electricity: 110 volts, AC 60 cycles, same as US.

Time: Puerto Rico operates on Atlantic Standard Time, which is one hour ahead of Eastern Standard Time and the same as Eastern Daylight Savings Time.

Language: Spanish is the official language, although many people speak English, which is taught from kindergarten through high school.

Taxes: The airport departure tax is included in the price of the airline ticket, and there's a 7% government tax at all hotels. Gratuities in restaurants are not included in the bill but 15% is the usual tip.

Religious Services: The majority of Puerto Ricans are Catholic, but religious freedom for all faiths is guaranteed by the Commonwealth Constitution. Catholic services are conducted throughout the island in both English and Spanish. There is a Jewish Community Center in Miramar and a Jewish Reform Congregation in Santurce. There are English-speaking Protestant services for Baptists, Episcopalians, Lutherans, Presbyterians and inter-denominational services.

For Additional Information: *Puerto Rico Tourism Company: In New York* – 666 Fifth Avenue, NY, NY 10103, ☎ 800-223-6530. *In California* – 3575 West Cahuenga Blvd., Suite 405, Los Angeles, CA 90068, ☎ 323-874-5991 or 800-874-1230. *In Florida* – 901 Ponce de Leon Blvd, Coral Gables, FL 33134, ☎ 800-815-7391 or 305-445-9112. *In the UK* – 67-69 Whitfield St., WIP 5RL, London, United Kingdom, ☎ 01932253302. *In Canada* – ☎ 416-969-9025. *In Puerto Rico*: PO Box 902-3960, San Juan, PR 00902-3960; Paseo de la Princesa #2, La Princessa Building, Old San Juan, PR 00901, ☎ 787-721-2400; www.gotopuertorico.com.

Saba

Located 30 miles off the coast of St. Maarten, Saba is a tiny, five-mile-square mountain that rises almost vertically to 3,000 feet. Once an active volcano, it is an island of paradoxes – a Caribbean hideaway without a single beach, with a road that engineers insisted couldn't be built, and with a capital called **The Bottom** that's on top of a mountain. The smallest of the Netherlands Antilles, Saba rises from the sea like the nose of a friendly dolphin breaking the water's surface. Its cliffs rise sharply from the blue Caribbean, culminating in mist-shrouded 2,855-foot Mount Scenery.

 Tiny white villages cling to the sides of the mountain – **Hell's Gate**, **Windwardside**, **St. John's**, **The Bottom** – linked by a road (referred to simply as "The Road") that dips and soars, curves and backtracks like a giant roller coaster. Visitors arrive at one end of the road or the other, since it begins at the airport and ends at the pier.

Diving is superb, and most reefs, walls, ledges and pinnacles are within 100 yards of shore – five or six minutes by boat. With little fishing, less than 1,000 divers per year and a government long-active in marine management, fish life is spectacular. Water clarity is too. The sea floor is a dense, heavy, black sand – not prone to silting or clouding the water. A constant wash of open-ocean currents supports a rich growth of soft and hard corals on submerged lava rocks and pinnacles. And it is one of the few destinations left in the Caribbean where you can still find huge turtles and grouper.

If arriving by air, the first sight of Saba may surprise you as your Windward Airways' STOL (Short Take-Off and Landing) aircraft swoops down to **Juancho E. Yrausquin Airport's** mini-runway. You may at first think it is a matter of visual perspective; that, perhaps, you are still quite high up. But, indeed, the runway measures just 1,312 feet. Nonetheless, touchdown is gentle. The airstrip stretches along **Flat Point**, one of the few level areas on the island. From here, the road rises in 20 serpentine curves to the village of Hell's Gate which, despite its name, nestles in the shadow of the island's largest church.

Swinging through groves of feathery tree ferns and past terraced banana plantations, the road continues on to Windwardside, a toylike village astride a saddle of land connecting **Mount Scenery** and **Booby Hill**. Its tiny houses, sparkling white under bright red roofs, are laced with wooden gingerbread.

Contributors: Joan Borque, Bill Wilson McQueen, Mike Meyers.

The narrow streets meander between stone walls enclosing miniscule yards that frequently contain the graves of previous owners. It is not unusual to find a doorside gravestone draped with the family's laundry drying in the sun. With level space so limited, the ingenious Sabans have converted every available square inch to some use.

Mini-shops with such eye-catching names as "Around the Bend" and "Green Shutters," are tucked in among the cottages. Most carry Saba's unique "Spanish Work," a form of airy linen drawnwork created by generations of Saban wives awaiting the return of their sailor husbands.

Leaving Windwardside, the highway snakes its way past **Kate's Hill**, **Peter Simon's Hill** and **Big Rendezvous** to the village of St. John's. From this point, you can see St. Eustatius floating on the southern horizon.

The road continues climbing, then swoops down to The Bottom, Saba's capital and, with 350 of the island's 950 inhabitants, her largest town. From The Bottom, the road makes its final descent, corkscrewing down to Fort Bay and the cruise-ship pier.

The Bottom did not get its name, as is often stated, because it is set in the bottom of a volcanic crater – it isn't. The name is a corruption of the Dutch words *De Botte*, meaning "The Bowl." A look at the surrounding hills tells why.

When to Go

Visibility is best during winter, though seas can be rough outside the leeward side of the island. Summertime brings warmer, 80° water with plankton blooms and lowered visibility, but a tremendous quantity of sealife. Water temperature varies from 76° in February to 82° in October. Sea conditions vary. The island is round, with no natural harbors and a very small leeward side. Seas are usually calm, but tropical storms can rule out many dive sites.

History

Saba's discovery is credited to Christopher Columbus, who first sighted the island in 1493. It remained sparsely inhabited by the Caribs until a group of Englishmen shipwrecked on Saban shores in the early 1600s. Later, in the 1640s, the Dutch built a community at Tent Bay. With bountiful fishing grounds nearby, Saba became a desirable property to several nations. Overall, the island changed hands 12 times, being claimed by the British, Spaniards, French, and, lastly, in 1816, the Dutch. St. Maarten and St. Eustatius changed hands even more times, but the Sabans, taking advantage of the unique topography, fought off invaders by pelting them from above with rocks and boulders. Saba has always been English speaking – influenced by early English missionaries and settlers.

Because of the island's largely vertical terrain and unapproachable coastline, roads, taxis, airports and even electricity are recent innovations on the Saban scene.

Until 1934, Saba had no telephones. Work on the road began in 1938, but the first automobile did not arrive until 1947. The Leo A. Chane Pier at **Fort Bay** was built in 1972. Approaching the island in Saba's early days meant riding the crest of a wave onto a rocky beach at **Ladder Bay**. Flights of steps carved by hand from volcanic rock connected one village to another. Two hundred steps rose from the small landing stage at Fort Bay to The Bottom; 900 more linked the capital to Windwardside, the island's second-largest village.

Everything, from pianos to prelates, was hoisted up these stairs: Twelve men were needed to wrestle a Steinway from the Bay to The Bottom; it took four men and a sedan chair to tote a visiting bishop up the steep stairs.

Without roads, wheeled vehicles were, of course, useless; Sabans walked or rode tiny donkeys. During World War II, tales of the wondrous "Jeep" reached local ears and thoughts that, perhaps, here at last was a vehicle that could conquer the precipitous Saban landscape. Officials were prompted to construct a road from Fort Bay to The Bottom... just in case.

Even not-so-old-timers reminisce about the arrival of the island's first car – a secondhand Jeep – in March, 1947. The novelty was swung over the side of a freighter that arrived every month from Curaçao, eased onto two longboats, hauled through the surf and finally deposited at the foot of the Fort Bay Road.

When the ignition key was turned, however, nothing happened; the shipper had forgotten to have the engine overhauled. Hurried consultations were held and the ship's engineer was summoned ashore. A few adjustments, a couple of stout whacks with a wrench and the engine sprang to life. Minutes later, the jeep roared into the capital, pursued by the entire junior population, shouting "donkey on wheels!" Today, about 200 cars negotiate the road.

When electricity finally reached the island in 1963, it was a sometime thing – from 6 pm till midnight. Not until 1970 was electric service extended to 24 hours a day.

Saba Marine Park

 The Saba Marine Park (SMP) was established in 1987 "to preserve Saba's Marine resources for the benefit and enjoyment of the people, in perpetuity." The project was funded by World Wildlife Fund-Netherlands, the Prince Bernhard Fund, and the Dutch and Saban Governments.

Dive & Snorkeling Sites
1 Tent Reef
2 Ladder Labyrinth
3 Third Encounter
4 Diamond Reef
5 Torrens Point

The park encompasses the entire island and includes the waters and the sea-bed from the high water mark down to 200 feet and two offshore seamounts. It was set up by Dutch marine biologist, Tom van't Hof, who also established successful marine parks in Bonaire and Curaçao.

Park officials maintain a system of mooring buoys and administer the Saba Marine Park Hyperbaric Facility, a four-person recompression chamber operated by a staff of trained volunteers.

Visitors to the marine park are charged a "dollar-a-dive" to help maintain the park and facilities. Spearfishing and collecting of any marine animals are pro-hibited. Divers must use proper bouyancy control and must not sit or stand on the corals. Anchoring on corals is prohibited. Vessels entering the park are advised to contact the marine park on VHF channel 16 for directions on anchoring. For additional information Write Saba Marine Park, Fort Bay, PO Box 18, The Bottom, Saba, Netherlands Antilles.

Stay Safe

Saba's altitude and any strenuous climbing – even from the dock back to your hotel room – must be considered when calculating the diving tables. Some of the new dive computers will figure in the altitude for you. Without careful planning, both the altitude and strenuous activity may bring on decompression sickness. Nitrox certification recommended.

Dr. John Buchanan, co-author of *Guide to the Saba Marine Park*, suggests divers climb Mt. Scenery "only if their dive tables or dive computers say that it is OK for them to fly."

Saba dive guides will help you plan each dive safely. All dive sites have permanent moorings with submerged lines for descents, ascents and safety stops. It is further suggested that, after making a decompression dive, divers *without* decompression sickness symptoms allow 48 hours before flying.

Best Dive & Snorkeling Sites

 ☆☆☆☆☆ **Tent Reef** is a shelf between 30 and 40 feet which becomes **Tent Wall** as the bottom drops quickly from 40 feet to over 100 feet. A series of overhangs on the slope make interesting photo frames. Currents around this southwest corner of the island nurture a multitude of delicate gorgonians, iridescent tube sponges and large barrel sponges – home to small shrimp and feeding polyps. From the dark sand, fields of garden eels emerge, playing hide and seek with legions of razorfish. Resident French angels patrol thickets of black coral bushes. At depth, the wall becomes a brilliant blue and red tapestry of encrusting sponges and long, velvet-like wire corals. Residents include black margates, horse-eye jacks, sergeant majors, tiger grouper and butterflyfish with occasional sightings of manta rays, spotted eagle rays, nurse sharks and seahorses.

☆☆☆ **Ladder Labyrinth** is an erratic maze of coral-covered mounds off Saba's western, leeward coast. Depths are from 30 to 60 feet. The reef is vibrant with enormous lavender sea fans, swaying sea plumes and a carpet of star corals. Within the labyrinth are hundreds of crevices teeming with banded coral shrimp and lobsters. Schools of curious barracuda circle the area. Seas are usually calm. Good for diving and snorkeling.

☆☆☆☆ **Diamond Rock** is a white-rock monolith astir with frigate birds and brown notty terns. Below the surface, between 35 and 80 feet, are hundreds of pink-tipped anemones, stinging corals and yellow tube sponges. Stingrays nap on the sandy bottom at 80 feet. Frequent sightings of hawksbill turtles, bigeyes, permits, spadefish, frogfish, rare orange filefish, flying gurnards, yellow jawfish, sailfin blennies and bull sharks make this an exciting dive. Light current. Outstanding visibility. Fifteen-minute boat ride. Recommended for novice and experienced divers. Photo opportunities abound.

☆☆☆☆ **Third Encounter**, off Saba's west coast, is a plateau on top of a submerged mountain range. Located a mile from shore, average depth is 100 feet. Explosions of Creole wrasses and brown chromis adorn the seamounts amidst huge clusters of orange elephant ear sponges. Black tip sharks guard a monument of coral named the "Eye of the Needle" – a 200-foot column that tops at 90 feet. Experienced divers only. Superb visibility. Current.

☆☆☆ **Torrens Point** off the island's northwest corner is the start of the Edward S. Arnold marked Snorkeling Trail. An outstanding shallow dive spot, depths range from five to 30 feet as you swim from marker one through 11. Black volcanic rocks, small caves and ledges swarm with fish and invertebrates. Pink sponges and lace corals grow in the crevices. Light pouring through the tunnels creates dramatic photo opportunities. This spot is weather-dependent. Ocean swells from the north, usually during winter months, make exploring the open caves hazardous, especially the areas known as #10 (The Rocks) and #9 (Into The Alley). Check with a local dive master before entering the water.

Snorkeling

Saba's entire coastline is excellent for snorkeling. There are three locations for easily entering the water: the **Fort Bay Harbor** area, **Well's Bay/Torrens Point** area, and **Cove Bay**, near the airport. Snorkel boat trips can be arranged through the dive shops. A snorkel trail is located at Torrens Point.

Dive Operators

 Rates for diving in Saba average: $45 for a single tank; $80 for a two-tank dive; $60 to $90 for a resort course; $350 for a C-course. Packages available (see *Accommodations*). All Saba dive shops require a C-card to join the dive trips. Courses and open-water check-outs available. Snorkelers join the dive boats or go in off the shore at Torrens Point. Sites are five to 15 minutes from the pier. Dive packages are non-refundable.

Sea Saba is a PADI training facility with two 40-foot custom dive boats. Dive trips are tailored to visitors' requests, usually making a deep dive at 10 am and a shallow dive at noon. C-cards required. Nitrox. Equipment rentals. ☎ direct 599-416-2246, www.seasaba.com, info@seasaba.com. Write PO Box 530, Windwardside, Saba, NA.

Saba Deep at Fort Bay Harbor, on the southwest side of the island, offers guided scuba and snorkeling tours. The shop is part of a dive complex in the now-restored old harbor master's building with the Inn Too Deep Restaurant, and dive boutique upstairs. Dive and accommodation packages. Resort and certification courses. Owner Mike Myers is a NAUI and PADI certified instructor. Nitrox. From the US, ☎ 866-416-3347, direct 599-416-3347. Write to Mike Myers, 8567 Coral Way, Miami, Florida 33155, USA, www.saba-deep.com, diving@sabadeep.com.

Saba Divers, a part of **Scout's Place** resort, is a fully acknowledged PADI international dive resort and NRC training facility. It has a great safety record, custom dive boats with freshwater showers and a shady relaxation area. The shop has three compressors, assorted rental equipment, cameras, underwater lights, a maintenance shop and plenty of dive tanks. They offer Nitrox for free to Nitrox certified divers, night dives, education and fun trips.Day trip with two-tank dive costs $95. Divers staying at Scouts Place can get lower-priced packages. ☎ 599-416-2740, www.sabadivers.com or www.nitrox-for-free.com, info@nitrox-for-free.com.

Where to Stay

Accommodations may be reserved through your travel agent, direct or packaged through the dive shops listed above. A government room tax of 5% and a service charge of 10% or 15% is added to your bill.

Julianas is a group of eight one-bedroom units, one apartment and a separate two-bedroom cottage built in 1989. New managers Wim Schutten and Johanna van't Hof added hammocks and an Internet café open for breakfast and lunch. Each room has an ocean view. Per-day rates for a double are from $135 for a room to $185 for a cottage in winter. Seven-night dive packages from $950 per diver cover accommodations, 10 dives (usually with Sea Saba), airport and boat transfers, daily breakfast, tanks and weights. Marine park fees not included. ☎ 888-289-5708 or direct 599-416-2269, fax 599-416-2389, www.julianas-hotel.com, info@julianas-hotel.com. Write Juliana's, Windwardside, Saba, NA.

The Cottage Club, a group of 10 Saban cottages with full kitchens, bath, cable TV, phone, fax and two beds, is a new favorite spot for divers and snorkelers. Winter rates, per person, double occupancy for five nights, six dives, are $539 ($831 for a single). Packages are available with all three dive shops listed above, or book through your travel agent. Rooms are $150 per night plus tax, and $25 per extra person. ☎ 599-416-2386, www.cottage-club.com, cottageclubsaba@yahoo.com or cottageclub@unspoiled-queen.com.

Recently renovated **Saba Gate House** sits high on a hillside with great views of the Caribbean Sea and neighboring islands. All three buildings are furnished with Caribbean paintings and artifacts from local artists. Hardwood or Mexican tile floors. The luxury villa features four bedrooms, three baths, large dining room, living room, fully equipped kitchen. Secluded pool with chaise lounge, hammock, patios, decks, balcony, all in a private setting. The cottage, with private terrace, living room/dining room, kitchenette, bedroom and full bath can accommodate a couple. The hotel has five double rooms with king-size, double, or twin bed, surrounded by wrap-around balconies or patios. All have full private bath. Pool. Dive packages start at $850 and include 12 dives, six nights accommodations, bedroom with king-sized bed, private bath, airport transfers, daily boat transfers, breakfast, local calls. ☎ 599-416-2416, 866-709-8058, www.sabagatehouse.com, info@sabagatehouse.com.

Scout's Place Hotel, adjacent to Saba Divers in Windwardside, accommodates divers in one of 14 guest rooms, each with private balcony and sea views. Rooms on the second floor are roomier and nicer. All have Caribbean-gingerbread décor and antique mahogany four-poster beds. A little musty for some, but the rooms are clean and low cost. Refrigerators, cable television and dial-up Internet access are also included. Pool, restaurant. Complimentary continental breakfasts each morning. Children stay free. Saba Divers on premises. Estimated taxi charge from the airport is $10. Room rates average $85 per night. Dive/accommodation packages for seven nights, 12 dives from $800. ☎ 866-656-7222, www.sabadivers.com, info@scoutsplace.com. Note: prepaid packages are not refundable.

Sightseeing & Other Activities

Saba nightlife is limited to stargazing and swapping dive stories. Restaurants serve as the town meeting places. Diving, hiking and birdwatching are the mainstay of daytime activities. Hiking, though strenuous, is exceptionally pleasant as there are no mosquitoes or biting insects. If your dive computer says it's all right to fly and you are in excellent physical condition you may want to climb **Mt. Scenery**. The hike takes about 90 minutes. On the climb you'll pass through several types of tropical vegetation. At 1,600 feet the rain forest is enveloped in clouds. Wildlife includes lizards, iguanas, hummingbirds and tree frogs.

Directional signs and interpretive signboards have been placed along many of Saba's trails. Pick up a copy of the *Saba Nature Trails* brochure at the Tourist Bureau to help you plan your hikes.

There are a few craft and souvenir shops in Windwardside and The Bottom offering local Saban threadwork, a lacy embroidery applied to linens, hand-woven fabrics, silk-screened clothing and Saba Spice – a 151-proof rum.

Dining

Scouts Place serves up lobster, roast chicken and island specials. ☎ 416-2205 or 416-2740.

In Two Deep Restaurant, upstairs at Saba Deep complex in Fort Bay, is open for breakfast, brunch, lunch and dinner. Menu offers "New England" style omelettes, chowders, salads and sandwiches. ☎ 416-3347.

Cantonese culinary creations are at **Saba Chinese Restaurant**, ☎ 416-2268, and **Chinese Family Restaurant**, ☎ 416-2353, which also features satellite TV – both in Windwardside.

Family Deli and Bakery on the main road to Fort Bay at The Bottom, opens at 7 am and serves local seafoods, grilled steaks, burgers, sandwiches, salads, pizzas, vegetarian meals, barbecue and other local, Creole and Latin cuisine. They also feature breakfast meals, fresh breads, cakes and pastries, and a variety of ice creams and drinks, including homemade fruit smoothies, fresh orange juice and milk shakes. ☎ 416-3858 or 416-2504.

Facts

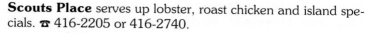

Nearest Recompression Chamber: Medical Emergencies: A.M. Edwards Medical Center, ☎ 63239; Saba Marine Park Hyperbaric Facility with a four-person re-compression chamber.

Airlines: International flights connect through St. Maarten via **American Airlines**, **BWIA**, **Continental**, **Northwest Airlines** or **US Airways**. Hop a **Windward Express Airways** (**WINAIR**) prop plane (15 minutes).

Driving: On the right. Rentals are available through **Johnson's Rent A Car** or your hotel. Beware of hairpin turns, potholes and bumps along the road.

Seaport: A deep-water pier accommodates ships at Fort Bay. Anchorage for yachts at Ladder Bay and Wells Bay.

Documents: Visitors require a passport and a return or onward ticket.

Customs: No customs.

Tipping and Taxes: Government room tax is 5%. Hotels and restaurants usually add a service charge of 10-15% to your bill. Tip taxi drivers a dollar or two.

Currency: Netherlands Antilles florin. US$ accepted everywhere. Credit cards are widely accepted. NAf 1.80=US$1 (variable).

Language: Dutch is the official language, but English is widely spoken.

Climate: Air temperature ranges from 78°F to 82°F year-round. Winter evenings may cool to 60°F. Rainfall averages 42 inches per year.

Clothing: Casual, lightweight. Sweater or light jacket suggested for winter evenings. Wetsuit needed for winter diving, when water temperatures drop to 75°. A light wetsuit or lycra wetskin is recommended for summer.

Electricity: 110 volts AC, 60 cycles (220 volts on request).

Time: Atlantic Standard (Eastern Standard + 1 hr).

Departure Tax: US$10 to other Netherland Antilles islands, US$20 for other destinations.

Religious Services: Limited.

Additional Information: *Saba Tourist Bureau*, Saba Tourist Office, PO Box 527 Windwardside, Saba, N.A. ☎ 599-416-2231, fax 599-416-2350, www.sabatourism.com, iluvsaba@unspoiledqueen.com.

St. Eustatius

S t. Eustatius (Statia) is a speck of land about 38 miles south of St. Maarten, six miles north of St. Kitts, and 17 miles southeast of Saba. It is one of the lesser-known islands in the eastern Caribbean – so small and with a name so long that it is often deleted from maps. A part of the Netherlands Antilles, this eight-square-mile territory is home to a population of 1,800.

 Statia's profile is distinct, with a flat plain in the center, sharp, green hills at the north end, and **The Quill**, a 2,000-foot extinct volcano, covering most of the south end. The Quill is noted by geologists as having an almost-perfect cone shape. Inside its crater lies a magnificent tropical rain forest of towering mahogany trees, wild bananas, air plants and trailing vines festooned with wild orchids and flowering air plants. Wood doves and sulfur-yellow butterflies flutter in the shadows, and at full moon, torch-bearing Statians hunt scuttling land-crabs.

Steep limestone cliffs interspersed with a few stretches of black-sand beach dominate the island's western coast. Its eastern shores shelve into a wide strip of dark sand and pebbles. There are few roads, and donkeys are still used for exploring rocky inland trails. Offshore lie the remains of more than 200 shipwrecks.

Beautiful shallow reefs, highlighted by giant golden sea fans and lush, soft corals, skirt the ballast stones and rubble of sunken 17th-century wooden trading ships. Now dive and snorkeling sites, they are all close to shore – at most, a few minutes by boat.

A leisurely stroll through the narrow cobblestone streets of **Oranjestad**, Statia's capital and only village, reveals the grey-stone and yellow-ballast brick walls of historic buildings dating back to the 1600s and the now-restored **Fort Oranje** (pronounced "oh-rahn-ye").

The fort, perched on the cliffs overlooking **Oranjestad Bay** (or Orange Bay), was the scene of the first salute to the US colors back in November 1776. Nearby, the ruins of an 18-century synagogue and graveyard, and a Dutch Reformed Church nestle among the pink and yellow homes of today's Statians. This area is **Upper Town**, the uphill section of town.

From the center of the village, just past a monument erected in honor of Queen Wilhelmina's Golden Jubilee, the stone-paved **Fort Road** zig-zags down to **Lower Town**, once the Caribbean's most bustling port. In the mid 1700s Lower Town stretched for two miles along the Bay. Warehouses, taverns, slave markets and merchants' stalls lined the double road-way. The

Contributor: Mark Padover, marine biologist and former Dive Statia instructor.

lively traffic, both licit and illicit, made St. Eustatius the richest port in the West Indies. Today, gentle-faced donkeys browse among its ruins.

Sheep and cows graze on small farms and pastures outside Oranjestad. On the opposite side of the island, surf tumbles onto a long strand where beach-combers find a treasure of shells, glass floats and sun-bleached driftwood.

Overall, the island is perfect for vacationers seeking an unhurried, peaceful haven. There is virtually no crime on the island. Everyone is safe walking the streets at night. Doors are rarely locked and the people are extremely friendly. When an elderly resident of St. Eustatius was asked if many tourists visited the island, the old gentleman looked hurt. "My dear sir," he replied, "we don't have tourists on Statia, we have guests!"

And Statians do have a knack for making "guests" feel welcome. Passers-by exchange greetings in the narrow streets; young boys offer to lead newcomers to hunt for the island's favorite treasure – blue "slave beads" – found nowhere else in the Caribbean.

When to Go

 Visibility is best in winter, though seas occasionally get rough. Summer brings calm seas, warmer water and more fish. Water temperature varies from 76° in February to 82° in October.

History

 Statia played a key role in America's war for independence. It was a major trans-shipment point for European arms and supplies intended for George Washington's troops. Muskets and gunpow-der, frequently shipped in casks marked "Tea," were stored in yel-low brick warehouses that stretched for a mile along the Bay. From there, blockade runners in swiftly moving brigantines would carry the supplies to the ports of Boston, New York and Charleston.

It was on November 16, 1776, that the cannons of Fort Oranje roared forth the first official salute to the American colors by a foreign power. The armed American merchant ship *Andrew Doria* sailed into the harbor and fired a 13-gun salute to the Dutch flag fluttering above Fort Oranje. Commander Johannes de Graaff, sympathetic to the cause of the American rebels, ordered the cannons of the fort to return the courtesy with an 11-gun salvo. By this act he unwittingly set in motion events that would bring to a violent end the age of prosperity on Statia.

Though De Graaff was obviously unaware of the historic importance of this salute, the British, getting wind of it, were understandably infuriated.

By 1781, the situation had become desperate for the British. Not only was the war going badly for George III's troops in North America, but the stream of supplies passing through St. Eustatius was unabated, despite a British blockade. Turnabout came on February 3, 1781, when British Admiral George Brydges Rodney attacked what he called "this nest of vipers."

Storming ashore with 650 troops he demanded the surrender of the Dutch garrison and began systematically looting not only the well-stocked warehouses, but the personal possessions of the merchants as well. In all, he destroyed the harbor and ransacked the town while accumulating five million pounds' worth of booty. Rodney also kept the Dutch flag flying above the ramparts of the fort, thereby luring more than 150 ships into his trap. Less than a year later the British troops were expelled from the island by the French.

Today, the island is an autonomous part of the Netherlands and is self governing. But, on each anniversary of De Graaff's salute, the island band strikes up *The Star Spangled Banner*, as the American flag is hoisted to the top of the flagpole in the center of the compound.

Sunken Treasure Hunting

The remains and treasures of 17th- and 18th-century sailing ships are played up in many Statia dive articles, but the island's real treasures are her lovely shallow reefs. The ships' wooden hulls rotted away centuries ago. What's left are some wonderful old anchors and piles of stone ballast where small fish play hide and peek.

A few sites have, in fact, given up treasures of jewels and exotic pottery, but any charted wrecks not yet salvaged are buried in the sand and would require extensive and expensive excavation work to uncover. Plus, if a diver happens upon an intact artifact, it must go to the St. Eustatius Historical Foundation. Treasure hunting is discouraged – metal detectors are prohibited, as is "fanning" of the bottom to find artifacts. Exceptions which divers may keep are fragments of clay pipe-stems or -bowls, and blue beads (slave beads). Uninhabited shells and broken pieces of dead coral may also be taken.

Statia Marine Park

In 1997 the waters surrounding Statia were brought under government supervision to protect the reefs, historic wrecks and turtle sanctuary. Divers and snorkelers must pay $6 per day or $15 for an annual pass.

Best Dive & Snorkeling Sites

There are approximately 40 major dive sites around Statia ranging from extreme shallows to 130 feet. Visibility often exceeds 100 feet, with water temperatures averaging 80°F. Divers must have a buddy, stay within the "no decompression" limits, wear a pressure gauge, depth gauge, flotation device and timing device. C-cards are required. Nitrox certification is suggested. All scuba divers must be accompanied by a local guide.

☆☆☆ **The Snorkeling Museum** is an underwater cannon display established for the St. Eustatius Historical foundation at Oranjestad Bay in Lower Town through the **Golden Rock Dive Center** (see below).

☆☆☆☆ **Carolines Reef** is a spectacular site in the center of the southern reef complex. Several long ledges meet, forming a circular hub. Big barrel sponges, tube sponges, sea fans, brain coral, sea whips and volcano sponges adorn the tops of the ledges. Hoards of small critters are in residence including blennies, lightbulb tunicates, pistol shrimp in their corkscrew anemones, lavender cleaning shrimp, cleaning gobies and arrow crabs. Big angels are common, as are rock beauties, barracuda, scrawled filefish, Bermuda chub, butterflyfish, sharptail eels and groupers. Nurse sharks and turtles cruise the area.

The hub is a keyhole in the coral, about 18 inches in diameter. Used as a shortcut by fish traversing one side of the ledge to the other, it also serves as an excellent frame for a photo. Maximum depth is 65 feet. Recommended for novice and experienced divers.

☆☆☆ **False Shoal**, outside of Kay Bay off the southwest shores, is an unusual formation of huge boulders that rise from the bottom at 25 to 30 feet to within a foot of the surface. Coral cover is minimal, but fish life is superb, with big congregations of tiger groupers, French and queen angels, several species of parrotfish and swarms of reef fish. Good for snorkeling and novice divers.

☆☆☆☆ **Anchor Reef** is named for an enormous anchor hooked under a ledge. The anchor is seven feet across and 14 feet long with an 18-inch ring. It is surrounded by a pretty reef with a colorful array of elephant-ear, moose antler, and green, lavender and red vase sponges. Cracks and crevices reveal feather dusters, shrimp anemones, barber shrimp and gorgonians. Bushy sea whips, sea plumes and sea fans decorate the ledges. Maximum depth is 60 feet.

☆☆☆☆ **Dropoff**, the southernmost dive on Statia and the most dramatic wall, starts at 85 feet and drops vertically to about 130 feet. The face of the wall is a collage of mountainous star coral, black wire coral, and sponges. Enormous French and queen angels, Nassau and tiger grouper, black durgons,

Above: Aerial view of Honduras

Below: Coral reef, Pigeon Island, Guadeloupe (© Rick Ockelman)

Above: Nisbet Plantation Beach, Nevis (© *Jon Huber*)
Below: Greetings from Dominica (*Dominica Tourist Bd*)

Above: San Juan Harbor & El Morro, Puerto Rico
Below: The Bottom, Saba

Above: Rick's anemone
Below: Anemone, Saba

Above: Diamond rock, Saba (© Joan Borque)
Below: Fish on a reef

Above: Aerial view, Marigot Bay, St. Lucia
Below: Pitons & Caribbean, St. Lucia

Above: Diver & tarpon (both © Staci Reed Kofick)
Below: Three divers, St. Thomas USVI

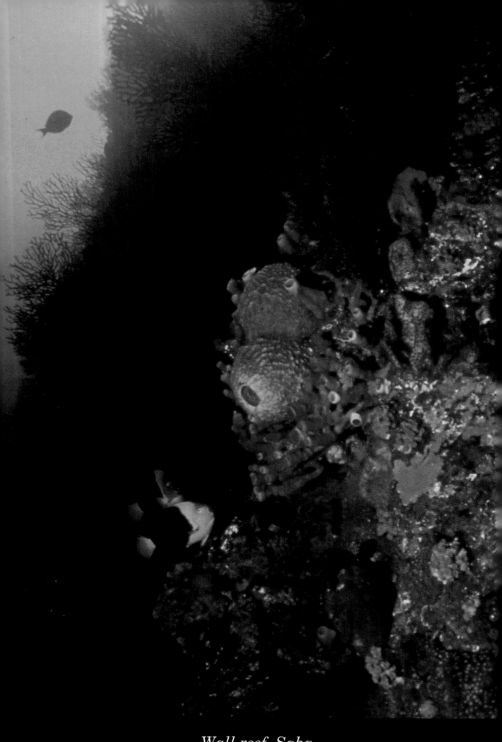

Wall reef, Saba

Barrel sponge & soft corals, Tobago (© Lorry Heverly)

Above: Butterflyfish, Saba (© *Joan Borque*)

Below: Tube sponges (© *Jon Huber*)

Sunset on the water; yacht Promenade
(photos courtesy BVI Tourist Board)

Above: Squirrelfish, St. Thomas USVI
Below: Orange coral, St. Thomas USVI (both © Staci R. Kofick)

Above: Shallow reef, St. Thomas USVI (© Staci R. Kofick)
Below: Trunk Bay, St. John USVI

Above: Cenote, Yucatán
Below: Dolphin Encounter, Yucatán *(courtesy Xcaret Tourism)*

Above: French angelfish, St. Thomas USVI (© Staci R. Kofick)
Below: Triggerfish, Barbados

Coral reef, Saba

St. Eustatius
(STATIA)

Boven Bay
Venus Bay
Jenkins Bay
Zeelandia
Interloper's Point
Fort Royal
Fort Oranje
ORANJESTAD
Great Bay
Lower Lynch
St. Louis Battery
Corre Corre Bay
Behind the Mountain
The Quill 2000 ft.
Fort Bouille
Toby Gut
For De Windt

Dive & Snorkeling Sites

1	Caroline's Reef	9	Double Wreck
2	False Shoal	10	Supermarket
3	Anchor Reef	11	Tommy's Temptation
4	Dropoff	12	North Point
5	Barracuda Reef	13	Darlene Bay
6	Outer Crooks Reef	14	Inner Crooks
7	City Wall	15	Corre Corre Bay
8	Stingray Wreck		

spotted eagle rays and occasional reef sharks and hammerheads frequent the area. For experienced divers.

☆☆☆ **Barracuda Reef** is a 700-foot-long mini-wall at 45 feet that drops to a sand-pit at 70 feet. A 12-foot-long, five-foot-wide, coral-encrusted anchor earmarks this site. As the name implies, schools of barracuda frequent the area, as do some more unusual creatures. On one occasion a friendly humpback whale cruised smack into a group of snorkelers and hung out with them for 15 minutes. Whale season on Statia is from December to mid March.

Healthy soft corals, a host of invertebrates, reef fish, spotted morays, stingrays and nurse sharks typify the area. Recommended for all level divers.

☆☆☆☆ The wreck of the **Charlie Brown**, a 327-foot cargo ship, rests on its starboard side in just under 100' feet of water with the bow pointing south east. The site is about 600 feet south west of Barracuda Reef. At the shallowest point it is only 50 feet to the port side of the hull, and on a good day you can even snorkel it. Dive pros Glenn and Michele Faires, owners of the Golden Rock Dive Center, find this depth is perfect for beginners and experienced divers. Their comments follow.

"There are at least three dives you can make on the exterior of the vessel full of points of interest and good photo opportunities. There are several different light-penetration options, from the bridge and chart room to the long swim-through at the main deck, called the highway. For the more adventurous diver the forward cable-reel room, cable tanks and main engine room will be available in the coming months. Once again, due to the depth of water, the *Charlie Brown* is perfectly suited for Nitrox dives, multi-level dives, deep dives, penetration dives, wreck specialties, and it is sure to attract an abundance of marine life."

Charlie Brown was built in the 1950s when workmanship was still a priority. This is not just another tugboat or cargo ship; with its teak decks, brass rails, and a hand-riveted hull it is truly a thing of beauty.

During its life afloat, it was involved in laying many of the subsea fiber-optic phone cables around the world. In many cases the *Charles L. Brown* created the only means of direct communications with the outside world. It has been seen on a postage stamp for the Maldives for it's involvement in the establishment of their connection to the rest of the world.

☆☆☆☆ **Outer Crooks Reef** is a pretty, shallow reef, five minutes by boat south of the city pier. The reef's ledges form a V-shape, which might stand for variety. Every imaginable hard and soft coral thrives within its bounds. Fish life, too, is diverse, with schools of smallmouth and striped grunts, black durgons, blue-head wrasse, coneys, rock hinds, banded and four-eyed butterflyfish, rock beauties, blue tang, bar jacks, damsels, fairy basslets, princess parrots, queen parrots, stoplight parrots, Spanish hogfish, sharknose gobies, spotted drums, honeycomb cowfish, burrfish, and huge porcupine fish – some over three feet long.

There are also secretary blennies. It takes a sharp eye to spot these tiny fish, but if you can, try watching them for a few minutes. You'll see them dart out for food that's drifting by, then quickly shoot tail-first back into their holes. They are unafraid of divers and make great subjects for close-up photography.

Invertebrates include flamingo-tongue snails, small crinoids, corkscrew anemones, giant anemones, pistol shrimp, pederson shrimp, thor shrimp, feather dusters, fire worms, crabs and spiny lobster. At night, divers have spotted rare copper lobsters and orange-ball anemones.

Outer Crooks is a best pick for getting reacquainted with the water and your gear after a long dry spell. It's also a great spot for night dives or snorkeling. Maximum depth, 40 feet.

☆☆ **City Wall** is 40 yards out from shore in front of Dive Statia and the hotels in Lower Town. The rock wall parallels the shore from 75 yards south of the Golden Era Hotel to the pavilion at Smoke Alley. This was the old sea wall for Lower Town back in the days of sailing ships. Storms, erosion, a freak earthquake and wave action have since repositioned the shoreline and the wall underwater. The top is at six feet, the bottom at seven to 13 feet. In many areas the wall is folded or crumpled, forming deep crevices where fish and creatures stand guard. There is not much coral cover, but reef fish are plentiful and invertebrate life is good. Watch out for sea urchins. The deepest point of the wall is 12 feet. Suggested for snorkeling and warm-up dives.

☆☆☆ **Stingray Wreck** is a half mile offshore to Orange Bay. Named for a great number of stingrays in residence, the site has been studied by William and Mary University and found to be the remains of a Dutch trading ship that went down in 1768.

The sea-moss beds at the south end of the wreck attract hawksbill turtles and flying gurnards. Average depth is 50 feet.

☆☆☆ **Double Wreck** is a colorful dive, five minutes from Orange Bay. Two wrecks, one on top of the other are overgrown with red-vase sponges and giant anemones. Bring your dive light to see the colors. Basket starfish curled into balls rest inside the sponges during the day. Patches of sea grass double as conch beds for four different species. The most common is the queen conch; the rarest, the rooster conch. At night, helmet conchs crawl out of the sand. Empty conch shells are often taken over by giant hermit crabs scavenging for food. Mantis shrimp, spotted snake eels and flying gurnards are curious residents. The northern wreck is littered with centuries-old broken bottles and pottery shards. Good for scuba, all levels.

☆☆ **Supermarket**, just outside of Double Wreck, is another dual wreck site. The remains are encrusted ballast, overgrown with branching corals, barrel and vase sponges, and plumes. A number of stems and bowls from old clay pipes – some dating back to the 1600s – have been unearthed by the shifting sands. But, remember, no fanning the bottom and anything *intact* goes to the museum.

Fish include cottonwicks, queen triggerfish, scorpionfish, stingrays, coneys, parrotfish, chalk bass and an occasional hawksbill turtle. Conchs reside in the sandy patches off the wreck. Depth is 70 feet.

☆☆☆☆ **Tommy's Temptation** is a photographer's delight. A 15-minute boat ride from town, this site is a lava finger that runs parallel to shore and just over a mile and a half straight out. The top is at 70 feet and the bottom at 100 feet. Soft corals and coral rubble umbrella the sides of the finger. The big attraction is the mega-sized old anchors hooked under the ledge. They average seven feet across and 14 feet in length with hawsers (the rings the ropes were tied to) about 18 inches in diameter.

Hundreds of schooling great barracuda, black margates, grouper, triggerfish and French angels sail by the ledges. This is also a good place to see turtles. If you spot one, stay still. Contributor, Mark Padover reports frequent advances on the turtles' part when the divers are motionless. "If you charge them, they get scared and vanish at lightening speed."

Currents often rule out a dive to this area, but when sea conditions are calm and currents light, this is a super spot for intermediate to advanced divers. If the ocean isn't flat, it is a bad choice.

☆☆ **North Point** is an outstanding dive and snorkeling site in the northern marine park area at the point of the island. The bottom slopes off steeply from shore, bottoming out in sand at 70 to 100 feet. The area is strewn with huge boulders, some up to 40 feet tall. The boulders are covered with corals, sea fans and gigantic barrel sponges – up to five feet across. Fish life is extraordinary. On one dive expect to see schoolmasters, black margates, hogfish, whitespotted filefish, blue tangs, rock beauties, sergeant majors and squirrelfish. Huge two-foot French and gray angels swim by. Spotted eagle rays and reef sharks cruise the area. Good for all experience levels.

☆☆ **Darlene Bay** is excellent for snorkeling when the seas are calm. The dive (or snorkel) boat anchors in a sandy area off the shallow reefs or will drift with you as you swim among lava outcrops and fingers. Maximum depth is 20 feet. The lava and corals come up to the surface at the south end of the bay. Good fish life – turtles, sea fans, sea whips and branching corals.

It is easiest to reach this site by a five-minute boat ride. It is a most difficult hike for a shore entry, with large rocks and loose gravel to negotiate, but if you are fit and agile, you can reach it by heading south along the coast for a half hour after passing the ruins of Crooks Castle.

Additional good snorkeling is found at **Inner Crooks**, just north of Crooks Castle (max. depth 18 feet); **Jenkins Bay** (max. 25 feet) on the island's northwest corner; and **Corre Corre Bay** (max. 40 feet), opposite town on the Eastern shores.

Dive Operators

To call Statia from the US or Canada, dial 011 (the international access code), then 599 (the country code for the Netherlands Antilles), and finally 318 (the area code for Statia) and the 4-digit local number. To call within Statia, only the last 5-digit local number is necessary.

Dive Statia is a full-service PADI training facility and NAUI PRO facility offering introductory courses through instructor and guided reef and wreck trips. Their boats range from ocean kayaks to a 31-foot cabin boat. Every dive is accompanied by a certified instructor or dive master. Rental gear and dive/accommodation packages are offered with a variety of inns and hotels. ☎ US 866-614-3491 or 405-843-7846. 599-318-2435, www.divestatia.com. Write to Box 58, St. Eustatius, NA.

Golden Rock Dive Center, located at the **Old Gin House Resort**, Oranjestad, and just a few minutes from southern marine park dives, features PADI resort courses, dive and snorkeling trips customized for all skill levels, shaded dive boat with dive platform, expert staff, equipment rentals. Dive packages. ☎ 800-311-6658 or dive shop direct 599-318-2964, www.golden-rockdive.com, grdivers@goldenrocknet.com.

Scubaqua Dive Center at the Golden Era Hotel features reef and wreck dives, basic through advanced PADI, SSI, CMAS courses in their shop pool. Snorkeling tours. ☎ 599-318-2345, www.scubaqua.com, dive@scubaqua.com

Where to Stay

There is a 7% service charge on room rates. At hotels, the service charge on food and beverage is 15% in lieu of gratuities.

The Old Gin House is a beautiful replica of an 18th-century building surrounded by beautiful palms and flowering trees. The original Gin House housed a cotton gin. Built of old bricks used by sailing ships as ballast, this landmark resort features 19 rooms with king-size beds, private baths, cable TV, air conditioning and direct-dial telephones. Two rooms and two suites face the sea. Poolside restaurant and oceanfront patio bars serve lobster specials and fine island drinks. **Golden Rock** dive shop on premises. ☎ 599-318-2319, info@oldginhouse.com, www.oldginhouse.com.

King's Well offers 12 spacious rooms, a few with air conditioning, on Orange Bay, each with a fridge and cable TV. Great views! Rates are $90-$140 per night, breakfast included. Walk to beach and Dive Statia. King's

Well features terrific views of Orange Bay. No phones. Pool, jacuzzi. The hotel pub, a favorite après-dive meeting place, serves steaks, jaeger and Wiener schnitzels. ☎ 599-318-2538, kingswellresort2000@yahoo.com, www.kingswellstatia.com.

The Golden Era Hotel offers 20 air-conditioned rooms on Orange Bay, with a pool and seaside restaurant. Suites and efficiencies available. Rooms feature cable TV, telephones and refrigerators. Rates average $150 per night. ☎ 599-318-2345; from the US, 800-223-9815; from Canada, 800-344-0023, www.statiatourism.com/goldenera/index.html. For special rates e-mail goldera@goldenrock.net. Dive shop next door.

Sightseeing & Other Activities

 Swapping dive stories, nature hikes, historic walks, and hunting for blue slave beads highlight a visit to Statia.

Historical Sites

In spite of British Admiral Lord Rodney's savaging of the island in 1781, numerous historical buildings remain, from large monumental structures to small workers' homes. Many are currently being restored in Upper Town.

Among those are **Fort Oranje** and **Fort de Windt**, the **Historical Foundation Museum**, old ruins at **Orange Bay** and remains of *Honen Dalim*, the second-oldest synagogue in the Western Hemisphere.

Don't miss the **Underwater Snorkeling Museum** tours offered by the Golden Era Dive Shop.

Blue Bead Hunts

Remnants of a curious past, these five-sided blue glass beads were used to buy and sell slaves during the 17th and 18th centuries, and to reward the slaves. Upon accumulation of enough beads, a male slave could buy freedom or a woman. The woman was priced by the number of beads that fit around her waist. Today, to some, a heavy woman is still considered more valuable than a thin one.

Beads are most often found on the beach between the end of the city pier and the ruins of Crooks Castle, headquarters of the slave trade way back when.

Hiking Trails

Be sure you are OK to fly on your dive tables before climbing The Quill. Hiking Statia is strenuous. Certain trails are often slippery and dangerous. Hikers should be properly attired and in good physical condition. Trails are marked with numbered signposts. Pick up a trail guide at the tourist bureau in the airport or at the Historical Museum, ☎ 2288.

The most exhilarating trails lead along the rim and down through the rain forest-covered crater of The Quill. The main trail starts at **Welfare Road** (south end of Oranjestad) at a telephone pole marked **Quill Track 1** (there are 20). This trail brings you up the mountain to the rim of the volcano. It is a strenuous hike and may be slippery in places. The climb up takes about 45 minutes; down in 30.

Dining

Blue Bead Bar & Restaurant on Gallows Bay sits amidst 18th-century ruins. Continental and Indonesian cuisine. ☎ 599-318-2873.

Cool Corner Bar & Restaurant in the heart of town features Chinese specials. ☎ 599-318-2523.

Golden Era Hotel specializes in West Indian, Creole and International dishes. ☎ 599-318-2345.

King's Well Bar & Restaurant overlooking beautiful Orange Bay, serves prime beef, Jaegerand Wiener schnitzels and more. Breakfast is served for hotel guests only. Lunch and dinner for hotel guests and the general public. ☎ 599-318-2538.

The Old Gin House Restaurant is unique, with a chef from Belgium who received many awards and a Michelin Star while running his own restaurant. He blends traditional and West Indian cuisine using fresh local produce. ☎ 599-318-2319.

Sandbox Tree Bakery opposite the Dutch Reformed Church makes your choice of sandwiches. ☎ 599-318-2469.

Smoke Alley Bar & Grill, an open-air beach bar and restaurant in Lower Town, Gallows Bay, prepares homemade dishes, Caribbean style. Open Monday-Saturday for lunch and dinner. Live music and DJ Friday nights. ☎ 599-318-2002.

Superburger offers innovative burgers, sandwiches, shakes, ice cream and daily specials. Local breakfast and local hot dishes from 11:30 am-2:00 pm. ☎ 599-318-2412.

Facts

Helpful Phone Numbers: Police, ☎ 911; hospital, ☎ 913; airport, 599-318-2887.

Nearest Recompression Chamber: St. Eustatius Medical School, 73 Goldenrock, ☎ 599-318-2600.

Airlines: To get to Statia you will first have to travel to *St. Maarten Netherlands Antilles* (airport code: SXM) via major carrier such as **American Airlines**, **Dutch Caribbean Airlines**, **Continental**, **US Airways**, **Delta**, **KLM** or **Air France**. Then on **WINAIR** (www.fly-winair.com) or **Windward Island Express** to *St. Eustatius* (Statia) airport code (EUX), reservations@fly-winair.com.

Driving: On the right.

Seaport: Gallows Bay.

Documents: US and Canadian citizens need a valid passport. Others need a passport or alien registration card. And, you need an onward or return ticket.

Customs: No customs.

Currency: Netherlands Antilles guilder, or florin (NAf). American dollars are accepted everywhere on the island. US$1=NAf 1.78 (variable).

Language: Dutch is the official language; English is widely spoken.

Climate: Air temperature ranges from 78° to 82°F year-round. Winter evenings may cool to 60°. Rainfall averages 45 inches per year.

Clothing: Casual, lightweight. Light wetsuit or wetskin suggested during winter.

Electricity: 110 volts AC, 60 cycles.

Time: Atlantic Standard (Eastern Standard + 1 hr).

Departure Tax: Everyone leaving Statia has to pay a departure fee of US$5.65 for local destinations within the Dutch Caribbean. All other destinations cost US$12.

Religious Services: Limited.

Additional Information: *St. Eustatius Tourism Development Foundation*, Fort Oranje, Oranjestad, St. Eustatius, Netherlands Antilles. ☎ 599-318-2433, fax 599-318-2433, www.statiatourism.com, euxtour@goldenrock.net.

St. Kitts & Nevis

Cradled between St. Maarten and Antigua in the Eastern Caribbean, the sister islands of St. Kitts and Nevis call themselves "The Secret Caribbean," but word of the area's unique natural beauty and subsea wonders have drawn tourists from around the globe.

Physically beautiful, the islands are a patchwork of rolling green mountains surrounded by miles of unexplored, shallow reefs, swim-through caves and grottoes. More than 400 shipwrecks, dating back to the 1600s, lie below their clear waters. Narrow strips of black and gold sand beaches skirt much of the coast.

St. Kitts

St. Kitts is an oval-shaped landmass that stretches out into a long, narrow peninsula extending like a guitar handle from its southeastern corner. Formed from volcanic eruption, its central area is a rugged mountain range, whose highest point is the dormant volcano, **Mount Liamuiga**, at 3,792 feet. Tropical forests, ridges and waterfalls at the high elevations contrast with its lowlands where spacious and fertile valleys produce an abundance of sugar cane, sea-island cotton and peanuts. Most of the beaches are black volcanic sand, although white, sandy beaches can be found along the southeast peninsula of **Frigate Bay** and **Salt Pond**. Overall, the island is 23 miles long, covering an area of 68 square miles.

On the seacoast lies **Basseterre**, the capital, with a population of about 15,000. Its ambience is decidedly old-world Caribbean with an informal produce market and rows of weather-beaten pastel buildings along the waterfront. Narrow streets lead from the town pier to a four-block made-for-tourists area in the center of town known as the **Circus**, a town square, or actually town circle, dominated by a tall grandfather clock, where three streets converge.

Old sugar plantations on both islands have been transformed into wonderfully stylish inns. These classic Great Houses, once the homes of the plantation owners, sit high in the foothills of the volcanic mountains that dominate the skylines. Surrounding the Great Houses are the remains of old windmills where the sugar cane was crushed, and the boiling houses where the sweet liquid was processed. Before the "around the island" narrow-gauge railroad was

Kenneth Samuel, Kenneth's Dive Centre; John Yearwood, Oualie Beach Hotel; Ellis Chaderton, Julian Rigby, Scuba Safaris Ltd; Auston MacLeod, Pro Divers; Gary Pereira, Turtle Beach Club; Jennifer Woods, Caribbean Explorer.

completed in 1926 to transport the cane to the central sugar factory in Basseterre, each plantation was a kingdom unto itself, growing, cutting, crushing, boiling and selling sugar. The downside of that free enterprise was air pollution. During the boiling season, the tall stone smokestacks on more than 50 estates would belch smoke into the atmosphere for 18 to 20 hours a day. To eliminate the problem, the government purchased the sugar-producing land and began transporting the cane to a central boiling house in Basseterre.

The majority of plantation owners sold their Great Houses to entrepreneurs who refurbished them as delightful inns. Most are furnished with a potpourri of antiques or West Indian furnishings.

Nevis

Separated from St. Kitts by a two-mile strait known as the "Narrows" lies **Nevis**, the sister island, which Columbus named for its mountainous resemblance to the snow-capped *Nieve* peak of Spain. Dubbed *Queen of the Caribees* by 17th- and 18th-century European visitors for its therapeutic hot springs and fertile soil, this island encompasses 36 square miles of spectacularly beautiful land. The tip of the island's dominant central peak, usually encircled by clouds, rises into an almost perfectly formed cone of 3,232 feet. **Charlestown**,the capital city and only town, has a population of 1,200.

The terrain of Nevis encompasses numerous fertile hillsides and narrow, golden sand beaches. Most of the inhabitants are vegetable and coconut farmers.

Low-cost passenger ferries operate daily once or twice a day – except Thursdays and Sundays – from Basseterre on St. Kitts to Charlestown on Nevis. The ferries run twice a day but are not synchronized with airline arrivals, so it is often difficult to make connections. Check the Website, www.nevis1.com, for ferry schedules, or contact the tourist board for a ferry schedule before planning a trip to Nevis. Phone numbers and addresses at end of chapter.

Diving

 Diving is diverse, with ledges, mini-walls, white holes teeming with fish, caves and drift diving in some areas. Most reefs on the Atlantic side and offshore on the Caribbean side are pristine, with monster-sized sea fans and sponges growing over piles of lava rocks. Regularly visited reef and wreck sites are on the sheltered Caribbean side of the islands and in the cut (the Narrows) between Nevis and St. Kitts, but trips to the Atlantic where the mysterious white holes lie and large pelagics are encountered may be arranged when seas are calm.

St. Kitts offers the most dive sites, with alternate sheltered areas on the Caribbean side when the seas are rough on the Atlantic side or at the Narrows. Nevis dive sites are more vulnerable to swells when the winds are high, even on its Caribbean side, but currents are usually light and the sites are spectacular. Average visibility is 80 to 100 feet, with exceptional water clarity at the cut and offshore Caribbean and Atlantic reefs. Water temperature is 80-85° year-round. Depths for scuba range from 30 to 90 feet, averaging 50 feet. Certification, referrals and resort courses with PADI and NAUI instructors are offered. The average boat trip to a dive site takes 15 minutes. Following rainy periods, freshwater runoff from the mountains will lower visibility on the close-in reefs and wrecks, especially off Basseterre. Coral collecting and spear fishing are prohibited only off **Turtle Beach** on the southeast (guitar handle) peninsula of St. Kitts.

Be sure to let the boat captains know if you prefer to dive a sheltered area as the diver population is tiny – diving is new on these islands – and some of the captains, who double as fishing guides, may want to share their best spots rather than the calmest ones.

Stay shallow and keep a close eye on your bottom time. The nearest recompression chamber is on Saba, a 15-minute flight from St. Kitts airport. But getting to that airport and arranging a flight over may take the good part of a day or more. Avoid exhausting mountain hikes and climbs after a dive or you risk the shaken-soda-bottle effect.

When to Go

 The best weather is from December to April, though air and water temperatures are good for diving year-round and reduced-rate dive packages are offered between May and December. The best months for diving the Caribbean side are April and May. June through mid November brings rain and a chance of a hurricane. Late December brings the "Christmas wind," which churns up the seas.

History

 First named *Liamuiga* – The Fertile Isle – by the Carib Indians, St. Kitts was renamed "St. Christopher" by discoverer Christopher Columbus in 1493. He apparently was so taken by its beauty that he honored it with the name of his patron saint. The name was later shortened to St. Kitts.

Latter-day historians equate St. Kitts with its most notable site, **Brimstone Hill**, a spectacular 18th-century fort turned national park and nicknamed the

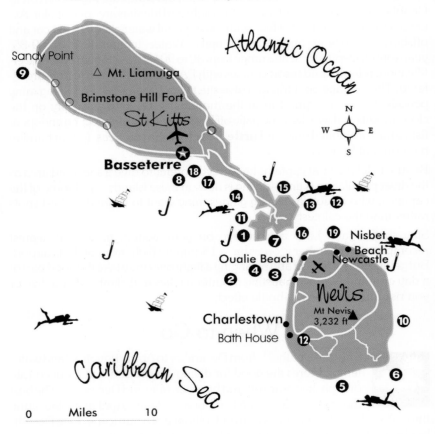

Dive & Snorkeling Sites

1	Turtle Bar Reef	11	Green Point
2	Monkey Reef	12	Gridiron
3	Coral Gardens	13	Turtle Beach
4	Lobster Walk	14	White House Bay
5	The Caves	15	Sand Bank Bay
6	Redonda Reef	16	Cockleshell & Banana Bays
7	Nags Head Reef	17	Timothy Beach
8	*Taleta* Wreck	18	Bird Rock Beach
9	Sandy Point	19	Long Hall Bay
10	The White Holes		

"Gibraltar of the West Indies." An architectural and engineering marvel, the fortress spreads across 40 acres on a bluff 800 feet above the sea.

Settled in 1623 by Sir Thomas Warner, St. Kitts was the first island in the West Indies to be colonized by the English. The French, under D'Esnambuc, colonized another part of the island the following year.

During the 17th century, intermittent warfare was waged between the French and British settlers. In 1713, St. Kitts was ceded to Britain by the Treaty of Utrecht. Fighting over possession of the island occurred for the last time in 1782, when the French captured the British fortress of Brimstone Hill. Later that year, the British were victorious over the French in a battle off the island of Dominica and regained possession of St. Kitts in 1783 under the terms of the Treaty of Versailles.

Nevis was colonized in 1628 by British settlers living in neighboring St. Kitts. Like its sister island, Nevis suffered stormy attacks from both the French and Spanish throughout the 17th and 18th centuries. On September 19, 1983 St. Kitts and Nevis gained independence.

Best Dive & Snorkeling Sites

Dive sites in the cut and around the southeast peninsula are shared by dive shops on both islands. Caribbean sites off Basseterre are most often dived by Kenneth's Dive Shop.

 The "sunken city of Jamestown" on Nevis, reputed to have been washed away by a hurricane, is listed in at least one guide as a great dive. Unfortunately it is nonexistent, more myth than fact. There is some small mention of it in historical records, but if it exists on the sea floor, no diver has discovered it. Historians feel that Jamestown simply fell into disuse as marshlands moved over it.

☆ **Turtle Bar Reef,** off the unpopulated southwestern tip of the St. Kitts, is a spur and groove reef growing over a rocky bottom. Pillar corals and sea plumes rise from a rocky bottom that slopes from 15 feet down to 65 feet. Seas are always calm. The shallows are a good dive for novices and snorkelers. Ten-minute boat ride from the Turtle Beach Watersports Center, 20 minutes from Basseterre.

☆☆☆☆ **Monkey Reef** is 2½ miles off the peninsula and Nevis, a longer boat ride than most, but worth the trip when seas are calm for the wonderful array of fish and invertebrate life, including blackbar soldierfish, coneys, sharks, barracuda, turtles and rays. The reef is a labyrinth of small caves, canyons and ledges ablaze with pink-tipped anemones, orange tube sponges, encrusting sponges, big barrel sponges, mounds of club finger corals, and sea fans. Excellent visibility. Average depths are from 45 to 60 feet. Suggested for experienced ocean divers only. Sea conditions are often choppy with four- to six-foot swells.

☆☆☆ **Coral Gardens**, a hilly reef off Oalie Beach, Nevis, has huge pillar coral formations and gigantic barrel sponges. It's a good place to spot big turtles, schools of spadefish, nurse sharks, rays, remoras, lobsters. Depths are 50-80 feet. Seas average three to four feet with little current. Excellent visibility. For experienced divers only. Ten minutes from **Scuba Safaris**.

☆☆☆ **Lobster Walk** is inside Coral Gardens, about 1½ miles from Oalie Beach, Nevis. The dive is similar to Coral Gardens, but inhabited by numerous lobsters. Depths start at 70 feet and drop to 110 feet. Experienced ocean divers only. Visibility and water clarity are outstanding. Expect some swells.

☆☆☆☆ **The Caves,** off the southwestern coast of Nevis, are a series of large caverns formed by ancient lava flows. The once-molten tubes are now home to schools of grunt, snapper, chubs, stingrays, nurse sharks and black tip reef sharks. Huge 200-lb turtles and rays have been spotted. Maximum depth is 40 feet. Good for all divers and snorkelers.

☆☆☆☆ **Redonda Reef,** off the southern end of Nevis, is a wilderness area with an extensive series of caverns and mini-walls just beginning to be explored. Depths average 60-70 feet. Sea conditions vary with the wind. Spectacular visibility and marine life. It is a 45-minute or longer boat ride. Seas must be exceptionally calm for the dive boats to visit this site.

☆☆ **Nags Head Reef** is at the southernmost tip of St. Kitts where the Caribbean and Atlantic meet. About a 55-minute boat ride from Basseterre, 10 minutes from Turtle Beach, this area is *the* place for spotting eagle rays, huge stingrays and other large pelagics. Even whales occasionally blast by. This site is weather-dependent, sometimes rough and with strong currents, suggested only for experts. But, when the sea is calm, it is good for novice divers. Depths range from 25 to 110 feet. The reef is a mix of mini-walls and canyons with superb and varied marine life.

☆ **The *Taleta*** sank in 1985 off the west coast of St. Kitts and lies in 50 feet of water. A quick boat ride from Basseterre, the wreck is a half mile offshore, surrounded by coral rubble. Its steel hull attracts schooling fish, barracuda and lobster. The wreck is subject to murky conditions after a storm.

☆☆☆☆ **Sandy Point** is the photographers' favorite, with huge barrel sponges, lavender sea fans, gorgonians and orange, elephant-ear sponges. A mini-wall and canyon, depths range from 45 to 100 feet. Unfortunately, this site is a long trip for St. Kitts dive operators and is visited only on request by groups who are then bussed to the site (15 miles north of Basseterre), where they rendezvous with the dive boats.

☆☆☆ **The White Holes**, off the Atlantic side of Nevis, are clear, sandy hollows packed with fish and surrounded by coral. Depths range from 15 to 45 feet. Fishlife and visibility are incredible, but the seas are often rough and the trip uncomfortable. On a calm day, this is an exceptional dive.

☆☆☆ **Green Point**, off the Caribbean side of the southeast peninsula on St. Kitts, is alive with black corals, big barrel and tube sponges and a variety of soft corals. Abundant lobster and fish. A 15-minute trip from either of the dive shops on St. Kitts. Twenty-five minutes from Nevis. Depth is 50 feet. Sea conditions are always calm. Good for all level divers.

☆☆☆ **The Grid Iron** is another Atlantic dive. This reef starts at **New Castle Airport** on Nevis and extends out past **Booby Island** and the north shoreline of St. Kitts. It is an undersea shelf that rises to within 15 feet of the surface. The shallows support a dense growth of well-formed elkhorn stands, fan-shaped hydroids, colonies of giant brain coral, yellow and orange tube sponges, barrel sponges, elephant ear sponges, and plate corals. There are plenty of fish, including blue tangs, French angelfish, porcupinefish, chubs, lobster, scrawled filefish, and yellowtail. Sea conditions vary. High winds and currents may rule out the area, but when conditions are favorable it is a spectacular dive and snorkeling site.

Snorkeling

All St. Kitts and Nevis beaches are open to the public. Access in some cases is through hotel property.

Nevis

☆☆ **Longhaul Bay** has good snorkeling on the inner side of the barrier reef off Nisbets Plantation. The water is shallow and visibility quite good. The beach is gorgeous. Get there by driving to the beach at **Nisbets Plantation Inn** (near the airport) and walk south along the beach. Facing the sea, turn right and follow the shore to the last jetty. Experienced snorkelers should go outside the jetty, swim out to the reef and turn right to find a protected inner reef. Novice snorkelers will find many fish among the rocks closer to shore inside the last jetty. The current will bring you back to the Nisbet beach bar, which serves cool drinks and an excellent lunch! Always calm inside the barrier reef. A wonderful spot for swimming and picnics too.

St. Kitts

☆☆ **Turtle Beach**. Facing the cut, walk to your left along the beach and swim out about 20 yards to the reef where you'll find the beginning of **Ballast**

Bay Reef. Turtle Beach is a watersports facility at the end of the southeast peninsula. Signs lead the way. Snorkeling gear may be rented from **Pro Divers** on the beach. Turtle Beach Bar & Grill serves drinks and lunch daily from noon to 5 pm.

☆ **White House Bay** is at the end of the first dirt road to your right as you reach the **Great Salt Pond** area. You'll know it by the two sections of tugboat sticking out of the water. If the road is muddy, you may have to park near the main road and walk part of the way back. Choose the dirt road to the left. Lots of fish and corals inhabit the wreck, which was washed ashore by Hurricane Hugo in 1989. Depths range from shallow to 25 feet in the bay.

☆☆ **Sand Bank Bay** is the first turn-off to your left before reaching the **Great Salt Pond** area. The Bay is on the Atlantic side and subject to waves on windy days. Walk to your right along the cove and swim over to the rocks, where a bevy of beautiful reef fish await.

☆☆ **Cockleshell & Banana Bays** are one bay south of Turtle Beach. To reach it, drive straight to the end of the scenic drive. There is a construction sight with framework for an unfinished – with no definite plans to be finished – hotel at the end of the road. Park next to it and walk toward the old **Cockleshell Hotel** (devastated by Hurricane Hugo) on the bluff. Directly in front of the bluff is a pretty reef. Watch out for fire coral. Both bays are calm with good visibility. Beautiful white sand beaches skirt the area. At press time the hotel property was sold to Sandals for a future resort.

☆ **Timothy Beach Resort**, just south of Basseterre, has a small reef off the beach. Shallow depths.

☆☆ **Bird Rock Beach Hotel**, two miles south of Basseterre on the Caribbean, has a narrow strip of jet-black sand at the bottom of its property. Just off the shore are several rocks and a pretty reef which drops off enough for a shallow dive. Always calm, never a current. Decent visibility. Reach the area by boat or by climbing down the three steep flights of stairs behind the multi-terraced hotel. On the climb back up you'll find cold drinks and meals at the hotel's open-air restaurant.

Snorkeling Tours

Snorkeling trips can be arranged with the dive shops, the hotels or the following operators.

St. Kitts

Banana Boat, Basseterre, St. Kitts, provides scenic tours to passengers of the cruise lines that regularly visit St. Kitts. The crew of the *Banana Boat* is USCG certified. ☎ 869-465-0645.

Blue Water Safaris Ltd., Basseterre, St. Kitts, sail along the scenic coastline to sheltered coves where you snorkel the clear turquoise water of St. Kitts. Day-trips or private charter. ☎ 869-466-4933.

Leeward Island Charters, Basseterre, St. Kitts, welcome snorkelers for day sails aboard luxurious 70-foot catamarans. Both of their vessels, the *Spirit of St. Kitts* and sister ship *Eagle* are equipped with an open bar, island music and friendly crew. Request snorkeling trips when you call. ☎ 869-465-7474.

Under the Sea-Sealife Education Centre: Owner Barbara Whitman, a marine biologist and teacher, leads guided snorkel trips, rents equipment and gives lessons off the Oualie Beach Hotel shore, and runs a summer camp for kids. ☎ 869-469-1291, cell 869-662-9291, terramar@caribsurf.com, www.undertheseanevis.com.

The *Rum*, a 24-foot former New England lobster boat, departs for snorkeling adventures from Oualie Beach at 10:30 am and returns around 2:30. Cost is $50 per person and they need four people to go out. They serve a picnic lunch with cold beverages and will photograph you snorkeling, if you wish. This operation is seasonal (winter months only). Captain Frank Morse is an ex-sailboat captain with a 100-ton master's ticket. ☎ 869-469-1060.

Nevis

Enjoy the soft island breezes aboard the 47-foot catamaran *Caona* with Captain Lennox at the helm. He takes people out for snorkeling and sailing trips (daily except Sunday). The three-hour snorkel and sailing trips (am or pm) include refreshments and snorkeling equipment. ☎ 869-469-8494 or 9494. Reservations also available though any hotel.

MV *Rum* owners Frank and Chris are history buffs and avid snorkelers. Join them on a cruise along Nevis' beautiful leeward coast for a chat on history and geology of Nevis. Once you reach the snorkeling site they personally guide you, pointing out interesting marine plants and animals. Beginners and experienced snorkelers are welcome! rockstonefish@hotmail.com. ☎ 869-469-1060.

Dive Operators

Prices for a two-tank boat dive range from US$80 to $90 and include all the equipment, if desired. One-tank dives are $45.

St. Kitts

Dive St. Kitts Scuba is a PADI/NAUI dual dive facility, based at the Bird Rock Beach Hotel. All dive packages include tanks and air, weights and weight belts, briefings before and after dives, fully customized dive boat, boat refreshments, no lifting or lugging of equipment, and freshwater rinse-off on dock and boat.

Dive boats, which accommodate up to 24 divers, leave the dock at 9 am for a 5-10 minute ride to the first dive site. Then return to the dock for a surface interval, giving you time to grab a snack, get a soft drink or relax by the pool. While you are relaxing the staff changes your tank and prepares all gear for your second dive. Two-tank dives run $90. Snorkel trip (minimum four people) costs $35. Six two-tank boat dives cost $370. Equipment and camera rentals are available. ☎ 800-621-1270, 869-465-1189, www.divestkitts .com, brbh@caribsurf.com.

Kenneth's Dive Centre on Bay Road East, Basseterre, offers full PADI certification programs, rental gear and two fast dive boats. Owner Kenneth Samuel has been diving St. Kitts for more than 20 years and is an expert on the reefs and wrecks, tides and currents. Friendly service is provided by a professional staff. Comfortable, roomy, twin-hull, twin-engine, flat-bottom dive boats tour the Caribbean sites around Basseterre. Trips to the cut and Monkey Reef on request. ☎ 869-465-2670 or 465-7043.

Pro Divers is based at the Ocean Terrace Inn's Fisherman's Wharf This PADI instruction center offers dive packages and dive/accommodation packages with **Ocean Terrace Inn**. All gear rentals, Nikonos camera and strobe rentals. The shop offers a full range of services, resort courses and PADI certification (Open-Water to Assistant Instructor). Reef tours aboard a fast 30-foot, twin-engine dive boat. Pro Divers circles the peninsula and always visits the best sites. When the wind is too high on the Atlantic, they dive the cut. When weather rules out the cut, the dive boats go around the bend to a protected Caribbean cove. Pro Divers also rents gear for beach dives. No spear fishing in this protected area. ☎ 869-466-DIVE (3483), www.prodiversstkitts.com, info@prodiversstkitts.com.

MV *Caribbean Explorer II* is a live-aboard that departs from St. Maarten and tours St. Kitts and Saba. The yacht has nine air-conditioned cabins, and is fully equipped for scuba, U/W photography and video. Winter rates from $1,595 per person. Summer from $1,395. The *Explorer II* visits some of the outer Caribbean reefs that are out of range for the dive shops. ☎ 800-322-3577 or write to Sara Moody, PO Box 488, Mabank, TX 75147 www.explorerventures.com.info.

Nevis

Dive uncrowded and unhurried Nevis with **Scuba Safaris**, a NAUI Dream Resort, a PADI Five Star Gold Palm facility, and a NASDS Examining Station on the grounds of the Oualie Beach Hotel. Owner Ellis Chaderton is a NAUI instructor offering personalized cave, wreck, and reef dives at **The Caves**, **Monkey Shoals** and **Redonda Bank**, noted for hammerheads, dolphin and whale sightings. During certain times of the year, Ellis also leads whale watching expeditions off Nevis. Dive/hotel packages are available through the Oualie Beach Resort from $720 per person. Package includes three dive days (one two-tank boat dive daily), five nights in deluxe room (based on double occupancy), room tax & service charges. ☎ 869-469-9518,fax 869-469-9619, www.oualiebeach.com, oualie@caribsurf.com.

Where to Stay

 A list of all accommodations, including rooms in the historic inns (most are not air conditioned), apartments, and guest houses, is available from the tourist board (see details at end of chapter).

Dive packages, including room (double occupancy), airport transfers, tax, service charge and 10 dives, are offered by the resorts listed below. A 9% government hotel tax and 10-15% service charge are added to the rates shown.

St. Kitts

Bird Rock Beach Hotel is high on a bluff overlooking Basseterre, with a panoramic view of the Caribbean. The inn has one, two and three bedroom suites with interconnecting suites and studios ideal for families. Each room has cable television, telephone, air conditioning, private bathroom and a Caribbean Sea-view patio or balcony.

Dive St. Kitts' boats are at the hotel dock. Gear may be stowed at the dive shop. The hotel features an adjacent restaurant, pool, coffee shop, bar. Nice snorkeling off the rocky beach. Winter room rates start at $125 per day, summer rates from $85 to $225. Dive/hotel packages. ☎ 800-621-1270, 869-465-8914, www.birdrockbeach.com, brbh@caribsurf.com.

Frigate Bay Resort, overlooking Frigate Bay, features spacious air-conditioned rooms and suites, restaurant and pool. The beach and golf course is a short stroll away. Winter rates start at $130 for a room to $290 for a two-bedroom suite; summer rates are from $100 to $225. ☎ 800-266-2185, 869-465-8935, fax 869-465-7050.

Ocean Terrace Inn (OTI), perched on a hill overlooking the capital city of Basseterre and its snug harbor, is a multi-terraced resort. Modern guest rooms are air conditioned, have satellite TV, and tubs with showers. The inn features two bars, two pools and a Jacuzzi. OTI's nearby wharf is headquarters for Pro Divers. Room rates per day are from $190 for a double to $460 for a two-bedroom (4 persons) per night. Seven night dive packages with Pro Divers are

$1000 per person, tax included. ☎ US 800-524-0512, direct 869-465-2754, otiskitts@caribsurf.com, www.oceanterraceinn.com.

Nevis

Nisbet Plantation Beach Club is by far the most pictur- esque spot on Nevis. Built as a sugar plantation in 1778, the resort is situated on a mile-long, white-sand beach on the island's reef-protected north shore. Units are housed in 13 duplex cottages with spacious bedrooms, showers and enclosed screened patios. All have small fridges, hair dryers (a rarity on these islands), tea- and coffee-making facilities, and telephones. Cooled by ceiling fans. The club's gourmet restaurant is outstanding and worth a visit.

Winter (December 21 to April 14) rates for two people are $500 to $680 per day, including breakfast. Summer rates based on double occupancy run $250-$370 per room.Children under two are free, extra person pays $125 per day. The resort's gourmet meal plan for $50 per person, per day is well worth every penny. You'll find nice snorkeling inside the reef off the resort beach. Shore dives are possible, but you need to make your own arrange- ments with the dive shop to get tanks and air. ☎ 800-742-6008 or 869-469-9325, www.nisbetplantation.com.

Oualie Beach Hotel, headquarters for Nevis dive vacations, sits on a lovely black sand beach on the island's leeward side. The hotel offers 22 clean ,stan- dard and deluxe rooms and suites in chalet-type structures with ceiling fans and telephones. A few have air conditioning and cable TV.

The resort's open-air restaurant opens early for breakfast and the meals are good, but we were put off by an abundance of small ants in the morning. Win- ter rates for a room, double occupancy, run from $245 to $360 per day; sum- mer, from $205. Scuba Safaris dive center is next to the hotel. Children under 12 are free with parents. Nice swimming beach. ☎ or 869-469-9135, fax 869-469-9176, www.oualiebeach.com, reservations@oualie.com.

Mt. Nevis Hotel & Beach Club, built in 1989, sprawls across 17 acres on the Round Hill Estate, a former lime plantation. This family run hotel features 32 rooms and suites in four two-story buildings. All have been recently reno- vated and redecorated with new furniture, colorful fabrics and tropical prints.

Superior suites have a queen-size bed, living area with CD/DVD players and a full kitchen. All rooms have private baths with showers, air conditioning, ceiling fans, direct-dial telephones, and cable TV. Some rooms have hot tubs. Rates from $360 to $675 per day. Their winter dive package costs $3,125 for seven nights accommodations, round-trip airport transfers, welcome rum punch, breakfast daily for two, five days compact-car rental (excluding license and insurance), three days of diving, two-tank dives (guided dives that include tanks, weights and weight belts). ☎ US and Can. 800-756-3847, direct 869-469-9373 or -9374, www.mountnevishotel.com, mountnevis@aol.com.

Hurricane Cove Bungalows, perched on a hilltop above the beach, provides a private setting in one-, two- and three-bedroom bungalows complete with kitchens. Freshwater pool, snorkeling equipment. Diving with **Scuba Safaris**. Cottages for two people run from $250 to $545 per day. Three-day minium. Book through your travel agent or ☎ (869) 469-9462, www.hurricanecove.com.

Sightseeing & Other Activities

St. Kitts

Tours of St. Kitts start at **Basseterre** and the **Circus**, an area patterned after London's famous Piccadilly Circus. Its centerpiece is a memorial to Thomas Berkeley. Surrounding it are a few craft boutiques, restaurants and galleries. Souvenir shops offer locally hand-screened fabrics, straw and coconut products, and jewelry fashioned from conch shells and volcanic rocks – many "Made in St. Kitts." Batik clothing and fabrics crafted on the island are found at **Island Hopper**, below the Ballahoo Restaurant on the Circus. From town, rent a car or taxi and travel north along the west-coast road. You'll pass several former **Great Houses**, some newly converted into restaurants or shops. Continue to **Old Road Bay**, the island's first capital city. Near the English colony, Carib drawings are sketched on the boulders. A short distance away is **Romney Manor**, the home of **Caribelle Batik**, where local artists work colorful designs into fabric with wax and dyes.

Continue to **Brimstone Hill**, a national park and fort that spreads over 40 acres above the sea and offers glorious views of St. Kitts and surrounding islands. The fort, which took 106 years of slave labor to build, is connected to a museum displaying photos and memorabilia honoring those who fought here.

Heading north from the fort brings you to **Sandy Point**, once headquarters for the Dutch tobacco industry. Continue along the island road, around the island past miles of sugar cane fields until you come to the **Black Rocks**, rugged cliffs formed of ancient lava flows from Mt. Liamuiga. A left turn will lead you to the **Frigate Bay** area, the site of luxury hotels, casinos, and the yacht club. From here head up the mountain on the new scenic road out through the uninhabited **South East Peninsula** and the **Salt Ponds**, habitat to green vervet monkeys, herons, sea turtles and wild deer. The ponds are a source of salt for the islanders.

The scenic road winds, dips and soars through seven miles of the most gorgeous, lush, green mountains and breathtaking ocean views on earth. On the Atlantic side there are panoramic views of waves crashing against rocky cliffs and washing over secluded, golden beaches and snorkeling coves. Rounding the mountains brings the turquoise Caribbean and distant mountains of Nevis into view. Near the end is the **Great Salt Pond**. Watch for monkeys and, near the ponds, cows crossing the road.

Hikes into the rain forest, board surfing, deep-sea fishing, horseback riding, sunset cruises, and historic tours are easily arranged through the resorts or individual operators.

Among the sporting activities are **golfing** (18-hole international championship course at Frigate Bay and a nine-hole course at Golden Rock, St. Kitts); **tennis**; **horseback riding** along the beaches of Friar's Bay and Conaree Beach. Traveling on land is done by taxi, auto, moped or bicycle. Or one can venture through town by horse and carriage. Taxis are expensive and allowed to jack up their rates at night. Be sure to have the published rates in hand and note the hours they are in effect. Taxis with a "T" on the license plate mean the driver is able to recite the local history and give sightseeing tours. Avis and several local companies have car-rental agents at the airports.

Nevis

 If you arrive on Nevis by boat, you can walk to Charlestown. You'll first encounter the **Cotton Ginnery**, still used to gin cotton, and the **Market Place**, where local merchants sell fresh fruits, spices and seafood. But more interesting is the **Nevis Philatelic Bureau**, which offers beautiful color plates of marine life, historic aircraft and space subjects, and local flora – unique souvenirs, all suitable for framing. **The Nevis Museum and Hamilton House**, birthplace of statesman and first Secretary of the US Treasury, Alexander Hamilton, will also be found here.

Heading north on the coast road past Oualie Beach, you'll come to **Newcastle Pottery**, where centuries-old methods create natural red pottery, from small ashtrays to flower pots and the coalpots used by many villagers. The best prices on the pottery are at the factory.

South of town turn left across from the Esso station to find the **Bath Hotel and Spring House**, once *the* grand hotel and health spa of the Caribbean. Much of the original structure was destroyed by an earthquake in 1950, but visitors can enjoy a mineral bath or just stick a toe in and tour the hotel.

Horseback riding and **rain forest walks** may be arranged through the hotels.

Dining

Local seafood, lobster dishes, and West Indian cuisine highlight St. Kitts and Nevis menus. Many fine restaurants are in the former Great Houses. Fast-food and pizza shops are found in towns. Menus list prices in EC (East Caribbean dollars), one of which is about US$2.70. When you are quoted a price in "dollars" ask which one. Credit cards are *not* widely accepted.

St. Kitts

Fisherman's Wharf, on the harbor in Basseterre, offers fresh seafood and local dishes. Seating is on a broad deck a few inches over the water. Much like eating on a yacht that doesn't rock. Great views of Basseterre at night. Don't miss the pumpkin fritters. Informal. Open for dinner nightly, and for lunch on weekends. Moderate. ☎ 465-2695.

The Ballahoo, center of town, Basseterre at the Circus, open Monday through Saturday, serves seafood and local dishes, 8 am to 11 pm. ☎ 465-4197.

Stonewall's Tropical Bar and Eating Place on Princes Street, Basseterre, mirrors a lush tropical garden. Stonewall's chef lures guests back with succulent steaks and freshly caught fish, all straight off the grill. Great ribs too. Open Monday through Friday, evenings only, from 5 pm to 11 pm. Dinner from 6.30 to 10 pm; closed weekends and public holidays. All major credit cards accepted. Reservations recommended. ☎ 465-5248.

PJ's Pizza Bar and Restaurant features pizza, sandwiches, vegetarian and Italian dinners. Eat-in or take-out. ☎ 465-8373.

Nevis

Oualie Beach Hotel, open daily from 7 am to 11 pm, serves lunch and dinner. Enjoy West Indian cuisine in an informal atmosphere at the water's edge. Excellent broiled lobster and pineapple mousse. Moderate. No credit cards. ☎ 469-9735.

Unella's Waterfront Bar & Restaurant serves refreshing tropical drinks, sandwiches, local and seafood dishes, including curried lamb, spare ribs and conch, at reasonable prices. By the ferry pier in Charlestown. ☎ 469-5574.

Nisbet Plantation offers elegant settings and taste-tempting creations such as chilled avocado and apricot soup, marinated salmon over asparagus mousse with caviar-stuffed quail eggs, amberjack with hollandaise sauce or sumptous meat dishes. Expensive. Meals average US$65 per person without drinks, plus gratuities and tax and an "optional" tip. If you are staying at Nisbet, be sure to get the money-saving meal package, which includes breakfast, afternoon tea and dinner daily. ☎ 469-9325.

Facts

Helpful Phone Numbers: Police, 911, **Air Ambulance**, ☎ 465-2801, **JNF General Hospital**, ☎ 465-2551.

Nearest Recompression Chamber: Saba, a 15-minute flight from St. Kitts. Getting from the dive boat to the airport and arranging for air transport may be dangerously time-consuming. Avoid decompression dives.

Getting Here: American Airlines, ☎ 800-433-7300, is the main carrier with direct flights from major US cities to San Juan, connecting to **American Eagle**, which serves **Golden Rock Airport**, St. Kitts. Other North American and international carriers have direct flights to San Juan, Antigua and other Caribbean islands that connect with American Eagle, BWIA, LIAT, to and from the island of St. Kitts. Golden Rock Airport can handle wide-body jets, while **Newcastle Airport** on Nevis can accommodate smaller twin-engined, prop aircraft. Daily ferry service connects Basseterre to Charlestown. Several cruise lines stop at St. Kitts.

The **MV Caribe Queen** is a governmen- owned and -operated ferry service between St. Kitts and Nevis. The passage between Basseterre and Charlestown takes about 45 minutes and provides beautiful views of both islands. Also crossing between the two islands is the privately owned, government-operated **MV Sea Hustler** and **Carib Breeze**. Information on all ferries is available at ☎ 869-466-INFO (466-4636).

Driving: On the left. Driver's permit required. This permit can be obtained from the Traffic Department for US$25, EC$64.80. Rental car steering wheels are on the left also.

Language: English.

Documents: Passports and photo ID are required of all visitors.

Airport Tax: Departure tax of US$22, paid in cash at the airport.

Currency: Eastern Caribbean dollar. US$1=EC$2.70 (variable).

Climate: Average temperate of 79°F. Annual rainfall is 55 inches.

Clothing: Casual, lightweight clothing. Beach attire, short shorts, bikinis or bare chests are *not allowed* in public places (in town, restaurants or shops). Snorkelers should wear wetskins or long-sleeve shirts to protect from the sun.

Electricity: 230 volts, 60 cycles AC. Some hotels have 110 volts, AC. Transformers and adapters are generally needed.

Religious Services: Seventh Day Adventist, Anglican, Baha'i, Baptist, Catholic, Church of God, Jehovah's Witnesses, Moravian, Methodist, and Pentecostal. Contact hotel desk for details.

Additional Information: *St. Kitts Tourism Authority*, Pelican Mall, Bay Road, PO Box 132, Basseterre, St. Kitts, WI, ☎ 869-465-4040, fax 869-465-8794, www.stkitts-tourism.com; on Nevis, ☎ 1-866-55 NEVIS (866-55-63847), on-island 869-469-7550 or 1-866-55-NEVIS, fax 869-469-7551, www.nevisisland.com, info@nevisisland.com, UK ☎ 01420 520810, office@nevisislandestates.com.

St. Lucia

Saint Lucia, (pronounced loo sha), is the second-largest of the **Windward Islands**. An independent state, the 238-square-mile island is about 1,300 miles southeast of Florida, 24 miles north of St. Vincent and 21 miles from Martinique.

Mountainous and scenic, the island boasts **Morne Gimie**, the highest peak at 3,145 feet, and two spectacular ancient forest-covered volcanic cones – **Gros Piton** (2,619 feet) and **Petit Piton** (2,461 feet) – that rise abruptly from the sea near **Soufrière**, an old colonial town on the west coast. Nearby, hot sulfurous springs bubble and spout steam from muddy, black craters. Lush, jungle-like vegetation covers much of the island and seems to grow as you pass through it.

St. Lucia's coast is lined by miles of beautiful beaches interspersed with sheer volcanic cliffs that plunge straight into the sea, where they are covered with a blaze of orange and yellow corals and sponges. Most diving and snorkeling is off **Anse Chastanet** (pronounced "ants-shas-tan-ay") and **Soufrière Bay**, both sheltered coves on the island's southwest corner. Within 150 feet of their shorelines lies a 30-mile-long coral reef on a shelf at 10- to 30-foot depths. Farther out are shallow caves and a sheer wall. Beyond the coves, strong currents mandate drift diving. The entire area is protected as a marine park.

St. Lucia's 150,000 residents are mostly African or of mixed African and European descent. English is the official language, although there is also a local patois. One-third of the population resides in **Castries**, the capital.

The economy is agricultural, with bananas as the main export crop. Cocoa beans, coconut oil, and copra (dried coconut) also are exported. Industries include rum making, fishing, and brick manufacturing. There are two airports, **Hewanorra International** at the southern tip of the island, and **George Charles Airport** in the north. American Airlines serves both airports. In summer, bug repellent is necessary from the moment you step off the plane.

When to Go

Dive St. Lucia from January to April, the dry season. It's rainy from June through November; August and September are the wettest. Annual rainfall varies from 55 inches on the south coast to 140 inches in the interior. Air temperatures average 80°F.

History

No one is certain when St. Lucia was discovered, or by whom, though some credit Christopher Columbus in 1502. The British tried to settle the island in 1605 and 1638, but were driven off with fierce attacks by the native Carib Indians. French claims to the island were confirmed by a treaty with the Caribs in 1660. St. Lucia subsequently changed hands several times before being captured by the British in 1803 and then ceded to them by the Treaty of Paris in 1814. In 1838, it became part of Britain's Windward Islands administrative group.

On February 22, 1979, St. Lucia attained full independence. The British monarch continues to be head of state, represented by a governor general, who appoints the prime minister. Parliament consists of a Senate and House of Assembly, and there is a supreme court.

Best Dive & Snorkeling Sites

☆☆☆ **The Wreck of the *Lesleen M*** is a 165-foot freighter sunk by the Department of Fisheries in 1986 to create an artificial reef. The wreck is intact, lying upright at 65 feet. Its hull, covered with soft corals, slender tube sponges and hydroids, provides shelter to many juvenile fish. Divers can explore the pilot house at 35 feet. It is possible to explore inside the hold and in the engine room. Good visibility.

☆☆☆☆ **Anse Chastanet Reef**, which lies off the **Anse Chastanet Hotel**, has three distinct dive areas. New divers and snorkelers enjoy a nice shallow area with a small cavern, sponges, large brain and boulder corals at depths of five to 25 feet. A resident school of squid is joined by goatfish, frogfish, parrotfish, chromis and wrasses.

Farther out, the reef slopes off to a wall that plummets to 140 feet. Most dives are at 50-60 feet, where the coral ledges sparkle with ruby sea whips, pink anemones, lacy corals, teal vase sponges, and crimson rope sponges. Crabs, lobster, trumpetfish, peppermint-stick lobster, blackbar soldierfish, brown chromis, batfish, peacock flounders, flying gurnards, moray eels, and margates inhabit the area. Below 100 feet are larger fish, black corals and porcelain-like plate corals.

☆☆ **Anse la Raye Reef** is a slope covered in huge boulders near the wreck of the *Lesleen M*. The shallow areas have lots of colorful fire corals, while deeper there are iridescent vase sponges, huge barrel sponges and bushy soft corals. Schools of jacks, bermuda chubs and spotted drums frequent the area.

St. Lucia

Pigeon Pt.

Rodney Bay

Gros Islet

Vigie Beach

✈ •Castries

1

3

Marigot

Anse La Raye

8

4

Anse Chastanet

Morne Gimie
3,145 ft. ▲

2

5 •Soufriere

Micoud

6

▲ Petit Piton
2,461 ft

7

▲ Gros Piton
2,619 ft

✈ Moule-a-Chique

Vieux Fort •

Maria Islands

Dive & Snorkeling Sites

1 Wreck of the *Lesleen M*
2 Anse Chastanet
3 Anse laRaye Reef
4 Fairyland
5 Pinnacles
6 Piton Wall
7 Superman's Flight
8 Turtle Reef

☆☆☆ **Fairyland**, outside the Anse Chastanet cove, is always done as a drift dive. Subject to occasional strong currents, this area has outstanding visibility and vibrant corals. The plateau slopes from 40 to 60 ft. and is strewn with huge boulders. Finger corals, anemones and lavender tube sponges attach to the rocks, with plenty of nooks and crannies for fish and invertebrates.

☆☆☆☆☆ **Pinnacles** are four spectacular seamounts that rise from the depths to within a few feet of the surface. These coral-covered subsea cliffs are a macro-photographer's dream; they are alive with octopi, feather dusters, arrow crabs, seahorses, squid, and shrimp. Cleansing currents nurture big barrel and vase sponges and a lattice of soft corals – sea plumes, sea whips and sea fans. Lots of fish. Black corals at depth.

☆☆☆ **Piton Wall**, at the base of Petit Piton, falls from the surface to hundreds of feet below. Sea whips, gorgonians and big feather dusters give way to a profusion of fish. Strong currents possible. Experienced divers only.

☆☆☆ **Superman's Flight** is a 15-minute boat trip across Soufrière Bay to the base of the Petit Piton Mountain. It was used as a setting for the film *Superman II*. Strong currents make this an exciting drift drive. You'll "fly" the wall underwater. Good fish life and excellent visibility.

☆☆ **Turtle Reef**, a crescent-shaped shoal north of Anse Chastanet Bay, starts at 40 feet, then drops to over 150 feet. Divers enjoy spectacular pillar coral and barrel sponges in the shallows. Lots of crustaceans, squid, parrotfish, starfish and soft corals.

When occasional calm seas occur off the southeast coast you can dive two wrecks – an airliner and a freighter. But more often than not rough seas and strong currents rule them out as safe sites.

Dive Operators

 Scuba St. Lucia is a PADI Five Star training facility located at Anse Chastanet. The seven-instructor shop offers introductory and advanced open-water and rescue courses plus specialty courses in marine life identification, underwater navigation, drift diving, wreck diving and U/W photography. E6 processing and camera rentals are available. Five custom dive boats. Dive/hotel packages with **Anse Chastanet Hotel**. ☎ 800-223-1108, 758-459-7000 or 758-459-7755, scuba@candw.lc. Write to PO Box 7000, Soufrière, St. Lucia. WI.

St. Lucia Undersea Adventures, at the Morgan Bay Resort, has a fast 40-foot dive boat that tours Anse Cochon, the Pinnacles and Anse Chastanet reefs. Packages available. ☎ 800-327-8150 or 758-451-7716, nealwatson@aol.com, www.twofin.com/twofin/stlucia.htm.

Buddies Scuba at Rodney Bay ,Castries, a full-service PADI facility, offers resort courses and reef and wreck tours. The shop is conveniently located at **Waterside Landing Marina** in the second lagoon inside **Rodney Bay Marina**. Dive packages are available. ☎ 758-450-8406 or 758-452-7044, buddies@candw.lc.

Island Divers at **Ti Kaye Village** offers resort and certification courses, shore dives, wreck dives, and boat trips to Anse Chastanet Reef and the Pitons. The wreck of the *Lesleen M* is just off the their doorstep. Equipment rentals include Mares Dive gear and Luxfer tanks. There are beachside showers, lockers, and freshwater deep sinks for the rinsing of dive gear.

Dive/accommodation packages include seven nights in an oceanview room, breakfast buffet daily, 10 dives, airport transfers, taxes and a welcome drink. Summer rates start at $900 per person based on double occupancy, $1,600 for a single; winter rates (December 16th to April 15th) range upward from $1,000 per person for a double, $1,800 for a single. Non-divers deduct $150. There is also a beachside bar for après-dive refreshments and a beachfront restaurant. ☎ 758-456-8101, fax 758-456-8105, www.tikaye.com, info@tikaye.com.

Where to Stay

 Rates are in US$.

 Anse Chastanet Beach Hotel is the island's first dive resort. It is named for the Chastanets, an aristcratic family originally from the Bordeaux region of France, who settled on the island during the 18th century (*anse* is antique French for "bay"). Today, Anse Chastanet is a beautifully scenic resort set amidst a lush, 400-acre plantation edged by a secluded, quarter-mile-long soft sand beach. Some of the resort's 48 rooms are scattered on a hillside, others are beachside. All rooms have fridges, electric tea/coffee makers, wall-mounted hair dryers, clay tile or tropical hardwood floors, private showers, and ceiling fans. **Scuba St. Lucia** resort's dive shop. Snorkeling and shore dives are possible from the resort beach. Their **Coral Kaleidoscope** package includes seven nights' accommodation, breakfast, lunch, afternoon tea and dinner, all taxes and services, airport transfers both ways, welcome cocktail, drinks package, in-room fridge and tropical fruit display on arrival. Also included are 12 beach or boat dives, and substitution of up to two night dives for day dives. Included in the package are use of tennis court and equipment, watersports gear (snorkeling, kayaking, mini-sailing, windsurfing), beach chairs/towels and complimentary water-taxi to Anse Mamin beach.

The winter weekly-package rate (December 20-April 15) starts at $4,989 ($627 per day) for two sharing a room, or $4,009 for one. Adjustments can be made for shorter or longer stays by either deducting or adding additional room nights. Spring (April 16-May 31) and fall (November 1-December 19) rates drop to $4,324 and summer (June 1-October 31) can be as low as $3,995. For a non-diver accompanying a diver, deduct US$25 daily. ☎ 800-223-1108 or 888-Go LUCIA (888-465-8242), www.ansechasta-net.com.

 Expect to lug some gear up and down the resort's hillside unless you arrange for a low room.

Marigot Beach Club Bay Hotel and Dive Resort is nine miles from Vigie Airport and Castries on picturesque Marigot Bay. The resort features 47 villas set in the hillside around the bay and marina. Studios rent from $175 per day in summer and from $210 per day in winter. On-site PADI dive shop packages start at $850 for four nights accommodations with two dive days, $1,510 for seven nights with five days of diving. Packages include breakfast, lunch and dinner (lunch on the dive boat or in Doolittle's restaurant); weights and tanks, a two-tank boat dive per dive day, use of resort facilities. ☎ 758-451-4974, www.marigotdiveresort.com, mbc@candw.lc.

Ti Kaye Village Resort features 33 private accommodations on a hillside overlooking the Caribbean Sea and a lovely, long sandy beach. Built in the Caribbean gingerbread style, each cottage has a large balcony with two person hammocks, spacious open-air garden shower, and a four-poster king-size bed. Cottages have an air conditioner, though you might enjoy letting the balmy Caribbean breeze drift through the shutters.

Guest rooms have fridge, mini bar, safe deposit box, coffee maker, hammocks and hair dryers. Resort property encompasses Island Divers Scuba Shop, a restaurant and bar, a beach bar, pool, fitness center, car rental, massage therapy, laundry, wifi Internet access available in restaurant, bar and pool areas.

Per-day rates for one or two in a room start at $180 in summer, $200 in winter, for the oceanfront cottages with small pool, $275 in summer, $380 in winter.

Dive/accommodation packages include seven nights in an ocean-view room, breakfast buffet daily, 10 dives, airport transfers, taxes and a welcome drink. Summer rates start at $900 per person with double occupancy, $1,600 for a single; winter rates (December 16th through April 15th) from $1,000 per person for a double, $1,800 for a single. Non divers deduct $150 from package. ☎ 758-456-8101, www.tikaye.com, info@TiKaye.com.

Beach and dive-boat access requires climbing down 166 wooden stairs ("hillside," remember?). The good news is that you may keep your gear in a locker at the shop rather than tote it up and down the stairs.

Almond Morgan Bay Resort's 250 guest rooms sprawl across 22 green acres on secluded Choc Bay, a short trip from the airport. Luxury rooms have every amenity. The property features six swimming pools, three restaurants, four bars, a kids club and a spa. Diving is arranged with local shops. Contact ☎ 1-800-4ALMOND or www.almondresorts.com.

Small Inns

St. Lucia also has a number of lovely small inns that rent rooms at lower rates than the big resorts. For a complete listing, call the tourist board at ☎ 800-456-3984, www.inntimateslucia.org.

Dining

Menu prices are in Eastern Caribbean dollars. $US1 = EC$2.70. Credit cards are *not* widely accepted, but major restaurants do take them.

Papa Don's Italian Bistro sits hillside at Windjammer Landing. The chef whips up terrific pizza in a woodburning oven. Also,pasta dishes and tiramisu to polish it off. Open form 11 am to 11 pm. Catch the Caribbean sunset and happy hour at 5 pm. ☎ 758-452-0913.

Find fast, but not too fast, food at **Capones Restaurant & La Piazza**, Gros Islet. You can eat inside if you want elegant or outdoors for quick service. Pizzas, subs and spicy Italian dishes. Closed Mondays. ☎ 758-452-0284.

Froggie Jacques Tropical Bistro offers a romantic tropical garden setting overlooking Vigie Cove with views of Morne Fortune across the harbor. Chef Jack offers gourmet French Caribbean seafood dishes – conch in passionfruit sauce, squid in lime and chive sauce and main courses of fresh catch of the day or boneless chicken stuffed with smoked fish in a citrus sauce. Open for lunch and dinner, Monday to Saturday. Closed for lunch during summer. ☎ 758-458-1900, cathy@froggiejacques.com.

Dasheene in Soufrière is on a 1,000-foot ridge in a lush setting at LaDera Resort. Good Creole and seafood dishes. Upscale. Open seven days for breakfast, lunch and dinner. ☎ 758-459-7323. Reservations.

Tuesday night is buffet night at **Anse Chastanet** resort. Each Friday night in **Gros Islet**, also known as "The Village," there is an all-out street party with music, dancing, food and loads of local color. It can get rowdy.

Sightseeing

A driving tour of St. Lucia's west coast affords breathtaking views of the bays, mountains, rain forests, and surrounding countryside. Starting at the southern tip of St. Lucia is **Moule à Chique Peninsula**, marked by a lighthouse.

From here you can see St. Vincent and the Grenadines. Heading north along the west coast brings you to the **Sulfur Springs**, billed as the world's only drive-in volcano. A walk-through takes you past steaming hot sulfur springs and bubbling mud craters. An ever-present smell of rotten eggs usually makes this a quick stop.

Just north of the springs is the 18th-century village of Soufrière, the island's breadbasket, where local fruits and vegetables are grown.

The **Soufrière Estate** offers tours where you can learn about the harvesting and processing of copra (dried coconut meat yielding oil) and cocoa. Adjacent to the estate are the **Diamond Falls and Mineral Baths,** where you can take a "therapeutic" hot dip and enjoy the surrounding gardens.

Continuing north brings you to **Anse-la-Raye**, a fishing village where dugout canoes are made. Beyond lies **Mt. Parasol** and **Mt. Gimie**. From here the road winds and dips through banana country to **Marigot**, a world-famous yacht harbor and resort community. There are two hotels and restaurants.

The road from Marigot to Castries curves and bends sharply with the rugged terrain through miles of banana plantations.

When you reach **Castries** take the John Compton Highway to the center of town where you'll find duty-free shopping. Behind the city is **Morne Fortune**, the "Hill of Good Fortune." A scenic drive up the Morne begins on Bridge Street. From the top are splendid views of the countryside and **Fort Charlotte**, an 18th-century French fort.

From Castries you can cross the island to the Atlantic coast or head north to **Gros Islet**, a sleepy fishing village, and **Pigeon Island National Park**, with 40 acres of forts, ruins and caves that are reputed still to hold pirate treasure. Beyond Pigeon Island lies **Cap Estate**, covering 1,500 acres of fine beaches, secluded coves and a golf course.

Full- and part-day water excursions are offered on the island's western coast. Most offer snorkeling and lunch.

The windward Atlantic coast is home to the **Frigate Island Nature Reserve**. A one-mile walk encircles the park area and takes you to a lookout where you can view outlying islets. During the summer the area is a nesting site of frigate birds and timid boa constrictors. Half-day tours may be arranged by the National Trust, ☎ 425-5005. Avoid swimming in the Atlantic. Strong currents and powerful waves make it dangerous. Offshore from **Vieux** on the south tip is the **Maria Islands Nature Reserve**, which houses unique grass snakes and ground lizards, plus many species of birds. Tours may be arranged when it's open.

Guided hikes in the Pitons and into the rain forest are offered by the Forest Service. ☎ 450-2231 or 450-2078.

Facts

Helpful Phone Numbers: Police ☎ 999; St. Jude's Hospital, Vieux Fort, ☎ 454-6041; Victoria Hospital, Hospital Road, Castries, ☎ 452-2421.

Nearest Recompression Chamber: Barbados, ☎ 590-828888, Dr. Dramor; ☎ 590-829880, Dr. Serina.

Getting Here: If you're coming from the US, **US Airways** offers a nonstop weekend service from Philadelphia and **BWIA** flies weekly from Miami and New York. **American Eagle** flies daily to and from Puerto Rico into George Charles Airport. **Virgin Atlantic, British Airways** and **BWIA** fly direct between London and St. Lucia. **Air Canada** has a nonstop weekly service from Toronto, Canada. **Caribbean Star** and **LIAT** offer inter-island travel. **Air Jamaica** has weekly services to and from New York.

Island Transportation: Car rentals – **Avis**, Vide Boutielle, ☎ 758-45-24554 or 22700, fax 758-45-31536; **National**, Gros Islet, ☎ 758-45-28721, fax 758-45-28577; **Dollar**, Reduit, ☎ 758-45-20994; and **Budget**, Marisule, ☎ 758-45-20233/28021, fax 758-45-29362.

Cab service is readily available from Hewanorra International Airport at the south end of the island. Taxis are unmetered and unregulated. Be sure to ask the cost *before* getting in the cab, and whether it is in EC$ or US$.

Airport Departure Tax: $22 US for anyone 12 years old or over.

Driving: On the left. You must be 25 or older and hold a valid driver's license. Buy a temporary St. Lucian license at the airport or police headquarters on Bridge Street in Castries. Steering wheels are on the right.

Documents: Citizens of the US, UK and Canada must produce a passport and an onward or return ticket.

Currency: The Eastern Caribbean dollar (XCD), which is exchanged at the rate of US$1 = EC$2.70 (variable; $2.60 in hotels and stores); US and Canadian dollars are also accepted. Credit cards accepted in many stores, but not all restaurants. Check when making reservations or accommodations.

Climate: In winter temperatures range between 65° and 85°F; summer, between 75° and 95°. Summers are rainy. Light wetsuits are suggested for winter diving.

Clothing: Lightweight and casual. Some of the fancier restaurants at the hotels in Castries require a jacket and tie.

Electricity: 220 volts. Adapters are required.

Time: Atlantic Standard (EST + 1 hr).

Language: The main language in St. Lucia is English although many St. Lucians also speak French and Spanish. *Kwéyòl*, St. Lucia's second language, is widely spoken by the St. Lucian people. It is not just a patois or broken French, but a language in its own right, which is being preserved by its use in day-to-day affairs and by special radio programs and publications printed in Kwéyòl.

Tax: An 8% government tax is added for accommodations. A service charge of 10% is added for restaurants. Hotels often calculate the taxes and charges in the rates.

Religious Services: Roman Catholic, Anglican, Methodist, Baptist, Seventh Day Adventists, Church of the Nazarene, Christian Science and the Salvation Army. Times of services vary at individual churches, so it is best to inquire at your hotel.

For Additional Information: Contact the *St. Lucia Tourist Board. In New York*: 820 Second Avenue, NY, NY 10017, ☎ 800-ST LUCIA or 212-867-2950. *In Canada*: ☎ 416-961-4317. *In London*: ☎ 011-44-71-937-1969. *In St. Lucia*: PO Box 221, Castries, St. Lucia, ☎ 758-45-24094/25968, fax 758-453-1121, www.stlucia.org.

St. Maarten/St. Martin

St. Maarten/St. Martin is a good spot for divers, snorkelers and non-divers to share a vacation. The island is surrounded by extremely shallow reefs, perfect for snorkeling or learning to dive. There are some areas suitable for children. For the more experienced diver, there are advanced reef, cave and wreck sites off the south coast. The island also serves as a jump-off point to three neighboring "best dive" islands – Saba, St. Eustatia, and Anguilla.

It is the largest of the **Dutch Windward Islands**, though still compact enough for you to stay on one end and easily explore the other. The northern half (St. Martin) is French, the southern half (St. Maarten) is Dutch. It is the only Caribbean island shared by two governments.

The island's dual personality, coupled with its reputation as the gourmet capital of the Caribbean, exciting nightlife, duty-free shopping, endless watersports and extraordinary scenery have contributed to its popularity as a prime vacation spot. The bustling tourist population may seem too busy for the devout naturalist, yet, given half a chance, this island's beautiful beaches and endless creature comforts can seduce, surprise and entertain just about anyone.

Residents of this small island point proudly to more than 300 years of peaceful co-existence. They are fond of describing their 37-square-mile island as "the smallest bit of real estate in the world shared by two countries," and, they are quick to add, "probably the friendliest."

A single border monument bracketed by a pair of flags stands beside the road connecting **Philipsburg** and **Marigot**, the Dutch and French "capital villages." There are no real boundaries or borders.

History

St. Maarten/St. Martin was discovered by Christopher Columbus on November 11, 1493. Though Spain claimed the island, it was abandoned in 1648 when the Spaniards no longer needed it as a Caribbean base. The Dutch commander of St. Eustatius promptly sent Captain Martin Thomas to take possession. Thomas found French troops who, after a few skirmishes, signed a treaty dividing the island between France and Holland. Legend portrays a Frenchman and a Dutchman walking from opposite ends of the island to see how much territory each could claim for his side in one day.

Unfortunately, that early agreement didn't last as long as the legend, and St. Maarten changed hands 16 times before becoming permanently Dutch.

During the 17th and 18th centuries, fishing, sugar plantations, and salt harvesting became the base for the island's economy. By the middle of the 18th century, however, the tiny nearby island of St. Eustatius began to overshadow St. Maarten/St. Martin in prosperity. Farms on St. Maarten/St. Martin supplied grapes for the tables of wealthy Statian merchants.

St. Maarten/St. Martin remained little noticed by the outside world until **Princess Juliana Airport** opened in 1943. With the end of World War II, American and European travelers, eager for an unspoiled Caribbean getaway, began to discover the island. In 1947, St. Maarten's first hotel, the **Sea View**, opened.

The decades following 1960 brought an increase in tourism. Today St. Maarten/St. Martin is one of the most popular vacation spots in the Caribbean.

Diving

 A number of divers stay on St. Maarten for the great dining and nightlife, then ferry over to Saba for diving. But St. Maarten diving is getting better with new marine management and the creation of sanctuarie. When the weather and seas cooperate, St. Maarten sites are worth a look.

There are a few snorkeling sites near shore, but the best dive and snorkeling spots are about a mile offshore and must be reached by boat.

The windward side of St. Maarten, extending from Philipsburg up the coast to Dawn Beach, is known for brilliant rock formations and a moon hole created by the impact of a meteor. The leeward side of St. Maarten has scattered coral heads.

Off the northeast coast of St. Martin, dive sites include **Ilet Pinel**, a small out island good for shallow diving; **Green Key**, a prolific barrier reef; and **Flat Island** (also known as *Ile Tintamarre*), for sheltered coves and subsea geological faults. To the north, **Anse Marcel** is a good choice.

Best Dive & Snorkeling Sites

☆☆☆ **Wreck of the HMS *Proselyte*** sits one mile off the south coast of St. Maarten in 50 feet of water. Remains include three 14-foot anchors, cannons, ballast bars and brass barrel hoops from the powder kegs. Divers still find square nails and spikes. Schools of sergeant majors, hordes of angelfish, yellow tail snappers and grunts inhabit the wreck, with an occasional sighting of an eagle ray or grey reef shark. The ship, first named *Jason*, began her 31 years afloat as a Dutch war frigate at Rotterdam, Holland. She was taken over

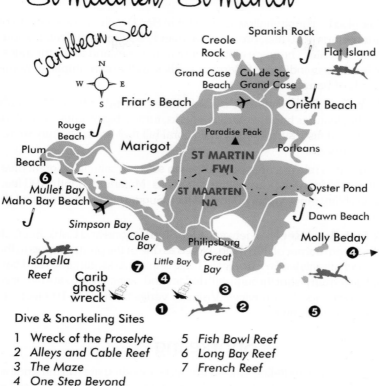

St Maarten/St Martin

Caribbean Sea

N
W — E
S

Creole Rock
Spanish Rock
Flat Island
Grand Case Beach
Cul de Sac
Grand Case
Friar's Beach
Orient Beach
Rouge Beach
Paradise Peak ▲
Porleans
Plum Beach
Marigot
ST MARTIN FWI
❻
Mullet Bay
Maho Bay Beach
ST MAARTEN NA
Oyster Pond
Simpson Bay
Dawn Beach
Cole Bay
Philipsburg
Molly Beday
❹ ▶
Isabella Reef
Little Bay
Great Bay
Carib ghost wreck
❼
❹
❸
❶
❷
❺

Dive & Snorkeling Sites

1 Wreck of the *Proselyte*   5 Fish Bowl Reef
2 Alleys and Cable Reef   6 Long Bay Reef
3 The Maze   7 French Reef
4 One Step Beyond

by a mutinous crew in 1796 and given to the British. The ship sank in 1801 after striking a submerged reef.

The reef surrounding the *Proselyte* sparkles with stands of elkhorn and soft corals. Reef depths are from 15 to 45 feet. A swim behind the reef reveals two new wrecks, a 30-foot sailboat and a 100-foot steel barge, sunk in 1989.

Seas average three to four feet. No spear fishing or coral or shell collecting. Good for novice divers.

☆☆ **The Alleys** and **Cable Reef** are a two-reef complex just east of the *Proselyte* wreck. Maximum depth is 65 feet. The reefs are riddled with small caves crowded with fish and lobster. Besides the usual parade of tropicals there are a few nurse sharks, an occasional hammerhead, eagle rays and turtles. In winter, the barracuda population quadruples. Coral rubble interspersed with sea fans and gorgonians carpets the bottom. Visibility varies with sea conditions from 50 to 100 feet. This area is good for novice divers when the seas are calm. Expect two- to four-foot swells. No spear fishing or collecting.

☆☆ **The Maze**, a huge shallow reef off Little Bay Beach on the south tip of St. Maarten, starts at 20 feet, dropping to a sandy bottom at 50 feet. Elkhorn corals predominate. There are a number of mini-caves and swim-throughs. One section of this winding reef, Barracuda Alley, as the name implies is home to hundreds of barracuda.

☆☆☆☆ **One Step Beyond**, a seven-mile boat ride off St. Maarten's southeast tip, features huge eagle rays, sharks, turtles, big morays, schools of grunts and spadefish, surrounding a big coral hill that branches into arches and swim-throughs.

High winds often rule this area out, but when seas are calm it is a great dive. Expect three- to four-foot seas on the calm days. Maximum depth is 90 feet. Average visibility ranges from 80 to 100 feet. Suggested for experienced divers only.

☆☆☆ **Fish Bowl Reef** lies between One Stop Beyond and Cable Reef, off the southeastern corner of the island. Noted as one of the prettiest spots in the area, the reef attracts walls of tropicals, huge nurse sharks, stingrays and barracuda. The terrain is shot through with ledges and caves. Depths are between 40 and 60 feet. Good for novices. Visibility varies from 60 to 100 feet. No spearfishing or collecting.

Snorkeling

Sail-snorkeling tours to the best snorkeling sites off the small islands surrounding St. Martin/St. Maarten may be arranged at **Bobby's Marina** and **Great Bay Marina** in Philipsburg, **Simpson Bay Lagoon** and **Port La Royale Marina** at Marigot Bay.

Snorkelers and novice divers will find some shallow reefs and wrecks off the northern and western coasts.

Long Bay Reef is close to shore at Long Bay off the western peninsula. This is a good choice when the outer reefs are weathered out. Watch for occasional currents. **French Reef** is close to shore off Cole Bay on the south coast. With depths from 12 to 25 feet, this protected reef is a good choice for beginners. Lots of tropicals.

Beach snorkeling exists off **Plum Beach** and **Rouge Beach** on the western peninsula; **Mullet Bay**, the point between Lay Bay and Cole Bay; and the point between Cay Bay and Little Bay. When the Atlantic is calm there is excellent snorkeling on the reefs off **Dawn Beach** and **Orient Beach** on the east coast. (Orient Beach is clothing-optional. Long Bay and Plum Bay have topless bathing.)

To reach Dawn Beach from Philipsburg, take the road on the northeast side of Salt Pond for two miles, then turn right and continue down the steep hill.

Grand Case Beach on the French side has crowds of small tropical fish and corals off the north end at Creole Rock. Depths are from 10 to 25 feet (boat or beach access). Seas are always calm with no currents and visibility is usually good. To reach it, follow the paved road through Grand Case; when it turns to the right, take the dirt road straight ahead.

Dive Operators

St. Maarten

 Ocean Explorers Dive Center is on a quiet beach on the south coast at Simpson Bay. It is owned and operated by LeRoy & Dominique French, long-time residents of St. Maarten, who personally escort tours aboard a fast, 26-foot Robalo dive boat. A maximum of seven divers per trip are taken. Ocean Explorers provides stab jackets with auto inflators, 80-cubic-foot tank, regulators with high pressure gauges, and wet suits. The shop has been appointed a NAUI Dream Resort. C-cards required. Resort and certification courses Two-tank dive trip cost $85. ☎ 544-5252. Yachts may contact the shop on VHF 16. Studio rental available, www.stmaartendiving.com. divesm@megatropic.com.

Scuba Fun Dive Center, a PADI Five Star Gold Palm Resort, on the Dutch side is located at Great Bay Marina (Pointe Blanche, Philipsburg), a short walk from the cruise ship pier and less than a 10-minutes boat trip to Proselyte reef, the Maze, Carib Cargo and Cable Reef. Dive tour departure times are 9 and 11 am and 2 pm. Rental gear available. Multi-lingual. ☎ 590-87-3613, www.scubafun.com, contact@scubafun.com.

The Scuba Shop and **Dive Safaris** cover St. Maarten/St. Martin with three locations – La Palapa Marina, Simpson Bay(☎ 599-545-3213); Bobby's Marina, Philipsburg (☎ 599-542-9001); and Captain Oliver's Marina, Oyster Pond (☎ 590-87-4801). Each center offers snorkel and dive trips, friendly service, scuba courses, rental equipment and retail sales of Mares, Scubapro, Uwatec, Suunto, Sherwood, Dacor, SeaQuest, Princeton Tec and many other brands at very competitive prices, and it's duty free. ☎ 599-542-9001, cell 599-57-3436, www.thescubashop.net.

Trade Winds Dive Center is on the dock at Great Bay Marina, Philipsburg near Chesterfield's Restaurant. The shop visits the south-coast dive areas with a 25-foot Mako and a 27-foot ridged-hull Avon inflatable powered by twin 120-hp outboards. PADI certifications available. Introductory lessons are taught in calm Mullet Bay. ☎ 599-5-54387, fax 599-5-23605; from the French side, 03-54387. Local 54387.

Where to Stay

St. Maarten/St. Martin resorts are not geared specifically toward scuba. Hotel/air packages are offered by tour operators and travel agents. Expect a 5% tax and 15-20% service charge added to most resort bills.

St. Martin

Grand Case Beach Club, a condo resort on the beach at Grand Case offers spacious air-conditioned studios and suites with balconies and kitchenettes. All newly decorated. Ocean-view studios $290 for two in winter; garden view rooms are $230 plus 15% service charge. Check their Website for money saving specials. Diving is arranged with Scuba Fun. Walk to the beach restaurants. ☎ 800-344-3016, www.grandcasebeachclub.com.

Green Cay Village, on Orient Beach, offers luxurious, fully equipped, private villas, each with a private pool, in a beautiful seaside setting. Diving with Scuba Fun. Studios rent for $210 per day in summer, from $275 in winter, one-bedroom from $363 to $616 in winter. Higher during Christmas and New Years. Lower rate packages are featured on their Website at www.greencayvillas.com. ☎ 866-592-4213 or 888-843-4760. (Note: Orient Beach is clothing-optional.)

La Flamboyant Hotel Resort, on the lagoon at Nettle Bay, features 271 privately owned suites in a colonial setting, two pools, tennis, volleyball, water-sports center, pool bar, beachfront restaurant, meeting rooms and children's playground. Each unit has a private balcony, some with a fully equipped kitchen. Rooms sleep two adults and one child (under 12). Winter per day rates for a junior suite, double occupancy are from $284. Summer rates are from $170. For an all-inclusive supplement, add $100 per person per day ☎ 800-480-8555, www.le-flamboyant.com.

St. Maarten

Great Bay Beach Hotel & Casino is a 225-room hotel on the beach at the edge of Philipsburg. Recently renovated rooms have marble baths, air conditioning, phones. Resort features include casino, restaurants, disco, shopping arcade, two pools, spa, water sports center, entertainment, tennis. Tradewinds Dive Shop on premises. Winter room rates start at $190 for ocean view, summer from $140. Add 21% for room tax. all-inclusive packages exclusive of diving available. Specials on their Website. ☎ 800-223-0757, www.greatbayhotel.com, info@greatbayhotel.com.

Oyster Bay Beach Resort has a dive shop on premises offering equipment rentals, diving and snorkeling tours. The three-story resort (no elevators), located where the Caribbean meets the Atlantic, offers 178 stylish suites, studios, and rooms with high ceilings, private balconies, tropical décor, mini frig, TV, safe, splendid views and tropical tranquility. French-Caribbean restaurant serves breakfast, lunch and dinner. Decent snorkeling off adjacent, mile-long Dawn Beach, around the rocky point, when seas are calm. Dive packages for two (four days including room, one beach dive, two days of two-tank dives), are $1,165 in summer, $1,520 in winter. ☎ 866-978-0212, www.oysterbaybeachresort.com.

Dining

 St. Maarten/St. Martin has more than 400 restaurants, featuring a wide variety of international cuisine. For classic French sidewalk cafés, head for Marigot. Philipsburg and Grand Case restaurants offer everything imaginable from Cuban or Mexican aperitifs, Brazilian or Indonesian entrées and Vietnamese desserts, along with Creole, Italian and Continental cuisine. There are also rib shacks, or *lolos*, where local cooks barbecue chicken, ribs and lobster. Orient Beach is clothing-optional, including dining establishments, and you'll see less and less wrapping as you go south on the beach. Stick to the northern end for mostly-clothed folks.

The California Restaurant, on Grand Case Boulevard at the California Apartments, offers seafood, serious pizza and crêpes. Seaside eating. Open for lunch and dinner. ☎ 590-87-55-57.

Turtle's Pier Restaurtant on Simpson Bay's waterfront is a favorite for seafood and steaks.

La Main à La Pâté, waterfront in Marigot at Marina Royale specializes in fresh seafood, pasta dishes and lobster. Moderate entrées. ☎ 590-87-71-19.

Find **McDonalds** on Front Street and **Kentucky Fried Chicken** at Cole Bay on the Dutch side and in Marigot on the French side.

Sightseeing & Other Activities

It is customary to ask permission before photographing residents on St. Martin/St. Maarten. Neglecting to do so may provoke a very angry response.

For guided island tours try **St. Maarten Sightseeing Tours**, ☎ 22753.

You can get a good bird's-eye view of St. Maarten from **Fort Willem** in Philipsburg, but walk up to it rather than drive as the road is treacherous.

The new three-acre **Sint Maarten Zoo and Botanical Gardens** are on the Arch Road in Madame Estate on the Dutch side. The collection focuses on plants and animals of the Caribbean area, including a large reptile collection. Open Monday to Friday, 9 am to 5 pm, weekends, 10 am to 6 pm. ☎ 22748.

Windsurfing, JetSkiing, water-skiing, parasailing, sailing, horse-back riding and **deep-sea fishing** can be arranged through hotel activity desks.

St. Maarten's **duty-free shopping** is among the best in the Caribbean. Philipsburg features a wide assortment of goods, including perfumes, liquors, cigarettes, crystal, linen and European designer fashions at 25-50% less than the US and Canada. Shops in Philipsburg are open from 8 am to noon, and from 2 to 6 pm, Monday through Saturday.

Casino gambling is offered by many hotels on the Dutch side.

On the French side, a climb to the top of **Fort Louis** at Marigot affords exceptional views of the surrounding bays and lagoons. Built in 1767 under Louis XVI, it is the island's biggest historical monument. On the road to Bay-Side and Galion, look for the **Butterfly Farm**, where rare species offer a visual delight. **The Pottery Workshop**, on the hilltop overlooking the eastern bay, creates original and unique souvenirs.

Facts

Helpful Phone Numbers: There is a hospital in Marigot (☎ 87-57-57) and another in Philipsburg (☎ 19-599-542656). Hotels will assist visitors in contacting English-speaking doctors. There are about 18 doctors practicing general medicine, six dentists, and specialists in many varied fields. In addition, French St. Martin has about six pharmacies. Other emergency numbers: Pharmacy (☎ 87-50-79) and Ambulance (☎ 87-86-25). For hours and names, see listing in St. Martin's Week, a free local publication. On weekends and holidays, numbers of "doctor & pharmacy on call" are posted in all pharmacies.

Nearest Recompression Chamber: Saba (30 miles from the south coast).

Getting Here: Air service from the US to *Princess Juliana International Airport* in St. Maarten is provided by **American Airlines** direct from New York, Miami and San Juan with connecting flights to numerous cities throughout the US; and seasonally by **Continental** from Newark, New Jersey, with connecting flights throughout the US; **Northwest** from Detroit and Minneapolis, with connections to other US cities; and **USAir** from Charlotte and Philadelphia with connections to other US cities. In addition, numerous charter flights are available from throughout the continental US. Other airlines serving the island include **LIAT** from Antigua, Anguilla, St. Croix, St. Kitts, St. Thomas and Tortola;

and **Windward Islands Airways (WINAIR)** from St. Thomas, St. Kitts/Nevis, Saba, St. Eustatius, Anguilla, St. Barts, Dominica and Tortola.

Driving: On the right. Major car rentals are at the airport.

Language: English is widely spoken, though Dutch is the official language of St. Maarten and French is the official language of St. Martin.

Documents: US citizens need a valid passport and photo identification and a return or onward ticket. Canadian and European citizens need a valid passport and a return or onward ticket.

Customs: None, but luggage is checked for illegal drugs and contraband.

Airport Tax: $30 for international departures, $10 for inter-island (usually included with ticket).

Currency: US dollars are widely accepted on both the Dutch and the French sides. Official currency of the Dutch side is the Netherlands Antilles florin (or guilder; NAf). Official currency of the French side is the euro (€). Nearly all prices are listed in US dollars and the local currency. ATMs are at several locations throughout the island.

Taxes: Government law requires a 5 percent room tax on all hotel rates. Most hotels and guest houses add 10 percent to 15 percent service charge in lieu of tipping. Some also add an energy surcharge.

Climate: Mean temperature is 80°F year-round; 45 inches rainfall annually.

Clothing: Lightweight, casual.

Electricity: 110 volts AC, 60 cycles.

Religious Services: Roman Catholic, Seventh Day Adventist, Anglican, Baptist, Jehovah's Witness, Methodist.

For Additional Information: *St. Maarten Tourist Office*, 675 Third Avenue, NY, NY 10017. ☎ 800-786-2278 or 212-953-2084, fax 212-953-2145, www.st-maarten.com. *Dutch side*, Walter Nisbet Road 23, Philipsburg, St. Maarten, Netherlands Antilles. ☎ 599-542-2337, fax 599-542-2734. *French side*, Boulevard de France, 97150 Marigot, St. Martin FWI, ☎ 590-590-87-57-21, fax 590-590-87-56-43, http://www.frenchcaribbean.com/StMartinFrenchCaribbean.html.

St. Vincent & the Grenadines

St. Vincent and the Grenadines, a multi-island nation in the eastern Caribbean, is known to just a few discriminating divers and snorkelers, but sailors have been enjoying her sheltered coves, beautiful beaches and protected harbors for centuries.

The capital and chief port is **Kingstown** on St. Vincent, the main island at 18 miles long and 11 miles wide. St. Vincent is also the most densely populated, with 100,000 residents. Black and white sand beaches loop around most of the island's coastline. **La Soufrière**, an active volcano and the highest point, reaching 4,048 feet, dominates the mountainous north end. It erupted last on Good Friday, the 13th of April 1979, causing extensive damage to farmland, houses and roads.

The Grenadines comprise 32 small islands and cays strung out like emerald stepping stones between St. Vincent and Grenada. All but two, **Carriacou** and **Petite Martinique**, are a part of this nation. Many are uninhabited or are the site of a single estate or resort. A favorite for many yachtsmen and divers are the tiny, uninhabited **Tobago Cays**, a five-island national park celebrated for its translucent waters; and adjacent **Horseshoe Reef**, a magnificent snorkeling area.

The larger Grenadine islands include **Bequia** (beck-way, Carib for "Island of the Clouds") **Canouan** (Can-o-wan), **Mayreau** (My-row), **Mustique**, **Union**, and **Carriacou**. All are postcard-perfect, fringed in part by soft, white-sand beaches and towering palm trees. Dive trips take off from St. Vincent, Bequia, and Union Island, a tiny, mile-long rock 40 miles south of St. Vincent.

Tiny **Palm Island** (formerly Prune Island) and **Petit St. Vincent** are world-class, one-resort islands offering guests luxurious jungle hideaways. Intrepid divers, snorkelers, birdwatchers and hikers are slowly expanding the small tourist population, but the country's economy is chiefly agricultural with exports of bananas, arrowroot, coconuts, cotton, sugar, cassava and peanuts.

Two main airports, one at **Arnos Vale** on St. Vincent's south coast, and another on **Bequia**, nine miles south of St. Vincent, serve the area. The most

---

Contributors: Dennis and Karen Sabo, Landfall Productions; Bill Tewes, Dive St. Vincent.

direct air service from the US is through Barbados. Mustique Airways offers excellent inter-island service. Mustique, Canouan and Union Island have airstrips with scheduled and charter flights. Sailing and yacht charters are available at the marinas. By boat, the trip from St. Vincent to Bequia, the largest of the Grenadines, takes about an hour.

When to Go

 The dry season is from December to April. Average rainfall on the coastal areas is 60 inches. The climate is tropical, tempered by the trade winds with a mean temperature of about 80°F.

Insects are a problem year-round, especially for hikers. Pack plenty of bug repellent.

History

 The first inhabitants of St. Vincent and the Grenadines came by small craft from South America. First the Ciboney settled in, then the peaceful Arawak Indians, who later fell to the Caribs. Slaves who escaped from Barbados' plantations literally "blew" in by makeshift craft with the prevailing winds, along with those who survived shipwrecks near St. Vincent and Bequia. These freed Africans, known as the black Caribs, fought off Europeans side-by-side with the yellow Caribs. Despite a claim of "discovery" by Christopher Columbus in 1498, Europeans did not settle here for 200 years. During the 17th and 18th centuries the island and surrounding rocks and islets changed hands between the British and the French. In 1763 the area was ceded to the British crown, but it wasn't until 1969 that the United Kingdom declared St. Vincent an associated state. The northern Grenadines, from Bequia to Petit St. Vincent, were administered by St. Vincent, while Carriacou and islets south of it were governed by Grenada. On October 27, 1979, St. Vincent and the Grenadines became an independent state.

Best Dive & Snorkeling Sites

Distinctive underwater landscapes encompass rocky canyons, caves, ledges and grottoes carved into mountain-sized boulders. Black corals exist at much shallower depths than normal.

St. Vincent

St. Vincent's best dive sites lie off the southwest corner of the island where calm sea conditions prevail. Strong currents, which maintain outstanding water clarity, occur in some areas. Private boaters should check local conditions before diving or snorkeling.

 ✰✰✰✰ **Bottle Reef**, a wall and reef dive located off a point under Fort Charlotte near Kingstown, takes its name from a huge collection of antique rum and gin bottles tossed down from the fort during the 18th century. Reef fish, including huge tarpons and morays, abound. Swim round the point of the wall to spot tuna, amberjacks, and bonito. Immense sea fans, towering gorgonians and sponges shelter hermit crabs, octopi and mini-critters. Bottle Reef is fine for all level divers and experienced snorkelers. Sea conditions range from calm to choppy, depending on the wind.

✰✰✰ **Turtle Bay Reef**, a shallow wall near Bottle Reef, brims over with giant gorgonians, sponges, club fingers, and star corals. Masses of fish swarm the area. Crabs, turtles, huge spotted eels and rare yellow frogfish are frequently spotted. The reef bottoms at 30 feet with more shallow areas for snorkeling. Good for novice divers. Visibility exceeds 80 feet. Seas are calm.

✰✰✰✰ **The Wall**, 200 yards off the western shore, starts with a shallow ledge at 18 feet, then slopes off into a stream of monster-sized boulders. Countless fish and mini-critters hide in the crevices and cracks. Big basket sponges bedeck the mammoth rocks. Large numbers of snappers, copper sweepers, squirrelfish, grunts, barracuda, and kingfish inhabit the reef. Black coral trees grow at depth. Average scuba depths are from 45 to 90 feet. Good for all level divers and experienced snorkelers.

✰✰✰✰✰ **New Guinea Reef**, just 10 minutes from Dive St. Vincent's dock, drops down a sheer cliff from a beautiful cove of orchids and lush vegetation. The reef starts at 40 feet, where an outpost of pastel gorgonians and finger sponges gives way to eight-foot-wide purple and orange sea fans. A cave at 80 feet shelters hard and soft black corals that bloom in shades of yellow, pink, green, white and red. Seahorses, large schools of reef fish, big angels and morays inhabit the ledges and overhangs. A great dive! Good, too, because of its shallow spots, for advanced snorkelers. Seas usually calm.

✰✰✰ **The Wrecks** refers to the rubble, anchors and cannons of two old wrecks in Kingston Harbor, and the nearby *Seimstrand*, an intact 120-foot freighter in 80 feet of water. All attract huge groupers, rays and eels. Better for diving, but the clear water allows good views to snorkelers also. Sea conditions are calm.

✰✰✰✰✰ **The Gardens** is a spectacular shallow reef located 15 yards from the shoreline, just north of Kingston. Frogfish, hordes of angelfish, Creole wrasse, gray snapper, kingfish, parrotfish and soldierfish crowd a profusion of soft, club and finger corals. Big boulders, brain corals, and colonies

St Vincent &
The Grenadines

Falls of
Baleine

Fancy

La Soufriere

Chateaubelair

St Vincent

Fort
Charlotte

Grant's Bay

Argyle

Milligan Cay

Young Island

Bequia

Baliceaux

Quatre

Mustique

Dive & Snorkeling Sites

 1 Bottle Reef
 2 Turtle Bay
 3 The Wall
 4 New Guinea Reef
 5 The Wrecks
 6 The Gardens
 7 L'Anse Chemin
 8 Ships Stern
 9 Northwest Point
10 West Cay
11 Wreck of the MS *Lirero*
12 Mayreau Gardens
13 Wreck of the *Purina*
14 Horseshoe Reef

Canouan

Mayreau

Union Is.

Tobago Cays

Palm Is.

of iridescent yellow tube sponges cover the bottom. Perfect for shallow dives and snorkeling. Seas are calm. Boat access.

Bequia

Bequia's leeward side is a marine park protecting eight miles of pristine reefs. Ferry and air service are available from St. Vincent.

☆☆☆☆☆ **L'Anse Chemin**, a 30-minute trip from Admiralty Bay, is a drift dive. Healthy corals and a big fish population popularize this spot. Seawhips, feather corals, orange-cup coral, lettuce and brain corals, blue sponges and mauve sea fans envelop the rocky bottom. As many as 20 flamingo tongues may be attached to one sea fan. Fish life is superb, with large parrotfish and groupers, queen triggerfish, queen and French angels, spotted and juvenile drums, gray snapper, Spanish mackerel, tuna, Creole wrasse and schooling reef fish. Nurse sharks are seen beneath the ledges of the reef. Depths range from 60 to 90 feet.

☆☆☆ **Ship's Stern** is a maze of swim-through tunnels, pinnacles, caverns and grottoes, all lavish with a thick cover of lacy corals, gorgonians and sponges. Big groupers and schooling fish abound. The site is a five-minute boat ride from the dock at Admiralty Bay. Depths are between 40 and 90 feet. Seas are calm.

☆☆☆ **Northwest Point**, a five-minute boat ride from the dock, is a sea-scape of coral buttresses. Throngs of squirrelfish, margate, trumpetfish, parrotfish, morays, chromis, grunts and Creole wrasse are in residence. Mi-cro-life is abundant with corkscrew anemones, flamingo tongues, flaming scallops, arrow crabs, neon gobies, barber shrimp and octopi. Seas generally calm. *The* spot for night dives.

☆☆ **West Cay**, off Bequia's southernmost tip, is the meeting point of the At-lantic and Caribbean. Mixing currents make this an exciting wall/drift dive and the best place to spot huge grouper, reef sharks, turtles, durgons, jack and spadefish. Photogenic with big sponges and dramatic overhangs. Depths are from 15 to 115 feet. For experienced divers.

☆☆ **Wreck of the MS *Lirero*.** This 110-foot freighter was scuttled in 1986 to create an artificial reef. She sits upright in 60 feet of water, covered over with red and yellow sponges and soft corals. The hull may be penetrated.

Out Islands

Dive trips to Union Island, Tobago Cayes, Petit St. Vincent, Palm and Mayreau take off from Union Island and Canouan. **World's End Reef** shel-ters these areas from wind-driven seas and storms.

☆☆☆ **Mayreau Gardens**, a 20-minute boat ride from the dock at Union Island, is a sparkling forest of branching and plate corals. Tornados of exotic fish and stingrays drift with you as the current carries you along the walls and channels of this colorful reef. Average depth is 60 feet.

☆☆☆☆ **Wreck of the *Purina*** is a 140-foot merchant trawler that went down in 1918 off Mayreau Island. The wreck is intact and, at 40 feet, is the center of activity for communities of yellowtail, huge French and grey angels, spotted morays, barracuda, nurse shark, squirrelfish and sergeant majors.

☆☆☆☆☆ **Horseshoe Reef,** which skirts four islands in the Tobago Cays, is one of the top five snorkeling spots in the Caribbean. Despite the remote location, it is populated by as many as 70 boats per day. Visibility is exceptional – you can see the reef and fish by just peering down from a boat. Depths range from the surface to 80 feet. Gigantic sea fans, gorgonians, and barrel sponges highlight the reef. Throngs of angelfish, grunts, big parrotfish and grouper cluster about.

Dive Operators

 The area code is scheduled to change to 784.

Dive/travel packages may be arranged through **Landfall Productions**, ☎800-525-3833 or 510-794-1599, fax 510-794-1617. Write to 39189 Cedar Boulevard, Newark CA 94560.

St. Vincent

 Dive St. Vincent sits on the southern tip of the island opposite the Young Island resort. Owner Bill Tewes, a NAUI, PADI, CMAS instructor, offers personalized scuba and snorkeling trips to the best reef and wall dives around St. Vincent. Resort and C-card courses. Bill is an outstanding underwater photographer. He and his work appear on St. Vincent postage stamps. Dive/accommodation packages. ☎ 784-457-4714 or 784-457-4928, fax 784-457-4948. Write PO Box 864, St. Vincent, WI; www.divestvincent.com, bill2s@caribsurf.com.

St. Vincent Dive Experience/Underwater Unlimited offers dive and snorkeling tours, NAUI certification courses, resort courses and a full line of rental equipment. Sleek, canopied boats whisk divers to the best sites, most only 10 minutes away. ☎784-456-9741 or 456-2768, fax 784-457-2768.

Petit Byahaut dives St. Vincent's leeward coast. The shop packages diving and five nights at a 50-acre nature resort with private beach and decent shore dives. ☎ 784-457-7008, www.petitbyahaut.com.

Bequia

Dive Bequia is on the beach at the Ginger Bread Hotel. ☎ 784-458-3504, bobsax@caribsurf.com, www.dive-bequia.com.

Bequia Dive Adventures, a full-service PADI Dive Center, is located along the harbor walk in Belmont, a few steps from several small hotels and restaurants. They arrange dive packages with island hotels and guest houses and offer a week of diving and lodging for as low as $900 per person/double occupancy. They offer harbor pick-up and return for yachting patrons. ☎ 784-458-3826, fax 316-221-6038.

Union

Grenadines Dive at the Anchorage Yacht Club tours the Tobago Cays and other southern Grenadine dive and snorkeling spots. Yacht NAUI or PADI instruction available. ☎ 784-458-8138, GDive@GrenadinesDive.com, www.GrenadinesDive.com.

Where to Stay

Rates listed are based on double occupancy and, unless othewise stated, do not include a 10% service charge and 7% government tax, which is added to the bill.

St. Vincent

The Grand View Beach Hotel at Villa Point is a plush 19-room resort set in a renovated plantation house on eight tropical acres. The dining room has a great view of the neighboring islands. Tennis, pool, A/C, TV, bar, fitness center. Good snorkeling off the beach. Transportation is provided to Dive St. Vincent's dock. Room rates in winter run from $160 for a single, $225 for a double. ☎ 784-458-4811, grandview@caribsurf.com, www.grandviewhotel.com.

Mariners Hotel & The French Verandah Restaurant is a cozy 20-bedroom hotel. Guest rooms have air conditioning, bath, cable TV, Internet, direct-dial telephone and a private balcony giving you panoramic views of the turquoise Caribbean Sea. Dive packages with St. Vincent from $900 per person for seven nights in the hotel, airport transfers, 10 dives, welcome drink, all diving equipment, personal gear washing and storage. Direct ☎ 784-457-4000, fax 784-457-4333, US 800-223-1108 or 310-440-4225, www.marinershotel.com.

Sunset Shores sits on the beach in St. Vincent amidst three acres of lush tropical gardens. This diver-friendly, family owned hotel has 32 furnished rooms all with patios overlooking the sea. Air conditioning, radio, television, and telephones ensure your comfort.

Dive packages with St. Vincent start at $909 per person for seven nights in the hotel, airport transfers, 10 dives, welcome drink, all diving equipment, personal gear washing and storage ☎ 784-458-4411, fax 784-457-4800, www.sunsetshores.com, sunshore@caribsurf.com.

Young Island sits 200 yards off the southern tip of St. Vincent. This 25-acre tropical island resort offers 30 individual cottages featuring king or twin beds, a refrigerator, ceiling fan and private patio. Life is ultra-casual. Diving is with Dive St. Vincent's. Snorkelers walk to the reef! Room rates for two in winter go from $355 per night to $745. Add $100 per person, per day for breakfast and dinner. Add $500 per diver per week (seven nights) for the dive package. Check their Website for a variety of packages that you can combine with diving (i.e. honeymoon or sailaway).

Dive rates include all equipment (except for computers) and free wash and storage of personal dive gear. Dive boats visit an extraordinary variety of sites.

When you arrive and depart on St. Vincent, a taxi will be arranged and included in your rate along with the local tax, service charge, fresh fruit and flowers in your room, ferry to and from St. Vincent day or night. US, ☎ 800-223-1108. In the UK, 0800-894057. In St. Vincent, 784-458-4826, www.youngisland.com, Y-island@caribsurf.

Beachcombers Hotel, originally a seaside family home, has 12 hilltop rooms with private bath and covered patios where your breakfast of fresh fruits, assorted homemade bread and beverages is served. The Beach House restaurant and bar offers fresh seafood and local vegetables. Weather permitting, dive boats will pick up and drop off at the hotel beach. Gear storage is provided at the Dive Center. Room rates are $90 to $150 per day. ☎ 784-458-4283, fax 784-458-4385, www.beachcombershotel.com.

Petit Byahaut, a secluded 50-acre valley on the leeward coast of St. Vincent, is accessible only from the sea. This spot is for the diehard naturalists only. There are no roads, no phones and no TVs. This unique outpost provides ferry service from Kingstown by prior arrangement. Diving and snorkeling are offered in Petit Byahaut Bay and other walls and reefs along the coast. Guests stay in room-sized tents on large covered decks on a hillside overlooking the sea and beach. Each tent features a queen-sized bed, hammock, solar powered lights and freshwater showers. Facilities include a restaurant, cocktail bar, boutique, secluded beach, dive shop, small sail and paddle boats, kayaks, water taxi service, moorings and air fills. Bring an entire suitcase full of bug repellant, then prepare for a continual onslaught of mosquitos. Still fun if you love camping. Transfers for stays of three nights or longer. Open from November till August. ☎ 784-457-7008, VHF 68, www.petitbyahaut.com, petitbyahaut@com.

Bequia

 From St. Vincent you can reach Bequia by Mustique Airways or ferry. The nine-mile ferry ride takes 70 to 90 minutes. Trips depart the main dock in Kingstown. Direct flights from Barbados are available.

The south side of Admiralty Bay is peppered with cafés, gourmet shops, beach bars, restaurants, boutiques and hotels that wind along a narrow waterfront path. The **Gingerbread Complex** encompasses the Frangipani cottages, Dive Bequia and The Gingerbread Hotel. A 15-minute walk over the bluff brings you to the **Princess Margaret Beach**.

Frangipani, on the shore of Admiralty Bay, accommodates guests in eight hillside garden cottages built of stone and hardwood. Units have two beds, modern bath, ceiling fan and sun deck over the bay. Bar and excellent restaurant on premises. Adjacent to Dive Bequia. Dive package rate are from $975 for seven nights, 12 dives and one night dive. ☎ 784-458-3504, bob-sax@caribsurf.com.

The Gingerbread Hotel, also adjacent to Dive Bequia, offers three apartments, a restaurant and boutique. Suites range from ornate with poster beds and mosquito netting to plain and simple. Apartments have porches, full kitchens and modern baths. Rates per day for a double are from $160 ☎ 784-458-3800, www.gingerbreadhotel.com, ginger@caribsurf.com.

Friendship Bay Resort sits on a hilltop overlooking distant green islands and the sea. The 60-room resort has a tennis court, dive shop and its own jetty for visitors with boats and for watersports. Decent snorkeling off the hotel beach. Swedish owners Lars and Margit pamper guests with gourmet cuisine in the lovely outdoor dining room and bar. Near Port Elisabeth, the capital of Bequia, and the Tobago Cays for diving and snorkeling. Room rates range from $165 to $310 per day. ☎ 784-458-3222, fax 784-458-3840, lambambas@vincysurf.com.

Petit St. Vincent is a private 113-acre island touted as the Caribbean's most luxurious and romantic hideaway. Accommodations are in 22 cottages, each with spectacular views. Each cottage has a living room, bedroom, bathroom and patio. Meals are served in the main pavilion, at your cottage or on the beach if you wish. Room rates are per day for two and include breakfast, lunch and dinner. Per day from $720 in winter, from $585 in summer. Flights between Barbados and Union Island cost $165 per person. Add 17% tax and service charge. No credit cards. Closed September and October. ☎ 954-963-7401, 800-654-9326, fax 954-963-7402, local www.psvresort.com, info@psvresort.com.

Julie's Guest House, in the center of Bequia's main harbor town, may be the bargain spot of the Caribbean. This small hotel features 19 clean rooms, each with private bath and shower. Julie's restaurant offers good seafood and fresh fruits and vegetables from their own garden. Diving with Dive Bequia. Guest room day rates are from $65. ☎ 784-458-3304, fax 784-458-3812, julies@caribsurf.com.

Canouan (Island of the Turtles)

 Jump-off point to the Tobago Cays and the magnificent Horseshoe Reef, Canouan sits 25 miles south of St. Vincent between Mustique and Union Island. A popular anchorage for sailors.

Tamarind Beach Hotel & Yacht Club offers 42 luxurious rooms on Grandbay Sandy Beach. The resort services yachts with provisions. Two good restaurants and a beach bar serve a variety of pizzas and pastas, grilled fish and meats. Room rates per day for a double, are $310 to 710 in season. Add $90 per day, per person for meals Guests are met at the airport. Kayak diving and snorkeling from the beach. Five-night dive packages include room and meals and three dives, from $1,700 to $2,200 per room. ☎ 784-458-8044, www.tamarindbeachhotel.com, reservations@tamarind.us.

Union

More developed than Mayreau or Canouan, Union is St. Vincent's customs and clearance point of entry for yachts. The island's lush appearance, splendid mountainous terrain and beautiful beaches attract more and more visitors each year. Near Tobago Cays.

Sunny Grenadines Hotel is a very simple, inexpensive place to stay (under $60 per night – room only). Guest rooms are in two-story stone cottages with twin beds and small porches. Kitchen units available. ☎ 784-458-8327.

Anchorage Yacht Club offers comfortable rooms, cottages and apartments at the marina and adjacent to the airstrip. Winter rates are from $130 to $180. ☎ 784-458-8221, www.ayc-hotels-grenadines.com.

Palm Island

Palm Island, a privately owned resort, lies about a mile east of Union Island. To get there, fly from Barbados to Union, where a resort launch picks you up for the 10-minute trip to Palm Island.

Palm Island Beach Resort once known as "Prune Island," has been transformed from a swamp-ridden, mosquito-infested jungle into a posh, intimate oasis. Guests stay in stone, beachfront cottages with king or twin beds, private bath, refrigerator, fans, A/C, coffee maker, hot water, screens, beach furniture, floats and patio. Diving and snorkeling trips are arranged with a Union

Island dive shop. Amenities include a boutique, yacht club, game room with ping pong, TV, Internet service, pool, table games and books (no TV in the rooms), superb gourmet restaurant, beach bar that serves burgers, fast food, ice cream and beverages. All-inclusive winter rates for two are from $750-$850 per day. Rates include three meals, tea, laundry, transfers, tennis and most watersports. Good snorkeling about 100 feet off the beach amidst boulders that shelter throngs of fish. You need a passport to visit Palm Island. ☎ 800-858-4618 or 866-317-8011, direct 784-458-8824, fax 784-458-8804.

Dining

St. Vincent

 Basil's in the Cobblestone Inn, a converted 1800s sugar warehouse, offers a buffet lunch, seafood pastas, lobster and excellent French wines. On Bay Street in Kingstown. Buffet on Fridays. Entrées from $10 to $30. ☎ 457-2713.

The Bounty Restaurant and Art Gallery on Halifax Street in Kingstown offers inexpensive steaks, rotis, pizza, burgers, pastries and homemade ice cream. No credit cards. ☎ 456-1776.

The Lagoon and Green Flash Bar, at the Lagoon Marina & Hotel, features breakfast, lunch and dinner. Good conch fritters, smoked fish and fresh seafood. Dinner entrées are from $22 to $35. ☎ 458-4308.

Join the locals at **Lime N Pub** facing Young Island resort's channel. Specials are pumpkin, lobster and callaloo soups, veal, chicken, steak, burgers and pizza. No credit cards. Moderate. ☎ 458-4227.

Young Island resort, directly across the channel from the French Verandah Restaurant at Mariner's Hotel on Villa Bay, features a super barbecue and steel band on Saturdays (about $20 per person). Call for the Young Island water taxi from the phone at the dock adjacent to the restaurant, ☎ 458-4826.

Bequia

Credit cards are not accepted. Most restaurants close on Sundays.

Mac's Pizzeria, seen on *Lifestyles of the Rich & Famous,* serves a world-class lobster pizza, tangy pita sandwiches and mouth watering brownies and lime pie. It's on the beach at Port Elizabeth. Call for reservations. ☎ 458-3474. No credit cards. Moderate.

Stop in the **Frangipani Resort** at the Gingerbread Complex any Thursday night for an all-you-can-eat barbecue and "jump-up" night with steel band. On the waterfront, and open daily for delicious breakfasts, freshly prepared lunches and candlelit dinners, with daily three-course special menu. Friendly popular bar open all day long. ☎ 458-3255.

For a special treat try **Le Petit Jardin** in Port Elizabeth. ☎ 458-3318. No credit cards. Expensive.

Sightseeing & Other Activities

 Prime topside sightseeing attractions are on St. Vincent. The most popular is the **Botanical Gardens.** Located north of Kingstown on the west coast, the 20-acre gardens are the oldest in the western hemisphere, established for growing herbs, spices and medicinal plants.

Garden paths wind through passion flowers, breadfruit, ironwood, and blooming jacaranda trees; sealing wax palms (a sticky gum taken from the base is used for sealing envelopes), coconut, avocado pears, huge mahogany, nutmeg, cocoa and fragrant ylang-ylang trees – oil from the ylang-ylang is used to make perfumes. The oldest tree sprouted around 1765.

Rugged hiking trails criss-cross St. Vincent's 33,000 acres of forest. The nicest are the **Vermont Nature Trails** in the upper part of the Buccament Valley, directly north of Kingstown – home to a community of 100 parrots which may be spotted early mornings or late afternoons.

Fort Charlotte, named for the wife of King George III, is only a few minutes drive from Kingstown. Situated on a 600-foot ridge, the fort is complete with a moat and drawbridge to the mainland. Visitors enjoy panoramic views of the Grenadines from the old gunner ports.

Baleine Falls is reached by boat and a short hike through a rocky stream. Wear boat shoes or aqua socks and plan on most of a day for the trip (about a one-hour boat ride, arranged through either dive shop), which includes snorkeling and diving stops. Rum punch and lunch are usually a part of the deal. The falls, which would befit a Hollywood set, are 60 feet high and drop into a deep crystalline pool. They are located on the northwest coast near the northern tip of the island.

Shop for batiks, tie-dyed sarongs, and crafts in **Kingstown** – a charming port town with cobblestone sidewalks, old stone buildings and a cluster of three churches.

Facts

Helpful Phone Numbers: Police, ☎ 457-1211; hospital, ☎ 456-1185; Department of Tourism, ☎ 456-2610; E.T. Joshua Iinternational Airport, St. Vincent, ☎ 458-4379. Pharmacies:Kingstown, Reliance, ☎ 456-1734, or Deane's, ☎ 457-1522; Bequia, ☎ 458-3296. Note: The small islands do not have phone service.

Nearest Recompression Chamber: Barbados.

Airlines: St. Vincent and the Grenadines are located between St. Lucia and Grenada on the southern end of the Eastern Caribbean. Barbados is 100 miles to the east and is a major gateway for incoming flights from the US; the others are Grenada, Martinique, St. Lucia, Puerto Rico and Trinidad. **American Eagle** (www.american.com) has service between San Jose and Canouan. **BWIA Express** (www.bwee.com), **Caribbean Star Airlines** (www.flycaribbeanstar.com) and **LIAT** (www.liat.com) all provide service from the gateways. **SVG Air** (www.svgair.com), **Trans Island Air** (www.tia2000.com) and **Mustique Airways** (www.mustique.com) offer inter-island charter services.

Daily connections on Mustique Airways from Barbados to Bequia (1 hr), and flights on Wednesdays, Fridays, and Sundays from Forte de France to Bequia (45 minutes). Alternatively, you may fly to St. Vincent from Barbados or Martinique and take a ferry (1 hr crossing) or the Air Shuttle (5 minute flight) to Bequia. Local airport departure tax: US$8.

Canouan Flights: There are direct flights to Canouan via Barbados and St. Vincent. Contact SVG Air in St. Vincent, ☎ 784-457-5124, or Trans Island Air in Barbados, ☎ 246-418-1654. One can also fly from Puerto Rico to Canouan on American Eagle, ☎ 784-456-5555.

Water and Land Taxi Services are readily available. On water, call VHF 16 to contact Catherine at R&C's, Cosmos at Specialist Transport Service, or André DeRoche at Rainbow Travel; on land, call Cassie at ☎ 482-0045 or 493-3557.

Island Transportation: Taxis and buses are available at the airports.

Driving: On the left. A temporary license is required. Rental cars are available on St. Vincent at the airport.

Documents: US and Canadian citizens must have a passport and onward ticket.

Currency: The Eastern Caribbean dollar (XCD). Exchange rate is approximately US$1=EC$2.70 (variable). Major credit cards are accepted at large hotels and restaurants on St. Vincent. With some exceptions, cash is necessary in the Grenadines.

Language: English is spoken everywhere.

Climate: Average air temperature is 86°F; water, 80°.

Clothing: Very casual. Pack light. Bring sneakers or light hiking shoes if you plan to hike the trails. Aqua socks are good for mucking about the shallows.

Electricity: 220 volts, 50 cycles. Bring an adaptor.

Time: Atlantic Standard (EST + 1 hr).

Departure Tax: A departure tax of $13 is charged to all visitors.

Religious Services: Catholic, Methodist.

Additional Information: *In the US*, ☎ 800-729-1726. *In Canada*, 100 University Avenue,Suite 504, Toronto, Ontario M5J 1V6. *In the UK*, ☎ 0071-937-6570, www.svgtourism.com, www.bequiatourism.com.

Tobago

Tobago, the *"Robinson Crusoe* Island," is Trinidad's small sister island. Separated by 22 miles of sea, both islands lie about seven miles off Venezuela's coast. Tobago sits on the South American continental shelf at the southernmost tip of the Lesser Antilles arc. It has a land area of 116 square miles and a mountainous interior, with a central backbone known as **Main Ridge** that runs most of its length. Pigeon Peak, its highest point, reaches 1,700 feet. The hillsides and lowlands are dotted with thatched cottages, each with an array of prayer flags on bamboo poles. Most of the people live on lower ground and are fishermen or farmers. Smooth beaches fringed by palms, breadfruit, mango and banana trees ribbon the northwestern Caribbean coast.

 Inland jungles support exotic wildlife and luxuriant vegetation, including flowering trees such as the crimson immortelle, pink poui, with its large bunches of trumpet-shaped flowers, its cousin, the yellow poui, and the purplish queen of flowers (pride of India). There are more than 700 species of orchids. The country's national flower is the chaconia, or wild poinsettia. Among the animal species are 60 kinds of bats, rodents such as the agouti and spotted paca (lappe), the pig-like peccary, the armadillo, the caiman (related to alligators), many types of snakes (including venomous ones), and a great variety of birds and butterflies. This is the only place outside New Guinea where birds of paradise exist in their wild state.

The main tourist areas are **Scarborough**, the capital, and along the Caribbean coast between **Plymouth** and the island's southern tip.

About half of Tobago's 40,000 people are of black African descent, including those of mixed race, 40% have South Asian ancestry (the "East Indians") and the rest are of European or Chinese descent. Many languages are spoken, but English is the official and common medium of communication.

Diving Tobago is adventure diving at its best. It's not just a visual experience, but a delight for the entire body and spirit. There are drift dives, "flights" through churning cuts, holes swarming with huge pelagics, monster coral forms, caves, grottoes, fish and more fish. For the diver grown weary of the ordinary, it is therapeutic.

Tobago's best dive areas are nurtured by fresh and saltwater currents that attract an ever-present population of manta rays, huge turtles, dolphins and sharks. Less spectacular, but calmer, shallow-reef areas exist that are good for snorkeling and novice divers. The most famous spot, but not necessarily the most interesting is Buccoo Reef off the island's northwest corner.

When to Go

The dry season, between February and August, is the best time of year for diving and snorkeling Tobago. By then, the heavy rains from the wet season have ceased and the waters are calm and clear. This time of year brings the best visibility and the fewest mosquitoes. Rainfall is heaviest from July to December, although it occurs in every month. Yearly precipitation varies in different parts of the islands but almost everywhere averages at least 50 inches. The islands are south of the normal hurricane belt.

The climate of the country is tropical, with little seasonal variation in temperature, but with a significant contrast between day and night readings. Northeast trade winds moderate the heat.

History

Christopher Columbus discovered Trinidad in 1498, but never mentioned Tobago. The island later made up for this neglect by changing hands more frequently than perhaps any other Caribbean island. For two centuries, the Dutch, English, and French fought for control. The Treaty of Amiens gave Tobago to France, but the island was ceded to Great Britain in 1814. For a while the island was declared neutral territory. This, however, made it irresistible to pirates, and Tobago turned into such a dangerous outpost of rogues that in 1762 the British invaded just to clear them out.

Subsequently, a prosperous sugar industry developed on the island and "as rich as a Tobago planter" became a familiar saying.

In 1976, Trinidad and Tobago severed its ties with the British crown and in 1980 Tobago was granted limited autonomy, exercised through its new House of Assembly.

Tourism increased greatly after World War II, becoming the country's second-largest industry as fast air service brought the islands within easy reach of North American tourists seeking a quiet, unspoiled tropical island vacation.

Best Dive & Snorkeling Sites

Freshwater overflow from the Orinoco and the Amazon rivers is carried past the south and east coasts of Tobago by the Guyana Current. This mix of salt and freshwater nutrients produces massive plankton blooms that support a

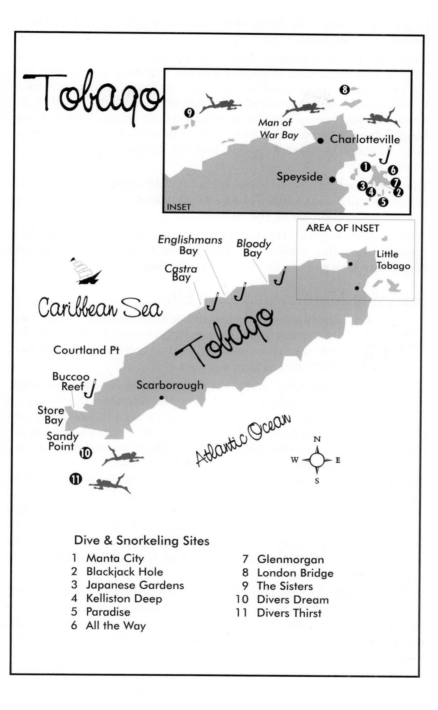

Dive & Snorkeling Sites

1 Manta City
2 Blackjack Hole
3 Japanese Gardens
4 Kelliston Deep
5 Paradise
6 All the Way

7 Glenmorgan
8 London Bridge
9 The Sisters
10 Divers Dream
11 Divers Thirst

huge range of marine life. Many deep-sea fish are found much closer to the surface here than normal.

Manta rays, turtles and dolphin are the star attractions, with huge, silvery tarpon, spotted eagle rays, stoplight parrotfish, queen angels, electric eels, durgons, squid, jewfish, lizardfish, spadefish, triggerfish, occasional black tip sharks and hammerheads as a splendid supporting cast. Little Tobago is also a haven for every imaginable critter, including multi-colored barber shrimp, banded shrimps, arrow crabs, spider crabs, Christmas trees, feather worms, slugs, nudibranchs and urchins. One diver reports three sightings of a whale shark.

The main areas for diving are off the southern tip of the island and off Speyside around the out islands: **Little Tobago**, **Goat Island**, and off the north coast around the islets known as **The Sisters**.

The best snorkeling areas are along the Caribbean coast at **Arnos Vale Bay**, **Englishman's Bay**, **Castra Bay**, **Fort James**, **Courtland Bay**, **Buccoo Bay**, **Store Bay** and off Speyside at **Tyrells Bay**.

Speyside Marine-area Dive Sites

All of the reefs in this area fringe the out islands. There is a prevailing northerly current and most dives are drift dives. Check with dive shops before diving or snorkeling on your own. Water temperature averages 82°F.

☆☆☆☆☆ **Manta City**, on the north side of Little Tobago, is *the* single most popular dive in Tobago. As the name implies, it is where manta rays are most commonly seen. Several of the mantas are used to interacting with divers and will approach to play. Avoid the temptation to hitch a ride as you may inadvertently harm the animal. Other residents are big French angels, urchins, crabs, blue tangs, jacks, damselfish, sharp nose puffers, and barracuda. Dive depths range from the extreme shallows near the shore to 50 feet. The bottom is a magnificent landscape of boulders and big rocks with good growth of star, brain and flower corals. Large barrel sponges and tube sponges are found at depth. The rays are usually spotted along the edge of a dropoff. Seas are generally calm with an occasional surge. The shallows are suitable for experienced snorkelers and novice divers. Unparalleled photo opportunities.

☆☆☆ **Blackjack Hole**, also off the south shore of Little Tobago, is a gentle slope allowing divers to choose their own depth preference. A beautiful dive with loads of fish, as well as loads of corals, big and small. Peak interest on the reef lies between 45 and 90 feet. The surface is calm, protected by the nearby island. Currents, if any, are gentle.

☆☆☆ **Japanese Gardens**, another manta-watch point, lies off the western tip of Goat Island. The reef's rich and varied soft corals take on a flower-garden appearance with a landscape of odd shapes, colors and patterns. The surface is usually choppy, but there is little or no current below except at the center of a reef where you will catch a good "flight" for some minutes through a narrow canal. The first part of the dive is on a slope, and the last part is in an area with big reef-boulders and reef-patches on a sandy bottom. Sunlight reflecting in the sand adds a lot of color to the dive. Angels, grunts, moray eels, and parrotfish are always about. Divers select depths for their skill level – between 30 and 60 feet or between 50 and 100 feet for the very experienced.

☆☆ **Kelliston Deep**, the site of the biggest recorded brain coral head in the world – 16 feet wide and 12 feet high – sits off the southwest tip of Little Tobago. It starts at a shelf between 30 and 50 feet, then slopes down to a sandy bottom at 120 feet. Typical reef fish are abundant with occasional sightings of nurse sharks and manta. The outer edge starts in 50 feet. This beautiful area is destined to become a marine reserve.

☆☆ **Paradise** is an almost circular arena with a sandy bottom. The site is off an islet just south of Little Tobago. You enter at the edge of a hole, go through a narrow canal, around a corner and over an edge. Above you, heavy wave action forms clouds and clouds of foam and, right under the white foam, schools of tarpons four to eight feet long drift by. A magnificent sight. Nearby and a part of this dive is a gently sloping reef with lots of coral and fish life. Suggested experience level depends on sea conditions. Average depth is 60 feet.

☆☆ **All the Way** is a playground of gigantic boulders – a secretive dive where you don't know what's around the next corner. The reef slopes are a marvelous seascape rich with coral and sponge growth. Depths average 40 to 50 feet. All the Way is off the northeast tip of Little Tobago.

☆☆☆ **Glennmorgan** lies in a sheltered area off the eastern coast of Little Tobago. Soft corals and slender tube sponges color the canyons and walls of the reef. Average depth is 60 to 80 feet. Seldom any current. Expect to meet white-tip sharks and other pelagics. Suggested experience level depends on sea conditions. Often calm.

Caribbean-side Dive Sites

☆☆☆ **London Bridge**, at St. Giles Island off the northern tip of Tobago, is a rugged dive on a good day. St. Giles is a small rocky island with a hole going through both above and beneath the surface – like a bridge. As you enter the hole you experience a Venturi effect and are whirled through by a rush of water. Exhilarating! The depth in the hole is 30-40 feet, and the rest of the dive is normally at 60 feet. Maximum depth is 110 feet. Fish life is superb with 30-lb parrotfish, huge green morays, lobster, schools of tarpon and pelagics between the walls and boulders. Big sponges, sea fans and corals. Experienced ocean divers except on extremely calm days. Boat dive.

☆☆ **The Sisters** is a group of small islands off Bloody Bay on the northern coast. Reaching the site requires a 30- to 45-minute boat ride over choppy seas, but if you crave a dramatic wall dive with huge pelagics, it's worth it. The wall is strewn with big boulders and rocks. At times you might find current and at times you might find surge. For experienced divers.

Atlantic-side Dive Sites

Water temperature on the southeast Atlantic side is about 79°F. Dives on this Atlantic side are drift dives with strong currents and some surge. Currents often run in one direction on the surface and the opposite way at depth, with occasional upwellings and downwellings. Not suggested for the timid or inexperienced diver.

☆☆☆☆ **Diver's Dream**, an awesome stone formation with towering fissures, cracks, canyons and caves, packs in an incredible wealth of fish and crustaceans. Once in the "Dream," you'll encounter giant vase sponges measuring six feet across, and finger corals that are 10 feet high. Large schooling reef fish mingle with black-tip sharks, nurse sharks, huge turtles, barracudas, and mantas. Surface conditions are calm, with gentle rollers. Always a drift dive with a one- to three-knot current. Recommended for experienced drift divers.

☆☆☆ **Diver's Thirst** is a mix of rock and reef that mold into an amphitheater populated by big grouper, black-tip sharks, eagle rays and midnight parrotfish. Maximum depth is 45 feet. Always a drift dive. Surface conditions are light. Experienced drift divers.

Dive Operators

All Tobago dive operators require a C-card and request a logbook. Rates for a two-tank dive average $50. Prices subject to change.

Tobago diving is fairly rugged, weather-dependent, with seas that often run five to six feet. Suggested for experienced ocean divers.

Aquamarine Dive Ltd., at the Blue Waters Inn, Speyside, tours Coral Gardens, Book Ends and Japanese Gardens. The shop has fast dive boats and modern equipment. ☎/fax 868-639-4416, www.aquamarinedive.com.

Man Friday Diving is at Man-O-War Bay, Charlotteville, near Speyside. Danish owner and dive manager, Finn Rinds, tours the best sights around Little Tobago and the northeastern spots. He is personal friends with a few mantas too! The PADI/NAUI shop has storage lockers and equipment rentals. Finn whisks divers out to the reefs aboard a 28-foot custom dive boat. Dive/hotel packages can be arranged with Blue Waters Inn (www.bluewatersinn.com). ☎ 809-660-4676, manfriday@hotmail.com.

Tobago Dive Experience at the Arnos Vale Hotel on the southern end of Tobago and at Manta Lodge in Speyside offers trips to all the Caribbean spots and around the south tip to the rugged Atlantic sites. This NAUI/PADI shop offers courses and equipment rentals. Arnos Vale has super snorkeling off their beach. ☎ 868-660-4888, www.tobagodiveexperience.com, info@tobagodiveexperience.com.

Tobago Marine Sports Ltd. is at the Crown Reef Hotel, Store Bay. Operated by Keith Darwent, this full-service PADI shop offers all courses, and tours the southeast tip of Tobago – Caribbean and Atlantic dives. Contact Keith or John Darwent at ☎ 876-639-0291. Write to PO Box 3000, Crown Reef Hotel, Store Bay, Tobago, WI.

Dive Tobago Limited at Pigeon Point is Tobago's oldest dive operation. It caters to the beginner and advanced diver. Resort courses, $60. One-tank dive with equipment, $30. ☎ 868-639-0202 or 868-639-7275, fax 868-639-2727.

Wild Turtle Dive located at Pigeon Point Beach Resort features drift dives, wreck dive such as the MV *Maverick*, a former passenger ferry that tops at 55feet. They dive all around the island including Crown Point, Speyside and Sisters. Small groups with great service and personable staff. Dive/accommodation packages available on their Website. ☎ 868-639-7936, www.wildturtledive.com, info@wildturtledive.com.

Where to Stay

Blue Waters Inn and Aquamarine Dive, Batteaux Bay, Speyside, have been named a PADI International Resort Association Gold Palm Resort and Five Star facility. They're at the heart of the Speyside Marine area, near the small villages of Speyside and Charlotteville. This low-rise resort, which circles the shores of a private bay, soothes guests with rooms a few feet from the sea. Rustic and rural, it is a haven for nature lovers, far away from the tourist area, with 46 acres of grounds. Snorkel from the beach. The inn has 28 guest rooms and four cottages. All are cooled by ceiling fans. Snorkel from the beach. Dive shop on premises. Room rates for double occupancy are from $160 in winter, $100 in summer. Cottages are from $230 per day. Rooms and cottages have been recently redecorated in bright Caribbean colors. ☎ 800-742 4276, 868-660-4341 or 868-660-4077, fax 868-660-5195, www.bluewatersinn .com, bwi@bluewatersinn.com.

Dive/accommodation packages, including seven nights, 10 dives, three meals daily, transfers and taxes, offered by **Into the Blue Tours**, start at $875 per person for a double. ☎ 800-6-GET-WET, www.intotheblue.com, cvdt@aol.com. **Scuba Voyages** offers similar tours. ☎ 800-544-7631, scubavoy@ix.netcom.com.

Manta Lodge, a lovely, low-rise dive resort in Speyside, offers 22 deluxe rooms with private verandas and an ocean view. Your choice of ceiling fan or air conditioning. Tobago Dive Experience on site. Pool, beautiful beach. Packages: (May 1 to December 15) The Hotel/Dive package includes: 10 dives (weights and tanks included) , seven nights accommodation, airport transfers, all taxes and service charges, breakfast and dinner daily, welcome drink on arrival. Rates for a standard room with a ceiling fan only, $899 per person; superior room with ceiling fan and air conditioning, $949 per person. Rates are based on double occupancy. ☎ 868-660-5268, fax 868-660-5030, www.mantalodge.com, info@mantalodge.com.

Grafton Beach Resort, in Black Rock, the island's leading hotel, sits on the Caribbean. This 100-room luxury resort straggles across five acres of tropical splendor. Features include a pool with a swim-up bar, air-conditioned squash courts, gym, restaurant, palm-lined beach, entertainment, dive shop and an 18-hole golf course nearby. Guest rooms have air conditioning, cable TV, private bath and mini-fridge. Book through your travel agent or direct. ☎ 868-639-0191, fax 868-639-0030, www.grafton-resort.com

Mt. Irvine Bay Hotel is a 54-room, two-story complex with 46 adjacent cottages on the site of a 17th-century sugar plantation. All accommodations have private balcony or patio and are fully air conditioned. The spacious garden cottages offer a choice of open or enclosed patio with refrigerator, wet bar, patio furniture and sun loungers. It is located on the south end of the the island's Caribbean coast. Beaches are across the street. Facilities include a pool, restaurant, spa, tennis and meeting room. Rates for a double are from $195 to $460 per day. ☎ 800-544-7631, direct 868-639-8871, fax 639-8800, www.mtirvine.com. mtirvine@tstt.net.tt.

Turtle Beach Hotel at Plymouth is just 15 minutes from the airport on Courland Bay. Rooms have private bath, air conditioning, balcony or patio overlooking the beach. Beach bar, small pool and The Rustic Kiskadee Restaurant. Entertainment. ☎ 868-639-2820, fax 868-639-1495. Write PO Box 201, Plymouth, Tobago, WI.

Man-O-War Bay Cottages, near St. Giles and Little Tobago Islands, are for nature lovers and bird watchers. Rooms are part of Charlotteville Estate, a

1,000-acre cocoa plantation 36 miles from the airport. The cottages are plain and simple, each with one to four bedrooms, twin beds, kitchenette, shower, jalousie windows. No A/C. (Air temperature averages 82°F year-round.) ☎ 868-660-4327, fax 868-660-4328. Cottages run from $65 to $110, www.man-o-warbaycottages.com, mowbc@tstt.net.tt.

Dining

Curried crab and dumplings highlight Tobago's menus, along with fish and lobster dishes prepared with callaloo (like spinach), coconut and cornmeal. Peas and rice are the usual side dishes.

Manta Lodge Restaurant in Speyside features local and continental seafood favorites. ☎ 660-5268.

Garden Grille Restaurant at the Ocean Point Hotel, Lowlands, serves up tasty seafood, Creole and East Indian specials such as curry crab, coconut bake or Callaloo in an open-air area adorned with tropical plants, crawling vines, and fragrant Jasmine trees. ☎ 868-639-0970.

Exotic gardens with splashing waterfalls and fishponds curtain **Shirvan Watermill Restaurant** on Shirvan Road, Mt. Pleasant. Menu specialties are all home made with fresh meats, seafood, fruits and vegetables. ☎ 868-639-0000, swmill@tstt.net.tt.

Surfer's at Mt. Irvine Beach lets you choose between a quiet, candlelit dinner in their International Restaurant or casual dining at their seafront bar and diner with panoramic view of Buccoo Reef. Local and international cuisine. Live steel band and barbecue every Friday night. ☎ 868-639-8407.

The Blue Crab in Scarborough is a tiny spot offering sumptuous conch, crab and Creole dishes. Fresh fish and local vegetables are prepared with island spices. Lunches daily and dinner on Wednesday and Friday. ☎ 868-639-2737.

Sightseeing & Other Activities

A two-hour drive from Scarborough, the capital, at the northern tip of Tobago, will lead you through most of the sightseeing spots on this tiny, rural island.

While in Scarborough visit the **Botanic Gardens**, the 18th-century **Fort King George** and the **National Fine Arts Gallery and Museum**. The fort commands a magnificent view of southern Tobago and the Atlantic coast.

Pigeon Point is the island's most famous beach, with offshore **Buccoo Reef**. A stop at **King's Bay Waterfall** is a necessity for the photo buff. It's about 20 miles from Scarborough, along the Windward Road to Charlotteville. Bring your bathing suit for a dip in the natural pool at the base of the falls.

 Two of Tobago's loveliest spots are **Argyll Waterfall** near Roxborough on the north end of the Atlantic coast, and **Courland Bay** on the leeward coast. The settlement at Great Courland Bay was established as a colony by the Duchy of Livonia in 1652.

Diving and birdwatching dominate the sports scene, but golfers will enjoy the **Mt. Irvine Golf Course** (☎ 639-8871), founded in 1892. Windsurfing is big off Speyside (☎ 660-5206), and horseback riding is offered at the Palm Tree Village Beach Resort (☎ 639-4347).

Facts

 Helpful Phone Numbers: Police, ☎ 999 or 622-5412; medical help, ☎ 623-2551; fire or ambulance, ☎ 990; Scarborough Hospital, ☎ 639-2551.

Nearest Recompression Chamber: Tobago's hyperbaric, or recompression, facility is housed at the Roxborough Medical Clinic, which is a drive of about 20 minutes from Speyside and about 40 minutes from Scarborough. The Facility is operated jointly by A.T.D.O., the Tobago House of Assembly and T.I.D.C.O. (the Trinidad & Tobago Industrial Development Corp.)

Getting Here: BWIA (☎ 800-327-7300) flies to Tobago from New York, Miami, and Washington, DC. Connect via Port of Spain on the Tobago Express and BWIA. **American Airlines**, ☎ 800-433-7300, flies to San Juan, connecting with **American Eagle**, which flies direct to Tobago.

Island Transportation: Taxis are very expensive in Tobago. If you drive, rent at Crown Point Airport (☎ 639-0644), or AR Rentals (☎ 639-5330). Some of the roads are narrow and muddy during spring and summer.

Driving: On the left. A valid license is required.

Documents: Passport valid for length of stay, return or onward ticket.

Currency: The Trinidad and Tobago dollar (TT$). currently US$1=TT$6 (variable). Credit cards are widely used in tourist areas.

Climate: Average water temperature is 78°F. Air temperature averages 85°. Humidity is high, with frequent showers, especially from June to December. Biting insects are a problem.

Clothing: Ultra-casual and lightweight. Long-sleeve shirts, long pants and closed shoes are best for hiking the rain forest trails. Light wetsuit suggested for deep dives. Snorkelers should wear protective covering from the midday sun.

Security: Avoid walking alone at night. Don't stop if flagged down while driving. Use hotel safes, lock cars and hotel rooms. Avoid wearing flashy jewelry.

Electricity: 110 and 220 volts, 60 cycles.

Time: Atlantic Standard (EST + 1 hr).

Tax: 15% government tax is added to hotel rates. A departure tax of TT $75 must be paid in local currency. A 10% service charge is added or expected at restaurants.

Religious Services: Catholic, Protestant.

For Additional Information: www.visitTNT.com, ☎ 888-535-567.

Virgin Islands

British Virgin Islands

Windswept and wildly beautiful, the BVI encompasses more than 60 sparsely inhabited islands and rocks that lie 60 miles east of Puerto Rico. Most tourist activity centers around the four larger islands: **Tortola**, **Anegada**, **Virgin Gorda** and **Jost Van Dyke**. Except for Anegada, which is a flat coral slab surrounded by shallow reefs, the islands are mountainous and of volcanic origin. The highest point is the 1,781-foot Mt. Sage on Tortola.

The capital and chief port is **Road Town** on Tortola, the largest island and home to 80% of the BVI residents, with a population of 17,000. A toll bridge connects Tortola to **Beef Island** and the international airport. An efficient ferry service or a short hop by light aircraft takes visitors to the other main islands. Other islands in the group include **Cooper Island**, **Ginger Island**, **The Dogs**, **Great Camanoe**, **Necker Island**, **Guana Island**, **Mosquito Island** and **Eustatia (Statia) Island**.

Save for a few clubs and discos that come to life on weekends, nightlife consists of stargazing and moonlit dives. The islands, devoid of casinos or high-rise hotels, offer a relatively untouched panorama of land, sea and sky. Overall, BVI life is relaxed, yet retains some British formality in terms of dignity and manners. Crime is rare and nudity is not encouraged. Visitors are asked to respect the residents' wishes by covering up in town and dressing "appropriately" in restaurants and bars.

The BVI's prime attractions are its hundreds of sheltered coves, isolated beaches and protected marine parks. Superb snorkeling and diving exists around the out islands with towering coral pinnacles, underwater caves, canyons, massive boulders, lava tunnels and almost 200 different wrecks. Most areas have little or no surge and only gentle currents. Visibility may reach from 50 to over 100 feet.

Clustered along the **Sir Francis Drake Channel** and protected from high wind and waves, the islands are enormously popular with sailors. In fact, half the BVI tourist "beds" are aboard the hundreds of yachts in Tortola's marinas.

The best time to visit the BVI is between October and June, with warmest water temperatures between mid March and early December. Reduced rates at hotels and on charter boats are available from July through mid December.

USVI contributors: Luana Wheatley, Virgin Rhythms; Michelle Pugh, Dive Experience; Lucy Portlock, Pelagic Pleasures.

Hurricane season is from July through October. Air temperature ranges between 80° and 90°F year-round with an occasional drop in February.

History

In 1493 Christopher Columbus discovered the islands and named them *St. Ursula y las Once Mil Virgenes* (St. Ursula and the 11,000 Virgins.) At that time, peaceful tribes of Indians roamed the BVI and remained its principal residents until the turn of the 17th century.

During the 1500s, pirates based themselves on Tortola, an ideal spot from which to attack ships trying to navigate the treacherous reefs of Sir Francis Drake Channel. Buccaneers such as Blackbeard (Edward Teach), Bluebeard, and Sir Francis Drake became legendary.

By 1672, the pirates were forced out by English planters who, with slave labor, developed the land for farming. They thrived on the export of bananas, sugarcane, citrus fruits, coconuts, mangoes and root crops until slavery was abolished in the early 1800s. Today, tourism has replaced agriculture as the islands' largest employer. Politically, the islands are a British colony administered by an executive council with a governor.

Best Dive & Snorkeling Sites

☆☆☆☆☆ **Wreck of the RMS** *Rhône*, featured in the movie *The Deep*, is by far the most popular dive in the BVI. Struck by a ferocious hurricane in October, 1867, the Royal Mail Steamer *Rhône* was hurled onto the rocks at Salt Island as its captain, Robert F. Wooley, struggled desperately to reach open sea.

The force with which the 310-foot vessel crashed upon the rocks broke the hull in two, leaving two superb dive spots, a great snorkeling area at the stern, which lies in 30 feet of water amid rocks and boulders, and a good area for diving at the bow, 80 feet down on a sandy bottom. The top of the rudder sits just 15 feet below the surface. Its superstructure, encrusted with corals, sponges, and sea fans, provides a dramatic setting for underwater photography.

Fish greet divers and snorkelers as they enter the water. Living among the wreckage are large groupers, curious barracudas, schools of snappers, grunts, jacks, arrow crabs, squirrelfish, and yellow tails. The *Rhône* is a boat-access dive. Sea conditions are usually calm; recommended for novices. Visibility is usually excellent, from 50 to over 100 feet. Also, the *Rhône* is a national park and off-limits to coral collecting and spear fishing. The wreck is located off Black Rock Point on the southwest tip of Salt Island.

British Virgin Islands

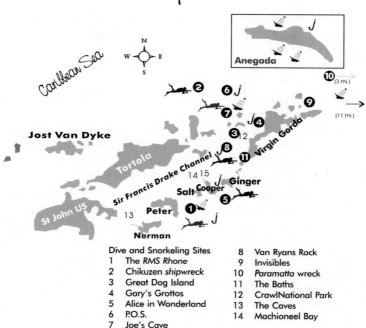

Dive and Snorkeling Sites		
1	The *RMS Rhone*	8 Van Ryans Rock
2	Chikuzen *shipwreck*	9 Invisibles
3	Great Dog Island	10 *Paramatta* wreck
4	Gary's Grottos	11 The Baths
5	Alice in Wonderland	12 Crawl National Park
6	P.O.S.	13 The Caves
7	Joe's Cave	14 Machioneel Bay

☆☆☆☆ **The *Chikuzen*,** a 268-foot steel-hulled refrigerator ship that went down off Tortola's east end in 1981, lies in 75 feet of water. Currently in use as a fish condominium, the wreck is blessed with visibility so good that you can stand on the bow and see the stern.

Tenants of the *Chikuzen* include several large stingrays, occasional black tip sharks, schools of yellowtail, filefish, barracudas, octopi, drumfish, and jewfish. The ship rests on her port side allowing easy entry. Coral covers the hull. A fine choice for novice divers. Boat access only. The outstanding visibility and large number of marine animals make for excellent photography.

☆☆☆ **The Chimney**, at Great Dog Island off the west end of Virgin Gorda, is a spectacular coral archway and canyon covered with a wide variety of soft corals, sponges and rare white coral. Hundreds of fish follow divers and snorkelers along the archway to a coral-wrapped, tube-like formation resembling a huge chimney. Inside the Chimney are circling groupers, crabs, brittle starfish, spiny lobsters, banded coral shrimp, queen angels, tube sponges and schooling fish. This is a favorite spot for close-up photography. Maximum depth of the Chimney is 45 feet. The many shallow areas and protected-cove location make this a "best snorkel dive" as well as a good selection for the scuba diver. Boat access only. Some surge and currents when wind is out of the north.

☆☆☆ **The MV *Inganess Bay*,** a new wreck sunk by BVI dive operators as an artificial reef after a storm snapped its anchor chain, lies off the southern tip of Cooper Island. The 136-foot freighter lies in 95 feet of water, its masts at 45 feet. Two national park moorings mark the sight. A good show of invertebrates and fish inhabit the wreck. Boat access.

☆☆☆ **Gary's Grottos** lie near the shoreline, four miles north of Spanish Town on Virgin Gorda. It is a shallow reef characterized by three huge arches that give the feel of swimming through a tunnel. At the end of the "tunnel" divers find a cave guarded by a friendly moray. This rocky area is teeming with shrimp, squid and sponges. Protected from wind and waves, the cove is also a choice spot for a night-dive. The average depth is 30 feet.

☆☆ **The Wreck of the *Rokus*.** On New Year's Eve, 1929, the Greek ship *Rokus* hit the reef on the southeast tip of Anegada. She sank in 40 feet of water with much of her hull remaining above the surface until hurricane Frederick struck in 1979. Remains of her cargo of animal bones can be found scattered around the wreckage. The reef surrounding the hull is pretty, with large formations of elkhorn and staghorn, as well as brain coral. An enormous eel has been spotted under the wreck by a number of divers. During the winter months, February through March, the song of migrating humpback whales can be heard from this site. This area is occasionally rough with small surges.

☆☆ **Great Dog Island's** south side drops off to a shallow reef with 10- to 60-foot depths. Nice elkhorn stands hide spotted and golden moray eels, spiny lobsters and barber shrimp. Good for novice divers when seas are calm.

☆☆☆☆☆ **Alice in Wonderland,** a coral wall at South Bay off Ginger Island, slopes from 15 feet to a sandy bottom at 90 feet, with most interest at 50 feet. Named for its huge mushroom corals, villainous overhangs, and gallant brain corals, this ornate reef shelters longnose butterflyfish, rays, conch and garden eels. Visibility is good and seas are usually calm. Alice in Wonderland is a boat-dive, good for photography, free diving, and novice through expert scuba diving.

Private yachts should choose the eastern mooring which is closer to the larger coral ridges.

☆☆☆☆ **PoS** was named after Project Ocean Search, a Cousteau project. The reef, which follows the shoreline of Cockroach Island (one of the Dog Islands), is a "must" for every underwater photographer. Beautiful, towering pillar, staghorn, and elkhorn corals at 35 feet are swept by huge silvery tarpons, French angels, crabs, lobsters, and schooling fish. The "Keyhole," a hole in one of the coral walls, is just big enough to frame a diver for an underwater portrait.

☆☆☆ **Blonde Rock**, a pinnacle between Dead Chest and Salt Island, starts at 15 feet below the surface. Coral-encrusted tunnels, caves and overhangs support a wealth of crabs, lobsters and reef fish. Good for novice divers when seas are calm. Boat access.

☆☆ **Santa Monica Rock**, a seamount, sits about a mile south of Norman Island. Depths range from 10 to 90 feet. Currents attract spotted eagle rays, sharks and other pelagics.

☆☆☆ **Joe's Cave**, an underwater cavern on the west side of West Dog Island, can be explored by swimming from the entrance at 20 feet down to 75 feet, where you'll find a magnificent opening to the sky. Corals and boulders form the cave's outer walls. Eels abound. Rough bottom terrain accents the masses of gleaming copper sweepers inside. This is a protected area with no current or surges. A good choice for divers of all levels.

☆☆ **Van Ryan's Rock**, in Drake's Channel, sits between Beef Island and Virgin Gorda. The top is at 16 feet and the bottom at 55 feet, with boulders and coral leading down to a sandy plain. Nurse sharks, eels, huge turtles, lobsters, jacks, spadefish, and barracudas circle it. Divers and snorkelers should take care to avoid the huge clumps of fire coral. A light current is occasionally encountered.

☆☆☆ **Invisibles**, a seamount off Tortola's northeast tip, is a haven for nurse sharks, eels, turtles and all types of reef fish, from the smallest to the largest. Diver Gayla Kilbride describes this area as a "Symphony of Fish." Depths go from three to 65 feet, a nice range for both snorkeling and diving.

 A wetsuit top, shortie, or wetskin is recommended for night-dives and winter diving. Snorkelers should have some protection from sunburn. The BVI reefs are protected by law, and no living thing may be taken. "Take only pictures, leave only bubbles."

Snorkeling

 Gear can be rented or borrowed from most hotels and charter boats, although it is best to have your own to insure a comfortable fit. Be sure to bring your camera. Snorkeling trips are offered by the dive shops.

☆☆☆☆ **Wreck of the *Paramatta***, which ran aground on her maiden voyage in 1853, rests at 30 feet off the southeast end of Anegada. The ship is on a dense coral reef – perfect for snorkelers. If you stand on the engine, you'll be shoulder-deep. Enormous reef fish swim around the wreck, including a 200-pound jewfish, 30-pound groupers, butterflyfish, turtles, and rays. Still remaining are the stern and bow sections, long chain, port holes, and cleats of the wreck, all sitting amid beautiful elkhorn and staghorn coral formations, large sea fans, brain corals and red and orange sponges. This is a great spot for underwater portraits.

☆☆☆☆ **The Baths**, at the southern tip of Virgin Gorda, encompasses the islands' most famous beaches. A natural landscape of partially submerged grottoes and caves formed by a jumble of enormous granite boulders, this is a favorite beach-access snorkeling area and one of the biggest tourist attractions in the BVI. The caves shelter a variety of tropical fish. Get here by taking the trail that starts at the end of the Baths Road. A small bar just off the beach rents snorkel equipment. Beware of dinghies! The Baths is a favorite of cruise ship visitors.

☆☆ **Spring Bay**, neighboring the Baths, has a gorgeous sandy beach and good snorkeling.

☆☆ **Crawl National Park**, a great spot for beginning snorkelers, also on Virgin Gorda, is reached via a palm-lined trail from Tower Road, just north of the Baths. A natural pond created by a boulder formation is ideal for children.

☆☆☆ **Smugglers Cove**, off the beaten path on the northwest end of Tortola, may be tough to find but is well worth the effort. The last mile leading to this spot is rough driving. There are two lovely reefs, about 100 feet out, with crowds of grunts, squirrelfish, parrotfish and some good-sized trunkfish to keep you company. Depths are shallow and seas usually calm. Good for children. The beach is shaded by palms and seagrape trees. No rest rooms or changing facilities, but there is an honor bar with sodas, beer and some snacks and a phone with a couple of taxi numbers.

Guests of the neighboring **Long Bay Beach Resort** are shuttled to Smugglers Cove twice a day.

☆☆ **Brewers Bay**, on Tortola's north coast road, has two good snorkeling sites, one to the left along the cliffs with depths from eight to 10 feet, the other in the center of the beach opposite the rock wall edging the road. The reef starts close to shore and stretches out in shallow depths for a long way. Schools of trumpetfish, barracudas, octopi, stingrays and sergeant majors inhabit the area.

☆☆☆☆ **The Caves** at Norman Island are accessible by boat. It is a favorite snorkeling-photo site, bright with sponges, corals and schools of small fish. The reef slopes down to 40 feet. Norman Island is rumored to have inspired Robert Louis Stevenson's *Treasure Island* and the Caves are reputed to be old hiding places for pirate treasure. Moorings are maintained by the National Park Trust.

☆☆ **Manchioneel Bay**, Cooper Island, has a beautiful shallow reef with packs of fish around the moorings.

Additional excellent snorkeling sites are found on the northeast corner of **Benures Bay**, Norman Island, or the **Bight** and **Little Bight**, also off Norman Island. At Peter Island, try the south shore at **Little Harbor** and the western shore at **Great Harbor**. **Diamond Reef** on the southeast side of Great Camanoe can be reached by dinghy fom Marina Cay. The shallow reef sits straight out from the utility pole on the shore.

Long Bay, near Smugglers Cove, Tortola, has pretty corals and the biggest fish, but water entry is difficult as the coral grows to the surface.

Dive Operators

 Most operators rent equipment, but it's best to bring your own stab jacket or vest, fins, mask and regulator.

AquaVenture sits adjacent to the cruise ship dock at the Village Cay Marina in Road Town, directly across from The Moorings operation. This shop specializes in small groups, eight or less, aboard their fast, 35-foot Striker dive boat, the *AquaVenture*. Trips to the favorite sites take 30 minutes or less from their dock. Soft drinks, water, fresh fruit, cheese and crackers are served after the dives.

If you're chartering a sail or power boat or cruising on your own, AquaVenture offers pick-up and return service or if you wish to dive from your own boat they offer a full line of rental equipment. ☎ 284-494-4320, www.aquaventurebvi.com, aquavent@surfbvi.com. Write to PO Box 11156.

Dive BVI Ltd., a PADI Five Star shop, operates out of Leverick Bay, Virgin Gorda Yacht Harbour, Peter Island and Marina Cay. Owner Joe Giacinto has been diving and snorkeling the BVI for more than 30 years and knows all the best spots. Rates are $85 for a two-tank dive, $225 for three two-tank dives. They will rendezvous with boats. Snorkeling trips are offered to Anegada and other spots aboard the *Sealion*, a fast 45-foot wave-piercing catamaran. Resort courses up through certification are available. ☎ 284-495-5513, 800-848-7078, fax 284-495-5347, www.divebvi.com, info@divebvi.com. Write PO Box 1040, Virgin Gorda, BVI.

Blue Water Divers has two Tortola locations, one on the south side at the Nanny Cay Resort and Marina, a 25-acre island overlooking Sir Francis Drake Channel, and the other at Sopers Hole on Frenchman's Caye off West End. Both shops offer boat tours and excursions, equipment sales and rentals.

A one-tank boat-dive costs $60; a two-tank boat-dive is $85. Rendezvous with your charter or private boat.

Blue Water Divers operates a 47-foot catamaran and a 27-foot dive boat. Dive tours are to the eastern sites in the BVI, such as Jost Van Dyke, as well as all the sites in the channel. Nanny Cay Dive Center, ☎ 284-494-2847, bwdbvi@surfbvi.com. Write PO Box 846, Road Town, Tortola, BVI. Sopers Hole Dive Center, ☎ 284-495-1200, www.bluewaterdiversbvi.com.

Dive Tortola, conveniently located on the harbor front at the Prospect Reef Resort, offers scuba rental equipment, rendezvous diving, certification courses and land-based dive packages. Their full-service includes gear storage, set up and rinsing for the next day's diving. The shop's staff will tote your stuff to and from the boat. ☎ 800-353-3419 or 954-453-5040, on island 284-357-3740, www.divetortola.com, diving@divetortola.com.

Kilbride's Sunchaser Scuba Ltd, at the Bitter End Yacht Club on Virgin Gorda, features guided scuba and snorkeling tours, courses and services. Their boats take you to 50 different dive sites. Sunchaser serves the North Sound resorts and their tours cover all the islands. Resort courses through PADI certification and open-water checkouts are available. Rates: $60 for a one-tank dive; $85 for a two-tank tour. Rates include all equipment except mask, fins and wetsuit. Snorkelers join dive trips for $30. ☎ 800-932-4286 or 284-495-9638, fax 284-495-7549, www.sunchaserscuba.com, info@sunchaserscuba.com.

Rainbow Visions Photography at Prospect Reef, next to Dive Tortola, offers underwater, still and video camera rentals. Processing, custom videos and portraits. ☎ 284-494-2749, www.rainbowvisionsbvi.com.

Sailing & Scuba Live-aboards

Sail-dive vacations are an easy way for divers to enjoy a variety of sites and destinations. Live-aboard yachts are chartered with captain, captain and crew or "bare" to qualified sailors. Navigation is uncomplicated; you can tour most of the area without ever leaving sight of land. Most boats carry snorkeling gear as standard equipment; some of the large craft have compressors. And every dive shop offers some type of arrangement to accommodate seafarers.

With sailing almost a religion in the BVI, it is easy to customize a live-aboard dive or snorkeling vacation. If you are an experienced sailor and diver you can charter a bare-boat and see the sights on your own. If you've never sailed before or have limited experience, you can "captain" a crewed yacht to find the best dive spots. If you've never sailed or dived, but want to learn both, you can charter a yacht with a crew that includes a dive master (often the captains are qualified dive instructors) or arrange to rendezvous with a dive boat. Or you can book a week-long cruise on a commercial live-aboard where you'll meet other divers. Prices on private charters vary with the number of people in your party. With four to six people, a crewed yacht will average about the same cost as a stay at a resort.

The **Cuan Law**, one of the world's largest trimarans (105 feet),was specifically designed with the scuba diver in mind. As with most live-aboards, you are offered "all the diving you can stand." *Cuan Law* accommodates 18 passengers in 10 large, airy double cabins, each with private head and shower. Rates from April through December start at $2,000 per person for seven days and six nights. Transfers, tips, alcohol and scuba instruction are NOT included.

Cruises are booked up from three months to a year in advance. ☎ 800-648-3393 or write Trimarine Boat Company, PO Box 4065, St. Thomas, USVI 00803.

Yacht *Promenade*, a sleek, 65-foot tri-hull sailing yacht for couples or groups of six to 12, features on-board scuba facilities, spacious air-conditioned cabins, movie projection theater with surround sound and six-foot screen, TV with VCR and DVD. Meals include full breakfasts, lunches, cocktails, hors d'oeuvres and three-course gourmet dinners. There are five guest state-rooms, one in each outer hull and three at the rear of the center hull, three queen-sized berths and two that are larger than king and can be converted into four single berths. Each stateroom has its own wash basin and mirror. Guests share four showers, a computer with e-mail access, fax, outlets for hair dryers and shavers.

Dive sites vary from coral reefs to grottoes, caves and old shipwrecks. *Promenade* crew includes two PADI and NAUI certifying dive instructors.

Diving from *Promenade* is very easy. There's a ladder that extends five rungs below the water to make it easier for you to climb aboard at the end of a dive, with a freshwater shower right beside it. In addition, they dive using a tender, which is also equipped with a customized ladder that's easy to use. They average two nice dive sites a day. Rates are based on number of passengers. You pay $3,700 per cabin booking individually, four guests pay $9,900, six pay $11,900, 10 guests pay $15,900 for six nights. Scuba divers add $100. With full rental equipment, add $225.

They have a resort course for non-divers as well as check out dives for those wishing to finish their training obtained elsewhere. Complete certification in PADI and NAUI. ☎ 284-499-2756, fax 284-496-0999, www.yacht-promenade.com, promcruz@surfbvi.com.

The Moorings provides chartered sailing tours for those wishing to enjoy a fully crewed sailing vacation without having to charter an entire yacht.

☎ 800-535-7289, www.moorings.com. Dive arrangements must be made separately; see below.

Bareboating

Private sailing yachts with diving guides and instructors are available from most of the charter operators listed below. You can arrange for your own personal live-aboard diving or snorkeling vacation. Be sure to specify your needs before going.

Bareboating can be surprisingly affordable for groups of four or more. Boats must be reserved six to nine months in advance for winter vacations and at least three months in advance for summer vacations.

Experience cruising on a similar yacht is required and you will be asked to fill out a questionnaire or produce a sailing résumé. Instructor-skippers are available for refresher sailing. A cruising permit, available from the Customs Department, is required. For a list of charter companies, contact the BVI Tourist Board at ☎ 800-835-8530 or online at www.bvitouristboard.com, then click on "*at sea.*"

The Moorings has been chartering sailing yachts from 32 to 40 feet for 18 years. Dive equipment can be rented from **Last Stop Sports** on the dock at the Moorings Mariner Inn. This operation is terrific for those of you who like to explore and dive on your own.

A three-day sailing vacation can be combined with a four-day resort vacation at the Moorings Mariner Inn. Write to The Moorings, 19345 US Hwy 19 N, Clearwater, FL 34624. ☎ 800-535-7289 or 813-535-1446, www.moorings.com. The dive shop is at www.laststopsports.com.

Divers who want to learn to sail should head directly to **Offshore Sailing School**. They offer a full range of courses from basic sailing through advanced cruising and racing, plus special programs such as the women's *You Can Sail* escapes; *Coastal Passage Making*, or live-aboard courses for monohulls and catamarans. They also have courses that prepare and qualify students to test for US SAILING certification – the most respected and widely recognized certification system. In 2004, Offshore Sailing School launched a new US SAILING-certified power-cruise school.

Offshore Sailing School is devoted to keeping its students sailing. It offers a host of graduate programs designed to expand sailing horizons, such as The **Offshore Sailing Club** and the **Offshore Cruising Club**, with flotilla cruises in some of the world's most exotic locations. ☎ 888-454-8002, or visit their Website at www.offshore-sailing.com.

Mooring Buoys

In order to protect the BVI's fragile coral reefs, boats are required to use National Parks Trust (NPT) mooring buoys when visiting the following areas: The Baths, The Caves, The Indians, Pelican Island, and Carrot Shoal; also dive or snorkeling sites at Peter, Norman, Ginger and Cooper Islands, the wreck of the *Fearless*, Dead Chest, Blonde Rock, The Dogs, Guana Island, the wreck of the *Rhône* and the *Rhône's* anchor. All users of the moorings must have a valid NPT moorings permit, available at their office in Road Town, or at BVI Customs Offices, local charter boat companies and brokerages.

Mooring buoy colors indicate the use for that mooring. White is for scuba diving only; orange or red are for snorkeling or any day use; yellow moorings are for commercial dive operations only; blue are for dinghies.

 Mooring on the reefs surrounding Anegada is prohibited.

Accommodations & Anchorages

Tortola

 Every type of accommodation is available in the BVI from tents to cottages, guesthouses, condos, luxury resorts to live-aboard sailboats and motor yachts. Reservations can be made through the BVI Tourist Board at ☎ 800-835-8530, or online at www.bvitouristboard.com or www.gobestdives.com.

Island Hideaways rents upscale private homes and villas. ☎ 800-832-2302 or 703-378-7840, www.islandhideaways.com.

Cooper Island Beach Club is a quiet beach hideaway in Manchioneel Bay on the northwest corner of Cooper Island. It features six rustic West Indian-style bungalows with 11 available guest units shaded by lovely palm trees, providing privacy and solitude. Each cottage unit has a living area, a small kitchen, and a balcony. Water and electricity are extremely limited. Think camping with a roof over your head. There are no roads, cars, nightclubs, casinos, shopping malls or fast-food outlets. There is a welcoming beach bar, outdoor restaurant and small boutique. **Sail Caribbean Divers** is the on-site host for scuba diving, kayaking, snorkeling and powerboat rentals. Winter rates for a seven-night dive package range from $1,099 in summer to $1,499 in winter. Non-divers pay from $699 in summer to $1,099 in winter. A la carte diving is also available.

The dive package includes accommodation for seven nights, round-trip ferry from Tortola, lunch and dinner daily, five days diving (10 dives) all diving and snorkeling equipment, use of a kayak, and a welcome drink. The 17% hotel tax and service charge is included. Nightly rates for the cottages run from $150 to $250. Cooper Island features a palm-studded beach, a boutique, beach bar and outdoor restaurant. The restaurant serves terrific grilled fish and chicken roti, calypso salad, conch fritters, hamburgers and soups. ☎ 800-542-4624, 413-863-3162, fax 413-863-3662, www.cooper-island.com, info@cooper-island.com. Write PO Box 512, Turners Falls, MA 01376.

Long Bay Beach Resort on Tortola's north shore has 82 deluxe hillside and beachfront accommodations. Rates start at $1,898 per couple + 17% tax and service charge for a seven-night dive vacation. Package includes three two-tank, daytime dives with a Dive Tortola dive master, tank, backpack and weights included. Two two-tank dives with the three-night package cost from $1,295. Also part of the package are accommodations with ocean views, transfers between airport or ferry dock and resort, special divers' breakfast each morning at the resort's **Beach Café**, four gourmet dinners at either of their restaurants, (two dinners on three-night package), rental car for three days, (two days on three-night package), free daytime use of tennis courts and nine-hole pitch and putt golf course, including equipment. ☎ 800-729-9599, www.longbay.com. Write PO Box 433, Road Town Tortola, BVI.

The Moorings-Mariner Inn. The newly refurbished Mariner Inn is just steps from the The Moorings, a premier marina. Amenities include air-conditioned rooms, waterfront restaurant and bar, boutiques, dive shop, 2,500-sq-ft grocery store, ATM and swimming pool. **Last Stop Sports**, on the dock, rents dive gear and sells air-fills to cruising divers. C-card required. ☎ 800-535-7289, 284-494-2332, The Moorings-Mariner Inn, 1305 US 19 South, Suite 402, Clearwater, FL 34624, www.moorings.com or www.laststopsports.com, yacht@moorings.com.

Nanny Cay Resort & Marina, two miles southwest of Road Town, has 41 air-conditioned rooms from $180 per day in winter; $110 in summer. TV, mini bar, phone, pool, restaurant, bar, tennis, windsurf school and on-site dive operation, **Blue Water Divers**. Winter dive/hotel packages start at $2,025 per person, summer at $1,600, for seven nights accommodations and five two-tank boat-dives; five-night packages include three two-tank dives; both include breakfast. Custom packages are easily arranged. ☎ 866-284-4683 or 284-494-4895, www.nannycay.com, hotel@nannycay.com.

Prospect Reef Resort sprawls across 10 acres along the west end of Road Town, Tortola, facing Sir Francis Drake Channel. The resort has over 130 rooms, ranging from studios to standard rooms, full apartments, and luxury villas. This is the largest resort on Tortola, with six tennis courts, miniature golf, two restaurants for casual food and drinks, and three pools. Décor incorporates vibrant Caribbean colors with traditional gingerbread woodwork. All rooms feature ceiling fans and/or air conditioning.

Rooms and suites are equipped with satellite TV, clock radio, direct-dial telephone with voice mail, personal safe, coffee maker, mini-fridge, iron and ironing board. Maid service daily. An excellent buffet is served at the resort's **Harbour Restaurant** on Saturday nights. Scuba packages are with **Dive Tortola**. A six-night package includes accommodations, a two-tank morning dive with tanks, weights and belt supplied. Cost per person in summer runs from $777 to $864; per-person winter rates climb to between $918 and $1,059. Room rates only, double occupancy, are from $115 to $380 in summer; $155 to $480 in winter (17% tax/service charge included in rates). ☎ 800-356-8937, 284-494-3311, www.prospectreef.com. Write PO Box 104, Road Town, Tortola, BVI.

Maria's By the Sea, conveniently located in Road Town along the shore of Road Harbour, offers reef tours with Dive Tortola. The hotel is within walking distance of most major shops yet isolated from the bustle of Road Town.

Beaches are a 10- to 20-minute drive and the ferry to Virgin Gorda is nearby. Guest rooms are equipped with refrigerator, bath, air conditioning, TV, phone and private balcony. Standard rooms contain one king bed or two double beds. Superior rooms are larger, and have ocean views and two double beds. Deluxe rooms are very large, have ocean views and are furnished in Caribbean-style décor, with two queen beds. Room rates from $130 to $170 per day in winter, from $110 to $150 in summer. ☎ 284-494-2595, www.mariasbythesea.com, info@mariasbythesea.com. Write to PO Box 206, Road Town, Tortola, British Virgin Island.

Sugarmill, on the northwest shore of Tortola, is a village of hillside cottages built around the remains of a 360-year-old sugar mill. Its proprietors, Jeff and Jinx Morgan, are famous for their gourmet meals (they write for *Bon Apétit*). The old sugar mill houses the restaurant, where you can dine by candlelight on conch stew, grouper salad, grilled swordfish and salads with lettuce from the lodge's garden. The Sugar Mill is separated from the beach by a small country road. Relax by the circular pool, or take a short walk to the beach where you can snorkel the natural reef and enjoy lunch at **Islands Beach Restaurant**.

All 23 rooms have air conditioning, ceiling fans, kitchenette (microwave only), iron and ironing board, hair dryers, clock radio and telephone (with data port).

Divers can arrange for guided boat tours every non-flying day or opt for the hotel's Adventure Package, which includes seven nights in deluxe accommodations, three two-tank dives or an introductory course plus two extra days with all equipment included. Also included are a day-trip to Anegada with Fly BVI to snorkel on fabulous reefs and wrecks, followed by a lobster lunch at Loblolly Bay (lobster subject to availability); six-day jeep rental (driver must be 25 or over); four gourmet dinners at the sugar Mill Restaurant; a one-hour massage each or a full day sail with lunch and drinks; a gourmet picnic for two; a copy of the *Sugar Mill Caribbean Cookbook* and a bottle of Sugar Mill rum.

Spring rates for the package are $3,087 per couple; summer $2,947; 17% tax and service charge are not included. This resort closes during August and September. ☎ US 800-462-8834, Canada 800-209-6874, direct 284-495-4355, fax 284-495-4696, www.sugarmillhotel.com. Write PO Box 9827, St. Thomas, USVI 00801.

Marina Cay

Marina Cay Resort, a lovely, eight-acre island off the northeast tip of Tortola, offers one-bedroom deluxe rooms and two-bedroom, two-bath villas. All have spectacular views of the reef below and the main channel. The villas sit on the south side of the island, with the double rooms on the east side. Constantly blowing trade winds and ceiling fans provide cool breezes. The reef and warm, shallow waters of the lagoon are ideal for snorkelers and beginning divers, and safe for families with children.

Also on Marina Cay are **Dive BVI**'s watersport center offering dive and snorkeling trips, ocean kayaks and catamarans; **Pusser's Store**, an award-winning restaurant; rental villas; and the Robb White Bar at the top of the island.

Rates for a villa that will accommodate four guests are $450 per day in winter, $295 in summer; deluxe rooms run from $154 to $195 in winter, $105 to $135 in summer. A 12.5% service charge and 7% hotel tax are additional. Diving is easily arranged with Dive BVI. Closed during September and October. ☎ 284-494-2174, www.pussers.com.

Treasure Isle Hotel, nestled on a hillside overlooking Sir Francis Drake Channel, features 40 air-conditioned rooms, pool, restaurant, bar and shuttle service to **The Big Banana Beach Club Restaurant** on Cane Garden Bay. The hotel also offers powerboats and sailboats if you wish to explore on your own or guided day-trips for snorkeling and diving. Room rates are from $170 to $253 in winter, from $143 to $209 in summer. ☎ 284-494-2501, 800-437-7880, www.treasureislehotel.net, info@treasureislehotel.net. Write PO Box 68, Road Town, Tortola, BVI.

Virgin Gorda

The Bitter End Yacht Club on Virgin Gorda's North Sound offers guest rooms in luxury villas along the shore and hillside or on a Freedom 30 live-aboard yacht. The club bar is the favorite story-swapping place for sailing and diving folk. Daily scuba trips, arranged through **Sunchaser's Underwater Tours**, leave from the Bitter End Docks every morning. Rates are for couples. A suite in winter (January 1-April 30) with all meals for two costs $630 per day or from $4,410 to $5,320 for seven nights. Diving is $225 for three two-tank dives. If you prefer to stay aboard a yacht, the package costs the same. Summer (May 1 to October 31)rates drop to $445 to $540 per day, or seven nights for $3,115 to $3,780, plus the diving. ☎ 800-872-2392, 284-494-2746, www.beyc.com, binfo@beyc.com. Write PO Box 46, Virgin Gorda, BVI.

Biras Creek Estate, located on a 140-acre peninsula, can be reached by scheduled ferry from Tortola. The resort has 34 luxury villas with garden and ocean views overlooking North Sound. Recently refurbished, the resort provides complimentary use of Boston Whalers, windsurfers and 25-foot sailboats. Diving, is extra; make arrangements with **Sunchaser** or **BVI Divers**. Rates for a room and three meals daily for two are from $910 in winter, $525 in summer, plus a 17% tax and service charge. Airport transfers included. ☎ 800-608-9661 or 284-494-3555, fax 284-494-3557, www.biras.com, caribisles@aol.com. In the US, ☎ 800-223-1108; from the UK, 0-800-894-057. Write PO Box 54, Virgin Gorda, BVI.

Leverick Bay Hotel, on North Sound, accommodates guests in spacious hillside rooms with tile floors and colorful island décor. Rooms overlook the surrounding North Sound islands and the Caribbean Sea. All have air conditioning, two double beds, a small fridge, coffee maker, ceiling fan, cable TV, phone, safe and balcony. A short walk takes you to a sandy beach and freshwater swimming pool, restaurant, shopping, the Spa and tennis. Diving, water-skiing, kayaking and small boat sailing are through **Dive BVI**, located on the resort's dock. The activities desk arranges diving, day sails, fishing, snorkeling, auto and boat rentals. Winter (December 15-April 14) rates start at $119 per day for a room; summer (April 16-December 14), $96. Dandy restaurant. ☎ 800-848-7078 or 284 495-7421, www.leverickbay.com, info@leverickbay.com.

Little Dix Bay features 90 luxury suites and guest rooms starting at $250 per day in summer (May-November), $450 per day during the high season (December 20 to March 31). The resort rests on a half mile of pristine beach, surrounded by tropical gardens. **Paradise Watersports**, on the premises, offers scuba and snorkeling tours. ☎ 800-928-3000 or book through your travel agent.

Peter Island Resort & Yacht Harbour has luxurious beachfront rooms overlooking Sprat Bay and the Sir Francis Drake Channel. Excellent snorkeling off the beach. A **Dive BVI** facility is on site. A four-night dive package includes accommodations in either an ocean-view room or beachfront junior suite, two boat-dives or a resort course and one shallow dive per person; seven-night packages feature accommodations and four boat-dives or a resort course with three shallow dives per person. All packages are for two guests and include the Full American Plan (FAP: breakfast, lunch, and dinner), unlimited use of Hobie Cats, Sunfish, and Laser sailboats; board surfing, snorkeling, mountain biking, day and evening tennis, swimming pool and fitness center, arrival gift, round-trip transfers, unlimited ferry service to and from Tortola. All accommodations are air conditioned and have ceiling fans and king-size beds. Four nights for two range from $2,785 to $3,185; seven nights are $5,019 to $7,714. ☎ 284-495-2000, fax 284-495-2500.

Anegada

Tiny Anegada, 12 miles northwest of Virgin Gorda, covers just 15 square miles. This off-the-beaten-track coral atoll, surrounded by uninterrupted beaches and gorgeous reefs, is home to 250 residents and a huge community of exotic Caribbean birds, including a flamingo colony, herons, terns and ospreys. Shipwrecks and coral heads abound, a delight for snorkelers, but sailors beware – approaching the island by boat can be treacherous without local knowledge and eyeball navigation. Snorkeling and fly fishing, done from shore, is outstanding. Scuba is prohibited.

Much of the island's interior is a preserve for 2,000 wild goats, donkeys and cattle. Not for the average tourist, but a great spot if you want to get away from it all. Expect encounters with a ferocious mosquito population – carry as much repellent as you can. Fly in from Beef Island, Tortola, or go by boat from any of the marinas.

Anegada Reef Hotel, on Setting Point, offers great beaches, snorkeling and fly fishing, 16 air-conditioned rooms, tackle shop and tank fills. Winter rates are $250 to $275 per day for a double. Rates include breakfast, lunch and dinner (surcharge for lobster) for two. Informal restaurant. Jeep and bicycle rentals. Rooms are simple, pleasant and clean. A 15% service charge and 7% tax are added to the bill. ☎ 284-495-8002, fax 284-495-9362, www.anegadareef.com, info@anaegdareef.com.

Pristine Anchorages

Deadman's Bay, on the eastern tip of Peter Island, is a short sail out of Road Harbour that takes no more than an hour or two. Once there, you will find a

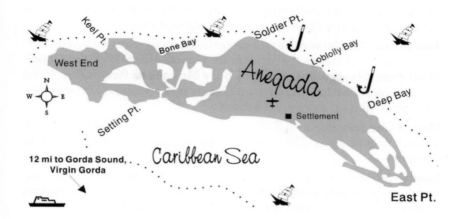

long white sand beach at **Peter Island Yacht Club**. Yachtsmen are requested to anchor in the Bay's extreme southeastern corner and should be aware that the area is prone to a swell, especially in the winter months.

Heading upwind from Deadman's Bay is **Salt Island**, once a regular stopping-off point for ships requiring salt for food preservation on the trade routes. This is also the location of the BVI's famed wreck of the *Rhône*, which sank off the island in 1867. At **Lee Bay**, just north of the *Rhône*, moorings are provided for those diving the wreck in order to minimize anchor damage. Both Lee Bay and Salt Pond Bay off the settlement can be rough anchorages and are recommended for day use only.

Cooper Island's Manchioneel Bay, on the island's northwest shore, is a good lunch stop for those sailing upwind to Virgin Gorda. There is a dock for dinghies and a beach for swimming. The **Cooper Island Beach Bar** serves lunch, dinner and drinks.

The Virgin Gorda Baths, one of the BVI's most famous landmarks, lies on the southwestern shore of Virgin Gorda. Randomly placed large granite boulders form small grottoes and pools on the beach's edge, great for exploring and snorkeling. As with all these north shore anchorages, a swell can prevent overnight anchoring.

North Sound, **Virgin Gorda**, offers the yachtsman a wide array of overnight anchorages, and a variety of good dining spots. The harbor sits along the eastern tip of the island and is well protected by surrounding islands – Mosquito, Prickly Pear and Eustatia. Boats over five feet in draft should use the Sound's northern entrance at Calquhoun Reef; shallow drafts can use the Anguilla Point entrance in calm weather only.

The Dogs make a good stopping-off point for sailors on their way from North Sound to Jost Van Dyke; they are also a popular diving and snorkeling venue.

On calm days the best anchorages are the bay to the west of Kitchen Point on George Dog, as well as on the south side of Great Dog.

Trellis Bay, **Beef Island**, is a well-protected anchorage fringed by a semicircular beach. It serves as the location for **Boardsailing BVI**, the **Conch Shell Point Restaurant** and **The Loose Mongoose Beach Bar**. At the Bay's center is **The Last Resort**, an English-style restaurant whose owner, Tony Snell, puts on a one-man cabaret act.

Marina Cay lies north of Trellis Bay and offers a restaurant, bar, small beach and moorings (see page 350). It is fringed by coral and one should enter from the north.

Sandy Cay, east of Little Jost Van Dyke, is uninhabited and offers a long stretch of white sandy beach. The water is deep almost until the shore; the area is prone to swells and not a good anchorage year-round.

Little Harbour, **Jost Van Dyke**, a quiet, easy-to-enter lagoon, touts three restaurants, all with local food and atmosphere at the shore's edge.

Great Harbour, **Jost Van Dyke** (south coast), is the setting for **Foxy's Tamarind Bar** and several other good West Indian restaurants. A small settlement bordering a white sand beach fringes this picturesque harbor. The anchorage is fairly well protected and the holding good.

White Bay, **Jost Van Dyke**, lies west of Great Harbour and features a white sand beach, small hotel and a restaurant. A channel through the center of the reef allows entrance to the anchorage, which is subject to winter swells.

Norman Island's main anchorage is **The Bight**.

Pelican Island and the **Indians** are near The Bight and offer good snorkeling and excellent scuba diving.

Soper's Hole, one of Tortola's three main ports of entry, lies at the very west end of the island and is both deep and sheltered. Ferries to St. Thomas and St. John leave from here daily. There are several nearby restaurants and marinas.

Road Harbour, Tortola's largest harbor, skirts Road Town, capital of the BVI. Here one finds customs and immigration facilities, good supermarkets and shops, marinas, restaurants and a boat yard – all within walking distance of the harbor.

Brandywine Bay and **Maya Cove**, which also offer restaurants, are two more anchorages just beyond Road Harbour.

Sightseeing & Other Activities

Hiking and exploring are popular in the BVI. You will find deserted dungeons, sugar mills, pirate caves, rain forests and wooded trails. Tennis courts as well as horseback riding are provided by some of the hotels. Boardsailing and windsurfing equipment is available at many of the resorts.

Tortola

The 2.8-acre **J.R. O'Neal Botanic Gardens** in the center of Road Town features a beautiful waterfall, lily pond and exotic tropical plants and birds. Nearby, on Main Street, is the **Virgin Island Folk Museum** which displays many artifacts from the *Rhône* and from early plantations. Hikers and botanists will find huge elephant-ear plants, and lush ferns under a canopy of mahogany and manilkara trees at **Sage Mountain National Park**. Mt. Sage peaks at 1,780 feet.

If you are cruising the BVI, be sure to visit **Stanley's** in Cane Garden Bay on the weekend, where the steel band is reputed to be the best in the islands.

Virgin Gorda

Visitors will find the ruins of an 18th-century sugar mill at **Nail Bay** on Virgin Gorda's west coast. And just south of the Yacht Harbor at **Little Fort National Park** is some masonry from an old Spanish fortress. Monster granite boulders are at the **Spring Bay** beach between Little Fort National Park and the Baths.

Gorda Peak is a 265-acre national park with a wealth of mahogany trees and exotic plants.

There are small shops (*not* duty-free) around Road Town, Tortola and Spanish Town, Virgin Gorda, specializing in local crafts and gifts.

Dining

Tortola

Rhymer's Beach Bar and Restaurant at Cane Garden Bay, Tortola, is a favorite with the locals. Serving fresh fish and lobster, it has a buffet night on Tuesday and Saturday. Open for breakfast, lunch and dinner. ☎ 54520.

Scatliffe's Tavern, another local favorite in Road Town, Tortola, specializes in local food such as fish soup made with coconut milk, conch fritters, ribs, and lobster dishes, followed by fresh lime pie. Near the high school. ☎ 42797.

Carib Casseroles, on Tortola, has a "Meals on Keels" service for bare-boaters experienced with boil-a-bags as well as sit-down service. Food is a combination of Caribbean, French, Greek and Creole. Peanut Creole soup, curry and casseroles are featured here. Moderate.

Virgin Gorda

The Bath & Turtle is a patio tavern in the Yacht Harbour serving breakfast, lunch, and dinner. Burgers, sandwiches, and homemade soups. ☎ 55239.

Mad Dog near the Baths specializes in sandwiches all day. Spectacular view! ☎ 55830.

The Olde Yard Inn features a library and classical music. Homemade soups, local seafood, gourmet specialties. ☎ 55544. Reservations.

Anegada

The Anegada Reefs Hotel, Anegada, serves lunch at their beach bar and specializes in barbecued lobster for dinner. Local fish or steak, chicken and ribs are also available. Moderate to expensive. ☎ 58002. VHF Ch 16.

Mosquito

Drake's Anchorage, on Mosquito, has been written up in *Gourmet* magazine for its fabulous Caribbean lobster and local fish dinners. Meals include fresh baked bread, soup, appetizer, salad, dessert and coffee. Moorings are available for a low overnight charge. ☎ 42254. VHF Ch 16.

Jost Van Dyke

Sandcastle, at White Bay on Jost Van Dyke, serves gourmet fish dishes, lobster, orange-glazed duck, fresh breads and desserts for lunch and dinner in the open-air restaurant on the beach. The **Soggy Dollar Bar** offers the original "Painkiller." No credit cards. Reservations on channel 16 VHF. Prices are moderate to high.

Foxy's, in Great Harbor (south coast), serves roti and sumptuous burgers for lunch, local lobster and steak for dinner. A favorite with the yachting crowd. ☎ 59258.

Peter Island

Peter Island Hotel and Yacht Harbour offers lunch at the **Beach Restaurant** from 12:30 to 2 pm. Dinners are formal: men must wear a jacket and women wear cocktail attire. ☎ 52000. Expensive.

BVI Facts

Nearest Recompression Chamber: The nearest chamber is on St. Thomas in the neighboring USVI.

Getting Here: The most direct way to reach the BVI is via San Juan, Puerto Rico. Frequent connecting service is offered by **American Eagle**, **LIAT** and

Cape Air, with occasional service by other airlines and charter flights. *Terrance B. Lettsome International Airport*, Beef Island, is the major airport for Tortola and the BVI. Ferries run from Tortola to Virgin Gorda, Peter Island, Jost Van Dyke. Baggage can sometimes be delayed by a day on the small airlines. Divers carrying a lot of equipment should fly direct to St. Thomas and take a water ferry, to avoid having to change planes.

If you are traveling on to Virgin Gorda, Anegada, Peter Island, or Jost van Dyke, check with your hotel, resort or villa to make sure that charter flights or ferry service will be available if you arrive after 4 pm. Otherwise, plan to spend a night or two in Tortola. If you choose to arrive via St. Thomas, you'll have to arrange a charter flight to Tortola, Virgin Gorda or Anegada or take one of the ferries that travel between downtown Charlotte Amalie or Red Hook, St. Thomas and Tortola. If you plan to make your own reservations on the Internet, remember that you will have to request flights to Tortola or type the airport code which is EIS.

Arriving by Ferry, Boat or Yacht: Ports of entry are located in Road Town and West End on Tortola, Great Harbour on Jost Van Dyke and St. Thomas Bay in Virgin Gorda. All vessels entering the territory must clear in with BVI Customs and Immigration immediately upon arrival into the territory. Customs and Immigration offices are on Tortola in Road Town and West End, on Virgin Gorda in the Virgin Gorda Yacht Harbour, and on Jost Van Dyke in Great Harbour. A valid passport and boat registration papers are required for entry into the BVI.

Ferries: St. Thomas to Tortola ferries operate only during daylight hours, the last ferry is usually around 5 pm. Ferry service starts at approximately 7:30 am.

Ferry companies with service to Tortola are:

Caribbean Maritime Excursion (operating as **Road Town Fast Ferry**). Runs from the Water Front and Red Hook, St. Thomas to Road Town, Tortola. ☎ 284-494-2323.

Inter-Island Boat Services. Operates from Red Hook, St. Thomas and Cruz Bay, St. John to West End, Tortola. ☎ 284-495-4166.

Marina Cay Ferry (Beef Island-Marina Cay). Complimentary ferry service from Trellis Bay, Beef Island to Marina Cay. ☎ 284-494-2174.

Native Son, Inc. (USVI-BVI). Operates from the Water Front and Red Hook, St. Thomas to West End and Road Town (via last ferry), Tortola. ☎ 284-495-4617.

New Horizon Ferry Services (Tortola-Jost Van Dyke). Runs from Great Harbour, Jost Van Dyke to West End, Tortola. ☎ 284-495-9278.

North Sound Express (Tortola-Beef Island). From Beef Island, Tortola to Spanish Town, Leverick Bay and Bitter End, Virgin Gorda. ☎ 284-495-2138.

Nubian Princess (USVI-BVI). Runs from Red Hook, St. Thomas and Cruz Bay, St. John to West End, Tortola. ☎ 284-495-4999.

Peter Island Ferry (Tortola-Peter Island). Goes from Baugher's Bay, Tortola to Peter Island Yacht Harbour. ☎ 284-495-2000.

Smith's Ferry Services Ltd., aka Tortola Fast Ferry (USVI-BVI). Runs from the Water Front and Red Hook, St. Thomas to West End and Road Town, Tortola, as well as to The Valley, Virgin Gorda. ☎ 284-495-4495.

Speedy's (USVI-BVI). From the Water Front and Red Hook, St. Thomas to West End and Road Town, Tortola, as well as The Valley, Virgin Gorda. ☎ 284-495-5240.

Car rentals: Tortola, **Hertz**, ☎ 54405; **Avis**, ☎ 4-3322; **Budget**, ☎ 4-2639; **International**, ☎ 4-2516. Virgin Gorda, **Speedy's**, ☎ 4-5240.

Taxi Service: Available from Beef Island Airport, Road Town Jetty, West End Jetty and from the dock on Virgin Gorda. Tortola: **VI Taxi**, ☎ 5-2378 or 4-2875; **Andy's Taxi**, ☎ 5-5252; **Style's Taxi**, ☎ 4-2260. Virgin Gorda: **Mahogany Taxi**, ☎ 5-5542.

Driving: Valid BVI driving license required. A temporary license may be obtained from the car rental agencies for $10. Driving is on the left-hand side of the road. Maximum speed is 30 mph. Bicycles must be registered at the Traffic Licensing Office in Road Town. Cost of registration is $5. License plate *must* be fixed to the bicycle.

Fishing: The removal of any marine organism from BVI waters is illegal for non-residents without a recreational fishing permit. ☎ 4-3429.

Documents: A valid passport is required to enter the BVI. For US and Canadian citizens a passport is preferred, but you may also use an original birth certificate accompanied by a valid photo ID such as a driver's license. Visitors may stay up to six months, provided they possess ongoing tickets, evidence of adequate means of support and pre-arranged accommodations. Visitors from some countries may need a visa. ☎ 284-494-3701.

Currency: US dollars. Personal checks not accepted.

Clothing: Casual, light clothing; some of the resorts require a jacket for dinner. Avoid exposed midriffs and bare chests in residential and commercial areas. Nudity is punishable by law. A wetsuit top, shortie, or wetskin is recommended for night-dives and winter diving. Snorkelers should have some protection from sunburn.

Time: Atlantic Standard (EST + 1 hr).

Language: English.

Climate: The BVI are in the trade-wind belt and have a subtropical climate. Average temperatures are 75° to 85°F in winter and 80° to 90°F in summer. Nights are cooler. The hurricane season extends from July through September.

Taxes: There is a departure tax of $20 if you are leaving by air. The hotel accommodation tax is 7%.

Religious Services: Methodist, Anglican, Roman Catholic, Seventh Day Adventist, Baptist, Jehovah's Witness, Pentecostal and Church of Christ.

For Additional Information and a list of all guesthouses, apartments, hotels, campgrounds, charter operators, and restaurants, contact the *The BVI Tourist Board: USA*, toll-free, ☎ 800-835-8530 (Mon-Fri 9 am-5 pm Easterrn); *London*,

☎ 44-207-355-9585, www.bvitouristboard.com or www.bviwel-come.com.

US Virgin Islands

Discovered by Columbus in 1493, the US Virgin Islands (USVI) comprise three main islands: **St. Croix**, **St. John** and **St. Thomas**. Each has a distinct personality and flavor, and since they are close together you can choose one island as your base and still catch the fun of the other two. They offer an enormous variety of reefs, wrecks and dropoffs, all in crystal clear water protected from strong currents and heavy seas.

Before becoming an American territory, the USVI lived under six different flags and it still preserves a rich and varied culture. Wander through old Danish arcades covered with tropical flowers in the historic town of **Christiansted** on St. Croix; visit **Bluebeard's Castle** on St. Thomas; or stroll around the partially restored ruins of the **Annaberg Plantation** on St. John.

St. Croix

The largest of the USVI, St. Croix plays host to over 50,000 visiting snorkelers and divers per year, the main attraction being **Buck Island Reef National Park** – the most famous snorkeling spot in the world. Scuba divers will find their share of reefs, walls and wrecks to dive. Much of the best diving and snorkeling around St. Croix is accessible by beach entry.

Picturesque St. Croix, once a Danish territory, is known for its easy lifestyle and warm hospitality. The streets of **Christiansted**, its tiny capital, are lined with 18th-century buildings in pastel pinks, blues and yellow. Tropical flowers greet the visitor everywhere. At night, shops, restaurants and nightclubs come alive with reggae music and island hospitality.

The small town of **Frederiksted** is laced with wide, tree-shaded streets that lead to a lovely waterfront with arcaded sidewalks. After a devastating fire in 1878, Frederiksted was rebuilt in the Victorian style. Flowering vines now cling to the balustrades of the decorative "gingerbread" frames that the Cruzans built over the Danish masonry.

Best Dives

☆☆☆ **Long Reef**, a six-mile-wide shallow reef on the outskirts of Christiansted Harbor, offers a variety of reef dives. The bottom terraces gently from the shallows to an average depth of 50 feet, reaching 80 feet at some spots. Hundreds of small coral caves and crevices along the reef shelter

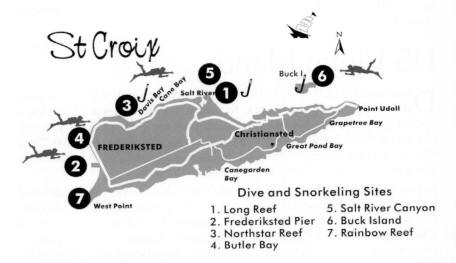

St Croix

Buck I.

N

Davis Bay

Cane Bay

Salt River

Point Udall

Grapetree Bay

Christiansted

FREDERIKSTED

Great Pond Bay

Canegarden
Bay

West Point

Dive and Snorkeling Sites

1. Long Reef
2. Frederiksted Pier
3. Northstar Reef
4. Butler Bay
5. Salt River Canyon
6. Buck Island
7. Rainbow Reef

French angels, parrotfish, rays, turtles, morays, octopi, lobsters and goatfish. A docile nurse shark makes frequent appearances. Huge brain and elkhorn coral formations prevail. An old barge intentionally sunk at 60 feet, near the harbor channel, attracts a healthy fish population. Visibility varies. Recommended for snorkelers and novice divers.

☆☆☆☆ **The Frederiksted Pier** offers the ultimate night dive on St. Croix. Underwater pilings, carpeted with red, yellow and orange sponges, provide cover for seahorses, iridescent tube sponges, octopi, baby morays, juvenile fish, brittle stars, puffers, feather dusters, parrotfish and tube anemones. Take your dive light. Beware of the stinging corals and red "do not touch me" sponge. Entrance to the dive site is by climbing down a steel ladder or taking a giant stride off the end of the pier. Before entering the water, be sure to see the Harbor Master at the pier, C-card in hand. Diving is prohibited when a ship is in. ☎ 772-0174.

☆☆☆☆ **Northstar Reef**, a spectacular wall dive at the east end of Davis Bay, is recommended for intermediate or experienced divers. Beach entry is possible here but most divers opt for boat access because of the rocky terrain.

Beautiful staghorn thickets and brain corals decorate the wall. A sandy shelf at 50 feet leads to a spooky cave and a hefty green moray eel. Huge anchors from 18th-century sailing ships lie scattered about. Marine life includes a superb collection of schooling tropicals, pelagics, turtles, morays and eagle rays. Expect an occasional moderate current.

☆☆☆ **Butler Bay**, on the island's west shore, harbors four shipwrecks: the 170-foot *Rosaomaira*, which sits in 100 feet of water; the 140-foot *Suffolk*

Maid, an old fishing trawler at 90 feet; the *Northwind*, a retired tugboat at about 60 feet; and the *Virgin Island*, a 300-foot barge sunk in 1991, resting at 70 feet. The wrecks are part of an artificial reef system which also includes old cars and trucks, music boxes, typewriters, and a vast array of other items. Wreck residents include goatfish, groupers, snappers, hogfish, parrotfish, turtles, rays, and angelfish. Recommended for intermediate to experienced divers.

★★★ **Salt River Canyon**, a deep, submerged canyon formed by the outflow to the Salt River, features two distinct dives off its east and west walls. **Salt River East**, with interest between 40- and 100-foot depths, is famed for the massive orange elephant-ear sponges and black corals that decorate its precipice. The area's usual good visibility allows a long look at resident bigeyes, grunts, barracuda, blue chromis andstingrays. Suggested for intermediate divers.

Salt River West plunges from 40 to more than 130 feet. Plate corals cascade down the reef slope and large purple tube sponges make a wonderful foreground for wide-angle photography.

When seas are calm, it is an excellent spot for novices. Visibility, normally good, may decrease during stormy weather.

★★★ **Cane Bay Dropoff** is the favorite beach dive. The dropoff lies about 140 yards off the beach and is suitable for scuba and snorkeling, with depths ranging from the surface to 120 feet. Inside the reef, calm waters and a decent fish population make this spot a favorite of snorkelers. Light surf along the shore. Light current at the dropoff. Park along the road at Cane Bay Beach.

Additional shore-entry dives are best at **Davis Bay** and **Butler Bay**. Visibility close to shore is weather-dependent and decreases when a lot of rain and wind churn the bottom. Equipment may be rented at any of the dive shops.

Best Snorkeling

★★★ **Buck Island Reef** continues to capture the hearts of Caribbean tourists despite noticeable wear and tear from hurricanes and a daily blitz of snorkelers.

As in most national parks, Buck Island has its own rangers, only here they sport swim trunks and patrol in power boats. There are also the standard park guide markers, but at Buck Island they stand at a depth of 12 feet, embedded in the sands along the ocean floor. Each day, catamarans, trimarans, sloops, and yawls unload what the islanders call "the wet set." The Buck Island welcoming committee includes green parrotfish, snappy sergeant majors, grouper, rainbow-striped angelfish and the silvery Bermuda chub. Beginners and experienced snorkelers alike can experience this underwater fantasy in an unusually safe atmosphere. The reefs of Buck Island lie only 100 yards off the coast and no trail is more than 15 feet deep. As snorkelers enter the park, they are welcomed by a blue and white plaque shimmering below the surface. One marker (number 8) next to an unusual round coral full of veins inquires, "What would you name this coral?" The next marker says, "You are right. Brain Coral." Arrows and signs guide the swimmer along the underwater trail and give the precise names of coral and other growths below the surface.

More than 300 species of fish are identified. One species that audibly demands attention is the small striped grunt, a fish that can be clearly heard underwater.The National Park Service maintains a careful watch, but one familiar park rule – Don't Feed the Animals – does not apply here. Swimmers can feed the fish as often as they like. Grouper, a favorite fish to hand-feed, come readily at the slightest beckoning.

Since the reef park is strictly non-commercial, you are advised to rent gear before heading out. Whether you're coming from St. Thomas, St. Croix or St. John, you can obtain equipment readily on all three islands. And getting there is half the fun. Most hotels on St. Croix offer a shuttle service to Christiansted, where you can select almost any kind of boat imaginable. Charter boats of every description line the docks of the Christiansted harbor. Boats to Buck Island are widely available at low cost.

Make sure you stop over on **Buck Island Beach**, a pristine stretch of powdery white sand created in part by sand excreted by parrotfish gnawing on the coral reef. From the beach, a wildlife trail leads 200 feet to an observation tower, which gives a grand view of the lagoon and reef. A trip to Buck will be one of the most memorable experiences of your visit to the Virgin Islands. Areas of Buck Island reef away from the snorkeling trail are suitable for scuba.

Dive Operators

All dive operators on St. Croix require you to present a C-card.

Cane Bay Dive Shop, on the beach at Cane Bay, offers "walk-in" dives to the Cane Bay Dropoff, which sits about 140 yards off the beach. Snorkeling tours and hotel/dive packages available. ☎ 800-338-3843 or 340-773-9913. Write PO Box 4510, Kings Hill, St. Croix, USVI 00851.

Dive Experience is at the Club St. Croix in Christiansted. Owner, Michelle Pugh is a diver-medic instructor as well as a PADI instructor. This PADI Five Star facility offers all certifications, including a four-day certification, a resort course, rentals, photography equipment . Dive Experience offers boat dives around the island and will shoot personalized videos. Hotel and dive packages are available. ☎ 800-235-9047, 340-524-2049 or write Box 4254, Christiansted, St. Croix, USVI 00822.

Scubawest, a full-service PADI shop at the Salt River Marina in Frederiksted, is a short trip to several of St. Croix's best dives, including **Rainbow Reef**, **five wrecks** and the **Frederiksted pier**, a fun night dive if you enjoy poking around for a peek at mini critters like seahorses and frogfish. Great staff, friendly service. ☎ 340-772-3701, www.divescubawest.com, info @divescubawest.com.

N2 The Blue Diving Adventures is located on North Shore Road, about one mile east of Cane Bay Beach, next to Lobster Reef Café. The shop specializes in small group diving, with a maximum of 6 divers at a time. Two-tank dives cost $65. They offer guided boat- or beach-entry tours. Personable guides. The shop also rents rooms in a luxurious villa. ☎ 866-712-BLUE or 340-713-1475, www.2dive4.net, info@n2blue.com.

St. Croix Scuba Shack's owner, Dave Ward, shares his extensive knowledge of marine science with visiting divers. Expect good tidbits about dive site critters and creatures. He's worked with NOAA's National Undersea Research Center marine scientists and enjoys guiding visiting divers on his subsea eco tours. Scuba Shack is a full-service dive facility with NAUI and PADI certified instructors, offering introductory through advanced diver training. Kayaks are also available for paddling around the west end. ☎ 340-772-DIVE, www.stcroixscubashack.com.

St. Croix Ultimate Bluewater Adventures (S.C.U.B.A.) bubbles with friendly service, offering reef dives all across the north shore to Cane Bay. No snorkeling. S.C.U.B.A. also has a large selection of swimsuits and Scuba Pro dive gear. ☎ 877-567-1367, 340-773-5994, www.stcroixscuba.com.

Anchor Dive Center at the Salt River Marina is a PADI five-star, IDC training facility. Resort to instructor courses. Near Salt River Canyon. ☎ 340-778-1522 or 800-532-3483. Write PO Box 5588, Sunny Isle, St. Croix, USVI 00823, www.anchordivestcroix.

Where to Stay

St. Croix offers a wide range of luxury resorts, villas, condominiums, inns and guest houses. Like the neighboring British Virgin Islands, the waters around the USVI are excellent for sailing. Many visiting divers combine a week of bareboating or live-aboard sailing with subsea exploring. The following resorts cater to divers and offer package deals. (Add 8% tax to room rates.)

The Buccaneer Hotel in Christiansted offers dive packages with local shops. This newly redecorated resort spans three beautiful beaches and features three restaurants, a spa, shopping arcade, eight tennis courts, an 18-hole golf course and all water sports. Dive and snorkeling trips leave from the resort dock for Buck Island. Rates are from $275 (summer) to $340 (winter) per night for a double in a standard room. Cottages range from $440 to $575 (winter) per night. Check the Website for current dive packages and specials. ☎ 800-295-3881 or hotel direct 340-773-2100, www.thebuccaneer.com, mango@thebuccaneer.com.

Chenay Bay Beach Resort offers 50 modern, West Indian style beachfront cottages, with fully equipped kitchens from $313 to $594 per day. Family friendly. Children under 18 with parents stay free. ☎ 800-548-4457, fax 340-773-6665, www.chenaybay.com, chenaybay1@msn.com.

Divi Carina Bay Resort & Casino defines tropical elegance. Choose from 130 beachfront guest rooms, suites or 20 ocean-view villas. All Divi Carina Bay guest rooms are spacious and air conditioned, and feature king-size beds and queen sofa bed or two queen-size beds, refrigerators, wet bars, coffee pots, microwaves, satellite TV, in-room safes, and telephones with voice mail and dataport. **Divi Dive**, a PADI Five Star dive center on premises, fills all your dive and snorkeling wishes. Property expands along a 1,000-foot white, sand beach. Two restaurants, two bars, two freshwater swimming pools, two outdoor whirlpools, lighted tennis courts, fitness center and Casino Divi keep you busy between dive trips. Children 15 and under stay free with an adult. The Divi staff is available to help arrange childcare (all childcare references are screened by the resort; contact them at least a week prior to arrival to make arrangements). The resort offers wheelchair-accessible guest rooms, and all public spaces and restaurants are wheelchair accessible. Guest rooms go for $160 to $200 per day. A variety of money-saving package deals are available, some with airfare. Look on line or call 877-773-9700, local 340-773-9700, www.divicarina.com.

 New owners of **The Hibiscus Beach Resort** have completely renovated the property, raising it from a two-star to a five-star inn. Each of the 38 rooms has a veranda overlooking the Caribbean Sea. White sandy beaches rim the property for more than a third of a mile. Freshwater pool. Snorkel off the beach among the fishes. Dive packages in winter start at $1,200 per couple for four nights and four two-tank dives. Room rates are from $150 to $190. ☎ 800-442-0121, direct 340-773-4042, www.hibiscusbeachresort.com, info@hibiscusbeachresort.com.

European-style **Caravelle Hotel** sits on the water's edge in historic Christiansted. The 43 newly furnished and spacious rooms have private bath, air conditioning, cable TV, direct-dial telephones, refrigerators and AM/FM radio. RumRunner's waterfront restaurant and bar on site. A variety of scuba diving packages are available with daily departures from the hotel dock. Walk to the St. Croix Aquarium. Duty-free shopping at the Caravelle Arcade and

Pan Am Pavilion outside your door. Beaches, tennis courts and two 18-hole golf courses are nearby. ☎ 340-773-0687, www.hotelcaravelle.com.

If you love the warmth of bed-and-breakfast accommodations, head for the **Carrington Inn**. Their five rooms are absolutely beautiful and their rates are easy to take at $120 to $150 per day. Scuba packages available. ☎ 340-713-0508, www.carringtonsinn.com.

Dining

 The US Virgin Islands are considered the mecca of haute cuisine in the Caribbean by some. From the islands' rich mixture of cultures – Spanish, French, English, Danish, Maltese, Dutch and American – its pungent local spices and fresh tropical fruits, local chefs create dishes to dream about. So many fine restaurants have opened up within the last five years, we can only give a hint of the many options.

Rum Runners, on the boardwalk by the Caravelle Resort in downtown Christiansted, opens daily for breakfast, lunch, and dinner, and Sunday brunch from 10 am to 2 pm. Choose your own live lobster from the island's only tank. Enjoy island cocktails, ice-cold beers, sushi, sashimi, and tropical appetizers. After sundown a dozen or so hungry tarpon swim up for a snack. ☎ 340-773-6585.

H2O, located at the Hibiscus Resort, opens for breakfast, lunch, dinner and late-night menus. Sunday brunch is not to be missed. Their all-day menu features tasty selections such as Cajun tuna sashimi, warm herbed goat-cheese salad, apple-cider curried pork loin, coconut shrimp, steaks, and a variety of pizza selections, sandwiches, wraps, and salads. Night menu includes wings, pizzas, wraps and burgers. Great views. ☎ 340-773-4042.

The Waves at Cane Bay on the north shore entices guests with grand sunset viewing, fresh lobster and local fish dishes. Very romantic. ☎ 340-778-1805.

The Fort Christian Brew Pub, on the boardwalk and Kings Alley in Christiansted, serves lunch and dinner overlooking Christiansted harbor. Menu features fine Cajun food and a nice selection of unusual handcrafted ales. ☎ 340-713-9820, www.fortchristianbrewpub.com.

St. John

The smallest and most verdant of the USVI, St. John is truly the most "virgin." The island is an unspoiled sanctuary of natural beauty and wildlife. Two-thirds of the 28-square-mile island and most of its stunning shoreline comprise the Virgin Islands National Park, part of the US National Park system. Here nature flaunts her majestic mountains, emerald valleys and lush

Dive and Snorkeling Sites
1. Trunk Bay
2. Caneel Bay Snorkeling Trail
3. Fishbowl Reef
4. Chocolate Hole
5. Cocoloba Cay
6. Salt Pont Cay
7. Waterlemon Cay
8. Francis Bay
9. Carval Rock
10. Congo Cay

tropical vegetation. St. John is the best choice for beachfront camping and shore-entry snorkeling.

Best Dives

The best dives of St. John are found in the out islands, **Congo Cay** and **Carval Rock**. Shallow dive sites are found around the south shores of **Reef Bay** and west shores of **Cruz Bay**.

☆☆ **Congo Cay** is a favorite dive site for boats based at St. John and St. Thomas. It is a rocky islet located between them. Visibility is usually good. As with many of the small cays, the submerged rocky areas are home to large schools of fish. The coral mounds, some of which have been beaten up by the sea, are decorated with soft corals and brightly colored sponges. Currents are occasionally strong here.

☆☆☆ **Carval Rock** is a short boat ride from the north end of St. John. Try this dive only if weather and sea conditions permit, as strong currents may exist. Recommended for very experienced divers only. Schools of very large fish and eagle rays appear daily. The submerged part of the rock is covered with sponges, gorgonians, basket stars, and false corals.

☆☆ **Fishbowl Reef**, just south of Cruz Bay, is a nice shallow dive for novices and snorkelers. Divers swim along ledges sparkling with beautiful elkhorn and staghorn coral. Soft corals undulate in the shallows. Many kinds of small reef fish are found hiding in the crevices.

Best Snorkeling

Half-day and full-day snorkeling excursions by boat to explore the outer reefs or shallow shipwrecks are available. Lucy Portlock, **Snorkel Mania**, ☎ 340-776-6567, at the Caneel Bay Resort, offers terrific boat snorkeling excursions to all the best sites around St. John. If you're not staying at Caneel Bay, sign up at **Hurricane Alley** in the Mongoose Junction Mini Mall.

☆☆☆ **Trunk Bay** on the north shore of the island has a clearly marked underwater trail, with abundant soft and hard corals, yellowtail, damselfish, and occasional turtles. The reef is shallow and is just off beautiful Trunk Bay Beach. Top-side here is great for snapshots. Average depths, 10 to 15 feet.

☆☆☆ **Salt Pond Bay,** at the southeast end, is never crowded and is blessed with ample shade trees. Coral reefs stretch from both points of the Bay, offering snorkelers a full day's worth of adventure. Many fish and marine animals make their home here.

☆☆☆ **Chocolate Hole**, located at the east side of the mouth of Chocolate Bay, is distinguised by several rocks sticking up out of the water. The reef is just to the west of these. Reef depths are from four to 15 feet. Hordes of fish, including grunts, squirrelfish, blue chromis, parrotfish, rays and turtles, wander about. Seas are usually very calm unless the wind is from the south. Good for all levels.

☆☆ **Waterlemon Cay**, a national park, offers terrific fish watching for experienced swimmers. Drive to Annaberg Sugarmill ruins, park and hike half a mile down the road to the beach. Swim along the east side of the bay to Waterlemon Cay. There are loads of big Caribbean starfish in the sand and walls of fish all around the island, including big yellowtail snapper and jawfish. This spot is usually calm in summer, but choppy in winter when the wind is out of the northeast. Tidal currents may exist.

☆☆ **Caneel Bay Snorkeling Trail** is limited to guests of the Caneel Bay Resort or boaters who enter from the sea, but Caneel Bay's main beach is open to the public and offers some nice fish watching.

☆ **Francis Bay** is easiest by boat, but you can reach it by driving to the Annaberg Sugar Mill, then left to Francis Bay. The last stretch of road is gravel and dirt. Rocks, corals and plenty of fish.

☆☆ **Cocoloba Cay,** a bare rocky site "attached" to St. John by rock, coral and sand, requires boat access. The east side has huge coral formations, some 15 feet high, which died long ago, but now have new coral growing on top. Large coral patch reefs exist along the west side. Depths range from five to 30 feet. Highlights are angelfish, schools of blue tang, spadefish, jacks, pompano and an occasional shark. This area is usually rough, good only on days with the wind is from the north or northeast. Experienced ocean swimmers only. Boaters should anchor about 100 yards east of the cay.

Dive Operators

Cruz Bay Watersports takes certified divers on two-location, two-tank dives 8:30 am to 12:30. Afternoons are devoted to introductory dives and take place on a shallow reef. Snorkelers are offered half-day trips aboard *Island Spirit*, a 60-foot catamaran, and full-day outings to the Baths off Virgin Gorda in the BVI aboard their 60-foot motor yacht. Cruz Bay offers a smart dive package. Every dive you log after the first one, the lower the rate until you reach package prices. This operator has two locations, one at Cruz Bay and the other at the West Resort. ☎ 340-776-6234, www.divestjohn.com.

Paradise Watersports is located on the beach at Caneel Bay. The shop has a nice selection of gear and souvenirs. Dive boat is shaded with a dive platform. New and rusty divers are offered an introductory/refresher course. Dives take off for local wrecks and the *Rhône* (see page 316). Nitrox. Open Monday to Saturday ☎ 340-779-4999, www.paradisevi.com, paradiseh2o@atttglobal.net.

Low Key Watersports on the beach at Cruz Bay next to the ferry dock. Dive trips visit the *Rhône* for $145, local reefs and wrecks $85. Referrals for open-water check out dive for PADI, NAUI, SSI and NASDS. ☎ 800-835-7718.

6-Paq Watersports offers dive trips and courses. Fast dive boat. ☎ 340-776-1057, www.6paqscuba.com.

Where to Stay

 Add 8% room tax and 10% service charge

Resorts

Caneel Bay Resort occupies a 170-acre peninsula that adjoins the Virgin Islands National Park. There are 171 guest units in low-profile buildings scattered about the grounds, three restaurants, seven white sand beaches and seven tennis courts. The resort is known for the gardens where over 500 tropical plant species grow. Room rates are from $450 per day. Check the Website for packages and specials. ☎ 888-ROSEWOOD (888-767-3966), direct 340-776-6111, www.caneelbay.com, or see your travel agent.

Westin Regency St. John sprawls over 34 exotic acres. The resort has a gigantic freshwater pool covering a quarter acre and offers 262 luxury guest rooms with all amenities. Under 18 stay free. Good snorkeling off the beach.

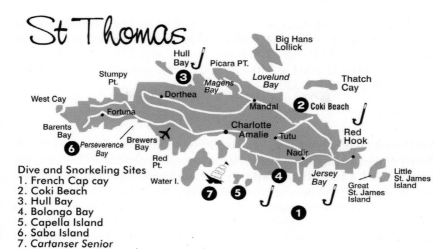

St Thomas

Dive and Snorkeling Sites
1. French Cap cay
2. Coki Beach
3. Hull Bay
4. Bolongo Bay
5. Capella Island
6. Saba Island
7. *Cartanser Senior*

Cruz Bay Watersports (☎ 693-8000 ext 1834), on premises, offers dive and snorkeling trips. Standard winter room rates for a double start at $519; summer, from $419. Specials and packages on their Website drop the rates tremendously. ☎ 800-WESTIN1 (800-937-8461) or 340-693-8000, fax 340-779-4985, www.westinresortstjohn.com.

Condos & Apartments

For a list of condos on St. John call ☎ 888-856-4601 or 340-779-4250, or visit www.vivacations.com. For B&B's and small inns visit www.usvi.net /usvi/stjohn.

Gallows Point Suite Resort, on the waterfront, features suites with full kitchens, private patios and bathrooms. Pool, gourmet shop and restaurant. Good snorkeling from the beach. From $495 to $575 per day in winter, from $335 to $475 in summer. ☎ 800-323-7229, fax 340-776-6520.

Campgrounds

Camping-snorkeling trips are popular on St. John. Bring your own gear.

Rates at **Cinnamon Bay Campground**, inside the National Park, go from $80 for a tent site to $110 per day for a 15'x15' cottages. Guided snorkeling tours, dive trips arranged, small sailboat rentals. ☎ 800-539-9998 or 340-776-6434, www.cinnamonbay.com, PO Box 720, Cruz Bay, St. John, USVI 00830.

Maho Bay Camps. Environmentally sound luxury camping in tent cottages with electricity, translucent walls that allow breezes to pass through, white sand beach. No water in cottages. Adjacent Maho Bay dive shop offers scuba and snorkeling trips, rents small sailboats, kayaks and windsurfers. Gourmet restaurant. From $115 per day for two people, add $15 for an additional person. ☎ 800-392-9004 or 340-715-0501, www.maho.org. Write PO Box 310, St. John, USVI 00830.

St. Thomas

St. Thomas, whose sheltered coves once harbored some of the most blood-thirsty pirates in Caribbean history, is the second-largest of the USVI and site of the capital, **Charlotte Amalie**. Provincial yet cosmopolitan, modern yet rich in history, it can be seen in a day. Divers should save an afternoon for shopping. Duty-free prices and keen competition make it a bargain-hunter's dream. In the narrow cobblestone streets and arcades of Charlotte Amalie you'll find designer shops housed in 200-year-old restored warehouses that were once full of molasses and rum. For those content to idle away some top-side time, St. Thomas boasts sugar-white beaches. It is in these calm sands that St. Thomas's history, rich and tumultuous, lies hidden.

The architecture and people of St. Thomas reflect the island's many-cultured past. Dutch, French and Spanish historic sites sit side-by-side with contemporary resorts. For those mixing scuba diving and sailing, St. Thomas is the home port to a number of charter operators.

Though some beach-entry diving exists here, the prettiest reefs and clearest waters are found around the outer cays. Some dive shops offer trips to the wreck of the RMS *Rhône*. Cruise ship visitors will find an abundance of snorkeling opportunities.

Best Dives

☆☆☆ **French Cap Cay** is well south of St. Thomas, but worth the long boat trip for both divers and snorkelers. This reef complex displays an enormous array of corals, caves, tunnels, and a spectacular seamount. Visibility is often unlimited. The reef is teeming with fish, rays and critters. Beautiful lavender, orange, and yellow vase and basket sponges grow on the walls, interspersed with orange and red corals and unblemished stands of elkhorn. A light current is usually encountered here.

☆☆ **Capella Island** is just east of Little Buck Island. The reef begins at 25 feet. Divers swim down through coral-encrusted canyons to a beautiful rocky bottom where basket sponges, soft corals and pillar coral grow. The visibility, often excellent, is weather-dependent. Fish life is abundant.

☆☆ **Saba Island**, a short boat trip from the St. Thomas's harbor, is a favorite one-tank dive. Depths are 20 to 50 feet. The reef at Saba Island is very pretty; divers swim through staghorn thickets and pillar corals. Large boulders cover the bottom, which is at a depth of about 50 feet. *Warning*: You may encounter surge; a number of divers have been tossed into the fire coral on the reef.

☆☆☆☆ Wreck of the **Major General Rogers,** a 180-foot Coast Guard Buoy Tender that went down in the 1970s, sits at 70 feet, with the top of the wreck at 40 feet. Vibrant corals and sponges drape the hull, and schooling fish study below deck. Occasional currents make this a good choice for experienced divers.

Best Snorkeling

Coki Beach, on the north shore of St. Thomas, is a favorite beach dive and snorkeling site. The beach is adjacent to Coral World, an underwater viewing tower. The reef here ranges in depth from 20 to 50 feet. Divers swim down a sand slope amid schools of snappers, French and queen angels, and an occasional baby shark. The reef has small coral arches and recesses, a favorite hiding place for small fish, sea turtles and stingrays. Star coral, sponges, crinoids, and rock are characteristic of the reef at Coki Beach. This is an excellent first dive.

☆☆☆ *Cartanser Senior*, a 190-foot wreck, sits just off Little Buck Island in 35 feet of water. It is filled with schools of squirrelfish, morays, angels, butterflyfish, sergeant majors, and damsels, all of whom are accustomed to being hand-fed and will approach you looking for a snack. Visibility is generally good.

French Cap Cay has the best visibility for snorkeling and free-diving photography (see overall description, page 350). The reef has many shallow areas full of large sea fans, antler coral, and elkhorn.

For good beach snorkeling try **Hull Bay**, on the north coast, and **Bolongo Bay**, plus the resort beaches at **Sugar Bay Resort**, **Renaissance Grand Beach**, **Secret Harbor Beach**, **Sapphire Beach**, **Point Pleasant Resort**, **Marriott's Morning Star Resort**, **Grand Palazzo**, and **Carib Beach**.

Dive Operators

Chris Sawyer Diving Centers, located at Red Hook in American Yacht Harbor (☎ 340-777-7804) and at the Wyndham Sugar Bay Resort (☎ 340-777-7804), offers "Discover Scuba" courses as well as PADI scuba certifications. All gear, including underwater photo equipment, is available for rent. Fast 42-foot dive boats shuttle divers to all the best dives around St. Thomas and its outer islands. Dive/accommodation packages with Point

Pleasant Resort and Wyndham Sugar Bay. Escorted night snorkeling tours. ☎ 877-929-3483, www.sawyerdive.vi sawerdive@islands.vi.

Aqua Action Dive Center at the Secret Harbour Beach Resort is a PADI Five Star facility specializing in dive and snorkeling tours, individual training and programs for divers with physical disabilities. Especially good for novice divers. ☎ 888-775-6285, www.aadivers.com, aquaaction@islands.vi.

Admiralty Dive Center is a full-service dive center, centrally located at the Holiday Inn Windward Passage Hotel in Charlotte Amalie. They offer both PADI and NAUI instruction plus a"Discover Scuba" class. Their dive center carries scuba and snorkeling equipment, along with rental gear for divers. ☎ 888-900-DIVE or 340-777-9802, www.admiraltydive.com/information, admiralty@viaccess.net.

Dive In! at the Sapphire Beach Resort, a full-service PADI facility, visits the sites around St. Thomas. Snorkelers may join the dive tours when sites are shallow. Equipment rentals and scuba courses. ☎ 866-434-8346 or 340-777-5255, www.diveinusvi.com.

St. Thomas Diving Club, at the Bolongo Bay Beach Club, specializes in dive and snorkel excursions to local and BVI reef and wreck sites. Nitrox. ☎ 877-538-8734 or 340-776-2381, www.st-thomasdivingclub.com.

Coki Beach Dive Club at Coki Beach offers dive and snorkeling lessons, referrals, and beach-entry tours. Excellent place for new or rusty divers and snorkelers. Popular with the cruise ship set. There are Two reefs, with maximum depths of 50 and 40 feet. ☎ 340-775-4220, www.cokidive.com.

Where to Stay

Resorts

St. Thomas has a seemingly endless variety of accommodations. You'll find charming antique guesthouses and cozy in-town hotels, resorts on secluded beaches, romantic mountain-top villas, condos, and hotels.

Bolongo Bay Beach & Sports Club offers diving packages in cooperation with the on-premises St. Thomas Diving Club. The all-inclusive resort has 65 air-conditioned beachfront units with telephone, color TV, kitchenettes, and balconies. Some suites. Nightly entertainment. Sport facilities include four tennis courts, a Sunfish sailboat fleet, resort yacht *Heavenly Days*, snorkeling, volleyball courts and board games. Informal atmosphere. Children under 15 free in room. Beach bar. Winter rates run from $399 per person, per day, including all meals, taxes, and service charge; $499 for a couple. Room only, double occupancy, is from $245 per day in winter; age 12 and under, $70 per day. Good snorkeling off the beach. ☎ 800-524-4746 or 340-775-1800, www.bolongobay.com.

Sapphire Beach Resort, on the northeast coast, offers suites with full kitchens, TV, phone, handicap access, day-long children's program. Under 12 free in room. **Dive In!** dive shop on premises offers PADI courses, equipment rentals, dive and snorkeling tours (see above). Freshwater pool, tennis, three restaurants. ☎ 800-524-2090 or 340-775-6100.

Best Western's Carib Beach Resort on south-coast Lindbergh Bay, features affordable oceanview rooms with private balconies. Two miles from town. Freshwater pool, phones, TV. Room rates per day from $134. ☎ 800-792-2742 or 340-774-2525, fax 340-777-4131.

Secret Harbor Beach Resort on Nazareth Bay, the southeast Caribbean side, offers 171 luxury rooms in a tranquil beachfront setting. Winter room rates run from $325 per day for one bedroom to $619 per day for a two-bedroom suite. Children under 13 stay free. Good snorkeling off the beach on a small reef with tropicals, turtles and rays. **Aqua Action Dive Center** on premises offers rentals, courses, dive and snorkeling boat trips. Dive packages available. ☎ 800-524-2250 or 340-775-6550, fax 775-1501.

Point Pleasant Resort, located on Pineapple Beach at the northeast end of St. Thomas, features luxurious suites strewn across a hillside with fully equipped kitchens, microwave oven, cable TV, AM/FM clock radio, air conditioning, ceiling fans, in-room safes, daily maid service, iron/ironing board, 24 hour security, free parking, cribs (no charge), snorkeling gear, welcome coffee basket, welcome bottle of rum, complimentary introductory scuba lesson, rollaways upon request at $20 per night, comfortable and spacious living and dining areas. Scenic ocean or garden views from your private balcony. Oceanfront pool. Restaurant. Rates start at $275 per day. Diving with **Chris Sawyer Diving Center** (see above). Dive/hotel packages available. ☎ 800-524-2300, www.pointpleasantresort.com.

The Wyndham Sugar Bay Resort & Spa is an all-inclusive beach comber's paradise. The resort is mountainside, sloping down to a gorgeous beach. Cozy guest rooms have colonial furniture, ceiling fans and refrigerators. Private balconies overlook green mountains, white beaches and the sea.. Besides scuba and snorkeling the resort offers golf, tennis, sailing, kayaking and board surfing. Three freshwater pools, four restaurants, beach bar. All-inclusive winter rates for two sharing a room are from $510 per day. Snorkeling is included; dive trips are extra. **Chris Sawyer Diving Center** (see above) is on premises. ☎ 340-777-7100.

Live-aboards

Virgin Islands Charter Yacht League will rent you a sailing yacht and teach you how to sail. On some yachts crew includes a dive master; some also have compressors aboard. Others arrange rendezvous with dive boats. Advance reservations required. ☎ 340-774-3944, www.vicl.org.

Sightseeing & Other Activities

The USVI provide opportunities for a wide variety of activities. Check with your hotel or the tourist newspapers (available everywhere) for historic tours, rum factory tours, golf, tennis, deep-sea fishing, bird-walks, day-sails, visits to the new national park on Hassel Island, parasailing, and board-sailing. Check nightclub listings for broken-bottle dancing, fire eating, limbo dancing, steel bands, and island entertainment acts.

Panoramic views from the watchtower at **Blackbeard's Castle** are worth the trek, Originally known as *Skytsborg*, the over-300-year-old structure is now a refurbished guesthouse and restaurant, possibly the oldest historical structure in the Virgin Islands. Some say that during 18th century, pirates, including Edward Teach (aka Blackbeard) lived here. ☎ 776-1234.

At **Paradise Point**, you can take a state-of-the-art tramway 700 feet up for a bird's-eye view of Charlotte Amalie Harbor and beyond.

Dining

The rich history of the USVI is reflected in the wonderful restaurants. You can dine on the finest continental cuisine or sample exciting local dishes. Savor a Caribbean lobster bouillabaisse in one of the restored 19th-century inns or try a delicious fish-fry on the beach while listening to strains of reggae or calypso. Check the tourist newspaper for complete restaurant listings.

For fashionable dining at moderate prices ride out to **The Old Stone Farm House Restaurant** at the Mahogany Run Golf Course. It's situated in a 200-year-old plantation field house overlooking the golf course. The Old Stone Farm House was the core of a Danish sugar plantation at Estate Lovendahl. Menu specials include mussels steeped in saffron with rosemary pommes frites and a caramelized onion with roasted tomato relish; chorizo sausage with a smoked onion sauce; phyllo-wrapped portobello mushroom and roasted parsnips; watermelon seared shrimp with pine nut cornbread and grilled zucchini. At the Buccaneer Mall, ☎ 777-6277.

Hotel 1829 was originally built by a sea captain and completed in the year of its name. This is a formal restaurant with an interior resembling an Italian villa. The chef specializes in rack of lamb and various pasta dishes. Located in the heart of the harbor, ☎ 776-1829.

Oceana, located in Frenchtown's historic Villa Olga, serves dinner on a lovely terrace. The favorite here is the 40-dish salad bar. Entrées include ribs, chicken, lobster, fish and shrimp. ☎ 340-774-4262.

Duffy's Love Shack on Rte 32 in Red Hook dazzles guests with exotic tropical drinks. Try the banana daquiri made with local rum or the Love Shack volcano. Menu specials include burgers, salads, grilled fresh fish, wraps, tacos and burritos. ☎ 340-779-2080.

Fast food has taken over the malls – **Domino's Pizza** can be found at Nisky Center and Tutu Park Mall; **Kentucky Fried Chicken** at the Buccaneer Mall; Sub Base at Fort Mylner and Tutu Park Mall; **McDonald's** in Frenchtown at Wheatley Center and the Tutu Park Mall; **Pizza Hut** on the waterfront at Wheatley Center ; **Subway** at the Nisky Center and Buccaneer Mall, Red Hook Plaza and Tutu Park Mall; and **Wendy's** in Long Bay sits next to Port of Sale Mall.

USVI Facts

Nearest Recompression Chamber: St. Thomas.

Getting Here: Major Airlines connect from Miami, New York, direct and through San Juan, to either *Cyril E. King* airport on St. Thomas (☎ 340-774-5100), or the *Henry Rohlsen Airport* on St. Croix (☎ 340-778-0589). **American Airlines** (☎ 340-776-2560 in St. Thomas; 340-778-2000 in St. Croix) has the most flights from Miami and New York. **American Eagle** has frequent flights throughout the day from San Juan. **Continental** (☎ 800-231-0856) flies from Newark. Delta (☎ 800-777-4177) from Atlanta.

Island Transportation: Taxi service is readily available on all three islands. Taxi rates are determined by law and those rates are available from your driver. Bus service and tours are available on St. Thomas and St. Croix. Car rentals: Avis, Budget (☎ 340-776-5774), Hertz, Discount Car Rental and L&L Jeep (☎ 340-776-1120).

Documents: Passport and onward ticket.

Driving: Traffic keeps to the left on all three islands. A US driver's license is required.

Customs: US citizens can bring back a total of $1,200 worth of duty-free imports from the USVI every 30 days. Family members traveling together can make joint declarations. USresidents can also bring back five liters of liquor duty free, plus an extra liter of rum if produced in the Virgin Islands. Hang on to all receipts. For updated information go to www.customs.gov ("Before you go").

Canadian citizens have a C$750 exemption plus duty-free one carton of cigarettes, 1 can of tobacco, 40 imperial ounces of liquor, and 50 cigars. Gifts may be mailed to to Canada valued at less than C$60 a day, provided they're unsolicited and don't contain alcohol or tobacco.

354 ■ USVI Facts

Currency: US$, travelers checks, major credit cards. No personal checks accepted.

Climate: Year-round temperatures range from 76 to 82°F.

Clothing: Casual, lightweight, with sweaters for winter; jackets and ties needed for some resorts and eating establishments.

Electricity: 110 volts AC, 60 cycles (same as US).

Time: Atlantic Standard, which is one hour earlier than Eastern Standard.

Language: English.

Taxes: No sales tax. 8% hotel tax. Service charge may apply at some hotels and restaurants.

Religious Services: All denominations.

For Additional Information: *US Virgin Islands Division of Tourism*, PO Box 6400, Charlotte Amalie, USVI 00804. http://www.usvi.net, ☎ 340-774-8784, fax: 340-774-4390, Toll free: 1-800-372-USVI.

Venezuela

Los Roques

If you crave wilderness diving, head to Los Roques, Venezuela, one of the most beautiful and least-known Caribbean destinations. Located about 95 miles off the coast of Venezuela, the archipelago of Los Roques sits amidst a Great Barrier Reef that shelters all of its 50 islands and 250 islets from high winds and waves. Ocean currents rush through periodically, carrying hordes of fish and nutrients that keep the visibility outstanding, and the reefs vibrant with hard and soft corals, beautiful sponges and sea fans. The islands form a circle around a shallow lagoon lined with walls of coral reefs, caves and pinnacles. National park status, granted by the Venezuelan government in 1972, has kept the reefs pristine and the islands free from major development. Spear fishing is prohibited.

 Most of the 50 islands in the archipelago are flat coral and sand, except for **Gran Roque** (great rock), which is volcanic stone. Its elevation tops out at 400 feet at the peak of Mount Cabelon. The other major islands are **Francisqui**, **Nordisqui**, **Madrisqui** and **Crasqui**.

Gran Roque is the only populated island in the archipelago. Most of its 1,000 residents, known as *Rococos*, are descended from fishermen who migrated here from Margarita Island. There is the main airport and a small fishermen's village with a few bars, small grocery stores, the sheriff's office, a church and a variety of accommodations. The streets are made of crushed coral. No cars. No bikes.

Besides terrific diving and snorkeling, there are plenty of good spots for wind surfing, water-skiing, fishing, fly fishing and kite surfing. Sailing excursions, both day and overnight, are readily available.

Birding is popular, with more than 90 resident and migrant bird species, including enormous gull colonies, brown boobies, frigates, pelicans, herons and scarlet ibis. There are no native mammals, but dogs and goats have been brought in by the locals. Many reptiles, including iguanas, chameleons and salamanders, live on the larger islands.

Best Dives

Dive boats from **Eco Buzos**, the major PADI shop (see page 360), visit two areas – the reefs surrounding Gran Roque and an area along the southern section of the archipelago. Whether you dive or not, expect to pay a one-time park entrance fee of $16.

A virtual kaleidoscope of marine life inhabits Los Roques, with regular sightings of parrotfish, barracudas, red snappers, dolphins, sharks, octopi, lobsters and the near-extinct queen conch. Green turtles visit the beaches to lay their eggs, and the island of Dos Mosquises Sur is the home of **La Fundación Científica Los Roques**, a biological research station dedicated to preserving the green turtle populations in the region.

Currents that carry hordes of fish and clear water into and through the area also make conditions right for drift diving and snorkeling. If the dive master finds the currents too strong to stay put, he will follow your bubbles and pick you up at the end of the dive area. Snorkelers drift "dive" also.

☆☆☆☆☆ **La Guaza** (the grouper), off Gran Roque, is a rocky formation, just five minutes by boat from the town dock. There are three coral pinnacles that start at 30 feet, then drop to 60 feet on the lagoon side and 130 feet on the ocean side. Visibility runs 60 feet or better. Marine life is superb, with resident barracudas, huge groupers, rays, snappers, turtles, eels, rays and tropicals. Soft corals, sea rods and encrusting sponges adorn the big rocks and walls. Damsels, squirrelfish, French and queen angels, sergeant majors, black groupers, grunts, trunkfish, tangs and filefish are permanent residents.

☆☆☆☆☆ **La Piedra Ahogada** (drowned rock) is a favorite night-dive spot. La Piedra's terrain is similar to La Guaza. Residents include jacks, barracudas, eels, and great variety of reef fishes and rays. Depths are from the shallows to about 130 feet, with most diving around 70 feet.

☆☆☆☆ **La Buceadora**, off the southwest tip of Gran Roque, is an area of rocky outcrops, caves and arches. One spot, Arco de los Sabalos (arch of the tarpons) attracts massive schools of snappers, black durgons, amberjacks and tarpons. One of the massive caverns has two domes. There is also a sailboat wreck at 90 feet.

☆☆☆☆ **Madrisqui** and **Francisqui** delight divers with gardens of soft corals, sea fans, and pastel sponges. It's a short seven-minute boat ride. Depths are from the shallows to 60 feet. Perfect for beginners.

☆☆☆☆ **Solapa De Rabusqui** is a 15-minute boat ride southwest of El Roques. The reef drapes over itself like surf. Lots of tarpons, spotted eagle rays, turtles, reef and nurse sharks pass through. Blennies, damselfish, barber shrimp, angels and squirrelfish peek out from the crevices.

☆☆☆☆☆ **Barrera Arrecifal Sur** is a protected area off the south barrier reef with at least 50 different sites. It starts at Boca de Cote along a wall that begins at five feet then drops to 200. Most diving is between 40 and 70 feet. The area is formed of enormous magical caves, spiraling pinnacles and beau-

Los Roques, Venezuela

1. La Guaza
2. Piedra Ahogada
3. La Buceadora
4. Madrizqui A
5. Francisqui
6. Rasqui
7. Madrizqui B
8. Rabusqui
9. Isla dos Mosquises
10. La Nueva Pared
11. Cueva de Cayo Sal
12. Cabeza de Salinas
13. Boca de Cote
14. Maceta de Cota

tiful coral walls. Usual inhabitants include sharks, snappers, turtles, big schools of jacks, and smaller tropicals. Expect a 40-minute boat ride from Gran Roque.

Dos Mosquises, the site of the biological research station, offers dives from 45 to 180 feet. Skill level is advanced. There are splendid reefs visited by turtles.

Dive Operator

Eco Buzos is our choice. They welcome English-speaking guests and offer everything from packaged vacations to courses from beginner to open-water rescue diving. They are licensed by NAUI/FVAS (*Federation Venezolana de Actividades Submarinas*). An open-water instructor supervises all the dives. They use 12-liter aluminum tanks with standard US valve fittings. We suggest that you carry your own personal gear, but if you don't, they provide Cressi Sub regulators and BCDs, as well as lead belts. Each dive, per-person, costs

$35 and includes park dive permits, tank and weights. Two dives run $65. Dive packages for a minimum of three days get 10% off.

Dive boats depart 9:30 am, noon, and 2:30 pm, and again at 7 pm for night dives. If you are on a private yacht and want to go diving, the dive boat will pick you up from your yacht and take you to the reefs, most of which are too shallow for your own boat to reach. www.ecobuzos.com, reservas@ecobuzos.com, ecobuzos@hotmail.com.

Where to Stay

 There are no big hotels or fancy restaurants on Gran Roque. Visitors stay in small inns or *posadas*, many owned by Italians who have fine-tuned simple, local cuisine to gourmet status. Other than the posadas, dining is limited to a few beachfront bars that serve the catch of the day, still caught by the fishermen who settled the Gran Roque village. Lobsters, king conch and Spanish mackerel are abundant and appear on most menus in season. At night the beach pubs offer music and dancing under the stars.

There are about 50 posadas on Gran Roque, each having between two to 10 rooms. Rates range from $30 to $300 per night, many with meal packages. The lower-priced inns are fairly primitive. Electricity is not always available, air conditioning is rare. If hot water is not listed as an amenity, don't expect any. Private baths are not widely available. Ask questions when booking.

A few of the very-low-priced places are somewhat shabby, with bedrooms too small to turn around in. Most, but not all, of those tagged "superior" have at least some rooms with private baths and air conditioning, as well as boat service for tours and trips.

Dive-accommodation packages can be arranged online at www.ecobuzos.com. Yacht charters and diving with Eco Buzos can be arranged through www.explorepartners.com.

Following are a few of our picks for guest rooms. Additional posadas are offered through http://discovervenezuela.com/coastposadas.cfm. Most of these places have no phones and no formal addresses.

Posada Malibu Los Roques features 14 double rooms with private bath. Suites are larger than most, with double or twin beds. Architecture is colonial with a definite Caribbean flair. Four of the rooms have air conditioning. All have private bath with hot water and 24-hour electricity. Amenities include DirecTV, open-air restaurant, multi-level terrace, and a bar-lounge restaurant. Lots of personal attention.

All-inclusive rates run from $220 per person per day to $275 (minimum two guests per room) and include all meals, day-trips to other islands by private boat, beach chairs, non-alcoholic beverages, parasol, and snorkeling gear. Children aged three to 12 get a discount of 25%; babies less than two years old get a discount of 95%. Tax included. It's located on Gran Roques, 4th Street #158, Parque Nacional Los Roques, posada@explorepartners.com.

Posada Galapagos Los Roques offers 13 rooms, all with private bath, hot water, ceiling fan, A/C, mini-safe, DirecTV, high ceilings, tile floor and tropical décor. Lagoon-front rooms open to a patio. Nice. Restaurant and piano bar. Excellent cuisine prepared by different chefs in the restaurant, **Churuata**. Italian and Spanish spoken. A six-day stay runs about $650 per person and includes all meals with beverages, a day-tour to remote islands with a boxed lunch, snorkeling gear and beach umbrella. Local airport transfers. Gran Roques, 4th Street #145 (facing the lagoon), Parque Nacional Los Roques, posada@explorepartners.com.

Macanao Lodge in Los Roques mixes Italian and Spanish-colonial architecture and features eight double beachfront rooms with private bath, comfortable beds and fresh-air ventilation, plus a great kitchen managed by professional crew and chef. Rooms are not air conditioned, but do have 24-hour electricity, satellite TV, open-air and indoor restaurant, bar and a private boat. Rates are from $230 per person, per night for all meals, transfer in Gran Roques, day tours to nearest islands with beach chairs, umbrellas and snorkeling gear. Scuba is arranged separately; posada@explorepartners.com.

Posada Acuarela, owned and operated by artist Angelo Belvedere, is an 11-room, two-story lodge with a delightful courtyard. Their rooftop patio offers views of Mount Cabelon, the island's highpoint. Five of the rooms have air conditioning. Beds have mosquito netting. Each room is decorated with a drawing or painting by the owner. Meals are served family-style in the dining area. Rates are from $145 per person, per night based on a double. Includes all meals and non-alcoholic beverages. Acuarela's restaurant features seafood and Italian specialties. ☎ 5814-323502, www.posadaacuarela.com/pages/ingles, airone@cantv.net.

Posada Piano & Papaya defines Caribbean with sparkling, white rooms, tropical art and plants, around a cool courtyard with hammocks for relaxing. Lovely open-air dining room. Private en-suite baths. Room rates run $170 per night with meals. Dive trips are available at $65 per day for a two-tank boat dive. Gear rental is extra. www.pianoypapaya.com/ingles2004, info@losroques.com.

Vistalmar, owned and operated by the airline LTA, offers 13 rooms and a romantic terrace bar overlooking the sea. Guests on the inn's meal plan dine at the nearby **El Muelle** restaurant; ☎ 58-27-62-3009, www.tuy.com.

Dive excursions are $65 per person for a two-tank dive including tanks, weights, boat and dive master. Picnic lunch, with chairs and umbrella for the beach, add $20 per person; for dinner, $30 per person.

The flight to Los Roques costs $170 per person round-trip. Reservations can be made through www.explorepartners.com or www.ecobuzos.com.

Facts

Getting Here: Travel to Los Roques from the US or Europe is easiest and most cost-efficient if booked through a dive tour company. Currently, **Eco Buzos** is the only dive-vacation company that packages flights, lodging, diving and snorkeling; www.ecobuzos.com.

Airlines: American, **Continental** and **Santa Barbara Airlines** depart gateway US cities to **Simon Bolivar International Airport**, Caracas, Venezuela. Flights to Gran Roque are only 30 minutes, but you may have to overnight in Caracas as flights to Los Roques are available during daylight hours only. There are several daily flights to Los Roques from Maiquetia, Caracas, Venezuela. Charter flights for dive groups are also available. **Lta/Aerotuy** offers the only regular air service to Gran Roque. Arrive early for departing flights as the planes fill up quickly. ☎ 212-761-6231; www.tuy.com. Two daily flights leave Caracas at 8:30 am and 5 pm, returning from Los Roques at 9 am and 6 pm, respectively. **Aero Ejecutivos**, ☎ 212-991-7942, www.aeroejecutivos.com.ve, **Avior**, ☎ 212-202-5811 or 0501-284-67737, www.avior.com.ve, and **Transaven**, ☎ 212-355-1179, www.transaven .com, also offer flights to Los Roques. Round-trip airfare from Caracas runs about $170. Prices fluctuate down to $130. All visitors to Los Roques must pay a $15 (or 25,000 bolivars) national port entrance fee. Caracas Airport charges a departure tax of 15,000 bolivars ($7) per person.

In season, December through January, the small airport on Gran Roque fills up quickly on weekends. Leave plenty of extra time for departures and expect delays anyway.

Private Yacht Charters are also popular. Book a live-aboard through **Explore Yachts**, 1ra Avenida Los Palos Grandes, edificio Oriental, piso 4, suite #401, Los Palos Grandes, 1062, Caracas, Venezuela, ☎ 58-212-2870517, 58-414-2877554, fax 58-212-2842015, www.explore-yachts.com, info@explore-yachts.com.

Private yachts arriving in Venezuelan waters must register at the harbor office in **Pampatar, Margarita Island**. Nautical charts are available at the harbor offices in La Guaira or the one nearer to their sailing port (for example, Puerto La Cruz, Puerto Cabello, Higuerote).

The shallow reefs around Los Roques have been the demise of several ships and yachts, thus private cruising is tricky. However, lighthouses at Cayo de Agua, at Boca de Sebastopol and atop the iron pyramid at Gran Roque guide marine traffic. Together they form a buoy triangle, visible from any approaching route to the archipelago. Sailors should tune to channel 218 VHF-marine (NAVTEX) which offers weather information and useful warnings.

Island Transportation: Sneakers, sandals or barefoot.

Clothing: Lightweight and casual. Shade is limited on Los Roques. Be sure to bring lots of sunblock, a hat with a wide brim that will shade your face, and sunglasses. Pack mosquito repellent. Drink plenty of fluids to avoid getting dehydrated.

Documents: Passport with at least six months of validity left. No visa required. A park entrance fee of 16,000 bolivars (about $16) is required.

Currency: The bolivar (VEB). US dollars are widely accepted. Credit cards and traveler's checks are not. Bring plenty of bolivars and US dollars in small change. There are no ATMs, but you can get cash with your credit card at the one bank on Gran Roque. At press time the US dollar was worth 2,700 bolivars.

Communication: Some of the inns have e-mail at the desk. No postal service. A few public phones operate on calling cards available at one of the general stores in town.

Language: Spanish and Italian, though the dive guides and tourist workers speak a little English.

Climate: Hot and dry. Los Roques gets very little rainfall, part of the reason for clear ocean water – no runoff. Trade winds keep temperatures in the mid 80s during the day, and mid 70s at night.

Area Code: From the US, dial ☎ 011-58 and then the local area code and number.

Documents: US citizens arriving in Venezuela are required to have a passport and return plane ticket.

Electricity: 110 volts, the same as in the US.

Time: GMT (Greenwich Mean Time) minus four hours; Eastern Daylight Time all year.

Taxes and Tipping: Dive boat captains should be tipped $10 per day.

Tourist Information: www.ecobuzos.com, http://think-venezuela.net. New World Travel at ☎ 800-308-SURF.

What About Sharks?

Sharks have generated more sensational publicity as a threat to divers than any other animals, even though their bites are among the least frequent of any injuries divers sustain. Two opposing attitudes seem to predominate: either irrational fear or total fascination.

Nowhere is this fascination more apparent than at the "Jaws" exhibit at Universal Studios theme park, where people line up for an opportunity to be drenched, buffeted and threatened by a huge, relentless great white shark.

Shark expert and author Paul Sieswerda, collection manager of the New York Aquarium, warns divers about taking either approach to this honored and feared species. Common sense and a realistic understanding of the animals should be used, he says, adding that "anything with teeth and the capability of biting should be treated with the same respect we give to any large animal having potential to inflict injury." The vast majority of sharks are inoffensive animals that threaten only small creatures; but some sharks will bite divers that molest them. Included are such common forms as nurse sharks and swell sharks. These animals appear docile largely because they are so sluggish, but large individuals can seriously injure a diver when provoked. Sieswerda cites an incident with a "harmless" nurse shark as the cause of 22 stitches in his hand – the result of aquarium handling.

The answer to "What about sharks?" from dive guides is usually a shrug of the shoulders. Experience tells us that most sharks are timid animals. Fewer than 100 serious assaults by sharks are reported worldwide each year, total, with the average being closer to 50, and less than 35% of these are fatal. Statistics isolating attacks on divers alone are not available, but it would be a small percentage of the toal, far fewer than 50. A majority of the few fatal attacks on man are not cases of the infamous great white shark biting someone in two; they involve much smaller (four- or five-foot) sharks causing a major laceration in an arm or leg. Loss of blood due to lack of immediate medical attention is usually the cause of death.

Overplaying the danger is equally unrealistic. Encounters with dangerous sharks by divers on shallow reefs or shipwrecks are uncommon. Divers interviewed for this book who have sighted dangerous sharks all report the same thing – getting a good, long look at any shark is rare; when a shark encounters man, it tends to leave the area as suddenly as it appeared.

Sharks are largely pelagic animals, meaning they are found out in deep, open water. Dangerous sharks are seldom found in the shallower areas where most novice sport diving takes place – certainly not on shallow snorkeling reefs.

Most dive guides agree. They would change their line of work if they thought a huge set of jaws was awaiting them on each day's dive.

So use common sense. Avoid diving in areas known as shark breeding grounds. Avoid spearfishing and carrying the bloody catch around on the end of the pole. If you do see a shark and are uncomfortable about its presence, leave the water. Above all do not corner or provoke the shark in any manner. Keep an eye on the shark at all times.

A number of shark bites occur each year on the east coast of Florida, where surfers dangle their feet and hands down in areas where sharks follow bait fish in from the open sea. Given the sharks' poor eyesight, a dangling hand or foot resembles a sickly fish trapped at the surface. Being at the surface for a small fish is akin to having one's back against a wall. Nowhere to go. Easy prey.

One crowd of bathers in Miami, fearful after seeing a shark terror movie, clubbed a baby whale to death in the surf, thinking it was a shark. Our favorite shark danger story comes from Florida dive master, Bill Crawford. A young diver begged to see a shark in the water. Finding one presented quite a problem. The area was largely shallow reefs so shark sightings were rare indeed. Thinking hard, the dive master remembered a big old nurse shark who could be found sleeping under a ledge on one of the outer reefs. She had been there for years totally ignoring the daily stampede of divers and snorkelers. So he took the young man to that spot and, as luck would have it, there was the shark. Upon seeing it sleeping under the ledge, the young diver became frozen with fear. In a wild panic he backed into a wall of coral, putting his hand deep into a hole where a big green moray eel lived. The nurse shark, true to its calm reputation, just kept sleeping. But the moray, incensed at the intrusion, defended its home by sinking its sharp teeth deep into the diver's hand.

Nitrox

Nitrox, a mixture of nitrogen and oxygen, replaces compressed air in your scuba cylinder. We are often asked about Nitrox diving and especially about its use in the Caribbean. Should you dive Nitrox? Do you have a technical bent? Do you want to learn a new skill? You need to examine your style of diving and goals to determine if the advantages of Nitrox will prove valuable. Nitrox can extend your bottom time and reduce your nitrogen load. Some people say you will feel less tired and warmer, both during and after a dive. As can be seen below, the time or depth advantage of Nitrox is significant.

Equivalent Nitrox Depths (in feet)

Air	32% oxygen, 68% nitrogen	40% oxygen, 60% nitrogen
40	51	63
50	63	76
70	75	89
80	86	99 (Max)
90	109	
100	121	
110	132 (Max)	

Nitrox diving can be as simple or complex as anything you will encounter in scuba diving. Basic Nitrox dive training will have you in the water with your standard scuba gear. No need to buy new gear or learn how to use and maintain it. This is the easiest, least expensive and probably the safest way for a sport diver to reap the benefits of Nitrox.

With that said, the maximum benefits of Nitrox can only be achieved with rebreather equipment. A rebreather is a self-contained breathing device which reuses at least part of each breath. Regular scuba equipment expels the entire breath into the surrounding water when the diver exhales. Although rebreathers have some significant advantages in technical diving applications, their use and the necessary training are outside the scope of this book.

Contact your local dive shop or certifying agency about training (listed under *Planning Your Trip*, page 2).